Good Living Street

Good Living Street

PORTRAIT OF A PATRON FAMILY, VIENNA 1900

TIM BONYHADY

PANTHEON BOOKS, NEW YORK

All rights reserved. Published in the United States by Pantheon Books,
a division of Random House, Inc., New York, and in Canada
by Random House of Canada Limited, Toronto.

Pantheon Books and colophon are registered trademarks of
Random House, Inc.

Library of Congress Cataloging-in-Publication Data

Bonyhady, Tim, [date]
Good Living Street : Portrait of a Patron Family, Vienna 1900 /
Tim Bonyhady.
p. cm.
Includes bibliographical references and index.
ISBN 978-0-307-37880-4
1. Gallia family. 2. Art patrons—Austria—Vienna—Biography.
3. Jews—Austria—Vienna—Biography. 4. Gallia family—Art patronage. 5. Vienna
(Austria)—Biography. I. Title.
N5252.G35B66 2011   709.2'243613—dc22   [B]   2010053160

www.pantheonbooks.com

Jacket image: *Portrait of Hermine Gallia,* 1904, by Gustav Klimt. National Gallery,
London, UK/The Bridgeman Art Library International
Jacket design by Carol Devine Carson

Printed in the United States of America

First Edition

2 4 6 8 9 7 5 3 1

For Bruce

Contents

List of Illustrations   ix
The Gallia Family Tree   xiii

I   HERMINE   1

Introduction   3
1   Klimt   15
2   God   29
3   Gaslights   42
4   Family   50
5   Galas   61
6   Pictures   77
7   Rooms   90

II   GRETL   107

1   Diaries   109
2   Tango   116
3   Love   125
4   War   132
5   Hoffmann   142
6   Death   154
7   Sex   165
8   Marriage   174

III ANNELORE   189

1 Memory   191
2 Austro-fascism   208
3 Anschluss   218
4 Visas   230
5 Subterfuge   240
6 Loss   254
7 Capture   263

IV ANNE   273

1 1939   275
2 Aliens   284
3 Correspondence   297
4 Eric   305
5 Return   313
6 Dispersal   323
7 Restitution   331
8 Identity   338

Notes   349
Index   359

Illustrations

6   Wohllebengasse 4, c. 1913.

10 Emil Orlik, *Gustav Mahler*, 1903.

11 The postcard sent by Theobald Pollak and Alma and Gustav Mahler to Hermine, July 1903.

18 Ferdinand Andri, *Moriz Gallia*, 1901.

21 Gustav Klimt, *Hermine Gallia*, 1903–1904.

25 The Klimt portrait of Hermine with two of Koloman Moser's cubic chairs in the *Klimt Kollektiv* at the Secession, 1903.

27 Gustav Klimt, *Beech Forest*, 1903.

37 Hermine, aged about sixteen, c. 1886.

38 One of Hermine's many merit certificates.

39 The Gallias and the Hamburgers, 1903.

46 Moriz and Hermine, after being married in Vienna's main synagogue, 1893.

52 Moriz and Hermine kiss on the steps of Adolf and Ida Gallia's villa, Baden, c. 1898.

54 Erni with one of his wet nurses, 1895.

55 Hermine with Gretl in her arms and Erni on a table, 1897.

56 Käthe and Lene, 1901.

57 Moriz with Erni on his shoulders and Hermine with Gretl on her lap, c. 1898.

63 Hermine dressed for going out, wearing her best pearls.

66 A page from Gretl's third diary, March 30, 1916.

71 The program for the *Parsifal* seen by the Gallias in Bayreuth, 1912.

81 A letter from Klimt to Moriz accepting an invitation to dinner at the Schleifmühlgasse.

82 Hermine's photograph of Klimt, taken by the Madame d'Ora studio of Dora Kallmus, c. 1908.

91   Koloman Moser, *Sweet Bowl*, 1903.

96   Moriz and Hermine's summerhouse in Alt Aussee.

98   The ground-floor entrance to Wohllebengasse 4, designed by Franz von Krauss.

101   The boudoir in the Gallia apartment.

102   The smoking room in the Gallia apartment.

105   The salon in the Gallia apartment.

117   Eleven-year-old Gretl, 1908.

119   Gretl, around the time of her two ball seasons.

131   Eighteen-year-old Gretl.

134   One of the Gallias' war glasses.

156   Klimt's funeral at the Hietzing cemetery, February 9, 1918.

170   Lene, Hermine, Käthe, and Gretl, late 1917 or early 1918.

175   Erni and Mizzi, 1921.

180   Gretl and Paul, 1921.

194   Annelore, aged three, 1925.

197   Annelore in her sailor suit and pearls, 1931.

204   The Klimt portrait of Hermine and some of the Hoffmann furniture from the salon crammed into Käthe's apartment in Vienna's Third District, c. 1938.

215   Annelore in her ball dress, Landstrasser-Hauptstrasse, March 1938.

228   Annelore, September 1938.

251   Gretl and Annelore as photographed in Brisbane by the *Telegraph*, January 4, 1939.

264   Paul's passport when he escaped the Nazis by illegally entering Belgium without a visa, 1939.

279   St. Vincent's College, Sydney, run by the Sisters of Charity, 1939.

289   Käthe and Anne, Sydney, 1945.

292   Gretl, Sydney, Christmas 1949.

295   The Grail, including Anne, performing in Sydney in 1941.

302   Paul, Toulouse, February 1948.

307   The Bonyhadys, 1944.

310   Eric and Anne, Sydney, January 1948.

316   Gretl, Kathe, Anne, Bruce, and Tim in the apartment in Sydney, Christmas 1967.

343   Anne, Canberra, 2002.

347   The book stamp by Fritzi Löw showing Hermine and Moriz as a young courting couple.

COLOR PLATES

The poster by Heinrich Lefler for Auer von Welsbach's Gas Glowing Light
    Company.
Ferdinand Andri, *The Gallia Children*, 1901.
Carl Moll, *Beethoven House, Heiligenstadt*, 1903.
Ernst Stöhr, *Moonlit Landscape*, 1903.
Carl Moll, *In the Gardens of Schönbrunn*, c. 1910/1911.
Giovanni Segantini, *The Evil Mothers*, 1894.
The sideboard designed by Adolf Loos, 1903.
Moriz's inkstand, designed c. 1911 by Josef Hoffmann.
Michael Powolny's ceramic version of Klimt's *The Kiss*, c. 1907.
Josef Hoffmann, *Design for Boudoir*, 1915.
Josef Hoffmann, *Design for Smoking Room*, 1915.
Josef Hoffmann, *Two Vases and a Pair of Goblets*, 1915 or 1916.
Carl Witzmann, *Bowl*, 1912.
Josef Hoffmann, *Work Table and Two Chairs*, 1913.
The copy of *Der Ewige Jude*, or *The Eternal Jew*.

THE GALLIA FAMILY

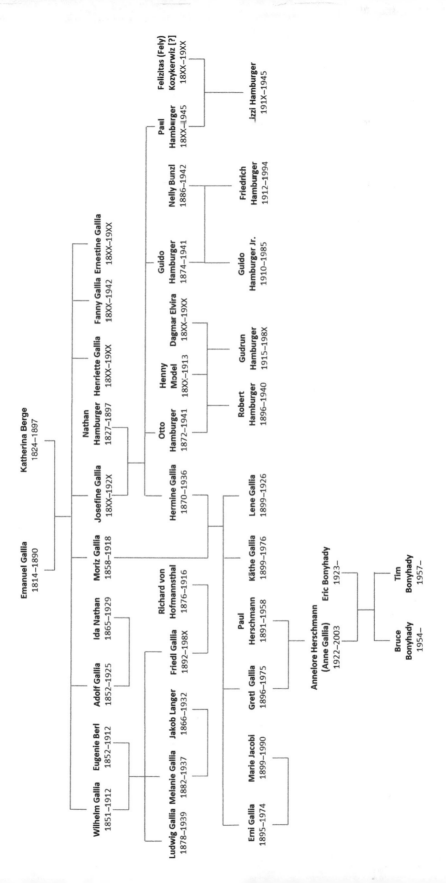

I

HERMINE

Introduction

Nineteen thirty-eight was a good year to be a mover in Vienna. As tens of thousands fled the city following the German annexation of Austria, the Nazis seized their businesses, required them to pay punitive departure taxes, prevented them from converting their remaining money into foreign currency, and stole much of their art. The refugees were usually able to leave with their other household goods, however, because the Nazis were eager to maintain the pretense that Austria's Jews were leaving voluntarily, and they wanted other countries to take them. The result was a surge in demand for movers in a city where it was common to rent the same apartment for life.

Vienna's leading newspaper, the *Neue Freie Presse,* did not need to report on this new economy built on persecution that led many movers to employ more workers and some to become specialists in the refugee trade. The newspaper's advertising columns told the story. Before the Anschluss, or annexation, that March, each edition of the *Presse* included at most one small advertisement from a mover, and more often contained none. Within a fortnight of the Anschluss, the *Presse* often carried three notices from movers quick to exploit the new market. By late April the newspaper carried up to seven of these advertisements. At the end of May, eleven.

The most remarkable consignment to leave Vienna belonged to two sisters—one unmarried, the other divorced, both unknown beyond the small circles in which they moved in Viennese society. Dr. Käthe Gallia, one of the first generation of women graduates of the University of Vienna, had abandoned her work as a chemist more than a decade earlier to become the manager of a family company that sold gas stoves. Her sister, Margarete Herschmann-Gallia, known as Gretl, had briefly been married to a Viennese leather merchant, Dr. Paul Herschmann. Like most married women of her class, Gretl had never worked.

Käthe was among the Nazis' first victims. Her job went first. Then the SS and Gestapo raided her apartment and imprisoned her. When they finally released her almost two months later, Gretl and she decided to escape Austria with Gretl's sixteen-year-old daughter, Annelore. While the United States of America would have taken them, the sisters chose Australia because other members of the family were headed there. By the start of November 1938, they were ready to join the fifty thousand who had fled Austria since the Anschluss. As Gretl and Käthe had all the necessary permits and approvals, they looked forward to a relatively simple departure. Once their movers packed up their apartments, they would take the train to Switzerland.

The sisters did not count on Kristallnacht, the pogrom ordered by Joseph Goebbels that erupted across the newly expanded German Reich in the early hours of the tenth of November and was more violent in Vienna than almost anywhere else. In all, the Nazis murdered at least twenty-seven Viennese Jews, severely injured another eighty-eight, and took nearly sixty-five hundred into custody, while looting more than four thousand shops and almost two thousand apartments and setting fire to almost all the city's synagogues and prayer rooms. The one exception was the main synagogue in the First District, which the Nazis left because its torching would have engulfed other buildings and because they needed the synagogue's records to determine who met their definition of a Jew.

When Gretl, Käthe, and Annelore realized a pogrom had started, they feared they would be among those whom the Nazis targeted. And even if they managed to escape the violence, would they be forced to flee empty-handed? They need not have worried. Their movers, who had started work a day or two before Kristallnacht, continued as usual on the tenth and eleventh of November, enabling Gretl and Annelore to leave on the twelfth and Käthe to follow on the fifteenth. As the Nazis terrorized Jews across the city, the movers swaddled the Gallias' furniture in blankets and wrapped their silver, glass, and ceramics in layers of tissue paper, ready for shipment around the globe.

Their containers included every conceivable household and personal item, ranging from chandeliers to doormats, cake molds to binoculars, lace and linen, skates and skis, letters and diaries, invoices and receipts. Rather than take one piano, Gretl and Käthe left with two: an upright and a grand. Their paintings included portraits, landscapes, seascapes, still lifes, genre subjects, a streetscape, and an interior. Each of their three sets of silver cutlery included more than 150 pieces. The biggest of their three display cabinets was more than five feet wide and almost six and a half feet high. Their main set of bookcases was nearly twenty feet long.

The sisters had inherited some of these objects from their uncle Adolf Gallia and his wife, Ida, who, in an era when only three in every hundred Viennese owned their own homes, occupied the grandest apartment in their own immense building on Vienna's renowned Ringstrasse. Almost everything else came from the sisters' parents, Moriz and Hermine, who lived just beyond the Ringstrasse in Vienna's Fourth District on the Wohllebengasse. Although named after Stefan Edler von Wohlleben, who was Vienna's mayor at the start of the nineteenth century, *Wohlleben*—or "good living"—evoked the area's character a century later. While *Gasse* literally means "lane" or "alley," the Wohllebengasse was so wealthy, spacious, and elegant that it was more like "Good Living Street."

The family was accustomed to buying the finest products, the best brands, the most prestigious labels. Just as the dinner service that Gretl inherited from her aunt Ida was one of the earliest sets of Flora Danica, the celebrated hand-molded, hand-painted porcelain decorated with Danish plants made by Royal Copenhagen, so the grand piano she inherited from her mother, Hermine, was a Steinway. Their furs included chinchilla and sable stoles and a sealskin mantle. But the paintings, furniture, silver, ceramics, and glass once owned by Moriz and Hermine were their most remarkable possessions. Almost all were from the turn of the century, when Vienna was among the world's most dynamic cultural and intellectual centers, one of the cities vital to the development of modernism, a source not just of great music, as it had been for centuries, but also of great art, design, architecture, literature, science, and ideas.

Moriz and Hermine were patrons of the Secession, the group of artists, architects, and designers led by Gustav Klimt that broke away from Vienna's long-established Künstlerhaus in 1897. They also were patrons of the Wiener Werkstätte, the most famous Viennese craft workshops, which the architects Josef Hoffmann and Koloman Moser established in 1903. The Gallias' grandest, most striking painting was a full-length portrait of Hermine by Klimt. Five of the front rooms of their apartment in the Wohllebengasse were designed by Hoffmann. While some families were significant early supporters of this culture and others began relatively late, Moriz and Hermine were among the few who sustained their patronage while this culture was at its peak from 1898 until 1918. When Gretl and

Käthe escaped in 1938, they took most of what Moriz and Hermine had collected and commissioned. Their crates, filled with the contents of Good Living Street, contained the best private collection of art and design to escape Nazi Austria.

Their destination was a Sydney apartment block built, like so many in the city, as if design did not matter, architecture did not pay, and aesthetics were for somewhere else. Its materials were the usual local combination of dull liver-red bricks topped by garish terra-cotta tiles. The approach to the front door down a narrow path on one side of the building was awkward, just as the main staircase was cold and mean. The building's one

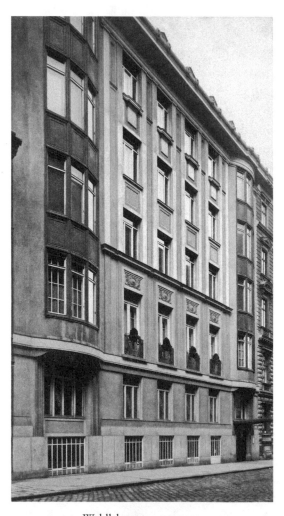

Wohllebengasse 4, c. 1913.

notable feature—its view of the harbor stretching almost from Sydney Heads to the center of the city at Circular Quay—owed everything to nature and nothing to culture.

The Gallias' apartment was different. One of the iconic portraits of Gustav Mahler, an etching by the Secessionist Emil Orlik, hung in the apartment's hall. The rest of the apartment's walls were thick with Secessionist paintings—most notably, Klimt's portrait of Hermine—while the apartment's rooms were filled with Hoffmann furniture, rugs, silver, and glass. A small sunroom was crammed with a suite of white-and-gold Hoffmann tables, chairs, and display cabinets. The other rooms were a domain of black—almost everything in them ebonized so the grain of the timber shone through. There were black Hoffmann tables, chairs, sideboards, and clocks, a black Hoffmann showcase, lamp, and piano stool, and seven black glass-fronted Hoffmann bookcases, which lined the walls of the two bedrooms as well as the long stretch of hall leading to the bathroom and toilet.

Because Hoffmann saw himself as creating a total work of art, or *Gesamtkunstwerk,* in which every element was integral and could fit into only one slot, his work could never be completely transplanted from one building, let alone one hemisphere, to another. Yet Gretl and Kathe—as Käthe became in Australia, just as Annelore became Anne—came remarkably close. For over thirty years, while the apartment in Cremorne was home to the Gallias, there was no comparable apartment in New York, Zurich, London, Budapest, or Prague. Nor, for that matter, was there one in Vienna itself, since most other Hoffmann interiors had been destroyed or dispersed. The apartment's contents were a mover's triumph, one of the great pieces of fin de siècle Vienna transported to Botany Bay.

I first went to the apartment as a baby—taken there by Anne shortly after she gave birth to me in 1957—and was soon going there regularly, usually with my older brother, Bruce. While adults who visited the apartment remember it as claustrophobic because the rooms were so full and so much of the furniture was black, I was completely at ease there as a boy. I had no idea that many of Gretl's and Käthe's things were designed for rooms at least two or three, if not four, times the size, rooms with high ceilings that easily accommodated chandeliers, rooms with fluted columns and marble paneling identical to those on the furniture, rooms designed at least as much for entertaining as for family life, rooms serviced by maids in uniforms. While I knew that Gretl and Kathe had fled Austria as refugees, I never thought of their things as being displaced. I thought everything in the apartment was in the perfect spot, exactly where it always had been intended.

Insofar as I realized there was a family treasure trove, it was not the apartment, where the doors had simple locks and Gretl and Kathe paid no attention to security, but a bank deposit box in a vast marble-clad, mosaic-decorated, barrel-domed vault in the center of the city where Gretl and Kathe kept their best jewelry in a safe twice the standard size. When I went there with Gretl, I looked with awe on the uniformed security guards, the grilled entrance opened only on proving one's credentials, and the immense steel door. I was impressed that it required two keys to open the safe—one carried by the guards, the other by Gretl. I was struck by the serious quiet of everyone who entered and how they each looked to find a cubicle where they could change the contents of their safe without anyone else observing what they were doing.

Had it been up to Gretl, I am sure she would have regaled Bruce and me with stories about her life in Vienna, just as she did her closest Australian friend, John Earngey, whom she came to regard as her stepson. But Anne asked Gretl not to, so we could become as Australian as possible, and Gretl agreed, although opportunities were everywhere. She could have talked as we sat in the apartment in Sydney surrounded by her Viennese inheritance. She might have told me more when we went into town and, without my knowing, visited one shop after another run by other Austrian refugees. She could have continued when she took Bruce and me to *The Sound of Music* in 1965 and for the first time we saw a film that not only represented the Anschluss but did so in one of the landscapes most important to Gretl—that of Salzburg and the surrounding Salzkammergut, where she spent twenty-seven summers.

I remember returning from the movie to the apartment, taking out my sketch pad, and drawing pistol-carrying Nazis based on seventeen-year-old Rolf, who begins as sixteen-year-old Liesl's love interest and ends as the weak, confused Nazi who catches the von Trapps as they flee but neither uses his gun nor raises the alarm until they have gone. As I recall it, I did these drawings without any sense that the escape of Gretl, Kathe, and Anne had been much more remarkable than that of the von Trapps. I did not realize that the captain, Maria, and the children could never have walked from the Salzkammergut over the Alps to freedom in Switzerland because it was almost one hundred miles to the west. I had no idea that in fact the von Trapps simply walked to their local station and took the train to Italy, where they were entitled to go because they had dual Austrian and Italian citizenship. I know that Gretl, who had read *The Story of the Trapp Family Singers,* which revealed that much of the film was invention, typically said nothing.

As I remember it, the only story Gretl ever told me about her escape— almost the only story she told me about her forty-two years in Austria— was about four thin disks, all the same size, all covered in the same dark blue material, which she kept in the safe. They intrigued me in a way that none of the jewelry did because it was not clear why they were there. Gretl explained that they were gold coins that she disguised before leaving Vienna so that she could take them into Switzerland undetected by the Nazis' border guards. After covering the coins with cloth, she sewed them onto her traveling coat in place of its original buttons and did not unwrap the coins even after she reached Sydney, so they remained talismans of her escape, symbols of her success in defying the Nazis.

The Orlik etching of Gustav Mahler—one of my favorite pictures in the apartment—sparked my first venture into family history. The catalyst was an inscription it carried by Mahler, perhaps the only time he inscribed one of these portraits. I was intrigued because this inscription was not to one of the Gallias but to Mahler's "dear friend" Dr. Theobald Pollak "in memory of the original." While Anne had told me that Theobald Pollak was one of Gretl's honorary uncles—she called him Uncle Baldi—I knew nothing else. In the library, I discovered a web of connections linking the Gallias and Pollak with Mahler and his wife, Alma Schindler. But a visit to my mother proved even more revealing when she took out a box containing a small cache of correspondence from the Mahlers, including one of their personal postcards. Sent to Hermine in 1903—the year of the Orlik portrait—this card was jointly written by Theobald Pollak and Gustav and Alma Mahler.

Until then, I had never ventured into the literature of fin de siècle Vienna, let alone thought of contributing to it. Although I had been to Vienna several times as a child and as an adult, it was not my city. While I enjoyed Vienna's art, architecture, and music, the culture and history, politics and law that I wanted to explore were those of Australia, my family's new home. The books I wrote, like the exhibitions I curated and the environmental causes I tried to advance, were an extension of my

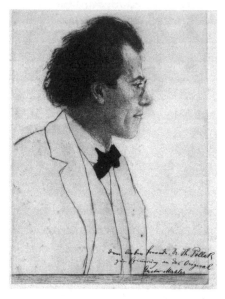

Emil Orlik, *Gustav Mahler*, 1903. Perhaps the only example of this portrait inscribed by Mahler himself.

mother's attempt to assimilate in Australia, a means of making me more Australian.

I had also never thought of adding to what had been written about the family since turn-of-the-century Vienna began exciting international interest in the 1960s. While the Gallias usually appeared as patrons of Klimt and Hoffmann in books and catalogs about art and design, Moriz and Hermine also featured in the literature about what made Vienna one of the intellectual and cultural centers of the early twentieth century. The Gallias were part of the argument about whether it was Jews and Jewish converts to Christianity who gave Vienna a cultural significance it had not achieved before or since.

I was ignorant about things Jewish as well, despite one visit to Israel with my mother on our way back from our second trip to Europe when I was fifteen. It was not only that I was an atheist who had never been to synagogue and knew nothing of the Talmud but also that I was almost completely removed from Jewish society and culture. When I first met Claire Young, with whom I lived for twenty years, I had no idea what she meant when she described herself as a shiksa. Without novels—especially

James Michener's *The Source,* which I chose as my prize for coming in fifth in my second year of high school in 1970, and *Exodus* by Leon Uris, which I read around the same time—I would have known almost nothing of Jewish history.

I also had little idea what was in my mother's cupboards. It had not occurred to me that she might have correspondence linking the Gallias and the Mahlers. As my stints in the library and the papers in her box began illuminating the place of the Gallias in turn-of-the-century Vienna, I gained a new sense of possibility. Where Vienna had been outside the bounds of what I might write about, it now moved within them.

My mother did not intend to get me started. The last thing Anne wanted was for me to write about her. Had she put more store on her life before she died in 2003, I might not have begun. But Anne was adamant that her life was not interesting. When my brother, Bruce, and I tried to get her to think differently, we failed. While it is in the nature of parents to expect the last word in arguments when their children are young, it is a prerogative of the living to have the last word about the dead. When I embarked on this book, it was because of Anne. Insofar as I intended to write about other

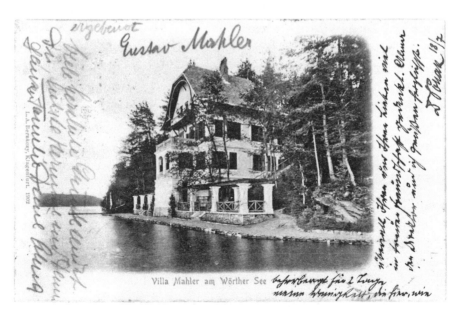

The postcard jointly sent by Theobald Pollak and Alma and Gustav Mahler to Hermine in July 1903 showing the Mahlers' summer villa.

members of the family, it was to explain her. Above all, I wanted to put a value on her life that she did not. Although her death was still far too close for me to be ready to write about it, my plan was to begin and end with her.

I thought I had ideal materials—accessible, diverse, and rich without being daunting. I had a memoir written by Anne at my request in the early 1990s as my interest in the Gallias grew. There was a cache of family papers in her cupboards. There was the family's Wiener Werkstätte collection, which had become the only substantial Hoffmann commission to enter a museum largely intact when the National Gallery of Victoria in Melbourne acquired it in 1976. Not even Vienna's Museum of Applied Arts had anything like it. There was the portrait of Hermine that had been the only painting by Klimt in an English museum since the National Gallery in London acquired it, also in 1976.

I still wanted more, of course, and was soon looking far and wide, not only spending long stints in archives, libraries, and museums but also visiting the towns where different family members came from, the buildings where they lived and worked, and the cemeteries where they were buried. Yet for all I found, nothing equaled my mother's cupboards, which contained much more than I realized. There were concert books, weather books, travel logs, autograph books, sketchbooks, recipe books, and a guest book. There were birth and death certificates, wedding and divorce documents, and a prenuptial agreement. There were records of leaving one religion and entering another. There were school exercise books and school prizes. There were passports, letters, postcards, poems, and menus. There were books with inscriptions, dedications, and marginal notes. There were theater, concert, and cinema programs. There were photographs not only of members of the family but also of the houses and apartments where they lived. There was an account of arrest and imprisonment.

This material took me deeper into the past than I ever thought possible, transforming my mother's place in this book in a way I could not resist. While my cast of characters multiplied as I embraced many members of the family whom Anne had rejected, the change in the place of Hermine and Gretl was greatest. Because their surviving diaries were much richer than I anticipated, I felt compelled to make the most of them. As this material was about how the Gallias lived in Vienna in the late nineteenth and early twentieth centuries, this part of the book grew and grew. I found myself writing a book about three generations of women: my great-grandmother, grandmother, and mother.

I also found myself coming closer to the present than I had planned. I had initially intended to stop when Gretl, Käthe, and Annelore escaped Vienna because their Australian lives seemed too big to deal with in this book. But having gotten them to Sydney, I found I had to go further, if only selectively. I wanted to discover how they dealt with their loss of privilege, what it was like for them to be classified as enemy aliens once World War II started, and how their religion continued to change. I needed to show how they responded to a very different culture, how after trying so hard to assimilate in Austria they tried again in Australia, and how they remained deeply attached to Austria despite the persecution they suffered there. As I came to think of it, I had to explore what it meant for Annelore to become Anne.

I was also eager to explore what happened to the family collection and to discover how Gretl and Kathe had succeeded in bringing their paintings and furniture to Australia when the Nazis looted so much art in Austria. But again I found myself working forward as I came to think that how Anne disposed of the collection was as integral to its history as how Moriz and Hermine acquired it. Anne's treatment of her inheritance exemplified how a collection built up by family members with access to the best advice and smartest taste is often dispersed one or two generations later by a descendant with nothing like the same understanding of the art world and little or no appreciation of what he or she has inherited. Anne's experience also demonstrated the vulnerability of the naive in the art market.

My pursuit of these questions was both impersonal and personal. At times I would be engaged with Hermine, Gretl, and Anne like any other historical subjects, looking for materials to reconstruct their lives without particular emotional investment in the process or heightened response to what I found. At times I would be drawing on my direct knowledge and inherited understanding of the family and grappling with trace memories, trying to conjure up what I once had been told or seemed to have experienced. Yet from the moment I started dipping into the diaries in Anne's cupboards and found her enjoying a night at the Vienna Opera on Kristallnacht, the past would confront and shock me in a way I had never experienced.

I was particularly struck by the continuities and discontinuities across the generations—how some patterns of behavior had been abandoned while others were repeated regardless of their flaws. Like Anne, I struggled with the legacy of coming from a rich Jewish family but, unlike her, I began to accept Judaism as part of my identity while still being shocked by the ostentatious consumption of Hermine and Moriz and embarrassed to find myself the great-grandson of such a tycoon. Wherever I turned, I found more than I anticipated or wanted, not just because it kept me writing longer than I expected but also because it often took me into terrain where I would have preferred not to tread.

I began to see that, however much the Gallias were exceptional in their embrace of modern art and design at the turn of the century, and how fortunate they were to escape with most of their collection after the Anschluss, in many respects they were creatures of convention and followers of fashion, whether it came to their passion for Wagner, embrace of the tango, or attitudes toward sex and marriage. For all their individuality, they were in large measure typical of those Jews who came from the provinces of the Austro-Hungarian Empire in the late nineteenth century, enriched Vienna at least as much as it enriched them until the late 1930s, and then with extraordinary speed were all gone from the city they had expected would always be their home.

I also saw that for all the debate about the extent to which the culture of fin de siècle Vienna was a creation of the city's Jews, only Alexander Waugh's *The House of Wittgenstein* had taken one of the families that had been among the big patrons of this culture and told their story over several generations. For all the interest in this Vienna, there was no other book that explored where one of these families had come from, how they had made their money, what they spent it on, who they mixed with, what happened to their religion, and what became of them and their possessions. If this material existed for other families, no one had exploited it. I would write this book about the Gallias by making what I could of the remains of Good Living Street.

I

Klimt

The bronze doors made by Gustav Klimt's brother Georg opened at eleven in the morning, but not everyone was welcome inside the small white-and-gold templelike structure on Vienna's Friedrichstrasse that combined the ornate with the austere and enriched the city's architecture as much as it transformed its artistic life at the turn of the century. Instead, entry to the Vienna Secession that Saturday, November 14, 1903, was restricted to the society's members and a select group of invitees, many of them collectors. The rest of the public had to wait until the following morning to view the Secession's eighteenth exhibition.

Those who attended were primarily women, dressed for these fashionable events in the most glamorous ways—some in hats decorated with spectacular bird feathers; others in veils; some still wearing conventional wasp-waisted, tightly laced, or corseted dresses; others in loose-fitting reform dresses widely promoted as rational; most in fur coats and muffs. The diaries kept by Alma Schindler, whose stepfather, Carl Moll, was a leading figure in the Secession, suggests many were Jews. After attending the private view of another of the Secession's exhibitions, Alma observed, "All the tribes of Israel were assembled, as ever, like on a feast day at the synagogue."

Hermine Gallia was one of them. While she was probably a regular at the Secession's private views, the society's eighteenth exhibition was especially important for Hermine because she appeared in it in a new guise. When the private view opened, her portrait by Klimt went on show for the first time. While identified in the exhibition catalog simply as a *Portrait of a Lady*—the standard practice of the Secession, which liked to keep the sitters of portraits anonymous—everyone who mattered to Hermine would have soon discovered that she had joined the ranks of the small group of women, still just seven in all, painted by Vienna's most successful and most notorious artist.

How might Hermine have been described that morning? She was the daughter of a wealthy industrialist in the small Silesian town of Freudenthal in the northern reaches of the Hapsburg Empire. She was married to her uncle Moriz, who had made a fortune as a businessman in Vienna. She was thirty-three years old, already middle-aged according to the contemporary calculus, a society matron. She was not just Frau Gallia but Frau Regierungsrat Gallia, as Emperor Franz Joseph had made Moriz a *Regierungsrat,* or imperial councilor. She was familiar with many of Vienna's leading artists, architects, and musicians—a friend of one or two, an acquaintance of many. She was a member of Vienna's main Jewish organization, its Israelitische Kultusgemeinde. She was the mother of four children, one boy and three girls, all of whom were Catholics.

The portrait by Klimt both signified her status and was designed to enhance it by demonstrating the Gallias' wealth, taste, and support for the avant-garde. While Hermine and Moriz conceived the painting primarily as a private picture that would hang in their apartment, they expected the portrait to shape how they were perceived by their many visitors. They anticipated that, like most of Klimt's paintings at the turn of the century, the portrait would be exhibited at the Secession when it was new so that Klimt could show off what he had just produced and they could show off what they had just acquired. They saw the portrait as an investment in the future, a claim on posterity, since, for all of Klimt's notoriety, it was the form in which Hermine was most likely to be remembered, the guise in which she had the greatest chance of becoming famous, able to perpetuate Hermine not just within the private sphere of the family but also in the public arena of art.

The outcry over Klimt's work had started in the late 1890s, when he rapidly went from being an artist of great technical facility but little originality to one of Europe's most innovative, imaginative painters. Klimt's rejection of traditional iconography resulted in several of his paintings being branded ugly, unnatural, and incomprehensible, as well as being lauded as daring and profound. The eroticism of much of his work led to its being declared obscene; in the case of the vast canvases of *Philosophy* and *Medicine,* which the imperial government commissioned for the University of Vienna, it excited petitions and counterpetitions from members of parliament and the university's professors. Meanwhile, his poster for the Secession's first exhibition in 1898 and a special issue of its magazine *Ver Sacrum* in 1901 had Klimt in trouble with the law—the first time for his depiction of a male nude, the second time on account of his female nudes.

Klimt was sustained through these years by a small group of private patrons who admired his new work and enjoyed the frisson that came from embracing the controversial. Interest in Klimt was so great that, when the Secession first devoted an issue of *Ver Sacrum* to him in 1898, the magazine's circulation more than doubled. The demand for his tiny output of just five or six paintings a year also allowed Klimt to increase his prices substantially in the early 1900s, making him Vienna's most expensive contemporary artist. His fee for a life-size portrait was 10,000 crowns, or about $100,000 in today's money.

As Moriz and Hermine would have known, Klimt's portraits were his only paintings to inspire general acclaim. His unusual ability to render materials, textures, hair, and skin was one factor. But so was his mix of realism and idealism, which saw his portraits praised as "faithful to reality, yet almost unreal." They were thought to represent their subjects at "the finest moment of their lives," even when, as with the thirty-six-year-old Rose von Rosthorn-Friedmann, whom Klimt painted in 1901, a Viennese critic publicly characterized her as "past her prime" and the twenty-one-year-old Alma Schindler privately dismissed her as an "old hag."

Those close to the Secession, such as Moriz and Hermine, also knew about Klimt's womanizing; a number of his sitters may have had affairs with him. As gossip circulated around the Secession, its supporters learned that Klimt had several children with his models, perhaps even discovered that he had two babies by different mothers within a month of each other in 1899. They wondered whether the dress designer Emilie Flöge was simply Klimt's companion, at least briefly his lover, or his one enduring mistress. They probably knew that Klimt attempted to seduce Alma Schindler, who was the woman most pursued by Vienna's greatest artists, writers, and musicians at the turn of the century. They heard that Klimt became Rose von Rosthorn-Friedmann's lover while painting her, which prompted Alma to write, "He takes what he can get," seemingly an expression of contempt for Klimt—except when Alma wrote exactly the same about the theater director and playwright Max Burckhard, she added, "Just what I'd do!"

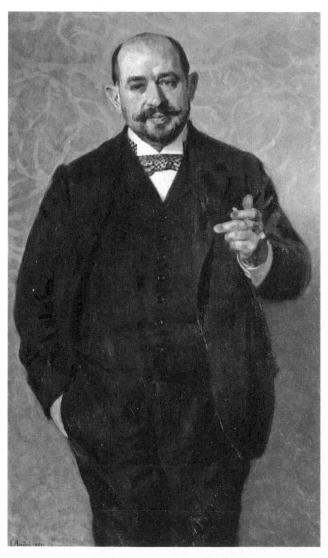

Ferdinand Andri, *Moriz Gallia*, 1901.

Klimt's reputation as a difficult artist to employ preceded him when Moriz and Hermine decided to have their entire family painted. They knew that Klimt refused to paint men. They understood that he demanded substantial advances but rarely completed his work on time. They realized that, in keeping with his highly developed persona as an artistic genius not subject to the strictures of ordinary society, he never acknowledged that he was fortunate to be able to work on this basis but treated even his biggest patrons as if they were lucky to have him paint them.

Hermine's appearance may have been an issue. A few years later Klimt reputedly refused to paint another Viennese matron, Marianne Löw-Beer, because she was plump, very different from his ideal of female beauty. As Hermine was growing increasingly stout, when the Gallias approached Klimt, he might have preferred not to paint her. But Klimt understood in the early 1900s that he could not be so selective when he painted both the thirty-six-year-old Rose von Rosthorn-Friedmann and the fifty-year-old Marie Henneberg. Because of the Gallias' support of the Secession, Klimt had no choice. Although he did not have to start immediately, he had to paint Hermine.

While Moriz and she waited, they decided to commission portraits of the rest of the family, starting with Moriz—a relatively unusual decision in turn-of-the-century Vienna where the husbands of Klimt's sitters generally went unpainted. Because no Viennese artist was renowned for portraits of men, Moriz and Hermine probably weighed a number of possibilities, while considering only members of the Secession. One was Carl Moll, a close friend of the Gallias, who had just painted his own family. Another was Max Kurzweil, whom Moriz knew because they were both Jews from the small Moravian town of Bisenz. Moriz and Hermine opted for Ferdinand Andri, who was acclaimed as "an artist who would never be forgotten" when he first showed with the Secession in 1899 at age twenty-eight and, by 1901, was on the society's governing committee and shaping its public image by designing the poster for its tenth exhibition. Because Andri was still eager for commissions, he embarked immediately on a three-quarter-length portrait of Moriz and, as soon as it was done, painted the Gallia children.

Moriz was forty-two years old in 1901—balding, bearded, big-eared, and portly. As several photographs record, the mustache, which had made him look stylish—even debonair—as a young man when he waxed it to form a perfect handlebar, had lost much of its shape. His face, once thin, had become soft and jowly. His standard dress was a dark three-piece suit with a white shirt and bow tie. While the writer Stefan Zweig recalled that his father never smoked an imported cigar despite making a fortune as a textile-mill owner—a kind of moderation that Zweig declared typical of Vienna's Jewish bourgeoisie—Moriz was unable to relax without a Havana in hand. His preferred stance was to have his right hand in his trouser pocket, a cigar holder held high in his left. Andri painted him like this, an archetypal successful businessman, while otherwise showing Moriz as quizzical and contemplative, tinged by sadness if not self-doubt, creating an engaging, personable image but hardly a flattering one.

Almost everything about Hermine's portrait was different when Klimt embarked on it, probably in 1902. He typically worked much more slowly than Andri. He also worked on a larger scale, painting Hermine full length. His much greater artistic ambition, pictorial imagination, and technical facility were even more significant, as were the different conventions for male and female portraiture. While Andri thought it appropriate to paint a man dressed just as he appeared every day, Klimt worked to make a woman look special, even extraordinary, while still providing a likeness. The result was anything but a mate for Andri's painting—Hermine's portrait utterly eclipsed Moriz's.

The clothing of Klimt's sitters was crucial, though how they came to wear it remains largely a matter of conjecture. Klimt's painting of Emilie Flöge is an example. By one account, her spectacular blue and gold dress decorated with spirals, circles, and squares was the one piece of clothing designed by Klimt for any of his sitters. By another account, this dress was a pictorial invention of Klimt's, created by him on canvas. For all her renown as a founder of Vienna's most innovative fashion salon, no one has suggested that Flöge might have designed this dress herself.

As Gretl and Kathe recalled it seventy years later—relying perhaps on what Gretl witnessed as a six- and seven-year-old as well as what Hermine told them—Klimt began by fitting out Hermine. Rather than simply deciding what she should wear, Klimt designed her clothes himself and had them made by Flöge. His choices were typically modern. As with many of his other early portraits, he painted Hermine in different shades of white in the style of the Anglo-American artist James McNeill Whistler. Klimt opted for a long, flowing reform dress, together with a ball-entrée or

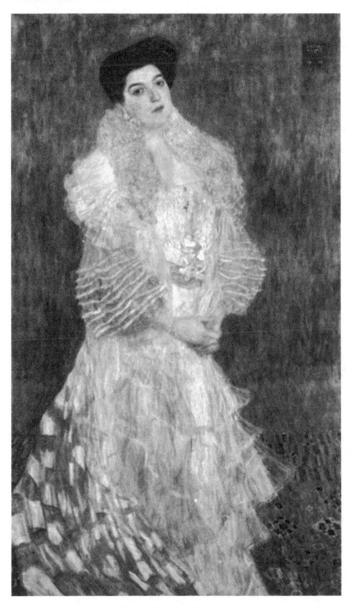

Gustav Klimt, *Hermine Gallia*, 1903–1904.

short cape for Hermine's shoulders and a boa for her neck with a pink broad band around her waist. At most, Hermine chose her own jewelry—a gold brooch with two enormous solitaire diamonds for her bodice, pearl earrings, and two rings, an emerald surrounded by diamonds and a sapphire with a gold bar.

Klimt's next step was to draw Hermine, making very quick pencil or crayon sketches to work out the composition of his painting. While Klimt made more than one hundred sketches for his first "golden" portrait of Adele Bloch-Bauer a year or two later, he usually required only about a dozen. Klimt did more than forty of Hermine. He began by showing her sitting, then did even more of her standing. He drew her with hands apart and hands clasped, her face looking directly at the viewer and her face in profile, sometimes turned to the left, sometimes to the right, before deciding on a pose different from all his other portraits, which made her painting distinctive. He had her stand on a slight angle, her upturned face toward the viewer, her hands clasped.

Like many society painters, Klimt regularly improved the appearance of his sitters, so the gulf between his portraits and photographs of these women is often profound. When Klimt painted Hermine, he disguised her portliness and depicted her with much more glamour and grace than any contemporary photographer. Yet a photograph taken over a decade later shows Hermine looking much like Klimt painted her, with her hair the same and her face on the same angle. This resemblance may be the result of Hermine's trying to live up to Klimt's picture and for once succeeding. Perhaps the photographer did all he could to emulate Klimt. Whatever the explanation, Hermine is much more sensual and beautiful in this photograph than in Klimt's painting.

The standard expectation of portraiture in Vienna was to provide a likeness and capture character, revealing the sitter's nature through her or his exterior. The prime vehicle for doing so was the face, which was regarded as the window on the soul. But Klimt generally worked in the very different tradition of aristocratic portraits developed by seventeenth-century painters such as Anthony Van Dyck, who distanced their subjects from the viewer rather than opening them to scrutiny. In keeping with this approach, Klimt showed his patrons as self-absorbed, staring off into space, more or less expressionless.

Did this mean that Klimt revealed little or nothing about his sitters? The novelist, playwright, and essayist Hermann Bahr, who was the self-appointed leader of the literary group Jung Wien, thought so. Despite his great regard for Klimt, Bahr maintained: "He paints a woman as though she were a jewel. She merely glitters, but the ring on her hand seems to breathe, and her hat has more life in it than she herself." Franz Servaes, the art critic of the *Neue Freie Presse,* disagreed. Partly because he assumed that Klimt's sitters determined how they appeared in his pictures, Servaes viewed their clothes, jewelry, and even their poses as expressive of their personalities. Servaes also credited Klimt with profound understanding of the relationship between the outer and the inner, unusually adept at conveying the souls of his sitters through his rendering of their silk dresses.

The portrait of Hermine tests this argument. The National Gallery in London has suggested that the portrait reveals "Klimt's fascination with drapery, which is the determining feature in the painting. The face and personality of the sitter interested him less than the sinuous rhythms of the costume." This assessment ignores how, like many of Klimt's other portraits, the painting of Hermine depends on the contrast between the stylized abstraction of her clothes and the relative naturalism of her face. For all the interest of the frills, patterns and folds, textures and translucence of Hermine's dress, her contemplative, even melancholy, face commands our attention.

The portrait occupied Klimt off and on for months through 1903. When he exhibited it at the Secession that November, he described it as unfinished. A photograph of the portrait in the Secession shows that it could easily have been taken as complete. But the exact appearance of the painting in 1903 remains unclear—and not just because Klimt later made slight changes to Hermine's hair, neck, and shoulders. The English art historian Frank Whitford has suggested that the portrait is one of many Klimts that have lost luster with age. It certainly is a very different picture from the one I knew as a child in Sydney. I remember being fascinated by the globules of paint that Klimt used to construct Hermine's gold brooch with solitaire diamonds. The paint was so thick that the brooch was almost three-dimensional—raised high above the surface of the canvas. This paint is now gone.

The exhibition at the Secession was special because it was the only one-man show Klimt ever held. This *Klimt Kollektiv* was doubly exciting because it did not attempt an overview of the work of the forty-three-year-old artist but was confined to the six years since the Secession's founding, when his work had been most innovative. The exhibition's interest was all the greater because ten paintings were new—a remarkable number for Klimt, who was exceptionally productive in 1903, spurred by the need to fill the Secession's rooms as much as the opportunity to have an exhibition to himself. The prime attraction was the last of Klimt's vast canvases for the University of Vienna, *Jurisprudence*. Because *Philosophy* and *Medicine* had excited such controversy, many wanted *Jurisprudence* to do the same. The *Neue Freie Presse* expected that *Jurisprudence* would be the "sensation" of the exhibition, provoking a "war of words" over whether Klimt was "a creator of masterpieces or painter of offal."

Expecting the worst, Klimt's admirers had a book ready in his defense, which Hermine and Moriz immediately bought. It was by Hermann Bahr, who identified Klimt as the one Austrian on a par with the finest contemporary European painters, the latest in a long line of great Austrian writers, composers, and artists pilloried by a blinkered, intolerant society. But the great polemicist and satirist Karl Kraus was almost alone in deriding *Jurisprudence*. Having already characterized Klimt's work as a domain of "goût juif," or "Jewish taste," in the course of identifying a larger connection between "modern art and idle-rich Jewry," Kraus lambasted Klimt for reducing jurisprudence to a barbarous system of revenge amounting to no more than "hunt them down and wring their necks." In branding Klimt a fraud, Kraus maintained that drunken students prosecuted for abusing policemen could only envy Klimt's success in getting away with painted insults.

The installation of the exhibition by Josef Hoffmann and Koloman Moser, who had just founded the Wiener Werkstätte with the businessman Fritz Waerndorfer, added to the excitement. While Hoffmann designed the exhibition's small, sumptuous anteroom, Moser designed the nine rooms containing Klimt's work with unprecedented simplicity. The walls were all white apart from a thin gray-and-gold frieze, which Moser used as a cornice and skirting and placed around all the doors. The rooms were empty apart from a scattering of new "cubic" chairs with square backs, square sides, and square seats that were among the most striking Viennese examples of geometric furniture. Instead of the pictures being hung two or three high, they were hung in a single line with ample space between them, much to the delight of Vienna's one notable female art critic, Berta Zuckerkandl, who admired Moser's creation of an environment "as still and discreet as possible," while still expressing her shock at the "royal squandering of space."

The portrait of Hermine was the dominant painting in the exhibition's sixth room, which also included a portrait of an unidentified girl and two landscapes. While these pictures were grouped together because of their "color harmony," each had a wall to itself. A photograph of the portrait of Hermine shows it in the most elegant setting ever created for it, framed not only by a simple thin piece of gilded beading but also by two of Moser's cubic chairs and by the gray-and-gold frieze that turned the entire wall into an outer frame.

The painting was no match for Klimt's other new woman in white, commissioned by Anton Loew, who owned Vienna's most exclusive sanitorium. Not only was Loew's nineteen-year-old daughter, Gertrud, much younger and prettier than Hermine, but she had also been painted by Klimt in an unusually narrow, striking format. Klimt's new portrait of Emilie Flöge was even more eye-catching because of her extraordinary blue-and-gold dress and her remarkable beauty, which Klimt did not exag-

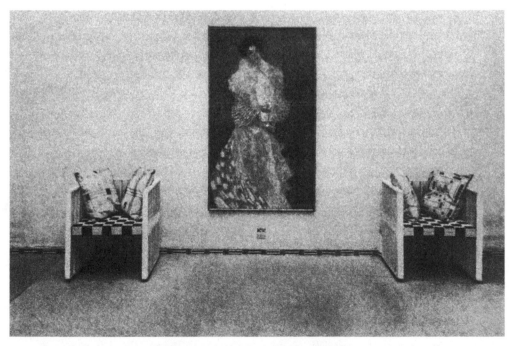

The Klimt portrait of Hermine with two of Koloman Moser's cubic chairs in the
Klimt Kollektiv at the Secession, 1903.

gerate. While the twenty-nine-year-old Flöge was just four years younger than Hermine, she looked like she belonged to a different generation. Klimt also painted her with much more inventiveness when he set her head against a halo of flowers, creating the first of his ornate, exotic backgrounds, one of his most sinuous, seductive images. The first response of local critics appeared in Vienna's morning newspapers before Hermine and Moriz went to the private view. The Secession's greatest champion, Ludwig Hevesi, lauded the new portraits for their "magical delicacy which was unique to Klimt." Berta Zuckerkandl credited Klimt with capturing the "sublimated essence of the modern type of woman."

The private view was the Gallias' first opportunity to see how Hermine's portrait looked properly framed, hung, and displayed, rather than on Klimt's easel in his studio. It was also their first opportunity to compare the painting with Klimt's other new portraits, just as everyone who saw Hermine would have compared her picture with how she looked that day. But the private view also provided collectors such as Hermine and Moriz with the best opportunity to buy more of Klimt's work when there was the greatest possible choice. While the Secession made much of how it organized exhibitions "on the basis of purely artistic considerations," the *Klimt Kollektiv* was also a commercial venture in which sixteen of his paintings—including two of the most controversial—were for sale. One was Klimt's *Pallas Athena,* which was widely regarded as shocking when he showed it at the Secession's second exhibition in 1898 because of his unprecedented depiction of the Greek goddess as a terrifying warrior. The other picture was *Goldfish*—in fact a painting of three young naked women dominated by one taking evident pleasure in displaying her ample bottom—which one critic greeted in 1902 as "a product of the most perverted taste, a soulless larking about with paint."

Seven paintings sold at the private view. While the overt sexuality of *Goldfish* again proved too much for Viennese collectors, *Pallas Athena* was bought by one of the founders of the Wiener Werkstätte, Fritz Waerndorfer. Hermine and Moriz chose one of Klimt's landscapes, which, while not as controversial, were his most modernist pictures and consequently still excited fierce responses and often took years to sell. "The people rolled about laughing," Ludwig Hevesi wrote of the response to Klimt's *Crab Apple Tree* in 1898. "They should be in an exhibition on Mars or Neptune. On our globe things still look somewhat different," another critic observed of the *Klimt Kollektiv.* The Gallias chose one of Klimt's forest

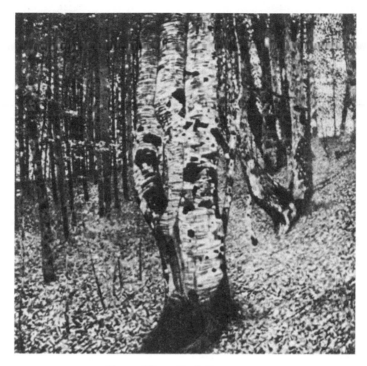

Gustav Klimt, *Beech Forest*, 1903.

interiors, in which he painted the trees from so close that their trunks typically extend beyond the top of the picture frame. It was a *Beech Forest* that Klimt probably had begun only that summer.

This purchase changed the status of Hermine and Moriz among Vienna's cultural elite. On the day that Hermine first publicly appeared as one of Klimt's subjects, Moriz and she demonstrated their wealth, taste for the new, and regard for Klimt by buying another of his paintings. While Hermine and Moriz needed to own one picture by Klimt to be regarded as serious collectors of avant-garde Austrian art, to purchase two put them in another league, given Klimt's high prices and small output. The only collector to own more Klimts in 1903 was Fritz Waerndorfer, whose collection grew to four when he bought *Pallas Athena*.

The appetite of Moriz and Hermine for culture was still not sated. The performances on offer that night in Vienna ranged from a production of part one of Goethe's *Faust* at the Hofburgtheater to the regular Saturday night performance of Johann Strauss Jr. at the Kursalon. After admiring and acquiring the most exciting new Viennese art during the day, Moriz and Hermine opted for more new Austrian culture. Leaving their children with their governess, Moriz and Hermine spent the evening at the Deutsches Volkstheater, watching *Maria Theresa,* the latest comedy by Franz von Schöntan, whose plays were very popular yet appealed to the avant-garde.

2

God

Most Viennese in 1900 came from somewhere else. As towns and villages shrank and cities swelled across Europe in the nineteenth century, Vienna grew unusually quickly. The 445,000 people who lived there in 1850 became 1.6 million in 1900, making Vienna the third most populous European city after London and Paris. Moriz and Hermine were among the provincials who flocked there from across the Hapsburg Empire, especially the Czech Crown lands. He came from southern Moravia, where Czech was the local language, but most Jews used German, which was the language of social and economic aspiration. She came from southern Silesia, where almost everyone spoke German.

Their families were both prosperous. Moriz's father, Emmanuel Gallia, was a successful produce merchant, innkeeper, and landowner in Bisenz, a town of just a few thousand people offering limited economic opportunities. Hermine's father, Nathan Hamburger, did much better in Freudenthal, which was more than three times the size of Bisenz. He began in 1864, aged just twenty-three, by renting one of the town's two breweries. In 1870, he bought it and rapidly transformed it into one of the most modern in Silesia. Before long he was also producing malt for export and acquired two inns, a restaurant, a hall, a business selling farming equipment, and a butter factory, making him one of Freudenthal's wealth-iest men.

Just as aristocrats often intermarried in the mid-nineteenth century to aggregate their wealth and power, so did members of the upper middle class. The Rothschilds were particularly committed to this practice, which usually involved first or second cousins but sometimes uncles and nieces. Between the 1820s and 1870s, thirty of thirty-six Rothschild marriages were within the family. The Gallias and Hamburgers had far less wealth to protect but continued this practice at the end of the century when marriages between relatives were rarer. While two of Hermine's first cousins married each other and another married a second cousin, Moriz and Hermine were uncle and niece. She was the eldest child and only daughter of his oldest sister, Josefine. He was twelve years Hermine's senior, a conventional age difference for men and women of their class.

Moriz and Hermine would have known something of the long history of Jews in Vienna when they moved there. For all its renown as the City of Music, Vienna was the City of Blood for Jews because of the destruction of its Jewish community in the 1420s, when it was one of the largest in Europe. Archduke Albert V began by imprisoning all the city's Jews. Then he expelled many poorer Jews by setting them adrift in boats on the Danube and accused the wealthy of sacrilege in order to legitimize their torture and forcible conversion and seize their property. Rather than submit to baptism, a hundred Jews committed suicide in Vienna's main synagogue, which the Archduke promptly demolished. He had the remaining 270 Jews burned to death outside the city's walls.

A century later, only twelve Jewish families lived in Vienna by one account, just seven according to another, and Jews visiting the city had to wear a ring of yellow cloth "uncovered and unhidden" so that they would be immediately identifiable. During the following century, the few Jewish families in Vienna were the target of more decrees of banishment, sometimes enforced, sometimes not. But in the 1620s, when there were still just fifty Jewish families in Vienna, Emperor Ferdinand II followed the Italian example of creating a "ghetto" away from the city center as a means of giving the city's Jews greater rights (rather than persecuting them). While Ferdinand required Jews to live in this ghetto across the Danube Canal, he freed them of control by the city council, permitted them to own shops in the inner city, and allowed them to erect a new synagogue.

This good fortune did not last. In 1641, Ferdinand III placed the ghetto under the jurisdiction of the city council, which wanted all its occupants expelled, and barred Jews from trading in the inner city. In 1642, 1649, 1665, and 1668, mobs stormed and plundered the ghetto. In 1669, Leopold I set about destroying it in return for a vast sum from the council, which offset the emperor's loss of the special taxes paid by the ghetto's inhabitants. Within a year Leopold had expelled all of Vienna's Jews, expropriated their property, and destroyed their synagogue so that a church could be erected on its foundations, though this time a tiny community established itself within a few years. At the end of the seventeenth century, ten "privileged" Jewish families lived in the city.

Jews in this period remained as vulnerable as ever. They were separated from the rest of the population by religion, language, clothing, culture, descent, and law. They spoke Yiddish, celebrated the Sabbath, observed special religious holidays, and followed their own dietary laws, while the men wore skullcaps and the women covered their hair or shaved it and wore wigs. Far from being citizens, they were classified as aliens and, because they were subject to so many restrictions and exclusions, they looked to the Jewish community for identity, maintaining its traditions and observing its religious tenets.

Emperor Joseph II reduced this separation in 1782 through his Edict of Tolerance, a prime expression of the European Enlightenment. This edict freed Jews from having to wear yellow badges, allowed them to attend Christian schools and universities, and enabled them to carry on all trades. Yet the edict also left Jews subject to discriminatory taxes and excluded them from the civil service and many professions. It failed to repeal the restrictions on the number of Jews entitled to live in Vienna. It undermined the identity of Jews by prohibiting them from using Hebrew and Yiddish and preventing them from establishing synagogues or forming community organizations.

Had this treatment been exceptional, Moriz and Hermine might have hesitated before moving to Vienna. But until the eighteenth century, European Jews were accustomed to bouts of intense persecution between periods of relative toleration. At best they enjoyed stability, prosperity, and substantial autonomy while remaining subject to significant discrimination. At worst they were killed or lost their homes and livelihoods when forced to move from one place to another. The Jews of Moriz's birthplace, Bisenz, were one example. In 1604, they occupied forty-nine buildings, ran their own hospital, and owned sixteen vineyards, whereas Jews across

Europe were generally barred from agriculture. In 1605, the prince of Transylvania, Stephan Bocskai, slaughtered almost the entire community.

Two hundred years later, Bisenz was one of fifty-two Moravian towns where the Hapsburgs allowed Jews to live. They numbered almost one thousand, more than ever, but had no say in the general administration of the town. Instead, their community was a self-governing entity with its own mayor, staff, services, and schools. Like all Jews in Moravia, those in Bisenz had to pay onerous special taxes, were excluded from many occupations, and had limited freedom of movement. They also were subject to the Familiants Law of Emperor Charles VI, which tried to contain the Jewish population of the Czech Crown lands by allowing only the eldest son of each family to marry and then only after his father's death.

Hermine's birthplace, Freudenthal, represented a different facet of Jewish experience. It was one of many central European towns where few, if any, Jews had lived for hundreds of years. If there was a Jewish community in Freudenthal in the medieval era, its members would have had to leave with the larger expulsion of Jews from Silesia in the fifteenth and sixteenth centuries, and none seem to have returned in the first half of the nineteenth century, when the Hapsburgs imposed even stricter demographic limits on the Jews of Silesia than those of Moravia.

Emperor Franz Joseph reformed this situation, out of necessity more than choice, as part of the larger constitutional changes triggered by the European revolutions of 1848 and Austria's defeat by Prussia in 1866. As part of extending the rights of all his subjects in 1848, Franz Joseph gave Jews freedom of movement and residence, legalized their religious services, permitted them to own land, opened the public service and professions to them, allowed them to marry, and repealed the special taxes. When Franz Joseph transformed his regime into a constitutional monarchy in 1867, he gave Jews the same civil and political rights as other Austrians.

Many Jews exercised their new rights to move to new towns, enter new occupations, and participate in Europe's burgeoning capitalist economy. Hermine's father, Nathan, who was born in Wischau in southern Moravia, was among a small group who went to Freudenthal, where they secured an upstairs prayer room in the center of the town and then established a Jewish cemetery on its outskirts. Yet even as the community established these institutions, it stopped growing and was soon in decline because of the pull of even bigger towns and cities, which saw Hermine and her parents settle in Vienna, while her three brothers also lived there for extended periods. Much the same occurred in Bisenz, where the Jewish community expressed its self-confidence in the 1860s by building a new synagogue, only for the population to halve by the end of the century. Moriz, his two brothers, and his three sisters were part of this exodus. By the early 1900s, no Gallias lived in Bisenz.

The number of Jews who moved to Vienna was particularly large because it offered the greatest opportunities and because Jews there initially experienced unprecedented tolerance, encouraged by Austria's Liberal government. A census in 1857 recorded just six thousand Jews, less than 1.5 percent of the population. By 1880 there were seventy-two thousand, or 10 percent, a proportion maintained as the city grew and grew over the next twenty years. Moriz and Hermine were among the new arrivals. They married in 1893 in Vienna's main synagogue in the First District. Their four children were born in Vienna between 1895 and 1899 and, like them, became members of the city's Israelitische Kultusgemeinde. They all were part of Vienna's extraordinary transformation in fifty years from a city almost without Jews to the most Jewish city in western Europe.

Vienna also became the only European capital with an elected anti-Semitic government as prejudice burgeoned again in the city. While the increase in its Jewish population was one factor, the envy with which many of its old residents looked on the economic success of the new arrivals was another. The key figure was Karl Lueger, the leader of the Christian Social Party, who controlled majorities in the Austrian parliament and provincial diet and was Vienna's mayor, the highest elected position in the Hapsburg monarchy, from 1897 until his death in 1910. While the Christian Socials eclipsed Austria's Liberals for many reasons, the way in which Lueger exploited and legitimated anti-Semitism was integral to his party's success. "We in Vienna are anti-Semites," Lueger observed in 1905, as if it were an uncontroversial, acceptable matter of fact.

Lueger also accused Jews of ritual murder. He identified them as a destructive element that brought down the state wherever they became powerful. He threatened them with pogroms. In practice he neither stripped Jews of their civil rights nor initiated attacks against them, and often worked with them when it was to his advantage. Yet discrimination against Jews intensified while Lueger was Vienna's mayor, making it almost impossible for them to secure government contracts or obtain municipal positions, let alone be promoted. The same was true of the

imperial army and the oldest, most prestigious imperial departments,
though newer ministries such as the post office and railways were a little
more open.

Theobald Pollak, the original owner of the family's portrait of Gustav
Mahler, illustrates both the discrimination Jews encountered in Vienna
and the opportunities they enjoyed. Pollak's religion meant that he could
secure a position in the Department of Railways only through patronage.
He also experienced enduring prejudice and vilification there but quickly
rose to be one of the department's most senior officials and acquired a string
of titles and honors, becoming a *Hofrat,* or ministerial counselor, a Knight
of the Iron Cross, and Commander of the Order of Isabella of Spain.

Alma Schindler, who was very close to Theobald Pollak, recorded
something of his experience in her diary. She wrote that Pollak looked on
religion as a cause of havoc—to blame for martyrs and crusades and much
else evil in the world. She also identified him as so sensitive to anti-
Semitism that he imagined it where none existed, prompting him to create "very unpleasant," "crazy" scenes and conflicts when he was with
friends and acquaintances of Alma's family. Yet she also recognized that
Pollak's fears were well founded when it came to his work. "The defamatory tactics of the anti-Semitic faction are making him ill," Alma observed
in 1900, when Pollak had been a departmental secretary for over a year.
"God knows, I'm glad I wasn't born a Jew."

Many of Alma's other entries explain why. Even though she was
attracted to Jews, she did not find it easy to accept them. She expressed her
abhorrence of the founder of the Wiener Werkstätte, Fritz Waerndorfer,
by identifying him as "a brazen Jew." While she developed a passion for
the composer Alexander Zemlinsky, a card he sent her from Vienna's most
Jewish district, the Leopoldstadt, prompted her to wonder, "Is he one of
those little half-Jews who never succeed in freeing themselves from their
roots?" When she heard that Zemlinsky had become engaged to another
woman, she railed, "You Jewish sneak, keep your hook-nosed Jew-girl.
She's just right for you," only to display her confusion by wondering
whether she should marry "some Semitic moneybag."

The possibility that Alma would marry a Jew was so clear that it
became a conversation topic with her friends and acquaintances. At a dinner attended by the architects Josef Hoffmann, Joseph Maria Olbrich, and
Koloman Moser, the German singer Hans Oberstetter "begged" Alma
"never to marry a Jew." Another of Alma's admirers, Max Burckhard, fol-

lowed suit when Alma's romance with Zemlinsky intensified after he turned out not to have gotten engaged to his "Jew-girl." When Burckhard warned Alma, "For heaven's sake *don't marry Z. Don't corrupt good* race," she concurred. "He's right—my body is ten times too beautiful for his," she declared, though she also acknowledged "that his soul is a hundred times too beautiful for mine . . . didn't occur to me." While there were occasions when Alma's desire for Zemlinsky was so great that she felt she would "gladly be pregnant for him . . . his blood and mine, commingled," in between she saw a fundamental obstacle: it would involve "bearing his children—little, degenerate Jew-kids."

She looked on converts to Christianity in much the same way, as part of thinking of Jewishness as a matter of race rather than religion that conversion did not alter. Although the composer Felix Mendelssohn had been baptized when he was seven, Alma still regarded him as a Jew. The same was true of Gustav Mahler himself, whom she met while still infatuated with Zemlinsky. Her identification of Mahler as a Jew underlay her observation: "So many things about him annoy me: his smell—the way he sings, the something in the way he speaks." But as Mahler rapidly replaced Zemlinsky in her affections, she longed not just to make love with Mahler but also to become pregnant by him. "Oh, to bear his child!" she exclaimed. "My body. His soul. When shall I be his?" By March 1902, when they married, Alma was one month pregnant.

She was contemptuous of Hermine and Moriz in 1901 when she first visited their apartment in the Schleifmühlgasse in Vienna's Fourth District, where the Gallias lived for twenty years before moving to the Wohllebengasse. All Alma noted after being invited for dinner along with her mother, Anna, and stepfather, Carl Moll, was the lavishness of the Gallias' hospitality, their corpulence, and their race, suggesting that Alma, who delighted in intellectual exchange and often recorded it in her diary, found what Hermine and Moriz had to say of no interest. She wrote: "Evening at Gallias, Caviar, champagne and a gross Jewish couple." She thought Hermine and Moriz ripe for caricature—describing them as "made for Rudolf Wilke," widely regarded as the most talented draftsman with the leading German satirical magazine *Simplicissimus,* who stocked his cartoons with obese Jews.

This entry raises many questions. Did Hermine and Moriz perceive what Alma thought of them that night? Did Alma think the same when Moriz, and especially Hermine, went on to see much more of her? Did

Anna and Carl Moll share Alma's views? And how did Hermine and Moriz respond to other Viennese who were much more anti-Semitic? I imagine that, just as Alma was acutely sensitive to Jewishness, seemingly able to identify it wherever she encountered it, so Hermine and Moriz were acutely aware of how their Jewishness defined their reception. They looked to see when they were genuinely accepted, when they were tolerated just because of their money, and when they were unwelcome, despised, or hated. As they encountered anti-Semitism repeatedly in Vienna, one of their great dilemmas was whether to confront this prejudice, try to ignore it, or do all they could to escape it.

Conversion was one possibility. While it did not free Jews from anti-Semitism, it sometimes allowed them to secure positions otherwise barred to them. Mahler was the most spectacular example. When he saw the opportunity late in 1896 to become director of Vienna's Hofoper, or Imperial Court Opera—the most coveted musical post in Europe—he was ineligible because the court required all of its officeholders to be baptized. By February 1897, Mahler was a Catholic, in April the Emperor Franz Joseph appointed him as one of the Hofoper's conductors, in July Franz Joseph made him its deputy director, and in October its director. Yet this imperial acceptance did not stop Mahler from being vilified in the anti-Semitic press. That Mahler had got himself "done"—as one newspaper described his conversion—was of no account to those who applied the maxim "Once a Jew always a Jew." There was outrage at "the setting of a non-German, especially a Jew, at the head of a German artistic institution."

The contemporary term for such conversions was *Karrieretaufe,* or "career baptism." The implication, always derogatory, was that Jews sacrificed their faith and tradition to increase their economic, social, and cultural prospects. While many Jews conformed to this pragmatic image, they often acted more for their families than for themselves. Mahler's sister, Justine, who served as his housekeeper until he married, was unusually explicit about how she converted to improve Gustav's prospects in Vienna. Justine described herself as acting out a piece of theater, likening her instruction in Christianity to learning "a poem in a foreign language" and boasting that she "did not believe a word." Yet for all of Gustav's pragmatism, Alma recognized that he was a far better Christian than she because of his deep-seated religiosity, which encompassed both Judaism and Catholicism.

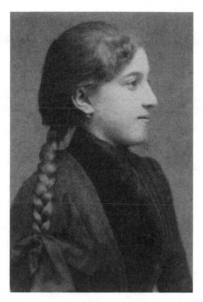

Hermine, at about
sixteen, c. 1886.

Hermine was one of many converts deeply affected by Christianity. Her attraction to Catholicism started when she was a girl in Freudenthal, where the small Jewish community lacked many of the institutions of Moriz's birthplace of Bisenz. While Hermine's parents wanted their children to be observant Jews, they also wanted them to be as assimilated as possible. Because education was a prime means of achieving this end, Nathan and Josefine sent Hermine to the local convent run by nuns from the Order of German Knights.

Her parents hoped to safeguard Hermine's faith by refusing to let her go to Catholic services or to attend the nuns' classes devoted to religious instruction, but the nuns were not so easily stymied, as revealed by Hermine's oldest surviving possessions—a collection of more than seventy merit certificates, which date from 1879, when she turned nine. While some of these certificates simply say "Reward" or "Distinction" or contain morals such as "Industriousness yields rewards," the majority carry Catholic imagery and Catholic texts, combining pictures of Jesus, saints, angels, and sacred hearts with homilies such as "God's Angel guards you day and night" and "Jesus is your Lord on earth." The nuns even gave Hermine one certificate ready for display, placing the image of a guardian

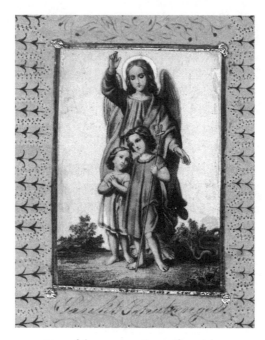

One of the many merit certificates that
the nuns in Freudenthal gave Hermine.

angel within a decorative surround of curled paper and glass beads inside
a glass-fronted frame.

Hermine's "dear parents," as she always described them, were a great
constraint when she considered converting twenty years later. Much as
Hermine's uncle Eduard Hamburger played a prime role in the construction of a new synagogue in the Moravian city of Olmütz, so Nathan Hamburger took a key part in establishing the Jewish cemetery in Freudenthal
and headed the association responsible for its prayer room. Moriz was in
an easier position, as his parents were both dead, but he also would have
been conscious of breaking tradition and subject to family pressure since
all of his siblings, apart from his brother Adolf, remained Jews. The surviving evidence suggests that Moriz was much more ambivalent about converting than Hermine—that it was something he did for her and their
children, an issue on which she led and he followed, one of many markers
of her influence over him.

A sharp increase in conversions at the start of the new century made it

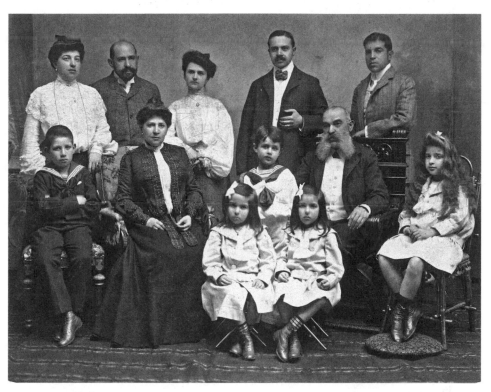

The Gallias and the Hamburgers in 1903, when all the adults remained Jews but all the children had been baptized. Standing from left are Hermine and Moriz followed by Henny Hamburger, Otto Hamburger, and Guido Hamburger. Seated from left are Erni, Josefine Hamburger, Robert Hamburger, Nathan Hamburger, and Gretl. In front are the twins, Käthe and Lene.

easier for Moriz and Hermine to leave the Kultusgemeinde. While the annual number remained less than half of 1 percent of Vienna's Jewish population, this figure still made Vienna the city where Jews were abandoning their religion faster than anywhere else in the world. Moriz and Hermine would have known many of the converts, as a disproportionate number were wealthy. Those who joined this exodus went in three directions: a quarter took the smallest step of becoming *konfessionslos*—literally faithless, identifying with no organized religion; another quarter, including Hermine's brother Otto, became Protestant (which was the dominant religion in Denmark, where Otto and his family were living when they began converting); and the other half became Roman Catholic, the Austrian state religion. Moriz, Hermine, and their four children were among them, as were Hermine's other brothers, Guido and Paul.

Many adults began by having their children baptized when they were small so that Christianity would always be part of their identities. In keeping with this practice, Moriz and Hermine had their oldest child and one son, Erni, baptized in 1902, when he was six, followed by their three daughters in 1903, when Gretl was six and Käthe and her twin sister, Lene, were four. While Austrian law required children to have the same religion as their parents, Moriz and Hermine avoided this obstacle by traveling across the Austro-Hungarian border to the city known in Hungarian as Pozsony, in German as Pressburg, and in Slovak as Bratislava, just an hour by train from Vienna. The church they chose was, typically, the grandest—the great Gothic cathedral of St. Martin's. On each occasion, the children's godfather was Carl Moll.

Father Alexander Gaibl, a canon at St. Martin's, not only presided over this process by officiating at the Gallias' baptisms and first communions but also saw the family on other occasions. An opera, theater, and concert book kept by Hermine reveals that she and Moriz celebrated New Year's Day in 1908 with Gaibl at the Hofoper seeing Saint-Saëns's *Samson et Dalila*—a peculiarly appropriate choice for a priest converting Jews to Christianity, as the opera's subject was the killing of the Hebrew strongman Samson because of his betrayal by the Philistine Delilah. In 1910 Gaibl officiated again when the forty-year-old Hermine and the fifty-two-year-old Moriz were baptized together at St. Martin's and the Gallias became a family of one religion for the first time in eight years.

The leaders of Vienna's Jewish community tried to discourage such conversions by publishing weekly lists of those who quit the Kultusgemeinde in the city's Jewish newspapers in an attempt to shame the apostates and ensure that Jews ostracized them. But these lists did nothing to stop the conversions and may even have added to them by advertising how many prominent Jews were abandoning their faith. When Moriz and Hermine were baptized, he remained close to his Jewish siblings just as she stayed close to her Jewish parents. They also retained many Jewish friends.

My mother thought these conversions were "some sort of wish fulfillment" for Hermine. While cynical about almost everything Hermine did, Anne was sure Hermine's baptism was an act of genuine conviction. She imagined that, as Hermine "always stayed in touch with the nuns who had taught her and whom she had loved," she "went and told the nuns about her baptism and they were very pleased." But while Moriz soon took on more Catholic responsibilities by becoming godfather to one of the sons of Guido and Nelly Hamburger, the family's attendance at church was sporadic at best. While Hermine's diary for 1911 lists what they did in great detail, it mentions neither mass nor confession.

3

Gaslights

The family's wealth owed much to the Austrian scientist Carl Auer von Welsbach, who employed Moriz for twenty years. While Austria's contribution to global culture in the fin de siècle is typically conceived in terms of art, music, literature, architecture, design, and ideas, Auer put Austria at the forefront of basic science and the most innovative technology. He discovered and isolated two of the rare earths that form the bottom section of the periodic table. He identified another two elements, though another scientist determined their atomic weight before he did. He played a pivotal role in the development of new forms of lighting, both gas and electric. Although it is commonly assumed that electricity's superiority was as obvious as its triumph was inevitable, once Thomas Edison first demonstrated his electric bulbs in 1879, the reality was very different. For another twenty, even thirty years, it was not clear whether electric or gas lighting would prevail, largely because of Auer, who was the one inventor to revolutionize both technologies.

Auer began by building on the work of the German scientist Robert Bunsen, who had taught him. Bunsen's great invention in 1855 was the Bunsen burner, which opened up a vast array of uses for gas as a fuel by mixing it with air before it ignited to produce a clean, intense flame.

Auer's great invention in 1885 was a knitted sleeve, or mantle, that he impregnated with a fluid made out of rare earths. Auer found that, when he heated this impregnated sleeve with a Bunsen burner, it became incandescent, generating much more light than the best existing gaslights while using much less fuel. One name for the mantle was the *Gasglühlicht,* or gas-glowing light. Otherwise, just like the Bunsen burner, it was named after its inventor—known in German as the Auerlicht, in French as the Bec Auer but called the Welsbach mantle across the English-speaking world because Auer was thought too difficult for English-speakers to pronounce.

The first version of these lights, which went into production in Europe and North America in 1887, failed because these mantles proved to be expensive and fragile, their light was no match for electric bulbs, and the mantles were positioned above the burner, which consequently cast a shadow on the surrounding environment. But a second version, which emitted a much whiter, longer-lasting light using even less fuel, was a triumph. Just as owners of old gaslights immediately began replacing them with mantles, so many households and businesses that had switched to electricity reverted to gas and used the mantles, too. By the end of 1891, Auer's Austrian company was marketing the mantles from a showroom in the Schleifmühlgasse in Vienna's Fourth District as well as from outlets in eleven other cities across the Hapsburg Empire. Although the German gas mantle company was most successful—returning 65 percent of its capital in its first year and 130 percent in its second year—all the gas mantle companies generated huge profits.

Sigmund Freud, who saw himself as another scientist making one discovery after another about the human mind, was envious of his compatriot. As Auer built a castle for himself in 1899 on a vast estate in Carinthia, Freud was living, by his own account, in fear of poverty in Vienna. Still a lowly lecturer at its university, his *Interpretation of Dreams* would sell only 351 copies over the next six years. When he summarized his ideas in an essay, "On Dreams," in 1901, he drew on an example from his own experience involving Auer to explain his concept of association. Freud recounted how he had been on a train one day, holding a glass cylinder, which got him thinking of the gas mantle. "I soon saw," Freud wrote, "that I should like to make a discovery that would make me as rich and independent as my fellow-countryman Dr. Auer von Welsbach was made by his."

Electric light companies were soon undertaking new research to improve their bulbs. Because Thomas Edison's original carbon filaments were short-lived, inefficient, and produced a yellow light, the challenge was to replace them. Although Auer had little or no reason to advance the technology that was the main rival to his gaslights, he joined hundreds of scientists around the world looking to do so. In 1898, he developed the first metal filaments made of osmium, which produced a long-lasting white light using half as much electricity, but they were very brittle and expensive. By 1900, these bulbs were on show at the Universal Exposition in Paris and illuminating Franz Joseph's office in Vienna. By 1902, they were in mass production in Austria and Germany, where 2 million bulbs sold over the next four years.

The gas mantle was much more successful. Its global reach is suggested by an advertisement in the Sydney *Bulletin* taken out in 1905 by the local Welsbach Light Company. "You all do know this mantle," the advertisement began, "its brilliant incandescence now gleams in every country and every clime, establishing its reputation as the brightest and most softly illuminating medium that human ingenuity has yet devised." The scale of production was prodigious. The Australian company manufactured up to 12,000 mantles a day, or close to 2 million a year, at its plant in Sydney. The British company made up to 30 million a year in London. The American plant in Gloucester City, New Jersey, produced up to 40 million a year.

The impact of the mantles not only in buildings but also on the streets of the world was profound. While Bombay was first, other cities soon followed, especially in Germany, where the number of streetlights using the mantles increased by 1,300 percent between 1895 and 1905. New York was not far behind. Its residents observed a great improvement in 1904 when 16,000 streetlights in Manhattan and the Bronx were fitted with mantles. A decade later, "Gotham by Gaslight" was the stuff not just of fiction but of reality. Over half of New York's 82,000 streetlights were lit with mantles as annual global production reached 300 million.

Auer's principal legal adviser was Moriz's brother Adolf, the first Gallia to go to university. When he moved from Bisenz to Vienna in 1870, Adolf studied law, the profession that Jews most often pursued and quickly dominated. Before long he was one of Vienna's leading patent lawyers and Auer was his most important client, generating so much work that Adolf had little time to represent anyone else. He advised Auer about how best to protect and exploit his rights around the world. He became a director and then vice president of the Austrian Gas Glowing Light Company. He helped to establish the German Auergesellschaft.

This association was integral to Adolf's rise to riches, which saw him acquire spectacular real estate with his wife, Ida. Their first purchase in the 1890s was an imposing summer villa in Baden, the nearest spa town to Vienna. They followed in 1903 by erecting two adjoining five-story apartment buildings in Vienna's First District. While one was on a relatively modest block on the Biberstrasse, which Adolf owned by himself and was all rented, the other was on a vast corner block extending to the Ringstrasse, which Adolf bought with Ida and developed in a much more imposing fashion appropriate to its location. This building, which became best known for its ground-floor Café Prückel, was where Adolf and Ida lived in the grandest apartment, Adolf had his chambers, and his initials adorned one of the street entrances.

In the most influential account of fin de siècle Vienna, the historian Carl Schorske argued that with the triumph of the Christian Socials in the 1890s, Vienna's Liberal bourgeoisie abandoned political engagement. Adolf acted very differently when Auer and he invested in *Die Zeit,* which went from being a weekly magazine to a newspaper in 1902, with the goal of providing daily, independent, radical commentary on social and political issues. In doing so, Adolf became a target of Karl Kraus, whose aspirations for his weekly *Die Fackel* were almost identical. As part of lambasting *Die Zeit* for being compromised by the financial interests of its investors, Kraus decried the newspaper's failure to report that the English Welsbach company had been forced to reduce its capital by 50 million crowns, with disastrous consequences for many of its small investors. "Baron Auer von Welsbach and Dr. Gallia could surely have given *Die Zeit* all the necessary information," Kraus snidely observed, "just as they were rumored to have given *Die Zeit* a third million."

Adolf's association with Auer was also the making of the two other Gallia brothers—Wilhelm, who was a year older than Adolf and spent much of the 1880s working as a merchant in Troppau or Opava in Silesia, and Moriz, who was six and a half years younger than Adolf and lived with him from 1891, when he moved to Vienna looking for work. When Auer employed both Wilhelm and Moriz, the gas mantle was already generating such big profits that he would have found it easy to attract capable businessmen to run his companies. The distinguishing qualification of Moriz and Wilhelm was that they were Adolf's brothers. Thirty-three-year-old

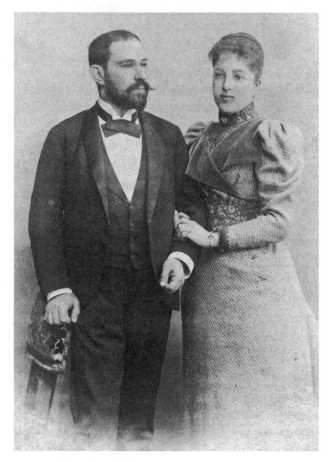

Moriz, thirty-four, and Hermine, twenty-two, after
being married in Vienna's main synagogue, 1893.

Auer began at the start of 1892 by employing thirty-three-year-old Moriz
as the director of the commercial operations of the Austrian Gas Glowing
Light Company in Vienna. A year later, Auer employed forty-year-old
Wilhelm to establish the Hungarian Gas Glowing Light Company in
Budapest and be its managing director. Before long, even more members
of the family were in the gaslight business as Moriz employed two of Hermine's brothers, Otto and Guido Hamburger, who were also the nephews
of Wilhelm, Adolf, and Moriz.

Moriz was responsible for marketing and supplying the gas mantles
across Austria as well as in other European countries where no local company had acquired the rights to Auer's patents. But Moriz's main market

was Vienna, where the opportunities were boosted by the growth in the city's population from 800,000 in 1890 to 2 million in 1910, the unprecedented prosperity of the city through most of this period, and Karl Lueger's investment in a new municipal gasworks while electricity lagged behind. Moriz was initially responsible for just the Gas Glowing Light Company's showroom in the Schleifmühlgasse. By the late 1890s, he was distributing the gas mantles through a network of forty-five retailers spread across the city. While he reduced this network to seven in 1902, his corporate role grew as a result of Auer's reconstituting the company's board and making Moriz its vice president in 1905. In between he also promoted and sold Auer's electric lights.

The benefits for Moriz were immense. His employment by Auer in 1892 enabled Moriz to marry Hermine, who came with a substantial dowry, in 1893. His position also entitled him to a spacious apartment above the gas mantle showroom that probably came rent-free because Auer owned the building. Moriz's salary in 1900 was between 35,000 and 40,000 crowns, the equivalent of about $400,000 today. He acquired shares in the Gas Glowing Light Company, which returned big dividends. He became a significant industrialist in his own right by investing in several other companies while still working for Auer. He became part of Vienna's "second society," the city's economic and bureaucratic elite who were eclipsed only by its "first society" of old aristocratic families with entrée at the imperial court.

One of Moriz's first big investments was in the Hamburger family company, which sold its brewery because of competition from bigger companies but continued to prosper as it produced malt, yeast, and spirits in Freudenthal and powdered milk in the neighboring towns of Fulnek and Hagenburg. When Hermine's father, Nathan, retired at the age of sixty-five in 1906, Moriz and Adolf each acquired one-fifth of the company, which had a staff of 160. Moriz also joined the board of a railway company, which constructed a new line in the south of the Hapsburg Empire between Trient and Malé. But Moriz's main involvement was in other lighting companies. Most likely, he sometimes lost heavily in companies involved in developing new technologies that failed. But Moriz also reaped spectacular profits from companies that brought some of the world's most successful new forms of lighting to Austria.

The oldest of these companies was the German firm Julius Pintsch, which developed the first safe, reliable, and effective form of lighting rail-

way carriages in the late 1860s using compressed gas. While initial demand
for these lights was modest, by the early 1900s Pintsch's lights dominated
the global market. In the intervening years, members of the Pintsch family came to have close links with Auer, and hence with Moriz, by investing
in Auer's first Austrian company, buying the rights to produce the first version of the mantles in Germany, and continuing to support Auer after
these mantles failed to sell. When Pintsch established a branch in Vienna
to supply Austria's railways, Moriz acquired one-third of the company,
which soon had three hundred employees.

Moriz became even more involved with another German company,
the Graetzinlicht Gesellschaft, which was first to exploit the invention by
the German scientist Otto Mannesmann of "inverted" gaslights with
mantles below, rather than above, the burners. The great advantage of
these lights, which the Graetzinlicht Gesellschaft produced from 1905, was
that they did not cast shadows on the floor. They were also much more
efficient than earlier burners and cheap to install, simply requiring the
adaptation of old fittings rather than the purchase of new ones. When the
Graetzinlicht Gesellschaft almost immediately began reaping huge profits
in Germany, Moriz founded its Austrian branch and retained half of its
shares.

Moriz was also a major investor in Watt, an electric lightbulb manufacturer with a factory outside Vienna and a showroom in the city. While
some of Watt's bulbs were used for ordinary electric lighting, its speciality
was small bulbs known as Monowatts, because they used just one watt per
candle. When the invention of these bulbs coincided in 1908 with the
invention of small dry-cell batteries, they were used together to produce
the first effective small flashlights, which immediately proved popular,
precipitating great demand for Watt's bulbs.

Moriz's stake in the Graetzinlicht Gesellschaft was particularly prob-
lematic given his positions as a board member and commercial director of
Auer's Gas Glowing Light Company. In 1911 Moriz recognized this conflict of interest and opted to keep his stake in the Graetzinlicht
Gesellschaft while preparing to quit the Gas Glowing Light Company.
But his departure was complicated because all three Gallia brothers had
been so close to Auer for so long. When Wilhelm died in 1912, he was still
running the Hungarian branch of the company that he had established
almost twenty years before. As recalled by one of his granddaughters, Wilhelm regarded Auer as his best friend. Adolf's association with Auer not

only started much earlier but lasted much longer as he rejoined the board of the Austrian Gas Glowing Light Company in 1913 just as Moriz quit. When Moriz sold almost all his shares in the company, resigned as director of its commercial operations, and stepped down from its board, Auer saw it as a betrayal.

Neither the Gas Glowing Light Company nor the Graetzinlicht Gesellschaft was flourishing by then because of the ascendancy of electric lighting. It prevailed in Vienna because of the invention of the tungsten-filament bulb and because of the extension of the city's electric grid across all of its nine inner districts. The lights that Moriz and Hermine chose for their own house in the Wohllebengasse were indicative. While they installed gas mantles where their servants lived and worked, they placed electric lights in the building's foyer, the front rooms of their apartment, and all the family's bedrooms. Although Moriz had made the bulk of his fortune out of gas lighting, most of his own lights in Good Living Street were electric.

4

Family

"*Ganz mutterseelenallein,*" not just "all alone" or "all by myself" but "utterly abandoned" or "godforsaken." It was February 1908 and Hermine had just been to a dramatization of Tolstoy's *Anna Karenina* at Vienna's Hofburgtheater and was recording the evening in her opera, theater, and concert book. While its column for "*Bemerkungen,*" or "Observations," was intended for comments about each performance, Hermine usually used it to list her companions. On this occasion, having none for what seems to have been the first time in her life, she thought her lack of company equally worth recording.

The extremity of her language is striking. "*Mutterseelenallein*" was how the Brothers Grimm described the seven-year-old Snow White after the huntsman took her into the great forest and left her there rather than kill her, as her wicked stepmother had ordered. In conceiving herself in these terms, the clear implication is that the thirty-eight-year-old Hermine did not plan to be at the theater alone. Someone had let her down. Most likely, Hermine had found out only at the last moment, giving her no opportunity to find another companion. She could have wasted her ticket, missed the performance, and stayed at home. Instead, she went by herself—a mark of her independence as a modern woman as well as her eagerness to go. Yet her diary suggests that she was highly uncomfortable doing so. She probably was acutely embarrassed as she entered Vienna's most prestigious theater by herself and, even worse, was by herself during the intermission. I imagine her thinking that everyone was looking at her, wondering why she was alone.

A month and eight performances later, Hermine was again out by herself. The attraction was the Polish piano virtuoso Leopold Godowski, who was the highest-paid soloist in Europe in the early 1900s. His concerts so excited Hermine that she saw him six times in two years, more than any other individual performer. Had Hermine had company when Godowski performed in March 1908 at Vienna's Musikverein, she probably would have declared the concert "inspiringly beautiful" and likened it to "heavenly light" as usual. Instead she thought her lack of companions more noteworthy. When she described herself as "*ganz allein,*" or "completely alone," she implied that she would have preferred company. But the relative restraint of her remark suggests that she was more comfortable than at the performance of *Anna Karenina.* Before long, she might have even become accustomed to going out alone, but because family and friends were always available, it seems she never did.

Hermine's marriage should have been unhappy. The standard image of fin de siècle Vienna, shaped above all by Arthur Schnitzler's stories and plays, is of loveless unions entered into with wealth and social respectability primarily in mind, resulting in adultery, separations, and divorces. Several of Klimt's other sitters fitted this image. Rose von Rosthorn-Friedmann was already remarried when Klimt painted her. Gertrud Loew remarried just a couple of years later. Margarete Wittgenstein separated from her husband. The marriage of Sonja Knips was notoriously unhappy. That of Adele Bloch-Bauer was "based on mutual respect rather than love." But Hermine was different, despite her marriage partly being a product of her father's wealth and Moriz's financial success.

A photograph taken at the villa of Adolf and Ida Gallia in Baden, most likely by Adolf himself in about 1898, when Hermine and Moriz had been married five years, suggests their happiness. This stereograph shows Moriz and Hermine at the villa's front entrance, smiling into each other's eyes as they kiss, their bodies touching, their hands stiffly by their sides as they resist their impulse to hold each other. Hermine's opera, theater, and concert book conveys more of their relationship. Her ways of describing the

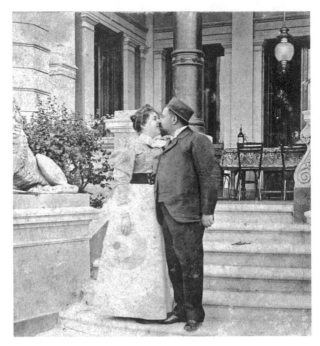

Moriz and Hermine kiss on the steps of Adolf and Ida
Gallia's villa at Baden outside Vienna, c. 1898.

rare occasions when she went out with just Moriz, rather than a larger
group of family and friends, express her pleasure in having him to herself.
"*Wir beide allein,*" "just the two of us," she would record, or "*allein mit
Schatz,*" "alone with my darling." Her habit of explaining why Moriz was
not with her when she went out with other members of the family is even
more suggestive. "*Schatz Berlin,*" she wrote almost every time.

The diary that Hermine began keeping in 1909 at the family's new
summerhouse in the small village of Alt Aussee, not far from Salzburg,
paints a similar picture. Hermine called it a *Wettertagebuch,* as if her sole
purpose was to record Alt Aussee's notoriously fickle weather, and occasionally she did so, recording nothing but rain. Yet she usually kept a more
extended log in which Moriz, whose work meant he could only escape the
city for short holidays, was not just Hermine's "*Schatz*" but occasionally
also her "*Schätzle,*" a typical use of the diminutive to convey affection.
After a relatively extended visit lasting five days in 1909, which saw Moriz
and Hermine embark on unusually ambitious exercise, trying out the
newly fashionable sport of mountaineering as they went close to reaching

the summit of the Dachstein, the region's highest peak, and crossed one of its glaciers roped to two guides, Hermine recorded Moriz's return to Vienna with manifest emotion. "As always we found the parting very difficult."

Moriz's one surviving letter to Hermine, written during the summer of 1913, when he was in Vienna and she was in Alt Aussee, is just as passionate. "My dearest heart," he started. Hermine was his "*Schatz*" and "*Schätzle*," he declared three times as he dwelled on how much he longed to see her. Yet this letter is most remarkable for how Moriz gave Hermine a detailed account of his business dealings, including payments and prices, suggesting that he was used to confiding in her and valued her judgment. His last will, which he finalized in 1917, was similar. While it was common for husbands to pay tribute to their wives in their wills, as part of expecting their wives to outlive them, Moriz was unusually fervent. Hermine had been a "faithful, brave, and hearty companion," he declared, giving him "never-ending love and devotion." According to family tradition, Moriz "adored and cosseted" Hermine.

A book stamp that Käthe and Lene commissioned from the Wiener Werkstätte as a silver wedding anniversary present for their parents in 1918 provides another view of their marriage. For all the idealization and hyperbole appropriate on such anniversaries, the stamp is a testament to the strength of the relationship of Moriz and Hermine. It shows a man and a woman holding hands with two sprigs of flowers entwined above them in a lover's knot. While both are stock seventeenth-century figures involving no attempt at likeness, they represent Moriz and Hermine, whose names appear in the box immediately underneath. To celebrate their parents' twenty-five years of marriage, Käthe and Lene thought it appropriate to have Moriz and Hermine portrayed as a courting couple enjoying young love.

Like most wealthy Viennese who had babies in the 1890s, Hermine employed wet nurses for her children—Erni, born 1895; Gretl, born 1896; and the twins, born 1899. The women who worked as wet nurses were generally unmarried mothers who, after a rigorous medical examination, left their own children in foundling homes and went to live in their employers' apartments. There they were subject to much more scrutiny than other servants so that they did not compromise the well-being of their charges, but they enjoyed unusually good pay and conditions. While Hermine was never photographed with Erni when he was a small baby,

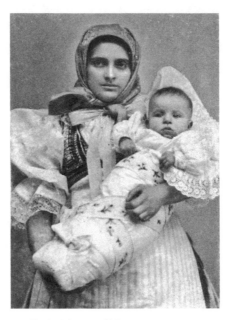

Erni with one of his wet nurses, 1895.

the earliest photographs of him include four different wet nurses. The most revealing shows a wet nurse who neither looks at Erni nor engages with the camera but stares off into space, implicitly recognizing her role as a baby stand, there simply to hold Erni.

If this photograph suggests a profound distance not just between Erni and his wet nurse but also between Erni and Hermine, the earliest studio portraits of Hermine as a young mother do not counter this impression. The reason is that these photographs were carefully staged by the Viennese studio of Carl Pietzner, whose many wealthy patrons included Sonja Knips, the subject of Klimt's first major portrait. While the photographs of Hermine show how Pietzner's Viennese studio thought the best way of suggesting a new mother's devotion—and adoration—was to show her seated in profile with eyes only for her children, these photographs reveal nothing of Hermine's relationship with Erni and Gretl.

A diary, which Hermine started when Gretl was born, reveals more of Hermine as a mother. It was one of many baby books that publishers began producing in the late nineteenth century for the upper middle class. The sixty-eight pages of *Unser Kind,* or *Our Child,* were divided into dozens of different categories, starting with a genealogical page for recording the names and dates of birth of the child's forebears and ending with five pages for recording the child's first school years. The obvious purpose of this record-keeping was to provide a child such as Gretl with an account of her life until she was able to maintain her own diary. But the book was also designed to encourage mothers and fathers, who were both addressed

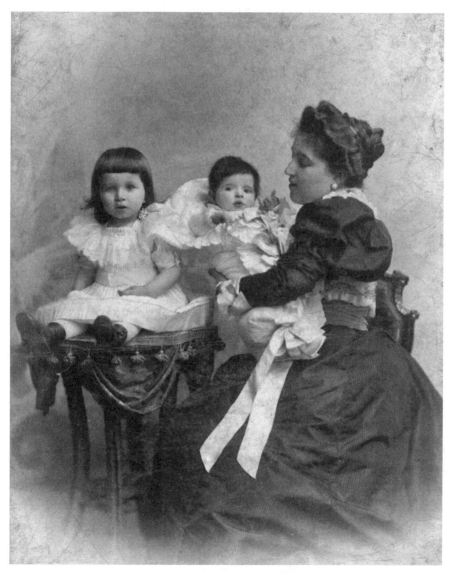

Hermine, with Gretl in her arms and Erni on a table, 1897.

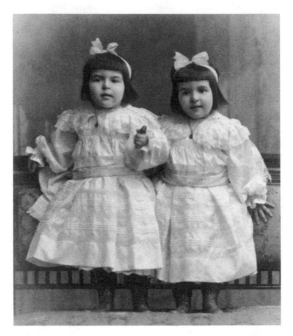

Käthe and Lene, 1901. While Hermine had herself photographed with Erni and Gretl when
they were little, she never had herself photographed with the twins.

in the publisher's introduction, to engage in the scientific observation of
children's development. The catalyst for this was Wilhelm Preyer, a German professor of physiology, who published the foundational work of
developmental psychology in 1882 based on observations of his own son.
In keeping with Preyer's work, *Unser Kind* had sections devoted to amusing incidents, remarkable sayings, and signs of good and bad character.

Some women maintained these books for years. The most famous
example is Martha Arendt, the mother of the political philosopher Hannah Arendt, born in Berlin in 1906. Until Hannah was eight, Martha used
Unser Kind to chronicle her physical, emotional, and intellectual development, recording many small incidents as well as Hannah's response to the
most profound events, such as the death of her grandfather and father.
Hermine wrote much less. She did not record anything amusing that
Gretl said or did and wrote nothing of Gretl's emotional development.
Her main interest was Gretl's growth, which she recorded weekly for a year
and a half on a page that the diary's publishers, anticipating a Christian

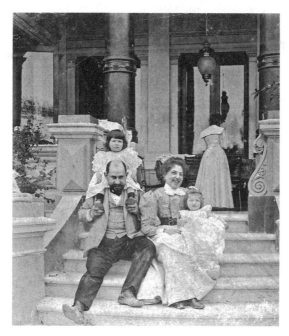

Moriz with Erni on his shoulders and Hermine
with Gretl on her lap, c. 1898.

audience, intended for recording Gretl's baptism. All Hermine otherwise
noted was Gretl's receipt of her first doll as a six-month-old, the arrival of
a new wet nurse when Gretl was eight months, her first experience of children's soup at the age of eleven months, and the appearance of her first
tooth a month later.

The most compelling evidence of Hermine's joy in her children is in
the series of photographs probably taken by Adolf Gallia at his villa in
Baden in about 1898. In one, Hermine holds Erni's hand while taking him
for a walk on the villa's extensive grounds. In another, Hermine holds
Gretl, who is sitting on a table next to Erni. In a third, Hermine sits on the
front steps with Gretl on one knee and Erni next to her. A fourth shows
both Hermine and Moriz delighting in parenthood. A beaming Hermine
has Gretl on her knee while an unusually casually attired Moriz in jacket,
waistcoat, and cravat has Erni on his shoulders.

The way in which Moriz chose to celebrate his birthday is similarly
revealing. Rather than go out just with Hermine or other adults, he chose
to take his children. He began on his forty-second birthday in 1900, when

he went with Hermine and the five-year-old Erni and four-year-old Gretl
to the Circus Tivoli. Two years later Hermine and he took all four children
to a matinee of ballets at the Hofoper, even though the twins were only
four years old. A year later, as part of the weekend when Moriz and Hermine spent Saturday attending the private view of the *Klimt Kollektiv* at
the Secession, buying their Klimt landscape, and seeing Franz von Schöntan's *Maria Theresa* at the Volkstheater, Moriz and Hermine celebrated his
forty-fifth birthday on Sunday by taking all four children to another matinee at the Hofoper.

Elisabeth Luzzatto sparked my curiosity because of her repeated appearance in Hermine's opera, theater, and concert book. In the early 1900s
Elisabeth and her husband, Maximilian, went out with Hermine and
Moriz four times as often as any of their other friends. While Maximilian
was another successful industrialist who owned an engineering works in
Vienna's Tenth District, Elisabeth was a supporter and at least occasional
patron of the best in modern Viennese design. Like Moriz, Maximilian
acquired a title, albeit Italian rather than Austrian. The Luzzattos were
married in 1895, just two years after Moriz and Hermine, and had children
at the same time. They, too, were of Jewish origin but had become Protestants before they married.

Elisabeth's politics were particularly interesting as I looked to see
whether Hermine's progressive taste in art might be matched by similar
politics, as was the case with Adele Bloch-Bauer in the 1920s. Elisabeth
was one of Vienna's most prominent feminists and socialists at the turn of
the century. In 1902 she became a member of the governing committee
of the new League of Austrian Women's Associations, the top women's
group in Austria. A year later she helped to found a Women's Discussion
Club, which aspired to make women more politically active and effective.
She was soon the club's main financial supporter and its president, chairing meetings devoted to free education, the secret ballot, and female
hygiene, and delivering lectures titled "Marriage," "Value and Capital,"
and "Socialism." She also became a founding member and patron of the
New Vienna Women's Club, a female preserve boasting a dining room,
salon, reading room, games room, and billiard room; it immediately
became a venue for lectures, courses, exhibitions, and concerts and provided advice to women on careers and employment.

The Frauenstimmrecht, or women's suffrage movement, also engaged her. When it became clear in 1905 that Franz Joseph would extend the franchise to all Austrian men while doing nothing for women, the Social Democratic Party instructed its female supporters not to campaign against this plan so as not to jeopardize the introduction of universal male suffrage, but a small group of women who were mostly liberals were more combative. The Austrian Women's Suffrage Committee, founded in 1906, was the first Austrian organization devoted to securing the vote for women. Despite her socialism, Elisabeth was not only on the committee's founding executive but also became one of its most active members and its biggest benefactor. When an International Women's Congress devoted to the Frauenstimmrecht was held in Vienna in 1913, she was among the leading Austrian delegates.

Elisabeth's politics became increasingly radical during these years. When she lectured at the Women's Discussion Club in 1908, she not only praised Vienna's "dear Lueger" for his investment in new publicly owned infrastructure in the city but also acclaimed the achievement of greater workers' rights and protections such as the ten-hour day and looked forward to the triumph of socialism, which she cast as the natural, inevitable successor to liberalism. Two years later her most ambitious piece of writing—a 444-page history of socialism from the ancient Greeks to the revolutions of 1848—was published by the Social Democratic Party's own publisher, a clear mark of her affiliation. As described by her son Richard, Elisabeth "dedicated her life-work to the redemption of the working classes."

This political engagement is all the more striking because a key part of Carl Schorske's interpretation of fin de siècle Vienna is that the city's bourgeoisie turned to culture as a substitute for politics, so that Vienna's extraordinary modernism at the turn of the century was a product of the apolitical. The patrons of the Secession and the Wiener Werkstätte are usually taken as prime examples of this phenomenon. Elisabeth Luzzatto, who was both a patron of the Werkstätte and a member of its kindred organization, the Österreichischer Werkbund, exemplifies how there was no end to politics for some of the bourgeoisie, even among the supporters of the new culture.

Because of their closeness, it is easy to imagine Hermine attending one or more of Elisabeth's lectures about marriage or socialism. When Elisabeth privately published her lecture on marriage in 1905, she would have given a copy to Hermine. She may have done the same after writing her history of socialism. When the two women went out together, Elisabeth would have discussed her activism and, as a committed proselytizer, tried to convert Hermine to her views. If the financial support of Adolf Gallia for the left-leaning newspaper *Die Zeit* is any guide to the politics of other members of the family, Hermine would have been sympathetic. Just as Moriz Gallia and Maximilian Luzzatto probably did business together, Hermine probably shared some of Elisabeth's politics.

Galas

A tour of Europe's great capitals saw Hermine and Moriz out every night. They started late in 1902 with five nights in London at the Empire, Hippodrome, Palace, Trocadero, and Gaiety theaters. They continued with three evenings in Paris at the Théâtre des Folies-Dramatiques, Opéra, and Comédie-Française. They finished in Berlin with five more performances in five nights, then spent their first evening back in Vienna at the Imperial Court Theater, the Hofburgtheater. The next night they attended a premiere at the Deutsches Volkstheater. Within a few days, they were at the Imperial Court Opera, the Hofoper.

The array of choices in Vienna, the possibilities nearly every night, were fantastic. While many accounts of "Vienna 1900" have adopted a parochial, even provincial approach, presenting the city as simply a site of local culture by fixing only on what was Viennese, the Hapsburg capital was also an imperial center and a global one, attracting most of the world's greatest conductors, singers, dancers, circuses, and variety stars through the 1890s and into the early 1900s.

This culture was a novelty for Hermine and Moriz because of their provincial backgrounds. Hermine's opera, theater, and concert book reveals how Moriz and she exploited their new opportunities. Hermine made thirty entries in the first season that she recorded, starting in November 1898 when she was already four months pregnant with Käthe and Lene, and stopping in April 1899, a fortnight before the twins were born. She generally listed about forty performances each season—or between one and two each week—from the start of October when she returned from her annual summer holiday, until late May, when she prepared to leave again to escape the heat. Yet Hermine went out much more often than she noted, as she made no entries for most of one season and failed to record some performances even when keeping her diary more regularly.

By the time Gretl began to accompany her, Hermine and Moriz were reserving very expensive seats. "We had a box very near the stage. It was an outstanding location," Gretl wrote after her first theater evening in 1906 and was soon even more precise, although the variations were small. They were once in the front row, once in the fifth, once in the seventh, once in the ninth, but otherwise always in the front row of a box on the parterre. Gretl was so particular, reflecting her parents' concerns, because the opera and theater were among the places to be seen in Vienna. While there was generally a profound gulf between members of Vienna's "second society," such as the Gallias, and its "first society" of old aristocratic families, the best boxes in the Hofburgtheater and the Hofoper brought the two unusually close together, placing the upper bourgeoisie and aristocracy literally on the same level, so for once they appeared as a community of equals. At the end of each performance, the occupants of all the boxes bowed to each other.

Opening nights and gala performances were integral to this pursuit of the most expensive, exclusive occasions. Hermine's concert book suggests that Moriz and she went to their first premiere in 1901 and were soon attending so many that Hermine did not always identify them. In 1903 Gustav Mahler and Theobald Pollak gave Moriz and Hermine entrée to a much grander event—a gala at the Hofoper in honor of Britain's King Edward VII presided over by Emperor Franz Joseph. As Mahler recorded in a letter to Alma, he gave his tickets to Pollak, who in turn gave them to Hermine, allowing the Gallias to see this spectacle from the director's box. A decade later, Hermine and Moriz introduced Erni and Gretl to a similarly prestigious occasion, the opening of the Konzertverein, Vienna's second concert hall, where Franz Joseph again presided.

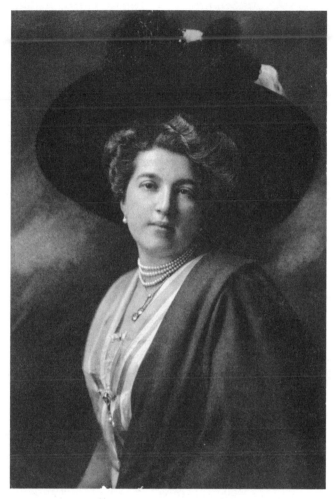

Hermine dressed for going out, wearing her best pearls.

Hermine and Moriz's choice of productions and performances reveals how two patrons of the most exciting Viennese art and design engaged with other parts of the culture. A common assumption is that there was a chasm between the taste of Vienna's conservatives and avant-garde—between the audience for the old and the new, the popular and the serious, the entertaining and the challenging. Hermine's diary suggests otherwise. For all her taste for the modern, her Vienna was a city of Gustav Mahler and Buffalo Bill, Oscar Wilde and somersaulting cyclists,

Shakespeare and Arthur Schnitzler, *The Merry Widow,* Isadora Duncan, and Mata Hari.

Gustav Mahler is often paired with Gustav Klimt. Just as the one Gustav dominated the visual art of Vienna, so the other dominated its musical life. Yet for all the controversy engendered by Klimt, Mahler excited a different order of opposition, acclaim, and argument, as Vienna took its music much more seriously than its painting. While Klimt was a public identity within the city, Mahler was its greatest celebrity, an object of incessant scrutiny, commentary, caricatures, and gossip. Mahler's international standing, especially as a conductor, also far eclipsed Klimt's reputation as a painter. Whereas Italy and Germany were the only countries outside Austria where Klimt was lauded by critics and found a market, opera houses and concert halls across Europe and North America clamored for Mahler to conduct.

Mahler's transformation of the Vienna Opera was profound as he turned its orchestra into the finest in Europe, recruited soloists for their acting ability as well as their voices, and worked with Alfred Roller, a member of the Secession, to create Europe's most innovative, evocative sets and lighting. Hermine and Moriz, who went to the opera more than any other venue, were quick to see many of these new productions. They attended the second night of Alexander Zemlinsky's *Es war einmal* in 1901. They were at the Viennese premiere of Tchaikovsky's *Pique Dame* in 1903 and the opening night of Puccini's *Madama Butterfly*—along with Puccini himself—in 1907. They often saw Mahler, who was the opera's principal conductor as well as its director, though Hermine never noted his involvement, just as Mahler omitted himself from the opera's posters and programs.

Hermine's first experience of the Vienna Philharmonic—a performance of Beethoven's Ninth Symphony in 1900—was different. When Mahler chose to rework Beethoven's score in order to exploit the expansion of the orchestra and to "clarify" Beethoven's intentions, many members of the Philharmonic protested these changes as well as Mahler's impassioned interpretation. Several critics accused Mahler of perverting Beethoven's work. The crowd that filled Vienna's Musikverein was thrilled. Hermine's initial record of the concert revealed nothing of her own response. Her assumption, commonplace in Vienna, was that a diary should simply record what happened, not what it felt like or why it mattered. "*Mahler dirigiert*," "Mahler conducted," was all she noted in pencil. But then, as an afterthought, she continued in ink, "*fabelhaft*," "fabulous"—a description she otherwise used only after hearing Sergey Rachmaninoff perform his Piano Concerto no. 3.

She soon was attending more of the Philharmonic's concerts where Mahler conducted Beethoven. But the opportunities to hear Mahler's own symphonies in Vienna were much rarer as he was anxious to avoid accusations of exploiting his position to promote himself. The extent of public interest in his work was also small as he stretched the symphony to unprecedented proportions, moved from the romantic toward the expressionist, and engaged in the creeping chromaticism that led to twelve-tone music. Mahler's usual practice on completing a new work was simply to conduct its Viennese premiere and give a repeat performance a few days later if there was sufficient demand. Still Hermine and Moriz were slow to attend, given their association with him and appetite for the controversial. They began late in 1905 with the Viennese premiere of his Fifth, which local critics characteristically dismissed as vulgar, superficial, sentimental, decadent, overheated, and retrograde, while the audience was ecstatic. Then Hermine and Moriz returned early in 1907 for the Viennese premiere of his Sixth.

Mahler was on his way to New York by the end of the year. He was lured by what the Metropolitan Opera claimed was the highest fee ever paid to a conductor, $15,000, or 75,000 crowns, for a three-month stint, twice his annual salary at the Hofoper. His repeated vilification in Vienna, as anti-Semitism intensified in the city, also spurred him to go. Like Klimt and Hoffmann, who signed a public letter defending him, Hermine and Moriz were probably outraged at Mahler's treatment in the Hapsburg capital and dismayed at his decision to leave. When he gave a farewell performance of his Second Symphony at the Musikverein, they were there for one of his most affecting concerts. As the symphony ended with its great choral outburst, the auditorium erupted, compelling Mahler to return again and again to his podium. "*Herrlich!*" Hermine wrote, "Magnificent!"

Hermine and Moriz never saw Mahler perform again because his imperial pension was conditional on his neither directing nor conducting in Vienna, but Hermine and Moriz experienced more of Mahler's music through other conductors, led by Bruno Walter. When Mahler died, at age fifty, of heart failure in 1911, Hermine and Moriz attended the first memorial concert together with Theobald Pollak, Erni, and Gretl, who

A page from Gretl's third diary with the leaf of ivy she took from
Mahler's grave in Vienna's Grinzing Cemetery, March 30, 1916.

was overwhelmed by her first encounter with Mahler's music. When the
concert ended with his Second, she started to cry.

The Mahler concert that excited Gretl most was one she attended in
1915 when, for the second time in Vienna, Bruno Walter conducted *Das
Lied von der Erde,* which was both a symphony and a song cycle, a new
form of composition, soon to be Mahler's most famous work. Gretl was
thrilled to see Walter, whom she had come to idolize as a "God-given
artist." The presence of Mahler's widow, Alma, and his only surviving
daughter, Gucki, who shared a box with Mahler's sister, Justine, and her

violinist husband, Alfred Rosé, heightened Gretl's sense of occasion. She was shaken by the music, which was especially important to her because of her connection to it through Theobald Pollak. In 1914 the critic Richard Specht revealed that Pollak gave Mahler *Die chinesische Flöte,* an anthololgy containing the Tang dynasty verses that Mahler set to music in *Das Lied von der Erde.* Gretl knew that Pollak had done more. Much as Alban Berg reported to Arnold Schönberg that Pollak was "the one who persuaded Mahler to do the Chinese poems," so Gretl wrote, "The composition was created at the suggestion of Uncle Baldi."

Her pride in Pollak's role was familial. When he died of tuberculosis soon after the Mahler memorial concert, Gretl declared, "After parents, siblings, and grandparents, I loved him most," putting Pollak before all her actual uncles and aunts. She was infuriated when her parents would not let her go to Pollak's funeral because they expected she would become overexcited. "And if I did, so what?" she exclaimed, recognizing that funerals were occasions for such grief. She was even more incensed that another of her honorary uncles, her godfather Carl Moll, failed to return from Bologna for the funeral even though Pollak and he were old friends and Moll's daughter, Maria, was a major beneficiary of Pollak's will. "I hate Moll," Gretl wrote.

The Orlik portrait that Mahler inscribed to Pollak was a tangible reminder of their friendship. It was the kind of object that Pollak would never have parted with while he was alive because Mahler was too important to him. Like other devotees of Mahler, Pollak probably preserved everything he received from Mahler, however trivial. But when Pollak drew up his last will shortly before his death in 1912, he specified that four of his closest friends, led by Moriz, should receive mementos from his estate and, typically, entrusted Moll with their selection. Most likely, Moll asked Moriz what he would like and he chose the portrait because it was both personal to Pollak and expressed the Gallias' awe of Mahler.

Gretl first saw Mahler's grave the following year, when Hermine took her to Vienna's Grinzing Cemetery to visit the grave of Hermine's sister-in-law, Henny Hamburger. While Mahler's memorial was designed by Josef Hoffmann so that it was as prestigious as contemporary Vienna could create, Gretl was appalled to find it overgrown with ivy. As she was accustomed to pressing plants into her diary, Gretl took a piece of ivy home and placed it across the page recording that day. Her birthday presents from her parents that July included the score of *Das Lied von der Erde.*

Five years later she acquired a special issue of the Viennese magazine *Moderne Welt* devoted to Mahler that reproduced an etching of his ivy-covered tomb and had the Orlik portrait on its cover.

The family's favorite was almost everyone else's favorite, Richard Wagner, whose appeal in Vienna extended across class, religious, and political lines. His work was still regarded as modern when Hermine and Moriz moved to the city in the early 1890s, forty years after Wagner emerged as a significant composer and ten years after his death. Another decade later, Wagner's operas had become classics, the stuff of musical history. But the national, even racial characterization of Wagner's operas as uniquely German did not change. By the turn of the century, Hermine and Moriz had seen at least six and were beginning to return to them. While they never attended a complete performance of Wagner's Ring Cycle, they once saw four of his operas in eight days. Moriz loved *Die Meistersinger von Nürnberg*, Wagner's most accessible composition, which Hermine and he saw at least ten times.

This passion required Moriz and Hermine to ignore Wagner's virulent anti-Semitism, which he not only expressed in private conversations and letters but also made public in some of his most widely read essays, such as "Judaism in Music" and "What Is German?" As part of blaming Jews for everything wrong with the modern world, Wagner identified them as the antithesis of what was German, describing them as an "utterly alien element" that had "invaded" the "German essence," accused them of "debasing German art," and dwelled on the "involuntary repellence" that Germans felt for Jews. He also declared that Jews had to "cease to be Jews" and could be redeemed only by their "*Untergang,*" or "going under."

Wagner's operas were widely identified as expressing the same politics although they were not explicitly anti-Semitic. When *Die Meistersinger* was first performed in Vienna, members of the city's Jewish community protested that Wagner had created the opera's villain, the music critic Beckmesser, to deride them. The theater director Franz Bittong thought this anti-Semitism ran even deeper in the *Meistersinger,* prompting him to dub it "Music and the Jews." Gustav Mahler had "no doubt" that Wagner "intended to ridicule the Jews" when he created the dwarf Mime in *Siegfried* and did so both "textually and musically." Meanwhile, racist political groups embraced Wagner's operas, and the magazine issued by the German Wagner Society became a leading anti-Semitic journal.

Vienna's Jubiläumstheater, which was established under the patronage of Karl Lueger in 1898 with the explicitly racist mission of promoting "Aryan" authors and composers through a company "untainted by Jewish influence," is one test of how Moriz and Hermine responded to anti-Semitism onstage. Although Moriz and Hermine patronized every other significant Viennese theater, they did not go to the Jubiläumstheater while it pursued this agenda, almost certainly a boycott triggered by its politics. Wagner was different both for Jews and for Jewish converts to Christianity. The Viennese musicologist Guido Adler was one of the founders of the city's Wagner Society. The creator of Zionism, Theodor Herzl, first formulated his ideas for a Jewish state after being exalted by a performance of *Tannhäuser*. Mahler turned Vienna into the best city to experience Wagner's work: he staged Wagner's established operas with unprecedented frequency and performed them at their full length rather than with cuts, as was common. While most critics thought Wagner's early opera, *Rienzi*, was of no interest, Mahler declared it the "greatest musical drama ever composed" and added it to the Hofoper's repertoire. He also worked with Alfred Roller on innovative productions, starting with a *Tristan und Isolde* that was immediately extolled for creating a new operatic style because of its remarkable mix of music, color, and light. Just as Moriz and Hermine went to the premiere of Mahler's *Rienzi* in 1901, so they were at the premiere of his *Tristan* in 1903.

Hermine typically recorded nothing of her response to these operas. But when Alma Schindler had supper with Hermine and Moriz after they saw *Die Walküre* for the third time in 1901, she noted something of what Moriz thought. While Alma had gone from being overwhelmed by all of *Die Walküre* to finding parts of it tedious, she continued to be inspired by the finales of its first and third acts. She also was typically sure of her judgment—a confidence that came with thinking she had the potential to be the first great female composer. As part of her larger disdain for the Gallias, she recorded contemptuously that Moriz found the third act *"charming."*

The one opera that Moriz and Hermine could not see in Vienna was *Parsifal,* which Wagner decided would be performed only in the small Bavarian town of Bayreuth where he established the first modern musical festival in 1876. This monopoly, which lasted as long as *Parsifal* remained in copyright, helped to make the festival a success, as did Bayreuth's status as the spiritual home of Wagnerism, the place to commune with the Master. The Wagnerites who went there also gained a great opportunity to lord it over those who did not, as George Bernard Shaw observed. "Ah, you should see it at Bayreuth," they would say. Moriz and Hermine joined these devotees in 1908, attending two performances, like many other visitors. They started with *Parsifal,* which was still the original production from 1882, then saw *Lohengrin,* which was the first new production of Wagner's son, Siegfried, who had just become the festival's director. Hermine was thrilled by these productions, which both excited critical acclaim. She described the *Parisfal* as the "most wonderful performance," the *Lohengrin* as "the most magnificent."

Hermine and Moriz were soon introducing their children to Wagner, and Gretl was characteristically receptive. When she saw *Das Rheingold* as an eleven-year-old in 1909, she much preferred it to Mozart's *The Magic Flute,* which was the only other opera she had seen, while her first *Lohengrin,* in 1911, left her crazy with excitement. "I am so easily enthused," Gretl observed, "but this time with good reason," since Moriz and Hermine thought the production could not have been bettered in Bayreuth. She was even more impressed a few weeks later when the family celebrated Hermine's forty-first birthday by seeing *Die Walküre.* When Gretl went to bed, she had to cry; she did not know why.

The family's biggest Wagner year was 1912, which Moriz, Hermine, Erni, and Gretl started in Vienna on New Year's Day with *Die Meistersinger.* A week later they saw another *Lohengrin,* which also made Gretl weep. They continued with *Gotterdämmerung,* which left Gretl so overwrought that she struggled to write about it afterward. The highlight was in July, when the entire family went to Bayreuth. Although Moriz and Hermine probably bought their tickets weeks, if not months, before, because demand for seats far exceeded supply, Gretl linked this trip to her matriculation just ten days earlier. She described it as her "*Maturreise,*" a reward for completing school with honors above and beyond the diamond and pearl pendant on a platinum chain that Moriz and Hermine gave her when she got her results.

Hermine and Moriz intensified this experience by stopping in Nürnberg, the setting of *Die Meistersinger,* Wagner's one major opera located in a specific time and place. Their immediate destination—the prime reason for their visit—was the house of the sixteenth-century poet and playwright Hans Sachs, one of *Die Meistersinger*'s main characters. Then they went to Bayreuth, where they paid more homage to Wagner by visiting his

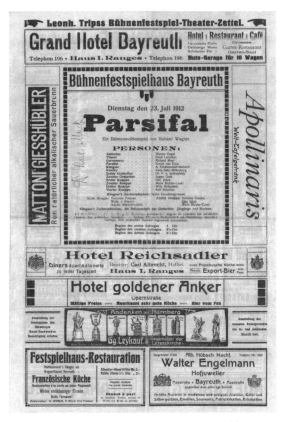

The program for the *Parsifal* seen by the Gallias
in Bayreuth, 1912—signed for Gretl by conductor Karl Muck.

house, Wahnfried, where he was buried. Just as Gretl picked a piece of ivy
from Mahler's tomb, so she took a sprig of cypress from Wagner's grave.
The first performance that the family saw was a production by Siegfried
Wagner of *Die Meistersinger* that, more than ever, was discussed and
lauded in Germanic and anti-Semitic terms. The second was the production of *Parsifal* that Moriz and Hermine had already seen but was new to
their children.

   This experience stayed with Gretl when she returned to Vienna and
continued to accompany her parents to Wagner's operas more often than
those of any other composer. She was, she wrote after seeing Verdi's *Rigoletto,* too great a "Wagneriana" to have much liking for Italian opera.
Although the performance of *Parsifal* that she saw in Bayreuth was widely

dismissed as tired and lifeless, it remained her benchmark when *Parsifal* came out of copyright in 1913 and companies across Europe immediately began performing it. When Hermine and Moriz took Gretl to two of these productions at Vienna's Volksoper and Hofoper, Gretl was appalled by the first and unimpressed by the second. Nothing compared with Bayreuth.

Isadora Duncan brought modern dance to Vienna in 1902, appearing barefoot and free of corsets and tights in the briefest of translucent tunics. Her three performances before small, invited audiences shocked and excited those who saw the twenty-four-year-old American because she appeared "nude or nearly so." Had Hermine and Moriz wished, they could have been among the 150 men and women who saw Duncan at the Secession, where she was introduced by the writer Hermann Bahr. Their patronage of the Secession would have given Hermine and Moriz access to this event, which started at ten o'clock one Friday evening and finished well after midnight. Their next opportunity was in 1903, when Duncan performed for a week at Vienna's Carl Theater and they bought tickets for her last night.

They went to the theater almost as often as the opera, but had little interest in classics. While Schiller's emphasis on freedom is often said to have made his work particularly important to Jews, Hermine and Moriz went to just three of his plays when they had only themselves to please. They saw even less of Shakespeare, who occupied almost as central a place in Austrian as in British culture. All that changed when Erni and Gretl began high school because Hermine and Moriz wanted to enhance their education. Over the next few years, they all went to most of Schiller's plays and saw a slate of Shakespeare, while Moriz and Hermine bought their collected works, a card game that tested knowledge of Schiller, and a children's edition of Shakespeare's plays for Gretl, whose response was often critical. "I find our classical dramas more beautiful than the English ones," she observed after *As You Like It.* "Too many ghosts, too many battles," she complained after *Richard III.*

The best contemporary playwrights from across Europe, such as Oscar Wilde, George Bernard Shaw, Henrik Ibsen, and Arthur Schnitzler, appealed much more to Hermine and Moriz. The work of these playwrights often addressed the "woman question," especially the domination of women by men within marriage and the double standard that applied to men and women when it came to sex outside it. Their work also occasionally featured the "new woman," who looked for equality in her relations with men, often chose to remain single and pursue a career, and was not ashamed of her interest in sex. The result was censorship in many European countries. Because Vienna's Hofoper and Hofburgtheater were both funded by the emperor, they were subject to particular controls. But foreign companies playing in private theaters enjoyed greater latitude and so became the prime medium through which Vienna saw controversial plays and operas.

One example was Franz Wedekind's *Frühlings Erwachen,* or *Spring Awakening,* the first German play about adolescent sexuality, in which the fourteen-year-old Wendla falls pregnant (without understanding how conception happens), has an abortion at her mother's insistence, and dies as a result of a botched operation. While Wedekind completed *Spring Awakening* in 1891, it was not performed until 1906, when Germany's leading director, Max Reinhardt, secured permission to stage it in Berlin by emphasizing that he practiced "a discreet performance style, free of every coarse or too drastic an effect" and by omitting all uses of the word "intercourse." When *Spring Awakening* ran for over three hundred nights in Berlin, other theaters became eager to stage it. The first Viennese production was by Reinhardt's company in 1907, when Moriz and Hermine were away from the city. The next was in 1908, when Reinhardt staged it at Vienna's most radical theater, the Deutsches Volkstheater, and Hermine and Moriz went to the third night.

Richard Strauss's opera *Salome,* based on Oscar Wilde's play of the same name, was even more notorious. Had Gustav Mahler gotten his way, its premiere would have been at the Hofoper in 1905, but the imperial censor rejected it as obscene and blasphemous. The censor thought Salome's desire to possess the head of John the Baptist and her rapture over his dead eyes, hair, and lips were "morally repugnant," exemplifying her "perverted sensuality." When Mahler questioned this decision, the censor required that the Hebrew name of John the Baptist and all allusions to Christ be removed or rewritten. The censor also reiterated that *Salome* was unsuited for the imperial stage because it belonged to "the domain of sexual pathology."

The obvious alternative venue was the Deutsches Volkstheater. By the time the Breslau Opera finally brought *Salome* there in 1907, it had played in many cities, attracting critical acclaim and vast crowds in some, while failing to secure an audience in others and being canceled at New York's

Metropolitan Opera at the insistence of one of the daughters of the banker John Pierpont Morgan. Interest in *Salome* in Vienna was consequently intense. Tickets for the *"sensationspremiere,"* as one critic characterized the opening night, sold out almost immediately. The audience was thick with aristocrats and musicians, the rich and famous, the men in frock coats or smoking jackets, the women in their most glamorous gowns. As the curtain rose, another critic sensed "a slightly unhealthy excitement" in the packed auditorium, which again included Moriz and Hermine.

Mata Hari was another sensation. She was a Dutchwoman, originally known as Margaretha Geertruida Zelle, who created an exotic identity for herself after spending three years in Java and Sumatra while married to a Dutch army captain. As she kept changing her story about whether she was a child of European parents born in the East Indies, part Indian and part Dutch, or the daughter of an Indian or Javanese temple dancer, critics occasionally branded her a fraud. But on the whole she was accepted as an Oriental who revealed the mysteries of the Brahmin cult as she played the part of a servant of God who spent her entire life inside a temple and through her dance grew nearer to the divine. This invocation of religion helped Mata Hari to avoid being charged with indecency when she first set Paris talking in 1905 with a performance that saw her strip off her multicolored veils until she was naked, except for bejeweled brass plates over her breasts and bracelets on her wrists, arms, and ankles.

Her first performance in Vienna was in 1906 when she was already among the most highly paid dancers in Europe. Like Isadora Duncan, she appeared at the Secession before invitees who, this time, included Hermine and Moriz and their friends, the Luzzattos. The centerpiece of the stage was a Buddha placed between tall vases and cherry trees covered with white blossoms, while a blue-white light reminiscent of a shimmering moon illuminated the floor. As Mata Hari removed her clothing, her performance grew wilder and wilder until she was naked except for her breast plates and bracelets. While the critic Ludwig Hevesi had no doubt that this performance was high art—an example of the "new dance" that Duncan had done most to create—he knew the audience did not care. "To what extent this rhythmic activity was dance, and to what extent it was Hindu hardly worried the spectators. They were indulging their eyes to the full."

Operetta occupied a very different place in Viennese culture. It was the most popular musical genre, the mainstay of several theaters, and vital to the city's identity. But it was dismissed by many of Vienna's cultural elite as pap for the masses. The one exception was *Die Fledermaus* by Johann Strauss Jr., the only Viennese composer of popular music in the second half of the nineteenth century whose work was regarded as serious art. When Mahler introduced *Die Fledermaus* into the Hofoper's repertoire following the Waltz King's death in 1899, he underwrote its place in the canon. Hermine, who discovered *Die Fledermaus* as a girl in Freudenthal, saw it with Moriz during its first week at the Hofoper. At the start of 1900 they saw it again. At the end of the year they saw it there on New Year's Eve.

No new operettas gained such acceptance, but the most successful works attracted almost everyone in the city. *The Geisha* by the British composer Sidney Jones was one example. As Jones exploited the contemporary European fascination with the East, *The Geisha* became the most popular British operetta of the 1890s, far eclipsing *The Mikado* by Gilbert and Sullivan. The Austrian writer Arthur Schnitzler saw *The Geisha* in London in 1896, and then went again in 1897, when the Carl Theater staged it in Vienna. Hermine and Moriz, who in some seasons went to no operettas but in others went to one or two, saw *The Geisha* in 1898, as did Alma Schindler, who was impressed enough to return.

An array of new Viennese operettas also attracted Hermine and Moriz, including the first Viennese song-and-dance show, Heinrich Reinhardt's *The Sweet Girl,* and Franz Lehár's *The Merry Widow,* the greatest international musical success of the new century, which redefined operetta through both its musical inventiveness and its naturalistic characters. Hermine and Moriz first saw *The Merry Widow* in 1906, three months after its premiere, when it was still struggling after receiving mixed reviews, but its audience was starting to grow through word of mouth. Hermine and Moriz returned with the Luzzattos in 1907 for its gala four-hundredth performance, featuring a new overture by Lehár conducted by Lehár himself.

Circuses also attracted Hermine and Moriz, both with and without their children, suggesting Hermine and Moriz's own enjoyment of these entertainments. The most spectacular was the *Wild West* show of William F. Cody, a.k.a. Buffalo Bill, which began touring Europe in the late 1880s and required a special train to move its eight hundred performers. When the entire family saw Cody's troupe at the Prater in 1906, on its final European tour, its most famous female star, Annie Oakley, was long gone. But the sixty-year-old Cody was still starting each show by donning his buckskins and galloping into the arena on his white horse to announce his "Congress of Rough Riders of the World."

Vienna's music halls combined the exotic, erotic, and extraordinary. When Hermine and Moriz first went to Vienna's oldest music hall, the Ronacher, in 1900, the evening started with "the French eccentric," Elise de Vere, in fact a Cockney actress and singer whom the British impresario Charles Cochran reckoned had the shapeliest legs he ever saw. The evening concluded with "the phenomenal contortionist," Juno Saimo. Its star was the Spanish dancer La Belle Chavita, whose performances, a Parisian critic observed, "would have made Saint Anthony himself swear." The failure of Hermine and Moriz to return suggests they did not enjoy it, but within a few years they were regulars at the Ronacher and its main rival, the Apollo.

The German essayist George Simmel looked on these theaters as proof of the debilitating consequences of modern urban life. While their audiences included men and women of all classes, Simmel wrote as if they simply attracted working-class men. He proclaimed: "Because life uses up his strength completely, all that may be offered him as relaxation is something that requires absolutely no effort," namely "gleaming colors, light music, and finally—and principally—sexual feelings." For all that sex was integral to these theaters, some of their stars were also at the forefront of the modern, led by Mata Hari, who, after performing at the Secession, began appearing before a general audience at the Apollo where she continued her elaborate removal of her clothes but wore a body stocking to keep within the law. As this legal stricture provoked a fierce debate over art and obscenity, nakedness and nudity, Hermine and Moriz went on another of their theater outings with the feminist and socialist Elisabeth Luzzatto and her industrialist husband, Maximilian, putting them among the few who could talk from experience about both of Mata Hari's acts.

6

Pictures

The fin de siècle was the first great era of the poster. The French artist Jules Chéret was largely responsible when he turned color lithographs into a powerful form of advertising in the late 1860s, relying on bold drawing, few colors, a simple text, and a beautiful young woman as the dominant figure. By the 1890s, many artists across Europe and the United States were following Chéret's example while others were more innovative. Their posters were largely used on billboards, but were also recognized immediately as worth collecting. As many were devoted to products that were the stuff of keen competition and strong demand, one of their prime subjects was new forms of lighting. The Gallias' involvement with modern art started when Moriz commissioned one of these posters for Auer von Welsbach's Gas Glowing Light Company. This poster by Heinrich Lefler, promoting the gas mantle, was the first significant poster by an Austrian artist. By commissioning it, Moriz was responsible for Austria's joining the international movement.

One of Moriz's own companies, Watt, soon followed suit, commissioning the Italian artist Adolphe Hohenstein to produce a poster promoting its Monowatt electric bulbs. Moriz also made the Gas Glowing Light Company one of the small group of companies that advertised regularly in the Vienna Secession's exhibition catalogs, both to attract customers and to subsidize the society's publication costs. Yet Moriz's main involvement with art was in a private rather than professional capacity. Over fifteen years, Hermine and he were not only significant collectors but also major cultural philanthropists who gave much more to the state than they spent on any of their own pictures.

Adele Bloch-Bauer, the subject of Klimt's most famous "golden" portrait, and her husband, Ferdinand, exemplify the difficulties in determining how Viennese couples went about such collecting. It has often been assumed that Adele was not only one of Klimt's many lovers but was also responsible for the Bloch-Bauers' acquisition of much of Klimt's work, including seven of his paintings. Yet there is no evidence that Adele was Klimt's lover, and a letter from Adele in 1903 reveals that Ferdinand initiated her first portrait. Adele's only documented Klimt purchase was in 1909, when she bought sixteen of his drawings. The ultimate ownership of the Bloch-Bauer paintings by Klimt is just as unclear. Again the standard assumption has been that Adele owned them. Adele herself seemingly thought so when she lent six of the paintings to an exhibition at the Öster-reichische Galerie in 1919. Her last will, which she wrote in 1923, has sometimes been read as stating so. But when the earliest list of Klimt's patrons was published in 1918, it identified Ferdinand as the owner of the Bloch-Bauer pictures, while identifying women as owners of several other paintings. A book about Klimt published in 1920 similarly identified Ferdinand as the owner.

The Gallias' situation appears simpler because Moriz was explicit in his last will. He stated that Hermine had always owned the family's household goods, including their paintings and furniture, rebutting the ordinary legal presumption that the household goods of an Austrian couple belonged to the man. Yet this statement may have been a fiction designed to diminish the size of Moriz's estate and hence reduce the death duties paid by the family when, as expected, Moriz died before Hermine. A who's who of Viennese art collectors published in 1914 identified Moriz rather than Hermine as the owner of the family's pictures, suggesting that that was how the Gallias thought of them. The list of Klimt's patrons published in 1918 did the same.

The family's taste was shaped, above all, by Carl Moll, who was not only one of Vienna's finest artists but also its greatest artistic entrepeneur at the turn of the century, known as "the impresario of the Vienna Moderne."

From the late 1890s, Moll proved himself as accomplished at organizing exhibitions as he was at selling pictures, as adept at gaining the ear of government as he was at becoming close to men and women with money to spend or give away. In 1900, Karl Kraus savaged Moll for becoming just another avaricious creature of the art market by working as the "art agent" of the coal merchant David Berl. Moll appears to have acted in much the same way for Moriz and Hermine, who arrived in Vienna with little knowledge of art, though it is not clear whether they paid for his help.

Moriz and Hermine's appetite for collecting was, in many respects, typical of successful Viennese Jews and recent converts to Christianity. Klimt's patrons included several industrialists whose families were of Jewish descent. Hoffmann and the Wiener Werkstätte attracted so many Jewish patrons that the Werkstätte produced bilingual New Year's cards with texts in German and Hebrew. The architect Adolf Loos was even more dependent on the city's Jews for commissions. The audience at Vienna's operas and theaters was similar, prompting Stefan Zweig to claim that "nine-tenths of what the world celebrated as Viennese culture . . . was promoted, nourished, or even created by Viennese Jews." They were "the real audience, they filled the theaters and the concerts, they bought the books and the pictures, they visited the exhibitions."

This support of the arts was part of the pursuit of education, refinement, and good manners—known in German as *Bildung*—by assimilated Jews. A new class looked to make up for their want of inherited social and economic status by buying cultural cachet. This desire was fueled, Arthur Schnitzler suggested, by the prejudice that Vienna's Jews experienced in other parts of their lives. As these men and women encountered discrimination, they turned to culture to distinguish themselves. Their appetite for paintings, music, and literature allowed them to fill a niche once occupied by Vienna's aristocrats.

The usual pattern of families who moved to Vienna was that members of the first generation were too intent on making their fortunes to spend much on art, but the second generation was more liberal. The Gallias were very different, spurred by the creation in 1897 of the Secession, just six years after Moriz moved to Vienna and four years after Hermine joined him. As the Secession became one of the most successful new artists' organizations in Europe, attracting the emperor's immediate imprimatur, a state subsidy, vast crowds, and many collectors, Moriz and Hermine were among its earliest supporters. Although they acquired nothing from the Secession's first exhibition, held at the city's Horticultural Society building in March 1898, at least one of their paintings was in the Secession's next exhibition, that November, in its own new building on the Friedrichstrasse. It was one of Carl Moll's largest canvases, depicting the interior of Vienna's Peterskirche, a baroque church in the First District modeled on St. Peter's Basilica in Rome.

The only question is whether Moriz and Hermine bought this painting from the exhibition or some time later. The painting's Christian subject is reason for Moriz and Hermine to have initially rejected it; most Jews would not have bought such a painting of a Catholic site and would have been embarrassed to have their Jewish friends and relatives see it in their homes. Moriz and Hermine may have done so because of her strong Christian inclinations. The strength of Moll's relationship with the Gallias by the start of the 1900s also suggests that their first significant dealings with him had been a few years before. The purchase by Moriz and Hermine of the Peterskirche painting from the Secession is the most likely catalyst for their friendship.

Either way, the Gallias' collection of Secessionist pictures soon grew. While they appear to have bought just one or two paintings in some years, they acquired at least four in 1903, including the Klimt *Beech Forest,* an even bigger landscape by Ferdinand Andri, a smaller oil by Moll of the house where Beethoven lived in the outer Viennese suburb of Heiligenstadt, and a sparkling neo-impressionist moonlit scene by Ernst Stöhr. When Klimt finally completed his portrait of Hermine early the following year, the Gallias' apartment in the Schleifmühlgasse boasted one of the great early Secessionist collections.

This patronage was thrown into question when, like many other breakaway artists' groups in Europe at the turn of the century, the Secession soon fractured. One source of discord was a proposal advanced by Klimt and his supporters that the Secession buy Vienna's leading commercial gallery, the Miethke, which Moll had run from 1904. Another, again advanced by this Klimtgruppe, was that Moll run the Miethke from the Secession's building while showing only some of the society's artists. When a majority of the Secession decided that Moll was guilty of a conflict of interest in 1905, the Klimtgruppe resigned in protest, depriving the society of its most innovative artists and architects, though its exhibitions continued to attract crowds, enjoy critical attention, and sell paintings.

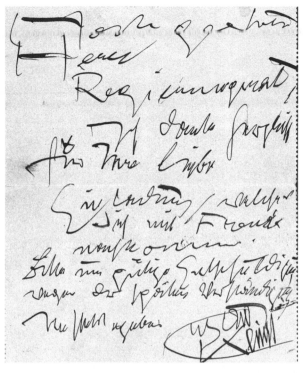

A letter from Klimt to Moriz accepting an invitation
to dinner at the Schleifmühlgasse, the Gallias' home
in Vienna's Fourth District from 1893 until 1913.

Moriz and Hermine continued to buy from the Secession after this
schism—above all, a beautiful landscape by Adolf Zdrazila, the foremost
Silesian painter of the early twentieth century, whose work appealed to
Hermine because it showed her childhood home. When the Gallias visited
the Munich Secession in 1912, Gretl declared its Viennese counterpart
"much more beautiful," most likely referring to both its building and the
art it showed. Yet Moriz and Hermine were much closer to the Klimtgruppe, including Klimt himself, who was an occasional visitor to the
family's apartment. Like Sonja Knips, Adele Bloch-Bauer, and Eugenia
Primavesi, who were also painted by Klimt, Hermine acquired his photograph, though, unlike these other women, Hermine did not put this photograph on display or place it in a special album.

Moll remained close to the Gallias. Just as he invited them to his
house on the Hohe Warte, so they invited him to their apartment in the

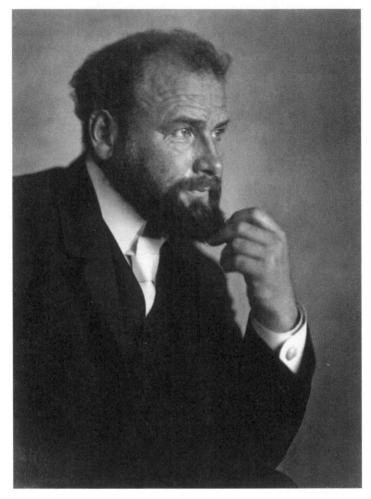

Hermine's photograph of Klimt. One of the celebrated series of
portraits of Klimt taken by the Madame d'Ora studio of Dora
Kallmus, c. 1908.

Schleifmühlgasse and sometimes went to the opera, theater, and concerts
with him and his wife, Anna. Not long after the Klimtgruppe quit the
Secession, the Gallias, Molls, and Theobald Pollak all went to a performance of Oscar Wilde's *The Importance of Being Earnest*. Six years later Moll
was so close to the Gallias that he gave them one of his own paintings, a
still life of roses. He also visited Hermine's birthplace of Freudenthal,
where he almost certainly stayed with her parents. In between, Moriz and
Hermine bought most of their pictures from him.

Moriz and Hermine had every opportunity to buy the best art from across Europe because both the Secession and the Galerie Miethke were internationalist in what they exhibited, but like most Viennese collectors of the modern, Moriz and Hermine preferred the local. A rare exception was a large watercolor by the Russian artist Constantin Somoff, who exhibited at the Galerie Miethke in 1905. Otherwise, Moriz and Hermine expressed their Austrian identity, which dated only from the 1890s when they moved to Vienna, by concentrating on Austrian artists. When they stopped collecting around the time they moved into their Hoffmann apartment in 1913, they owned at least twenty-five paintings stretching over almost eighty years, illustrating the rise of modern Austrian art as Klimt and his followers saw it.

The family's collection started with Ferdinand Georg Waldmüller, the finest Austrian artist of the first half of the nineteenth century, who enjoyed great contemporary success from the late 1820s, when the imperial family commissioned him to paint a series of portraits and Vienna's Academy of the Fine Arts made him a professor. But after Waldmüller published two polemics attacking the academy, it dismissed him on a janitor's pension. When he died in 1865, he was almost forgotten and remained so until the mid-1890s, when he was embraced both by traditionalists who admired his realism and by members of the avant-garde who lauded his attacks on the academy, support for younger artists, and anticipation of impressionism by painting en plein air. When his work was allocated its own room at the exhibition of Austrian art staged to mark Franz Joseph's jubilee as emperor in 1898, the critic Ludwig Hevesi set Waldmüller at the start of a lineage of radical art in Austria, identifying him as an "*Ursecessionist*," or "proto-Secessionist."

The prices fetched by Waldmüller's paintings were soon immense. By one account, in 1907 his pictures were worth ten times what they sold for in his lifetime. The main dealer in them was Moll, who almost always had Waldmüller's work in stock after choosing him as the subject of his first exhibition at the Galerie Miethke. Moriz and Hermine bought a pair of Waldmüller's small portraits of a man and woman from 1837, when he was at his most prolific, completing a portrait every two to three weeks as well as an array of other pictures. Both of these paintings possess the comfortable self-assurance that characterizes Waldmüller's commissioned portraits. Both are in near frontal poses against neutral backgrounds, which was Waldmüller's standard composition. Both are on smooth, shiny surfaces painted with the remarkable detail that prompted Waldmüller's identification as the Ingres of Austria and looked anything but radical. They probably appealed to Moriz and Hermine because they suggested old money, identity, and culture while possessing great modernist cachet.

Moriz and Hermine also bought the work of the most innovative Austrian landscape painters of the 1870s and 1880s, Emil Jakob Schindler and Rudolf Ribarz, whose estates were both handled by Moll. They acquired the work of members of the Klimtgruppe, including two harbor scenes by Max Kurzweil, who exhibited at the Galerie Miethke in 1907. But the artist who occupied the most substantial place in their collection was Moll himself. Hermine and Moriz were Moll's foremost patrons, acquiring about ten of his paintings, including a landscape that he painted in Freudenthal and his finest series of prints, a boxed set of woodcuts published by the Wiener Werkstätte depicting twelve houses in and around Vienna where Beethoven lived.

The catalyst for these subjects was a Beethoven exhibition staged by the Secession in 1902 around a massive polychrome sculpture of Beethoven by the German artist Max Klinger. But this exhibition also marked the one-hundredth anniversary of the Heiligenstadt Testament, Beethoven's most famous piece of writing, in which he expressed his anguish at his increasing deafness. Moll made a woodcut of Beethoven's house in Heiligenstadt that was published in the exhibition catalog. In 1903 he completed a painting of this scene, and Hermine and Moriz bought it after Moll had shown it at the Secession. Three years later Moll completed his set of twelve woodcuts, which was first shown in 1908 at the most important exhibition organized by Klimt after leaving the Secession, the Kunstschau Wien, which included Klimt's first "golden" portrait of Adele Bloch-Bauer and his *Kiss.*

The Secession's Beethoven exhibition is renowned for its collaboration across the arts. While Mahler conducted a passage from Beethoven's Ninth Symphony at the opening, several members of the Secession, led by Klimt, produced friezes and reliefs in order to create "a spatial work of art" around Max Klinger's sculpture. Yet it was not just musicians, sculptors, and painters who joined in celebrating Beethoven. As patrons such as the Gallias were swept up in the Beethoven cult, they also bridged the divide between the arts. After hearing Mahler conduct one Beethoven concert after another, Hermine and Moriz collected some of the most significant Secessionist art celebrating Beethoven's life in Vienna.

Adele Bloch-Bauer and her husband, Ferdinand, the sugar baron of the Hapsburg Empire, were the most famous collectors with the same taste as Moriz and Hermine. But while the Bloch-Bauers bought the same artists as the Gallias, they generally acquired more pictures because of their greater wealth. In addition to seven paintings by Klimt, which included a second portrait of Adele and another beech forest, the Bloch-Bauers acquired nine paintings by Waldmüller, three by Schindler, and one by Moll. When it came to collecting pictures, Moriz and Hermine were mini Bloch-Bauers.

The dazzling snow-covered landscape, almost always on display in Vienna's Österreichische Galerie, is dominated by a woman caught in the large tree in the foreground on the right. She is standing low on the trunk, wearing a golden diaphanous dress, her head back, holding a leafless branch with one hand, her long, windswept hair wrapped around another leafless branch, her face, neck, and shoulders aglow in the afternoon light, a baby at her breast. Several more women, similarly clad, also with long hair, are underneath the mountains to the left. While two have babies at their breasts, the nearest does not. Her baby lies on the snow, seemingly dead, at the end of the roots of the tree in which the woman is caught.

This picture from 1894 by Giovanni Segantini is one of the great examples of neo-impressionism, the art movement pioneered by Georges Seurat in Paris in 1886 using dots of pure color, which Segantini developed in his own style using long thin lines of paint dubbed the "Segantini stitch." The painting is also one of the great works of symbolism and, like many symbolist pictures, begs an explanation. While there is manifest storytelling and moralizing going on, this theatrical scene does not fit any standard religious, mythological, or literary subject. Who are these women? What is their relationship to their babies? Why are they in this remote, frozen landscape?

The picture's title, *The Evil Mothers,* provides a partial answer without explaining what these women have done wrong. "The Nirvana of the Lustful Women," the poem by the Milanese writer Luigi Illica that inspired Segantini, is illuminating. Its view of women was profoundly conservative—very different from the plays seen by Hermine and Moriz grappling with the "woman question" and the "new woman." It was about women whose unbridled lust led them to fall pregnant, then to reject their babies because of their hedonism and selfishness. Their punishment was to be cast into a barren, freezing landscape until they repented and their natural maternal instincts began to blossom, allowing them to move toward salvation by suckling the babies who had died through their neglect. In taking up this subject, Segantini cast female sexuality as both dangerous and evil.

A description of *The Evil Mothers* by the Viennese critic Franz Servaes is indicative of the painting's initial impact. Servaes wrote: "Incredible misery is expressed in the figure of this bereft damned woman. The very curve of her body is like a weeping cry of woe; the outstretched arms speak of helpless despair; the fluttering hair hanging in the tree is like the pain of one who is taking her own life." Segantini's deeper motivations occupied one of Freud's earliest German followers, Karl Abraham, when he wrote the first extended psychoanalytical study of an artist. Abraham argued that the key to Segantini's work was his sexual fixation with his mother, who died when he was five. According to Abraham, *The Evil Mothers* revealed Segantini's "unconscious desire to punish his own mother and to take revenge upon her."

The painting is in Vienna because the Secession set out to transform the permanent display of contemporary art in the city by persuading the imperial government to establish a Moderne Galerie. This cause was championed by Moll, who was guilty of a typical conflict of interest in using his position on the government's arts council to make the case for the gallery when he aspired to be its inaugural director. Meanwhile, the Secession set about acquiring works from its own exhibitions in order to donate them to the government so that the new gallery would have more to show. It also tried to persuade some of its wealthiest supporters to buy major oil paintings for it. Moriz was the first to respond when he paid for *The Evil Mothers.*

The Secession fixed on *The Evil Mothers* as part of an international competition over Segantini among Austria, where he was born, Italy, where he spent most of his life, and Switzerland, where he died. While Italy initially claimed Segantini by including his work in its displays at world exhibitions and Switzerland posthumously granted him honorary citizenship and erected a Segantini museum in St. Moritz, Austria began embracing Segantini in 1896, when Vienna's Künstlerhaus invited him to participate in its annual exhibition and awarded him its gold medal. The imperial government followed by reversing his classification as a deserter, which resulted from his failure to undertake Austrian military service. The

Secession did most by filling a room with Segantini's paintings at its first exhibition and staging a retrospective of his work that attracted a record number of visitors to its building.

Austria still needed a major Segantini. If a modern gallery was to open in Vienna, one of Segantini's best paintings had to be in it. The obstacle was cost, as the prices for Segantini's work skyrocketed after he died in 1899, making him one of the most expensive artists in the world. When the exhibition opened at the Secession in 1901, one of Segantini's small, late works cost 40,000 crowns (now about $400,000). This sum was the same as Moriz's annual salary from the Gas Glowing Light Company in 1901. It was four times what Klimt received a few years later for his much bigger portraits. But Franz Servaes of the *Neue Freie Presse* was not alone in expecting that Segantini's work would soon become immeasurably more expensive. After Franz Joseph visited the exhibition, Servaes was confident that the government would "prove itself worthy of its great son" by buying Segantini's most ambitious work, his *Alpine Triptych,* in which he grappled with the themes of life, death, and nature. When the government did not, Moriz provided the money for *The Evil Mothers,* the centerpiece of the exhibition's first room.

The importance of *The Evil Mothers* was underlined repeatedly over the next decade. When the Moderne Galerie opened in 1903, *The Evil Mothers* was on show, hung with one of Monet's rare figure paintings and two of Klimt's landscapes. When the Secession looked back on its contribution to art in Austria a year later, it identified *The Evil Mothers* as its most significant gift to the state, eclipsing van Gogh's *The Plain at Auvers,* which another of the Secession's patrons bought for it. *The Evil Mothers* also influenced the course of Austrian art as the Secession had hoped—its impact clear, above all, in the series of landscapes with highly stylized leafless trees painted by the young Egon Schiele.

Auer von Welsbach may have influenced Moriz's gift by not only making repeated substantial donations to charities for children and students but also by endowing the Secession. Auer engaged in this philanthropy because he believed in giving something back to the society that had enriched him. He also understood how the imperial government rewarded philanthropy with an array of titles, which conferred great prestige in a society preoccupied with modes of address. While the steel baron Karl Wittgenstein refused to be ennobled because he thought this elevation would underline his status as a parvenu, almost everyone else in Austria who could get a title was eager to secure one. In 1901 the government rewarded Auer. As he was already "von Welsbach," the government gave him a hereditary baronetcy.

Just as the donation of a foundation picture for the Moderne Galerie by one of Freud's admirers secured his elevation to a professorship at the University of Vienna, which conferred prestige but involved no work, so Moriz's purchase secured his title. Carl Moll, who was the Secession's main fund-raiser, probably approached the government as soon as he realized Moriz might pay for *The Evil Mothers.* The case for Moriz's elevation was simple. Because of his work with Auer in the gas mantle company, he had played a key role in developing a new industry, one criterion for business-men seeking a title. Because of the cost of *The Evil Mothers,* Moriz had engaged in substantial philanthropy. Most likely, the painting cost more than 100,000 crowns (now about $1,000,000), which was close to Karl Wittgenstein's contribution to the construction of the Secession's build-ing. If so, Moriz's expenditure was remarkable because the wealth he had accumulated as a company manager may not even have been one-twentieth of Wittgenstein's fortune.

Due to the price of *The Evil Mothers,* the imperial bureaucracy responded immediately. Moriz probably provided the money to buy *The Evil Mothers* in early or mid-February 1901. The documents recommend-ing that Moriz become a *Regierungsrat,* or Imperial Councilor—another position involving no formal powers or responsibilities but significant prestige—were completed by the end of the month. When Franz Joseph signed the documents at the start of March, his approval was a formality. After Moriz visited Moll on February 25, Alma Schindler observed that Moriz had secured his title in return for a "prodigious loss of money on his side."

Hermine was a beneficiary of this process as she became Frau Regierungsrat Gallia, just as Moriz became Herr Regierungsrat Gallia. Moll was probably another beneficiary; he received an Order of the Iron Cross at the same time. While Alma Schindler recorded that Moll "did not make too much of this honor, because he claimed not to know why he had received it," its timing suggests the government was partly rewarding Moll for engineering the purchase of *The Evil Mothers.* Alma also noted that "innumerable people immediately began harassing Moll with congratula-tions." No doubt they did so with Moriz on an even greater scale because his title was more prestigious.

The usual practice of the Secession, like other Austrian institutions that benefited from philanthropy, was to conceal the identity of those who endowed it. When the *Neue Freie Presse* reported the acquisition of *The Evil Mothers,* it simply attributed the purchase to "private means." The Secession wrote much the same in *Ver Sacrum.* Moriz knew the Secession would implicitly acknowledge his gift by making him one of its members. He also expected this gift to change his status among the artists and architects of the Secession who knew about it, establishing him as someone worth courting and flattering, even if they were contemptuous of him behind his back because of his new money and wrong religion.

If Alma's diary is any guide, the purchase of *The Evil Mothers* was also pivotal in her relationship with Hermine. While Alma did not mention the Gallias until Moriz's elevation, she was soon doing so regularly. She went to the family's apartment in the Schleifmühlgasse for dinner that March, met Hermine in the Prater before having tea with her in the Schleifmühlgasse a few days later, and then saw both Moriz and Hermine again after the opera. Alma also saw Hermine later in the year when they again had tea, and Carl Moll, who was always looking to orchestrate more commissions and purchases, invited Moriz and Hermine and Theobald Pollak to dinner with Josef Hoffmann and Koloman Moser.

7

Rooms

Koloman Moser made spectacular presents. One of Gustav Mahler's gifts to Alma was a silver box by Moser topped with red coral, dated Christmas Eve 1902, and inscribed with Alma's initials. One of Klimt's presents to Emilie Flöge for Christmas 1903 was a silver necklace by Moser with a large egg-shaped stone at its center and five semiprecious orange stones on silver chains hanging in a star pattern. When Theobald Pollak wanted a gift for Hermine in 1903, he also went to Moser, commissioning a silver sweet bowl that had lapis lazuli beads around its rim and Hermine's initials set in a square of pearl shell on its handle. Because Pollak was among the many assimilated Viennese Jews who celebrated Christmas with gift giving, he may have given the bowl to Hermine then, though he may have waited until New Year's, which he also marked with gifts.

This present fits the image of Pollak in Alma Schindler's diaries as embarrassingly extravagant in his gift giving. It is another manifestation of Pollak's closeness to the Gallias, which led Gretl to identify him as Moriz's "best and only friend" and the entire family to call him by his Christian name. Yet this present also illustrates how easy it was for Hermine to be at the forefront of fashion in Vienna. While she kept a keen eye on what was

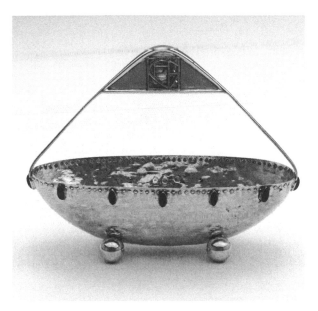

Koloman Moser, *Sweet Bowl*, 1903. Hermine's first
piece of Wiener Werkstätte, given to her by Theobald
Pollak.

most chic, her friends such as Pollak and Moll also introduced her to the
new. When Pollak gave her the bowl in December 1903, it was just six
months since Moser and Josef Hoffmann had founded the Wiener Werkstätte with the businessman Fritz Waerndorfer. While Hermine's portrait
by Klimt was first being shown in the *Klimt Kollektiv* at the Secession in a
Moser room framed by Moser chairs, she acquired her first piece of Moser
silver for her apartment in the Schleifmühlgasse.

Hermine's apartment already included a wealth of silver—an essential
ingredient of any upper-middle-class Viennese household. The establishment of the Wiener Werkstätte opened up possibilities not only for more
silver made in its first and biggest workshop but also for gold, leatherwork,
bookbinding, and furniture. The Gallias could ignore the Werkstätte, buy
just the occasional object, or go there for almost every household item.
This decision was not only a question of cost but also one of taste, which
members of the one family often shared, leading one relative after another
to employ the same designer. Yet there often were also profound differ-

ences within families, as some members embraced the modern while others pursued the old. The families of Moriz and Hermine were like this, providing very different models of how to live.

The revival of the old, whether in the form of the neoclassical, neo-Renaissance, neo-Gothic, or neo-baroque, was the dominant style across the Hapsburg Empire. Hermine's uncle, Eduard Hamburger, chose it in 1895 when commissioning a villa from one of Vienna's most successful architects, Jakob Gartner, who was indirectly related to Eduard through marriage, since Gartner's mother was a Gallia. This villa was one of a group for leading members of the Jewish community in Olmütz, which resulted in the most important precinct of historicist architecture in Moravia. In keeping with Eduard's position as chairman of the Jewish community, he commissioned the first, most spectacular villa.

The appetite of Adolf and Ida Gallia for conventional trappings of wealth and power was manifest in the late 1890s when they bought their villa in Baden, which had carved lions at the base of its front stairs. They displayed the same taste in 1902, when they commissioned Gartner to design their two apartment blocks in Vienna, including the one where they lived. This house was one of many Ringstrasse buildings that came with an imposing foyer decorated with frescoes and a master staircase leading to the best apartments on the second and third floors, as well as a secondary staircase leading to the higher floors. The neoclassical facade exemplified what the city's modernists decried as architectural malaise.

Melanie Gallia, the oldest child of Moriz's brother Wilhelm, lived very differently from 1902, when she married Jakob Langer, who operated a chain of currency exchanges with his brother Leopold. Many wealthy Viennese couples began married life in apartments with architect-designed rooms, usually paid for by the bride's parents as part of her dowry. The Langer family's architect was Adolf Loos, who had made a name for himself as an essayist but was struggling to secure architectural commissions. His work combined two radically different aesthetics. Most of his furniture was severe, using simple geometric patterns, but he also copied the elaborate rococo chairs of the eighteenth-century English cabinetmaker Thomas Chippendale, which he regarded as the most comfortable chairs ever made, impossible to better, ideal for contemporary use, and hence "modern." In 1901 Loos designed the interiors of the Langer brothers' currency exchanges. In 1902 he fitted out four rooms in the apartment of Jakob and Melanie. A year later he designed a room in Leopold's apartment and another in his country house. By then, the Langers were among Loos's most important early patrons.

Loos and Josef Hoffmann had much in common. They both were born in Moravia in 1870, were in the same class in high school, and attended the same technical college. Both also looked to England for inspiration, employed the finest craftsmen, selected the most expensive timbers, and used simple forms at the start of the century before gradually becoming more decorative. But Loos abhorred the idea of a total work of art, or *Gesamtkunstwerk,* as applied to interior design, arguing that the rich should buy the work of skilled craftsmen instead of trying to express their individuality by commissioning architects to design objects for daily use. Hoffmann's objects also failed Loos's test of utility. While Loos acknowledged in 1898 that Hoffmann was "an artist with an exuberant imagination" who could "successfully attack the old traditions," he still declared himself "utterly opposed" to Hoffmann's direction. A decade later Loos dismissed Hoffmann's work as a "mistake." When he first delivered his polemic "Ornament and Crime" as a lecture in 1910, Loos went even further. As part of decrying decoration as retrograde and degenerate, a waste of labor, materials, and money, he declared Hoffmann's work "intolerable."

The gulf between Loos and Hoffmann was so great that families who commissioned apartments from Loos are generally assumed to have never given commissions to Hoffmann. The commonplace is that, while intellectuals went to Loos, businessmen went to Hoffmann—whereas Loos appealed to socialists, Hoffmann appealed to liberals and conservatives. According to this view, for any individual to have gone from employing Loos to commissioning Hoffmann would have been like trading with the enemy. For members of the same family, like the Langers and Gallias, to do so was little different. But Hermine's commitment to the Secession meant that she would never have considered employing Loos even if he had designed the kind of silverware that Hermine began collecting. The closest that Moriz and she came to acquiring any of Loos's work was when they bought a copy of *Sprüche und Widersprüche,* Karl Kraus's second book published in 1909, which Loos designed. Otherwise, like most of Klimt's patrons, they went to Hoffmann, who enjoyed much greater contemporary success than Loos, becoming a professor at Vienna's School of Applied Arts and obtaining a string of commissions from wealthy supporters of the Secession.

Moriz and Hermine first encountered Hoffmann's work in 1898, when he began creating interiors for the Secession's exhibitions. They saw more of it from 1901, when he designed a house for Carl Moll in the artists' colony of Hohe Warte on Vienna's outskirts. It came closer to them in 1903, when Theobald Pollak acquired a Hoffmann carpet and Hoffmann silver for his apartment in the building on the Schleifmühlgasse where Hermine and Moriz also lived. They would have seen still more in 1905, when Moll staged the Wiener Werkstätte's first Viennese exhibition in the new premises of the Galerie Miethke, designed by Hoffmann, on Vienna's most fashionable shopping street, the Graben.

The family's first recorded purchase from the Werkstätte was big, but late: five "flower baskets," or vases, which all employed the simple geometric grids made of either silver or plated silver known as *Gitterwerk,* which put Hoffmann at the forefront of modern design. They were bought in 1906 by Hermine, who was responsible for most of the decoration of their apartment in keeping with the standard assumption that the domestic environment of a Viennese matron was an extension of her personality. The placement of Hermine's initials rather than those of Moriz on the family's silver cutlery was a clear mark that the dining room was hers. Anyone who smoked implicitly got the same message when offered cigarettes from a Hoffmann box, especially designed for Hermine even though she did not smoke, which also carried her monogram.

The Werkstätte's next great public display in Vienna was at the Cabaret Fledermaus, which opened in 1907 on the Graben and rapidly became the most effective showroom for the Werkstätte's work. More than a dozen artists, led by Klimt and Hoffmann, designed almost everything in the cabaret's auditorium, foyer, and American Bar, including the tables, chairs, vases, sculptures, light fittings, posters, menus, menu folders, and programs. The result was the closest the Werkstätte came to creating a public *Gesamtkunstwerk,* though the styles that the cabaret contained were mixed. While Hoffmann was at his simplest, working in black and white, the ceramicist Michael Powolny was typically extravagant, employing a riot of color.

Moriz and Hermine were again slow to go to the Fledermaus, which was one of Europe's most innovative and exciting cabarets. When they finally went six weeks after its gala opening, the interior probably was the main attraction, especially since Moriz had an interest in the Fledermaus's electric lights, which were fitted with bulbs from Watt. After a concert at nine and a cabaret at ten, there was Spanish music and dancing in the American Bar from one till four in the morning. "*Sehr nett*," "very nice," Hermine recorded with characteristic blandness. A fortnight later they were back, accompanied by Adolf and Ida Gallia and Nelly Hamburger, the new wife of Hermine's brother Guido, who had moved from Freudenthal to Vienna to run a branch of the Hamburger family company as well as work with Moriz in the gaslight business.

The marriage of Guido and Nelly prompted another architectural commission. Rather than marry in Vienna, Guido and Nelly went to the Semmering, a fashionable mountain resort an hour's train ride from the city. The service was in the Catholic church in the village of Maria Schutz. The celebrations were at the grand hotel Panhans, where most of the wedding party stayed. The festivities started one evening with a dinner for nineteen and continued, after the wedding the following morning, with a lunch for twenty-four, after which Guido and Nelly left to honeymoon amid the palm trees of Abbazia on the Dalmatian coast. On their return, they occupied an apartment in Vienna's Third District, where Hoffmann had designed four relatively modest rooms.

Moriz and Hermine probably were intent on having a Hoffmann apartment but gave precedence to buying their first real estate. Just as Adolf and Ida began by acquiring a villa that they could use to escape Vienna's summer heat, so did Moriz and Hermine. After investigating the Austrian and Czech countryside on their annual holidays, they decided on Alt Aussee, a fashionable resort in the lake district near Salzburg known as the Salzkammergut. As the Austrian economy boomed in 1909, they paid 40,000 crowns, or $400,000, for a fully furnished fourteen-room, three-story villa with an attic, a basement, and extensive grounds including a tennis court. While most houses in Austria were owned by men, Moriz and Hermine bought theirs together—an arrangement that probably had financial advantages but also was decidedly modern.

A car was another priority. By 1911, there were well over three thousand on Vienna's streets, and most of the families against whom Moriz and Hermine measured themselves owned one. They chose a Gräf & Stift, the most prestigious, luxurious Austrian make, preferred by the emperor and

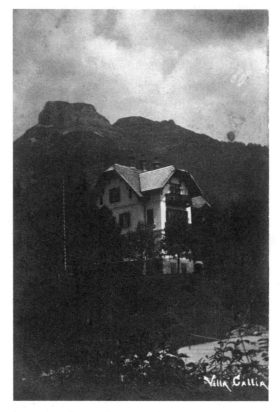

The villa in Alt Aussee, bought in 1909 by
Moriz and Hermine as a summerhouse.

the archdukes Franz Ferdinand and Karl Stefan. The car bought by Moriz
and Hermine was so big that it could easily carry all six of the Gallias, the
twins' governess, and an abundance of luggage. As soon as their new
chauffeur arrived with it that summer at the Villa Gallia, they began using
it like the proverbial boy with a new bicycle, taking it out at least once or
twice every day for what Hermine soon described as the "obligatory car
ride."

Meanwhile Hermine demonstrated her attachment to Hoffmann by
acquiring only his silver for the family's apartment in the Schleifmühlgasse. Most of the boxes, bottle tops, serviette rings, and coasters that she
selected were for the dining room along with a basket for fresh fruit and a
table centerpiece for preserved fruit. Other baskets and vases adorned the

salon. The only commission was the cigarette box inscribed with Hermine's initials. But a pair of ribbed vases on bell-shaped feet designed by Hoffmann In 1911 were all the Werkstätte made in this form. An inkstand for Moriz's desk was most spectacular. Like many of Hoffmann's best pieces of tableware, it looked more like the model for a fantastical building than a functional object.

Moriz and Hermine bought Wohllebengasse 4 at the end of 1911 when Austria's economy was still booming—mounting inflation and growing liquidity problems notwithstanding. Although just a few minutes' walk from the Schleifmühlgasse, the Wohllebengasse was in a classier part of the Fourth District, where there were much grander apartment blocks, palais, and embassies, and almost no shops. While the Fourth District had one of the smallest Jewish populations of any part of the city, Vienna's wealthiest Jews lived there. The Rothschilds' palais was around the corner in the Prinz-Eugen-Strasse. The Wittgensteins lived around the other corner in the Argentinierstrasse.

Just as Moriz and Hermine bought their villa in Alt Aussee together, so they acquired their block in the Wohllebengasse. It came with a substantial three-story house erected seventy-five years before but was slated for redevelopment as part of the larger reconstruction of the Wohllebengasse that started in the 1880s and saw the Wittgensteins erect the street's largest apartment building on a double block. By January 1912, Moriz and Hermine were talking to architects. By May they had the approval of Vienna's municipal authorities for a five-story structure with an attic above and a cellar below.

The house in the Wohllebengasse was the most significant manifestation of the wealth of Moriz and Hermine, a mark of how rich they had grown in twenty years in the Austrian capital. It was the sharpest expression of their social aspirations, their ambition to live in one of the most exclusive parts of Vienna, and their desire to entertain in the most lavish, luxurious style. It became vital to their finances, a vast source of income, because they rented out the front of the ground floor as offices and the top three floors as apartments. It was the greatest demonstration of their taste for the best in modern Viennese design.

Moriz and Hermine kept the most prestigious part of the building—its *Nobelstock,* the "noble floor," or first floor—for themselves. They also occupied the back part of the floor below, so their apartment was unusually big, totaling over seventy-five hundred square feet. Yet the apartments on the top three floors were also vast: rather than divide these floors into several small apartments, as was common in older buildings, Moriz and Hermine devoted each one to a single apartment. In doing so, they ensured that only the rich could be their tenants.

Moriz and Hermine also built two garages, as they became one of the first two-car families in Vienna when even one was a mark of modernity and wealth. Whereas they rewarded Gretl when she finished school in 1912 by giving her a diamond and pearl pendant and taking her to Bayreuth, they gave Erni his own car when he matriculated in 1913. It was made by the Turin firm, Itala, which secured an international market after one of its

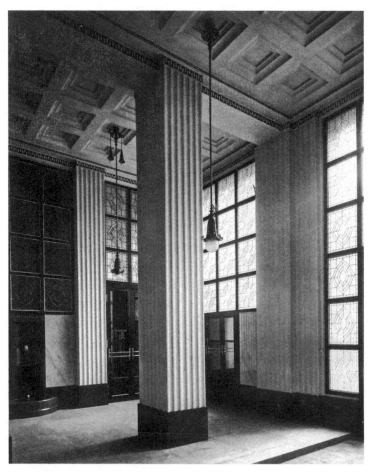

The ground-floor entrance to Wohllebengasse 4, designed by Franz von Krauss.

vehicles won the first transnational car rally, the 1907 Great Race from Beijing to Paris. While much smaller than the family's Gräf & Stift, the Itala also had great cachet.

Because Hoffmann never designed apartment buildings, another architect had to design the house. Moriz and Hermine chose Franz von Krauss, whose commissions included Vienna's Jubiläumstheater and Hof-burgtheater. As the British magazine *The Studio* recognized, Krauss's most successful designs included "modern houses built straight to defy time and weather" that were free of "superfluous decoration, culled from all lands and all periods." These houses often made unusually good provision for servants, prompted by the difficulty of securing good domestic staff at the start of the century. One of Krauss's villas included a servants' balcony that they could enjoy "unseen and unheard."

Krauss's design for Moriz and Hermine was similar. The entrance to the building was especially lavish and elegant, combining fluted white columns, a black marble fountain, and gray marble wall cladding, with gold and white tiles around its cornice. The facade of the house was plain except for neoclassical touches. Four sets of French doors identified the *Nobelstock* where the family had their entertaining rooms, bedrooms, and bathrooms. The kitchen and pantry were below, along with the bedrooms of the female servants, which had their own windows rather than just a light well, as was usually the case. The Gallias' servants also had their own bathroom when it was conventional for all the servants of a building to share one in the attic.

The immediate context of Krauss's building made it all the more strik-ing. When Moriz and Hermine commissioned it, the other houses on the Wohllebengasse were historicist. The same was true on the next street, the Schwindgasse. The embrace of the modern by Moriz and Hermine was a public assertion of difference, a clear rejection of everything surrounding them. An immediate vindication of their taste came when the City of Vienna awarded a prize to Krauss because of the building's clear articula-tion and restrained, elegant decoration. When Krauss published a book of his work, he included three photographs of the building.

Hoffmann's commission was five rooms—a salon for formal entertaining, a smoking room for Moriz, a boudoir for Hermine, a dining room for for-mal meals, and a hall for less formal ones. But Hoffmann typically designed almost everything in them as part of creating a *Gesamtkunstwerk*.

While his insistence on doing so was no problem for a newly married couple such as Guido and Nelly Hamburger, who otherwise owned little or no furniture, it was an issue for a long-married couple such as Moriz and Hermine, who had furnished their apartment in the Schleifmühlgasse at considerable expense. As Moriz and Hermine planned their apartment, they had to decide whether to jettison or retain their old things. While Moriz and Hermine wanted an apartment that was strikingly new, they did not want to waste what they had acquired, and so they moved their best Biedermeier into the smaller of their two salons in the Wohllebengasse. In doing so, they created an awkward juxtaposition with the five other front rooms, where Hoffmann was responsible for all the furniture and fittings except the family's Steinway grand piano, and everything he designed apart from one of the carpets and some of the wallpapers was unique.

The opulence of Hoffmann's work for Moriz and Hermine was in marked contrast to his work for Guido and Nelly. The hall in the Wohllebengasse was hung with floral fabric and contained ebonized furniture with red morocco upholstery. The salon was painted yellow and contained fruitwood furniture covered with black-and-white upholstery. The boudoir was hung with blue silk embellished with red-and-green rose sprays and contained white-and-gold furniture, again upholstered red. The smoking room was painted white above a thick wooden frieze hung with a floral fabric below and contained ebonized furniture upholstered with green wool. The dining room combined white walls with a black marble wall fountain, black marble buffet, black marble dado, black marble architraves, and walnut furniture. Each room had a different carpet— placed on the best parquetry floor in the hall, salon, and dining room but wall to wall in the boudoir and smoking room.

The family's pictures were vital to this schema. The director of Vienna's Kunsthistorisches Museum, Gustav Glück, spoke for many of Klimt's patrons when he declared that Klimt's paintings demanded a "special kind of environment" and that Hoffmann was the architect who made them look "most effective." But Hoffmann failed to do so in the Wohllebengasse, where his installation of the paintings was no match for Koloman Moser's design of the *Klimt Kollektiv* at the Secession a decade before. While Hoffmann squeezed the beech forest landscape into the salon above a marble-framed, grille-fronted central heating unit, he hung Hermine's

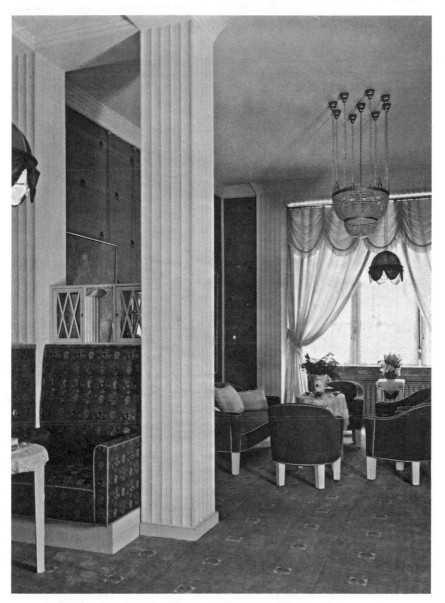

The boudoir in the Gallia apartment. The Klimt portrait of Hermine is visible on the left wall. The Koloman Moser sweet bowl that Theobald Pollak gave Hermine in 1903 is on the table in the middle of the room.

portrait in her boudoir next to Andri's portrait of Moriz, an obvious—but unsuccessful—pairing because the portraits were so different.

The start of a "trade crisis" did not dint the Gallias' spending. Instead, Hermine acquired ever more objects, including her most striking piece of glass—a red-and-white bowl by Hoffmann's student, Carl Witzmann— and three new jardinieres by Hoffmann himself, which would become a set with the two bell-shaped vases from 1911, creating Hermine's most spectacular display of silver at the end of her new dining room. Moriz's one concern, when he sent a letter from Vienna to Hermine in Alt Aussee that August, was the gulf between the original quotations for the apart- ment and the bill he received from Jakob Soulek, who made much of Hoffmann's furniture. Moriz, who was bald, exclaimed that his hair stood on end when he first saw Soulek's invoice. Moriz was sure that, if he did

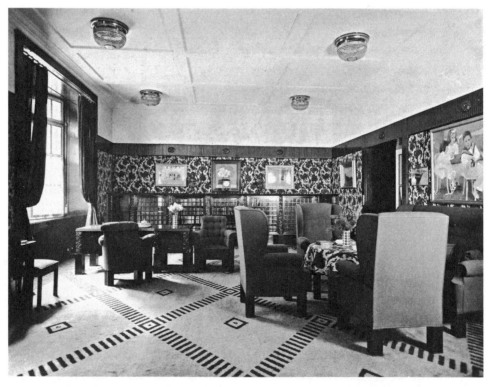

The smoking room in the Gallia apartment. The Andri portrait of the four Gallia children is on the right wall. Moriz's silver Upmann cigar box made by Klinkosch is on the table in the foreground, while Moriz's silver Hoffmann inkstand is on his desk behind.

not challenge it after scrutinizing Soulek's original quotes, he would pay double what he had anticipated.

These rooms put Moriz and Hermine where they wanted to be—at the forefront of fashion. Like Hoffmann's other major commissions in this period, the Gallia apartment excited immediate interest in fashionable design circles in Austria and Germany. As the furniture was being built, Austria's leading interior design magazine, *Das Interieur,* published six of Hoffmann's drawings for the rooms. When they were complete, the German magazines *Innen-Dekoration* and *Deutsche Kunst und Dekoration* published photographs of them, as well as one of the new Hoffmann jardinieres. The most important contemporary book about Viennese design, Max Eisler's *Österreichische Werkkultur,* included two of the interiors, the jardiniere, the white-and-gold bureau from Hermine's boudoir, and the Witzmann glass.

The photographs of the interiors by Bruno Reiffenstein, one of Vienna's foremost architectural photographers, were a crucial means of promoting Hoffmann's work. Everything about them was carefully staged, from the placement of the furniture to the selection of objects on the tabletops. They showed an environment in which almost everything was Wiener Werkstätte, including the silverware that Hermine had been acquiring for a decade. While the Moser sweet bowl that Theobald Pollak gave Hermine in 1903 was on a table in her boudoir, a Hoffmann fruit stand from 1907 was on the buffet in the dining room and the Hoffmann inkstand from 1909 was on the desk in Moriz's smoking room.

The box on the circular table in the smoking room was an exception. This box was a piece of trompe l'oeil—a silver replica of a wooden cigar box of the Upmann company, which produced some of the finest Havana cigars from the mid-nineteenth century. This box not only had the Upmann name on the center of the lid but was embellished with two rows of paper tobacco tax stamps bearing the Cyrillic script for "Imported Tobacco," as if the box had been brought into Russia. Such boxes, which were fashionable under the Romanovs from the late 1870s, were generally made in Moscow, though soon found a wider market. Moriz's box was unusually large, heavy, and superbly engraved. Despite its Russian facade, it was made by the Viennese silversmith J. C. Klinkosch, who had designed the family's first set of silver cutlery. The inclusion of this box in the photograph suggests that she and Moriz regarded it as particularly valuable and stylish.

The main piece of ceramics in the salon was different again. It was *Nordpolen*, or *North Pole*, a table centerpiece depicting two polar bears around a frozen pool, made by Royal Copenhagen, which, after an extended period of stagnation, had a renaissance in the mid-1880s. As the company secured an international market, its prices soared, prompting one commentator to describe them as "simply amusing in their exorbitance." The piece displayed by Hermine and Moriz was one of Royal Copenhagen's most acclaimed crystalline works, using white and sea-green glazes. Designed in 1900 by Carl Bonnesen, it was reproduced in 1905 by the art nouveau magazine *Der Moderne Stil* and shaped the work of the Japanese potter Makuzu Kōzan, who was particularly open to the latest European fashions.

There was much more on show beyond the lens of Reiffenstein's camera. While Nelly Hamburger had a small collection of Hoffmann silver that she distributed around her Hoffmann rooms, she filled the vitrine in her salon with Royal Copenhagen vases and figurines, which she soon supplemented with antique clocks and Czech crystal glasses. Hermine was similarly eclectic. She filled the main vitrine in her boudoir almost entirely with Royal Copenhagen. She placed a group of Meissen figurines and vases and an array of Biedermeier silver and glass in the floor-to-ceiling cabinets that separated the salon from the hall.

A story handed down over the generations provides a measure of both the opulence of this environment and how it was perceived by visitors. One day a family friend arrived carrying a walking stick, which he had never done while the Gallias lived above the gaslight showroom in the Schleifmühlgasse. The Gallias were concerned. They wanted to know how their visitor had injured himself. "Why are you carrying the stick?" they asked. "Because there is so much marble here," he responded. "I brought the stick in case I needed to touch wood."

The political situation was deteriorating all the while. It is now a cliché that the Hapsburg Empire was close to collapse in the early twentieth century, set to fracture as the myriad national groups within it secured independence. For all of Vienna's wealth, vitality, and creativity, it was a capital living on borrowed time, making it no place to invest, especially with the lavishness of the Gallias' Hoffmann rooms. Yet for all the vulnerability of the empire, its fate was far from self-evident in 1913, even to close observers such as Henry Wickham Steed of the London *Times*. After ten years in

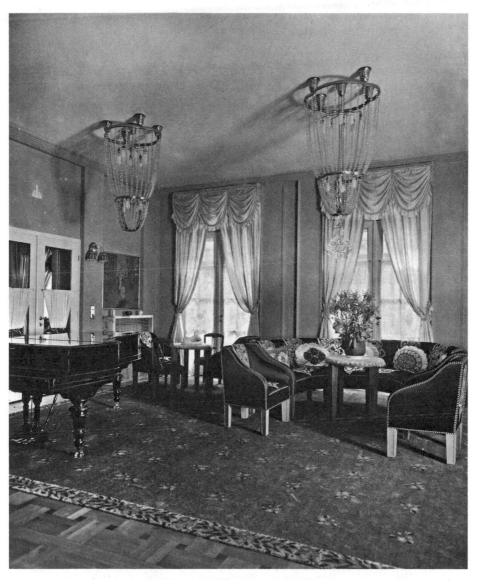

The salon in the Gallia apartment. Klimt's *Beech Forest* is visible on the left wall. *Nordpolen*, the Gallias' most spectacular piece of Royal Copenhagen, is on the table nearby.

Vienna, Steed could see no reason "why, with moderate foresight on the part of the Dynasty, the Hapsburg Monarchy should not retain its rightful place in the European community." While Steed recognized that the empire faced internal crises, he argued that they were "crises of growth rather than of decay."

Moriz still manifested this confidence early in 1914, when the Wiener Werkstätte almost collapsed despite Fritz Waerndorfer's spending most of his fortune on sustaining it. While a number of artists and designers, led by Hoffmann, contributed to its refinancing, most of its new funds came from Hoffmann's patrons, including Moriz, who became the vice-chairman of its board after investing 20,000 crowns (or about $150,000 in today's money). As this process saw Waerndorfer ousted from the Werkstätte, he lambasted its new shareholders, claiming that these "new money people" immediately resorted to "sharp practices" in order to make "plenty of money" from the Werkstätte. But while Moriz expected to manage the workshops better than Waerndorfer, who was a typical example of second-generation wealth, more adept at spending money than accumulating it, money making was not Moriz's goal. Like Hoffmann's other patrons who became shareholders in the Werkstätte, he saw himself as a philanthropist ensuring the survival of one of Vienna's finest artistic institutions when its record suggested it would always run at a loss. His goal was to sustain creativity, not profit from it.

The start of the Great War made the task of the Werkstätte's new directors all the harder as the market for the workshops' luxurious products became smaller than ever. The war also transformed how families such as the Gallias lived in their Hoffmann rooms. These rooms were designed for display, made for grand events, conceived on the assumption that their occupants would entertain like never before amid social, economic, and political stability. The war prevented them from doing so. Although the Gallias had no reason to suspect it in July 1914, their heyday on Good Living Street was over. It had lasted just six months.

II

GRETL

I

Diaries

I want to write about my life. I cry when someone pulls my leg. *I often think I exist only to get annoyed.* I lead a lovely life in the middle of my happy family. *I do not deserve to be loved.* I record this tragic story so as to try to control my feelings and stop myself talking about it. *I have been excitable and vehement, which is understandable.* When I get older, I will look back and say I was rather childish and stupid. *I used to want to marry but who would take me now?* Unfortunately I am like a flower, easily damaged if moved. *If I did what I would like to do, I would finish up in hell.* I don't think people fully understand me but that is how it goes in the world! *I am still very young but I understand much more than people think.*

Gretl made these observations as a girl in the diaries that she kept for most of her life. She started at the age of ten in the European summer of 1906, when she was about to begin her secondary schooling—a turning point in the lives of all Austrian children but a particularly profound one for Gretl, who had received her primary education from governesses. She stopped at the age of seventy-seven, in 1974, when she was in a nursing home in Armidale in northern New South Wales, though she still thought of the apartment in Cremorne as her home. The diaries that she filled in between—the first handsome leather-bound volumes, the last crude card-board exercise books—were all in the apartment when she died in 1975.

These diaries were just a fraction of the papers in the apartment, because Gretl and Kathe, like many refugees, retained almost all the documents they had brought with them. Anne's general rule was to keep illustrative examples. She kept one of Hermine's concert books, one weather book, and one guest book. She did much the same with the correspondence relating to the Hoffmann rooms in the Wohllebengasse. All the letters between Moriz and Hermine and Hoffmann were there, along with all the quotes, receipts, and invoices for the apartment. This archive was as rare and remarkable in its own way as the furniture, carpets, silver, glass, and ceramics, providing a unique opportunity to cost all the components of a big Hoffmann commission. Anne threw out the lot apart from two of Hoffmann's letters, which she gave to the National Gallery of Victoria.

Anne found Gretl's diaries most difficult. While she was too close to Gretl to see the interest of their great sweep of history stretching from the Austro-Hungary of the Hapsburgs to the Australia of Gough Whitlam, Anne must have realized that these diaries contained the most extensive record of how Moriz and Hermine had lived in Vienna. Anne knew that these diaries contained the only chronicle of Gretl's life and the most extensive account of her own childhood. Because Gretl had instructed that these diaries be destroyed unread when she died, Anne threw out twenty, perhaps thirty. But wanting to preserve something of how Gretl had experienced the world, Anne kept her first three diaries and the last two.

Gretl's materialism as a girl was intense. Just as she listed her birthday and Christmas presents, so she recorded many of the family's latest acquisitions and newest forms of consumption. When the family occupied their house in Alt Aussee in 1909, she began her first entry with a typical exclamation: "Our villa!" After an evening at the opera early in 1911, she recorded her first ride in a taxi. A few months later, after the family acquired their own car, came "Our first automobile tour" when they took an hour and ten minutes to drive the twenty-two miles from Alt Aussee to the spa town of Bad Ischl for an afternoon tea of chocolate-topped, jam-filled *Krapferl* at the celebrated Konditorei-Kaffee Zauner. "We have acquired a car and, what is more, a Gräf & Stift," Gretl wrote, clearly aware that this was no ordinary vehicle. It was *"pikfein!!!"* she declared, "tiptop!!!"

A typical Christmas saw her receive clothes, jewelry, books, and much else—for example, a ball dress, dancing shoes, dancing gloves, a silver wristwatch, a gold brooch, perfume, a table lamp, nightdresses, a box of stamps, a cape, a small embroidered handbag, a leather jewelry box, a volume of Goethe's poetry, another of Schiller's verse, and a copy of *Hamlet.* In 1909 Moriz and Hermine gave her a new room in the Schleifmühlgasse and promptly set about refurbishing it. The scale of the family's apartment is suggested by how her new furniture comprised not only a bed, bedside table, dressing table, two wardrobes, and a desk but also a sofa, a table, and four chairs.

How did Gretl view these presents? Was she aware of her privilege, which saw her parents punctuate their summer holidays in Alt Aussee with one- and two-day excursions around the Salzkammergut and southern Germany and a weeklong tour of the Dolomites? Did Gretl appreciate her good fortune in escaping the long winter in Vienna when the family went for a fortnight to the sea at Abbazia, where they divided their time between the aptly named Palace Hotel and the Savoy? What did she think of being able to go to the theater and opera in style and see many of the world's greatest musicians, such as Bruno Walter, Pablo Casals, and Arthur Rubinstein?

Gretl's usual response was a brief expression of delight. "I'm so happy," she would write, "I could go mad!" Just once, she acknowledged that she was being overindulged, and her manner of doing so was conventional, as Alma Schindler's diary reveals. When Alma listed her twenty-four Christmas presents in 1898, she concluded: "In a word: a vast amount. Spoilt. And what do we do in return? . . . Nothing!" Gretl echoed these sentiments in 1907. "I received far too much. Unbearable."

Gretl revealed much more of herself in many other entries that, because of when and where they were written, might seem particularly ripe for Freudian analysis, though I have not undertaken that here. While some of her entries were filled with humor and self-mockery, many others were imbued with intense emotion, especially when writing about her relationships with Moriz and Hermine, which could not have been more different. She fought constantly with Hermine but idolized Moriz. After a particularly tempestuous disagreement with Hermine, Gretl observed: "If

Father were here, everything would be better, because he is fair." He was her "sweetheart," "the person she loved most," her "*Herzallerliebstes*," a term usually reserved for a lover, not a parent.

Her siblings—especially her twin sisters, Käthe and Lene—occupied her almost as much. When she first wrote about them following her eleventh birthday in 1907, she thought herself so close to the "little ones" that she did not need other friends. But within a year she recognized that she treated Käthe and Lene much worse than Erni and, when the twins responded by declaring Gretl "appalling and disgusting," she reciprocated. Gretl described Käthe and Lene ironically as "sweet small things." She called them "common dogs." Because Hermine made no attempt to disguise her preference for the twins, Gretl's attachment to Moriz grew.

Gretl also dwelled on her own character, especially her weaknesses. So she observed that she was too quick "to call a spade a spade"—one of those English phrases that upper-middle-class Viennese often used to display their education and sophistication—and recognized that she would pay for her bluntness and honesty. She knew that she had "a little bit of a temper" and was very easily offended but could or would not change it. She accepted the judgment of others that she was difficult and at times contrary. She was incensed that her beloved father, even more than her mother, thought her "arrogant, snobbish, and God knows what else besides."

Her progress through the Catholic Church gave her great joy. When she had her first Communion in 1908, the eleven-year-old Gretl was overcome by emotion at receiving the body of her Lord for the first time, aspired to be better than ever, and wondered whether she could be as happy again. Moriz and Hermine gave her a celebratory drink of vanilla liqueur. She declared it the most beautiful day of her life. Her confirmation in 1909 was an even bigger event, involving Hermine's three brothers and a wealth of presents. Guido Hamburger and his wife Nelly, who had already converted to Catholicism, hosted a family lunch. Otto Hamburger, who remained a Jew but whose son, Robert, had been baptized in 1903, gave Gretl a prayer book. She was delighted by her acquisition of a new Christian name, Cornelia, in honor of Nelly, who sponsored her confirmation. "So many names!" Gretl exclaimed. "This marvelous day! I have been confirmed!!!"

Her God was not only interventionist but also prepared to help those who did not believe in him, as became apparent when Theobald Pollak returned to Vienna to die in his apartment after searching in vain for a cure for his tuberculosis in sanitoriums. As Pollak's condition deteriorated in 1912, Gretl's first close experience of long, painful death, she was so upset to see his suffering that she asked her Lord to end it. When Pollak died in his sleep a few days later, Gretl credited her prayers with his release even though Pollak had remained a Jew.

Her ignorance of things Jewish was manifest a few months later when she saw a play about the Rothschilds and wrote, with surprise, of the play's "Jewish milieu." Yet Gretl herself was part of Jewish society. The number of Jews at the Frauen-Erwerb-Verein where Gretl went to school was disproportionately high because Vienna's Jews put exceptional store in education. Although they were only 10 percent of the city's population, Jews accounted for almost half of Gretl's fellow students. While Alt Aussee attracted an array of wealthy visitors, including many aristocrats, it was especially popular with Viennese Jews and recent converts to Christianity. A small number bought villas, but most rented, including Freud, who went there with his family for four summers in succession.

Gretl's status was usually that of a child, even after she finished school in 1912. When she scratched Lene early in 1913, Moriz and Hermine slapped her face and hit her as punishment, which sixteen-year-old Gretl accepted because she had attacked Lene "without reason." When Gretl had another fight with Käthe and Lene late in 1913, Hermine advised the seventeen-year-old to find a husband who would discipline her with force but did not do so herself. Instead, Hermine prohibited Gretl from accompanying the rest of the family to church, only to change her mind because the priest would notice Gretl's absence. The greatest punishment Hermine could conceive that evening was to refuse Gretl her customary good-night kiss.

Nonetheless, Gretl edged toward adulthood. She was delighted when Moriz and Hermine let her join their dinner parties from mid-1912. She was thrilled six months later when they let her have her first "adult New Year," which saw her go to bed at two-thirty after a performance of Strauss's *Fledermaus* at the Hofoper and a dinner of hors d'oeuvres, soup, duck liver fillets, venison with Cumberland sauce, gelato to cleanse the palate, and fruit and cheese. A year later, she did much the same, seeing Puccini's *La bohème* before dining with her uncle Adolf and aunt Ida. Yet she craved more, eagerly looking forward to when she turned eighteen and would be out in "society" so much more often.

Her position in the family was that of the eldest of three daughters, almost three years older than her twin sisters, and the one "beauty" of the three, according to contemporary taste, blessed with long wavy hair and a shapely figure. Gretl's appearance mattered intensely not only to her but also to Moriz and Hermine, who did their best to embellish it through repeated gifts of fabulous clothes and jewelry. As her wardrobe kept on changing and growing, one of her nicknames was *"die fesche Gretl,"* "the natty Gretl."

Gretl's infatuations were all at a distance. Like many other students at all-girls schools in the early 1900s, she had a crush on one of her female teachers. She began to adore Frau Kappelmann in her first year at secondary school and was soon dreaming about her every night. She also idolized the singer Richard Mayr, one of the stars of the Hofoper, even more than she worshipped the conductor Bruno Walter. She almost always recorded Mayr's name with two or even three exclamation marks after seeing him perform. He loomed largest in her collection of autographed photographs. She thought of him as "the King," a "God-blessed singer," her own *"sweet Mayrlein."*

Her aspirations were shaped by the educational opportunities for girls in Vienna. When she started her secondary schooling in 1906, only the *Gymnasien,* or elite senior schools for boys, offered the eight-year program, with a curriculum dominated by Latin and Greek, that led to admission to university. The Frauen-Erwerb-Verein, or Association for the Livelihoods of Women, which ran her school, had been at the forefront of women's education in Vienna in the late nineteenth century but then slipped behind. Its six-year program, dominated by modern languages, literature, and music, enabled its students to attend university lectures but did not entitle them to embark on degrees. Its goal was to enhance its students' prospects of marrying well.

Gretl wanted to become her father's personal secretary—a role filled by the daughters of some other upper-middle-class Viennese families. As a governess had begun teaching her shorthand, she had some skills but knew she needed more. Gretl thought she could obtain them by working with Moriz during the day and attending a commercial school at night. Yet Gretl had to pluck up the courage to present this possibility to Moriz because she expected him to think such work beneath her, and she was deeply hurt when he dismissed her suggestion with a laugh.

She expected to marry sooner rather than later. When her parents refused to let her accompany them to Moravia for Theobald Pollak's funeral in 1912, because they feared she would become overwrought, the fifteen-year-old Gretl declared that she would visit Pollak's grave on her honeymoon, which she expected to be her first opportunity to decide where she went. On other occasions she expressed her frustration with her parents by expounding about how she would run her own household and raise her own children. Because she could not enroll at university or enter the workforce, there was little else for her to do.

2

Tango

Gretl was happiest on the dance floor. She deemed herself the queen of the
first ball she attended in 1908 as an eleven-year-old because she received
more bouquets than any other girl. Her first dance with adults, in 1911,
was even more exciting. It was at her family's apartment in the
Schleifmühlgasse on the afternoon of December 26, which Roman
Catholics celebrated as Saint Stephen's Day and Gretl described as the second Christmas Day. She wore the red ball dress, shoes, and gloves that her
parents had given her on Christmas Eve. After dancing until she was
exhausted, she declared it "the most beautiful day of my life," just like her
confirmation three years before, only this time she added: "That is no
exaggeration."

With her schooling over in 1912, she went dancing much more often.
After Moriz and Hermine gave her a bright blue outfit that Christmas, she
began her first season, attending six balls in two months. Her next season,
a year later, was twice as busy, prompting Moriz and Hermine to fit her
out with two more ensembles. Only one of the balls she attended was a
public event, held at the Kursalon, or casino, in the City Park. Another
was a private function at the Kopetzky dancing academy. The others were
in family apartments. Moriz and Hermine held one in the Schleifmühl-

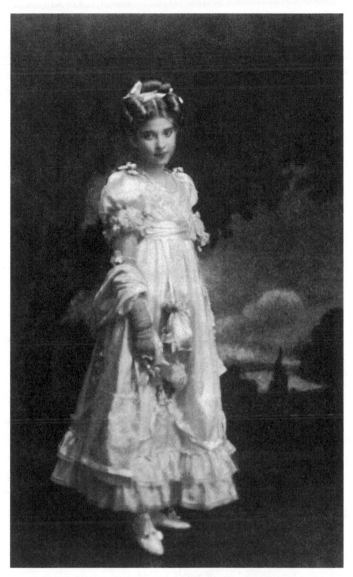

Eleven-year-old Gretl when she attended her first ball, 1908.

gasse in 1913, followed by another in the Wohllebengasse a year later. The rest were staged by other wealthy families with children about the same age.

As Gretl prepared to attend these dances, a hairdresser would come to the family apartment—at least once drawing her hair back in the fashionable Grecian style. She occasionally was accompanied not only by Erni, who was a year older, but also by Käthe and Lene, who were three years younger. Usually, though, she went alone or with Erni. She was always escorted to and from these balls—sometimes by Hermine, sometimes by her aunt Ida, who had no children of her own, sometimes by the parents of other young women who were attending the dance. If Gretl was in bed around midnight, she thought it unfortunately early. She generally had no grounds to complain, since she often danced into the morning, arriving home at three, five, and once not until six-thirty. On these occasions she recorded with satisfaction how late she got up the next day.

One in ten of the guests at these balls was a "von," a measure of the limited extent to which the family mixed with the aristocracy. Most guests were of Jewish origin. While some of these Rosenbergs, Eggers, Mandls, Mondscheins, Luzzattos, Pollaks, Schweinburgs, and Bambergers had left the Kultusgemeinde, many had not. Gretl's one response to this company voiced the antipathy to Jews felt by many converts as they rejected their old identity. She described a play staged at the Mandls' ball as a piece of "Jewish upstartery."

Gretl recorded the names of the young men she talked to and those she found most interesting, always assessing the quality of their conversations. She also identified whom she sat between at supper or who served her at the buffet and described the decorations, food, and drink with a keen eye for their presentation. The one brand she identified was WW— the monogram of the Wiener Werkstätte that adorned its salesrooms, wrapping paper, and many of its products. At one ball staged by her parents' friends the Luzzattos, the women all received flowers in WW bands. At another their hosts used WW table cards.

The entertainment at these balls was diverse. It once included films. It occasionally included raffles, lotteries, or gambling. It often included performances—sometimes amateur by a few of the guests, more usually by professional magicians, comedians, cabaret artists, or actors. The larger part of each evening was spent dancing. Gretl always noted how often she was asked to dance—usually a lot, once more than any other young

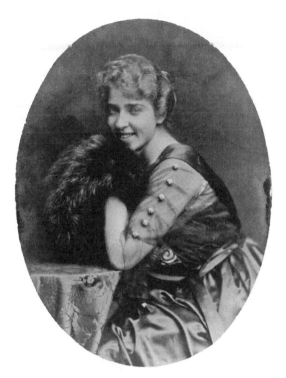

Gretl around the time of her two ball seasons.

woman there. She listed who asked her and whether they included the best dancers. She identified the young men who gave her bouquets and the total she received, which ranged from eight to twenty-one, though those bouquets were unusually shabby.

The Hoffmann apartment was designed for these occasions. Had construction gone according to schedule, it would have been ready in September 1913, enabling the family to use it through the ball season, which started a couple of months later. But wet weather slowed progress, so the family could not occupy the apartment until the end of the year, and even then work continued since the Wiener Werkstätte did not finish the last of the Hoffmann light fittings until March 1914. Moriz and Hermine were not willing to wait that long before entertaining. In December 1913, a pianist named Blum provided the music for a soiree on Saint Stephen's Day for thirty-eight people, which Gretl considered small but attractive while fearing that the Gallias were being slighted by those with more social status, if less wealth. Gretl was particularly disturbed that one of their invitees failed to tell them he would not be coming, another declined their invitation but came regardless, and a third maintained that Erni had told him the wrong time when he arrived three hours late. While Gretl often arrived an hour or two late at other families' dances, she thought three hours unacceptable and the explanation infuriated her. "If the idiot cannot come up with better excuses, he should stay at home," she fumed. "We will never invite him again."

Erni caused the family much greater concern as he struggled with the privileges and expectations that came with being Moriz and Hermine's eldest child and only son. Their decision to send him to the Theresianum, Vienna's most prestigious gymnasium, initially intended only for boys from the aristocracy, marred his childhood. While Jews constituted on average over 30 percent of the students of Vienna's other *Gymnasien,* they comprised less than 1 percent of the Theresianum's students. Just two of its boys were Jews and they were both nobility, sons of Vienna's Baron Rothschild. Despite his conversion long before he started there, Erni was treated like a Jew.

Erni's difficulties with Latin and Greek made his schooling even more traumatic because of the prospect of his failing his *Matura,* which would force him to do two years of compulsory military service as an ordinary soldier rather than one year as an officer trainee, permanently diminishing his social status. When Erni graduated in June 1913 with the help of a private tutor who lived with the family during his final school year, Moriz and Hermine rewarded Erni by buying him his first car. But because he passed only with *Stimmenmehrheit,* which meant some of his teachers thought Erni should fail, Moriz and Hermine made him leave the car in Vienna that summer. Much as Freud discussed in his *Interpretation of Dreams,* Erni never lost his fear of failing this examination, experiencing recurrent *Matura* dreams.

Erni's military training, which he started in October 1913 in an artillery regiment based in Vienna, proved at least as difficult when he was confined to barracks for a fortnight as a punishment just before Moriz and Hermine were due to hold another soiree in January 1914. While the family was embarrassed by Erni's absence that Saturday, they were more concerned that their ball for the season was to take place a week later and everyone who attended would discover the family's humiliation. Although Moriz and Hermine had sent out the invitations and organized the food, music, entertainment, and decorations, they considered canceling the ball. "What will happen is still quite uncertain!" Gretl exclaimed. "I am very anxious!!!!!!!"

Gretl's entry three days later conveys the family's horror—as well as their pride in their reputation and identity as Gallias, which Moriz and Hermine began developing as they prospered in Vienna in the 1890s. "Good God!! The shocking has happened," Gretl wrote, as if Erni had only just been imprisoned and she had not already written about it. "Our Erni, a Gallia, has been confined to barracks for fourteen days. He will never become an officer and must serve as a common soldier! He, a Gallia! It is unbelievable! And why? Because of his laziness and because he owed a crown to a common soldier and failed to pay despite repeated (four) warnings. Mama fainted when she heard the news. Both Papa and she have not slept for three nights. It is too dreadful, so beyond belief!"

Gretl was so eager for the ball to proceed that she thought of writing secretly to Erni's commanding officer, Colonel Czerny, to beg for lenience. Moriz, whose wealth and status as a *Regierungsrat* gave him significant influence in Vienna despite his Jewish origins, was unable to secure Erni's immediate release but ensured that Erni's misconduct went unnoted on his military record and he remained an officer trainee. Three weeks later, Moriz and Hermine rewarded Czerny by taking him to a performance of *Parsifal* at the Hofoper, then entertained him until early in the morning at one of Vienna's best cafés. In between, the family's ball proceeded without the prodigal.

The seventy-one guests—twenty-five more than the year before—included one baroness, eight "vons," one professor, and one doctor. Although the Hoffmann rooms, other than the boudoir, were all more than 540 square feet, it was a challenge to feed so many with style. Gretl's diary indicates that everything went well. The table in the Hoffmann dining room ordinarily seated eight, but it came with eighteen chairs and could be extended to fit them in comfort. On this occasion the family sat twenty-seven there, then seated forty-nine more in the smaller smoking room. If the guests did not know why Erni was absent when they arrived, they soon found out, but Gretl was too happy to care.

Their entertainer was the nineteen-year-old Oskar Karlweis, whose father wrote several of the plays Hermine and Moriz saw at the start of the century. While Karlweis was a guest at a number of the balls that Gretl attended in her first season, by 1914 he was acquiring a reputation as an

actor and finding work at private balls, which soon saw him become a success onstage and on-screen. To Gretl's delight, Karlweis arranged to perform with the twenty-year-old Ernst Marischka, who had already written
the screenplay for one successful film and was to write and script dozens
more, winning fame for his 1950s *Sissi* trilogy about Empress Elisabeth of
Austria.

In between conversations that Gretl thought insanely good, she
danced until four in the morning. As usual, her parents employed Blum to
play the family's Steinway. Most likely, their servants pushed the piano
into a corner of the salon to make more space for dancing, rolled up the
Hoffmann carpet, and moved the Hoffmann furniture to the edges of the
room, thereby highlighting the three massive Hoffmann gilt-metal and
glass-bead chandeliers that the Wiener Werkstätte had installed only the
day before. Because there were so many guests, the adjoining hall probably
became yet another dance floor.

Gretl received twenty-two bouquets, more than ever before, but
danced almost all night with just three partners. One was Ernst
Marischka, who ate and danced with the guests as well as performed with
them. Another was Oskar Karlweis, who did the same. The third was First
Lieutenant Balberitz, an officer in the 6th Dragoons, one of Austria's most
prestigious cavalry regiments. Although Marischka was a bad dancer and
Karlweis little better, Gretl was happy to dance with them because of their
cultural cachet. She most enjoyed her turns around the floor with Balberitz, who was the best dancer present. She was thrilled when he arrived
first and led her for most of the evening.

The new dance that season was the tango, which originated in
Argentina, where it was condemned as a "pornographic spectacle," a dance
"belonging distinctly to ill-famed clubs and to taverns of the worst repute
never danced in tasteful salons or among distinguished people." In Europe
it became a dance of the upper classes after being modified to make it
more modest. At the start of 1913, the dance that young men especially
wanted with Gretl was the quadrille, which had become popular in
Vienna in the first half of the nineteenth century. At the end of 1913, it was
the tango. She was typically good at it, winning second prize at one ball
for both the old waltz and the new craze.

As this passion continued into 1914, one Argentinean observed that
for Europeans the tango was "no more than a vaguely sinful exotic dance,
and they dance it because of its sensual perverse elements and because it is

somewhat barbaric." Because of its popularity, the tango was a high point of the Gallias' ball. While the three officers present, including Lieutenant Balberitz, had to sit it out because Franz Joseph had prohibited his soldiers from dancing it in uniform, Gretl did the tango in the family's Hoffmann salon hung with their Klimt landscape.

Other families entertained even more lavishly than the Gallias, whether because they were richer or because they were readier to spend. Just as the city's public balls culminated with the Opera Ball at the Hofoper, so the seasons of private balls attended by Gretl grew ever more extravagant. She thought a ball staged by the family of her best friend Lili Pollak in mid-February 1914 could not be surpassed. Gretl recorded that when she made her entrance—characteristically late at nine-thirty—everyone was talking and she had outstanding conversations. A supper followed at which the guests chose where they sat, to Gretl's delight, providing her with even better company. Then, at last, the dancing began to music from Blum and continued for hours, stopping only for a raffle of rococo puppets. Gretl remained on the floor until she was exhausted. It was "outstandingly beautiful," she observed after arriving home at four, "the most beautiful ball for the season."

Her last ball that season was better again—"like a dream," she wrote, "the Ball of Balls." When she again arrived at nine-thirty, she was the ninety-second guest to check her coat. When she left at two-thirty, because her uncle Adolf and aunt Ida had come to collect her, the ball was still in full swing. In between, Blum played with a quartet, and an actress from the Hofburgtheater and an actor from the Volkstheater performed. The supper, served on tables strewn with red roses, was "as for grownups," the seventeen-year-old Gretl observed delightedly, prompting her to record all its treats. Caviar was followed by bouillon, guinea fowl salad, chestnut-and-pineapple compote, goose liver bread rolls, and gelato served in the shape of roses and fruits, accompanied by sherry, red and white wines, and champagne. She was particularly gratified that the hostess, Frau Kern, declared her the most attractive, smartest dancer.

Had the men at these balls paid her such compliments, Gretl would have recorded them, too. But just as she expressed no particular interest in any of them, regardless of how long they danced and talked together, so these men seem not to have been particularly interested in her. The one exception was at a dinner in March 1914, after the season ended, when,

Gretl wrote, she was courted in "a very amusing manner" by the only "von" who was present. She was particularly pleased because it made one of the other young women "jealous as a Turk."

Meanwhile, her cousin Friedl, the youngest daughter of Wilhelm Gallia, made the kind of marriage that Moriz and Hermine wanted for Gretl. Friedl's husband, Richard, was both a "von" and a Hofmannsthal, a cousin of the great Austrian poet, playwright, and librettist, Hugo von Hofmannsthal. Richard was also a convert to Christianity and the director of a Danish petrol refinery. Yet Gretl was unimpressed when she met him at a New Year's Eve party at Adolf and Ida's apartment. After von Hofmannsthal dominated the occasion by singing in the "most horrible" fashion, Gretl declared him "disgusting." She was delighted when he stopped, and Käthe and she made a much better start to the New Year by dancing a tango.

3

Love

The summer of 1914 started like any other for Gretl. She left Vienna in mid-June with the rest of the family for their holiday in Alt Aussee. At the Villa Gallia, they saw friends, read, went for walks, played tennis, and went on excursions in the family car. As the Archduke Franz Ferdinand was being driven through Sarajevo on June 28 in his Gräf & Stift, first narrowly avoiding being killed by a grenade that destroyed the car behind, then being shot and killed as he went to visit those injured in the grenade attack, I imagine the Gallias' chauffeur driving them around Alt Aussee in their Gräf & Stift.

The assassination did not immediately affect the family. While Hermine and the Gallia children stayed in Alt Aussee as usual, Moriz divided his time between the country and the city. Once the Austrian government declared war against Serbia and mobilized its armed forces, including Erni, in late July, the family abandoned their holiday like thousands of other Austrians and hurried back to the city, where Gretl had not spent a summer since she was a baby. As she looked for things to do and ways to escape the heat, one of her aunt Ida's friends, Mrs. Stern, invited Gretl to her villa at Neuwaldegg on the edge of the Vienna Woods. Before long Gretl was there again at the invitation of Mrs. Stern's son, Norbert, to play tennis. In mid-October Hermine reciprocated by inviting Norbert and his mother to the Wohllebengasse for afternoon tea.

The following day Gretl took out her diary for the first time in four months. "A scandal!" Gretl observed. "Nothing of the five weeks in Aussee, nothing of my birthday, nothing of our sudden departure from Aussee and our arrival in Vienna immediately after the mobilization, nothing about how we remained in Vienna all of August, only Papa returned to the villa to put it in order and Erni returned in mid-September with appendicitis." Nothing, she might have added, about where Erni returned from—how since July he had taken part in Austria's rapid advance east into Russian Poland, then its even quicker retreat west, which saw Austria suffer shocking casualties and abandon most of its granary in Galicia.

As Gretl wrote, Moriz, Hermine, and Erni were on their way to the Sanitorium Loew so Erni could have his appendix removed. "I am now home alone," Gretl recorded, disregarding the family's servants, "and fear so much for Erni." Yet it was not Erni but Norbert Stern, a qualified engineer eager to establish himself as an architect, who spurred Gretl to resume her diary. "He is extraordinarily engaging, surely the nicest human being (male) that I have met," she began. "Already twenty-eight and three-quarters years old and not at all conceited!" she continued, suggesting that the eighteen-year-old Gretl was used to men his age patronizing her and did not like it.

As she recorded her ever more frequent encounters with Norbert in greater detail, Gretl created an almost daily chronicle of their relationship—a remarkable account of young love and courtship in early twentieth-century Vienna. She also revealed the Gallias' hopes, fears, and values when they had only just moved to Good Living Street, though the onset of war meant they were no longer living as they had planned. As Gretl recorded their conduct, conversations, and conflicts, she left a rare description of how one of the main patron families of Viennese modernism lived in their new Hoffmann rooms.

Gretl saw Norbert twice that November. Her aunt Ida began by taking her to a lecture about Egypt so that Gretl and Norbert could sit next to each other. Then Moriz, Hermine, Gretl, Käthe, and Lene went with Norbert and Mrs. Stern to the Vienna Woods, one of the city's most popular excursion grounds. "I have never enjoyed an outing so much," Gretl recorded.

"He is truly an unusually nice, good-natured human being—and so upright!!"

His Catholicism was one attraction, though Gretl's religious observance was not strong. While she started her second diary in 1913 *"Mit Gott!"* or "With God!" and did the same when she started her first recipe book in 1914, that was simply a matter of convention. She recorded only one instance of churchgoing in 1914 and just one more in 1915 when Käthe and Lene were belatedly confirmed at the age of sixteen. Still, Gretl was delighted to discover that Norbert had converted from Judaism a few years before. Their common origins and shared religion were, she observed, "another starting point for conversation!"

Gretl was just as impressed when Ida brought them together again three weeks later for supper at her apartment. Gretl wrote, "It was beautiful, such good conversations, he is such a nice person." After he went home, he telephoned her for the first time to ask her to call him Norbert rather than Herr Stern. "I wonder," she wrote, "if I shall do that?!"

Had there been no war, she would soon have been dancing through her third season, but in keeping with a government edict banning public balls, there were no private ones. Gretl was oblivious because of Norbert. As they began exchanging presents, he gave her three anemones, which she pressed into her diary, and one of his own engravings. She reciprocated with a portfolio in which to keep his work. But for his twenty-ninth birthday she sent only a letter. They also gave each other nothing for Christmas, though they saw each other immediately beforehand, when Moriz and Hermine invited Norbert to dinner for the first time, and immediately after, when Gretl invited him for afternoon tea on Saint Stephen's Day.

Gretl was in the kitchen five days later, preparing for New Year's Eve, when a parcel arrived with a bouquet of snowdrops attached to it. "Addressed to me?" she wrote. "Odd." Then she recognized Norbert's handwriting on the envelope, which contained a note suggesting Gretl, Käthe, and Lene share the two pounds of assorted chocolates in the parcel but instructed Gretl to keep the flowers. "I am so delighted!" she recorded. "This is the first time I have received flowers and sweets from a man!!!"

Moriz and Hermine were accustomed to ringing in the New Year in style with Adolf and Ida, but because they were at their villa in Baden, Moriz and Hermine stayed at home with Gretl, Käthe, and Lene. After toasting the New Year at nine o'clock, they engaged in the New Year's ritual of *Bleigiessen,* dropping pieces of molten lead into cold water to predict the future by interpreting the shapes that resulted. By eleven o'clock Gretl was in bed, tired from drinking wine and punch. But she lay awake thinking of Norbert, not only because of his gift that morning but also because when she played *Bleigiessen* she saw a "*Stern,*" or star. "Was that coincidence?!" she wondered.

A fortnight later an anonymous telephone caller asked whether she could congratulate Gretl on her engagement, then hung up before Gretl could reply. Then the caller rang back to say that rumor had it that Gretl and Norbert were engaged even though he was unable to support a family. This time Gretl responded that it was impertinent to repeat such baseless stories, then she herself hung up. While she could not identify the caller, she suspected one of the young women whom she sometimes invited to the Wohllebengasse. She thought it had to be one of her guests from Saint Stephen's Day, as only they had seen her with Norbert.

Gretl was young to be engaged at eighteen but not especially so. Her aunt Henny married when she was nineteen, her cousin Melanie when she was twenty, her cousin Friedl when she was twenty-one, Hermine when she was twenty-two. Norbert was the right age to marry at twenty-nine. It was only when men turned twenty-five that they reached the age of majority and were likely to have the means to support a wife and children, though Norbert could not do so on his salary of 3,000 crowns, or about $24,000 in today's money. In the parlance of the day, he was "*keine gute Partie,*" not a good catch, as the traditional bourgeois emphasis on economics as the basis for marriage remained strong in Vienna, despite the rise of romantic love.

Moriz and Hermine did not appear to care as they joined with Adolf, Ida, and Mrs. Stern in chaperoning Norbert and Gretl on one excursion after another. Their usual destination was the Vienna Woods, where they went by tram or train but never by car, as the Austrian military found itself desperately short of vehicles almost as soon as the war started, prompting Moriz to give his Gräf & Stift to the army. While they usually went walking, they once skied and once inspected a villa and duplex designed by Norbert in the village of Pötzleinsdorf, which led Gretl to admire him as "not only a rare, dear, good human being but also a very skilled architect."

Hermine tried to constrain Gretl just once, when Norbert and she were to accompany Adolf and Ida to Baden. Because one of Hermine's servants was on holiday, she asked Gretl to stay home so she could help Hermine dust the front rooms of the apartment. The result, according to

Gretl, was a "hard battle," which saw her escape the dusting and go to Baden. While she knew Hermine would protest that she had been forced to clean until midnight and Moriz would admonish her for attending too many balls in one year and going on too many excursions the next, Gretl was triumphant. She wrote: "For a few days, they will berate me and whatever I do will be bad but no one can deprive me of the memory of such a beautiful outing."

These occasions fueled Gretl's excitement. She was astounded that such a wise, educated, intelligent man could enjoy talking to someone so young and stupid. She preferred Norbert's simplicity and honesty to the flattery of a "*Salonmensch*" adept in the ways of fashionable society. She believed Norbert when he told her that she was his "dear one," despite her father's always telling her that men would want to marry her for his money. Her goal was to have Norbert to herself as much as possible so they could talk uninterrupted.

She was delighted to be alone with Norbert when Mrs. Stern and he were among the guests at a dinner party at the Wohllebengasse that March. While Gretl liked to think she was adroit at creating these opportunities without anyone noticing, she owed this one to Ida. Norbert and Gretl were in the smoking room when their conversation turned to the anonymous phone calls she had received at the start of the year and Norbert asked whether she would mind if the rumors proved true. When Gretl blushed and said no, Norbert declared she must have realized that he loved her and asked whether she liked him a little and might be willing to give it a go with him. She said yes, and thus they were secretly engaged.

Norbert's only concerns were that the times were so ominous—war and love might not go together—and that she had been spoiled by the lavish environment of the Wohllebengasse and would struggle to adjust to a much more modest married life. When he called the next morning, he addressed her as "*Du*" rather than "*Sie*," a mark of their new intimacy. He also reported that he had told his mother and they had her blessing. They agreed to talk about everything in more detail that Sunday, just two days later, when they were supposed to go on an excursion. Then Norbert would ask Moriz and Hermine for permission to marry her.

Gretl expected her parents to put up more opposition than Mrs. Stern. They would declare her too young, stupid, and impractical. They would say that Norbert did not have a secure job and could not support her in the manner to which she was accustomed. She would respond that she loved Norbert so much that she was ready to curb her expenditure. She would tell them that he was such a "gentleman"—one of many English words that she continued to use in her diary, despite a wartime prohibition on the use of English in public—that he had never asked about the Gallias' wealth, leading her to think him oblivious to it.

Sunday was too far away for Gretl. After talking to Nobert on Friday morning, she could not contain herself. Before the day was out, she "confessed everything" to Moriz and Hermine, who seem not to have objected. Yet Gretl almost despaired on Sunday when the weather was so bad that an excursion was unthinkable and Norbert did not call. When he rang on Monday evening, she told him to come to the Wohllebengasse as soon as possible. When he rang the following morning to ask whether he could come that afternoon, she said the sooner the better.

Gretl received Norbert in her mother's boudoir, which was dominated by the Klimt portrait of Hermine and the Andri portrait of Moriz and filled with the Hoffmann white-and-gold furniture. Had Gretl and Norbert thought it appropriate, they could have sat together on the Hoffmann sofa or the suite of Hoffmann armchairs. Instead, they sat apart, opposite each other, in an inglenook created by Hoffmann in which the two built-in seats were separated by an occasional table and false fireplace. There Gretl and Norbert had the kind of formal discussion that she considered proper, confirming they would marry. Then, for the first time, they kissed. "Norbert gave me the engagement kisses," Gretl wrote, "and overcome with happiness, everything went black before me."

Moriz and Hermine were in the smoking room with the twins, who realized what was afoot as soon as Norbert and Gretl emerged. Norbert's mother, whom Gretl observed was now also her mother, transformed from Mrs. Stern into Mama Luis, was by the telephone in her apartment waiting to hear their news. "Everybody saw it coming," Gretl observed, "but never thought it would happen so fast." Norbert and she had seen each other fifteen times in the five months since he first visited the Wohllebengasse.

Not everybody had seen it coming, however, as became clear when Gretl told Adolf and Ida. Although Ida had facilitated Norbert's courtship of Gretl and was an old friend of Mrs. Stern's, she was shocked. "Say that again!" Ida exclaimed. "You must be mad!!" But Gretl was too happy to worry or to take offense. She wrote of her engagement: "It happened so quickly and I am overjoyed. Today for the first time I slept." As she was

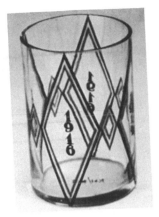

One of the Gallias' war glasses
made by the Wiener Werkstätte

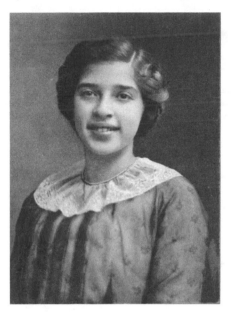

Eighteen-year-old Gretl gave a
copy of this photograph to Norbert Stern when they became
engaged, March 1915.

when he finished school and further exemption following Franz Ferdinand's assassination. But as Austria's peacetime army was decimated in the
first months of the war, it became desperate for more men. By one
account, "Only the physically handicapped, civil servants, priests, farmers,
and war-industries producers escaped service." Norbert's eyesight was so
bad that the military rejected him again in November 1914. "It is really
wonderful," Gretl wrote, "that my dearest and kindest friend remains in
Vienna!!"

Other Viennese diarists wrote almost exclusively about the war during
these months, filling their entries with observations on Austria's cam-
paigns. Gretl ignored the war for weeks on end because she was preoccupied with Norbert and because her diary was always more personal than
political. The war was also slow to affect Vienna's wealthiest citizens, as
revealed by the frequency with which Gretl continued to eat in style at the
city's most expensive hotels while the first food shortages occurred and the
government instructed the city's bakers to use rye, barley, corn, and potato
meal instead of wheat flour. But Austria's military campaign in the south-
east was such a disaster that Gretl wrote about it. She was distressed to
learn that after the Hapsburg troops announced they were laying Belgrade
at Franz Joseph's feet, having finally taken the Serbian capital on their third
attempt, they proved so overstretched, ill equipped, and outnumbered
that the Serbs immediately retook Belgrade, inflicting huge losses on the
Austrians. Gretl was all the more upset that this humiliation occurred on

washing her face the following day, a large bouquet of white lilacs arrived
from Norbert with the message: "Good morning!"

Norbert was immediately making plans. He suggested they should be
married that August. He wanted to honeymoon in Switzerland, which
had maintained its traditional neutrality at the start of the war, and Italy,
which had dishonored its Triple Alliance with Germany and Austria in
August 1914 by declaring its neutrality. They should start in St. Moritz, the
most famous alpine resort, then head south to Lake Como and Venice.
Meanwhile, they exchanged rings and photographs. That of Gretl shows
her in clothes exceptionally plain. She appears sweet, eager, and hopeful.
She does not look her age. She seems too young to marry.

4

War

Most Austrians welcomed the war as they wanted to avenge the assassination of Franz Ferdinand. But Jews and recent converts to Christianity were particularly enthusiastic because they saw the war as an opportunity to counter the heightened anti-Semitism of the late 1890s and early 1900s. They wanted to show that they were exemplary citizens, displaying their gratitude to Emperor Franz Joseph for introducing the laws that allowed them to move to Vienna and succeed there. When the imperial government counted the Jews in its forces in 1916, in response to accusations that Jews were evading military service, it found a disproportionately high number in its army.

Like women around the world, Gretl was soon contributing to the war effort by knitting—not only when she was by herself at home but also when she went out. Her first knitting afternoon was at the apartment of family friends in November 1914. The next was a fortnight later, when Hermine and she first visited the Sterns' apartment in the Second District. After that Gretl wrote only once about knitting. Most likely, she refrained from mentioning it because these afternoons had become too commonplace to mention, rather than because they had stopped.

Like other countries, Austria funded its military primarily through

special war bonds scheduled for repayment a d these bonds was so great that the government su significantly raising taxes. In all, two-thirds of A scribed, whether out of patriotism, the lure of unusu or public pressure. Moriz did not acquire any of the fi autumn of 1914, but then spent heavily on the second series, investing 510,000 crowns, the equivalent of about

The government raised more money by encoura donate their jewelry. The most conspicuous, common re married women to give their gold wedding rings in return f provided by the government inscribed "*Gold gab ich für Ei* "I gave gold for iron 1914"—which publicly testified to their pa relinquishing one of their most personal possessions for a standa Hermine retained her wedding ring, a simple gold band engraved inside with her wedding date, but donated a much more valuable the spectacular gold brooch with two solitaire diamonds that she worn when Klimt painted her.

Moriz and Hermine also demonstrated their patriotism through th Wiener Werkstätte, which was soon doing what it could to promote the war effort—designing posters promoting war bonds, selling these bonds in its stores, and putting war imagery onto its wares. Hermine bought one of the Werkstätte's first pieces of war jewelry—a square enameled brooch produced in August 1914 that included the flags not only of Austria and its German and Turkish allies but also of Italy, in recognition of the still just extant Triple Alliance. She also acquired several of the Werkstätte's main war products, its war glasses, which were adorned with the figures of soldiers and the national colors of Austria and Germany.

Erni ordinarily would have entered the civilian workforce in one of Moriz's companies late in 1914 and become a member of Austria's military reserve after completing his year's training as an officer trainee, but the war kept him in the army as a full-time soldier. After recuperating from his appendix operation at the Sanitorium Loew, he left Vienna before the new year to join his artillery unit at Bärn in northern Moravia, where Moriz and Hermine visited him regularly before he telegrammed in May 1915 that he was about to return to the front, prompting them to rush to Bärn so they could see him before he saw action again.

Norbert was in a different position because he suffered from severe astigmatism, prompting his exemption from compulsory military service

Emperor's Day, which marked the anniversary of Franz Joseph's ascendancy to the throne sixty-six years before. She wrote: "God grant that the war soon have an end."

The course of the war in the northeast also engaged her. When the Austrian army retreated westward before the much larger Tsarist army in 1914, the one town that the Austrians retained was Przemyśl, the site of their biggest fortress, which they protected with 30 miles of new trenches, 650 miles of extra barbed wire, and two hundred batteries. The Austrians rightly thought it capable of withstanding any attack; an extended siege was a different matter. Three days after Gretl and Norbert became engaged, the Austrian commander began butchering his horses, firing almost all his remaining artillery shells, blowing up his big guns, and destroying most of his defenses so the Russians would capture as little as possible. When he surrendered along with 120,000 officers and men in March 1915, Franz Joseph was reduced to tears. Gretl observed, "This unfortunate war is the one thing that disturbs our happiness."

Gretl was even less interested in a counterattack by the Austrians and Germans two months later, which saw the combined force break through the Russian lines and begin pressing east, rapidly taking thirty thousand prisoners. Gretl wrote about this victory only because when Hermine decided to celebrate it, she had such trouble raising the Hapsburg flag over the family's apartment that she left Norbert and Gretl alone for a wonderful half hour. Gretl was much more concerned by the actions of Italy, which was looking to gain territory from the war. When Austria refused to agree to a dismemberment of its empire, which would have secured Italy's continued neutrality, everyone knew Italy would declare war, forcing Austria to fight on a third front to the southwest, requiring even more soldiers. "God give me the great good luck that they do not call up my dear one!" Gretl exclaimed on May 17. Then struck by her unprecedented reliance on God, she added: "One grows so pious now! What don't I pray for every evening!" She still continued, "God grant all my wishes be fulfilled! Let us stay at peace with Italy."

Gretl was even more fearful two days later because Norbert had decided to volunteer. "I could accept a separation but not the possibility that they would send him to the front," she wrote. "If he is sent there, God help me." When the Italian parliament met to vote in favor of war on May 20, the Gallias and Sterns waited at the Wohllebengasse for a special edition of the newspaper reporting Italy's decision to fight its former partners in the Triple Alliance. Like most Austrians, Gretl's sense of betrayal was intense. Austria's chief of staff, Conrad von Hötzendorf, likened Italy to a snake. Gretl railed: "The Italian swine have declared war on us."

Karl Kraus wrote as if Austrians with good connections could easily avoid military service. In *The Last Days of Mankind* he included an exchange between two draft dodgers who both "went up and got it fixed, of course," escaping the army altogether. More often these men were taken by the military but received special treatment. So Egon Schiele's patrons secured him a position in the Department of Supply that allowed the artist to continue painting and organizing exhibitions. The writer Hugo von Hofmannsthal was even more privileged. After a stint at a desk job far from the front, Hofmannsthal returned to civilian life through the joint intervention of the principal adviser to Austria's foreign secretary, one of Austria's regional governors, and two leading Austrian politicians.

Moriz hoped to use his status as a *Regierungsrat* and industrialist to protect Norbert, just as he had used it to maintain Erni's position as an officer cadet a year before. When Norbert went to the Ministry of War to report sick the day after Italy declared war, Moriz accompanied him, but the ministry advised them to wait and see what happened when the army recalled Norbert for another examination. As they waited, Gretl developed her own version of the Lord's Prayer, which concluded: "Give us peace and victory and us two especially luck and happiness and ensure that, when they call up Norbert, they either reject him or employ him as an engineer away from the front, Amen."

The army decided to take Norbert in early June as flags flew across Vienna to celebrate the retaking of the fortress of Przemyśl. When Norbert heard he had to start training immediately and would be in an infantry division at the front within four months, Gretl drew on Shakespeare's *Hamlet,* which Vienna's Hofburgtheater persisted in staging by interpreting an imperial ban on the performance of all British works as applying only to living authors. As Gretl contemplated the prospect of Norbert's being killed at the front, she despaired and, in her misery, imagined herself as "a second Ophelia," ready to die without crying. Moriz revived her hopes. After he again went to the ministry to contest the army's decision, Gretl's admiration reached new bounds. "Everything has not been lost," she exclaimed. "Papa is an angel and a genius!"

Gretl was even happier a week later because the army postponed Norbert's call-up until mid-July. When a dove flew into her room and dropped a feather, she took it as an omen that Norbert might yet escape the front. But Norbert knew he would have to serve. When he left his job in Vienna at the end of June 1915, he expected to be in Italy soon, while his workmates looked forward to postcards from him recording Austria's conquest of Milan. "*Heil und Sieg!*" one farewelled him. "Hail and Victory!"

One of the most virulent, popular pieces of propaganda in Germany and Austria at the start of the war was the *Hassgesang gegen England,* or *Song of Hatred Against England* by the poet Ernst Lissauer. When Italy declared war on Austria, the Viennese writers Arthur Löwenstein and Grete von Urbanitzky tried in vain to emulate Lissauer's success with a *Song of Hatred Against Italy,* set to music by the composer Attilio Bleibtreu. When the Gallias went as usual to spend the summer in Alt Aussee and Norbert visited them for a week at the start of July, he gave Gretl the new *Song of Hatred* to play for him on the family's baby grand in the Villa Gallia.

Gretl gave Norbert several presents after they were engaged. One was a traveling alarm clock with an illuminated radium face. Another was an illustrated edition of Hans Christian Andersen that Gretl selected both because it was a beautiful production and because of her own taste for fairy tales. A third came from the Wiener Werkstätte, where the Gallias shopped more than ever after Moriz became one of its directors. When Gretl and Norbert celebrated Easter together, she gave him a black WW briefcase—a lavish gift when one of the Werkstätte's handkerchiefs cost more than the weekly wage of a trained dressmaker.

Norbert gave Gretl many more presents in keeping with convention, though he could rarely afford to make them as luxurious. He not only brought her something almost every time they saw each other but also sometimes sent her gifts in between. On the whole, he gave her flowers— violets, lilies, snowdrops, white, pink and red carnations, red tulips, dark red rhododendrons, long, dark red roses. But occasionally he gave her jewelry, knickknacks, books, and music. She was delighted one Tuesday when, instead of the flowers she expected, he had her sent a selection of handbags so she might choose her favorite. Whatever she received, Gretl was thrilled by these marks of his devotion.

Gretl found being alone with him "beyond words," "beautiful," even "godlike"—but they required permission to retire together and had to be careful not to absent themselves for too long or they would be reprimanded for exceeding the bounds of propriety. Their most frequent opportunities occurred at the Wohllebengasse, where Norbert visited much more often than Gretl went to Mrs. Stern's apartment. Gretl was so grateful for one of these occasions that she exclaimed, "Mother is an angel." She was thrilled another night when Hermine allowed Norbert and her to retire twice. They also had some time alone when they visited Gretl's aunt Ida, who celebrated their engagement with an afternoon tea that, Gretl wrote, was even grander than the one staged by Hermine at the Wohllebengasse. Gretl was especially touched that Ida's tea was the first at which she used her newly acquired service of Flora Danica, a mark of how Ida and Adolf's patterns of consumption remained unaffected by the first months of the war. Yet the highlight of this tea for Gretl was that Ida unexpectedly allowed Norbert and her to retire briefly together.

Their first outing by themselves was a month after they were engaged, when Norbert met Gretl at the apartment of her grandparents, Nathan and Josefine Hamburger, who had just moved from Freudenthal to the fashionable outer Viennese suburb of Hietzing. Because Norbert was on his way to a lecture, he had only an hour. By the time he had engaged in the usual formalities of greeting and saying good-bye to her grandparents, Gretl and he had little more than half that. They used it to see the newly completed villa that Hoffmann had designed for the landowner and industrialist Robert Primavesi and his companion, Josephine Skywa. If Norbert and Gretl had to justify this outing, they probably explained that Hoffmann was the Gallia family's architect and Norbert had a professional interest in his work. But Gretl did not mention Hoffmann in her diary. Instead, what excited her was that Norbert and she were "alone together for the first time on the street."

Their only other outings alone lasted just a couple of hours. The first was in a *Fiaker*, the traditional Viennese two-horse cab, to make brief calls on several members of the extended Gallia family. The second was to the grave of Norbert's father on Whitsunday, the Christian festival commemorating the coming of the Holy Ghost. Gretl recorded: "For the first time we went on our own to the grave of Papa Stern and brought him flowers. My darling must have been very devoted to his late father. I was also very affected by visiting his grave and prayed there with all my heart."

Otherwise Norbert and Gretl were always chaperoned and at most had a few minutes alone. The excursion that gave Gretl greatest pleasure was with Norbert's mother to the baroque monastery of Melk on Ascension Thursday, a public holiday. The celebrated way of making this journey was to take the train from Vienna to Melk and return by steamer along the River Danube. Gretl, who had never made this voyage, described it as the most beautiful Ascension Day she had experienced. Norbert and she were "blissfully happy." And her delight grew when they returned to the Wohllebengasse and Mrs. Stern waited downstairs in their taxi while Norbert took her inside, so they "could at least have a quick kiss on the stairs," which she declared "better than nothing!"

As a newly engaged couple, Gretl and Norbert were also expected to attend a host of special teas at the homes of relations and friends. Yet six weeks passed before one of these functions left her neither embarrassed nor distraught. She was horrified by all the advice she received about how to be a married woman. She was even more upset when Norbert and she had no time by themselves. Her refrain was that she did not benefit from Norbert's presence because they were always with others. Gretl thought it an eternity to wait a week for the chance to be alone. Sometimes she had to wait a fortnight. Far from relishing her status as an engaged woman, it frustrated her.

Her family caused her more grief. One "explosion," as Gretl described it, climaxed with Hermine exclaiming in English: "When you're married, I will surely have as much trouble from you as I usually had." If Norbert knew how she sometimes behaved, Hermine continued in German, he "would leave her at the altar." Another of Hermine's outbursts saw her accuse Norbert in his absence of having no manners: he left the apartment without saying good-bye to Hermine's mother. Yet another occurred after Moriz and Hermine invited Norbert to Wagner's *Parsifal* at the Hofoper; he left before the second act and was indiscreet enough to tell Käthe that he had never wanted to go in the first place. Gretl began by being appalled at her family's tactlessness in denigrating her fiancé in front of her. She soon feared that they were set on making her quarrel with him. If that was their aim, they succeeded one evening in late April when Gretl felt that Norbert paid more attention to the family's dog than to her. When Gretl started to cry, she thought her parents and sisters were delighted.

Norbert and Gretl began expressing their disappointment in each other a few days later with the "best understanding." He was surprised to find her so sensitive; she was surprised to find him such a dunderhead. While Norbert apologized the following day and declared his criticisms unjust, only a few days later he was labeling her a coquette and a spendthrift, and Gretl was accusing him of being inattentive and parsimonious. Her ideal was her father, she confided to her diary. "Someone like Papa exists just once in the world," she wrote. "I pray every evening that Norbert might become as much like him as possible."

His family's dog soon also had them arguing. While Norbert wanted it to live with them when they married, she did not. "I made my first request of him and he did not immediately agree!" she recorded. Norbert's failure to comply was "the bitterest disappointment" of her life. Rather than keep this quarrel to themselves, Norbert immediately informed his mother, who announced she would keep the dog, but Gretl was not placated. A thorn remained, a thorn that stung, she wrote, adopting the language of fairy tales. That night, Hermine told Gretl that Moriz and she, but especially Moriz, feared Norbert was the wrong man for her.

By then Gretl was full of remorse, aware that she had responded disproportionately and sure that she was largely to blame for their quarrels. When Hermine asked whether she was certain she wanted to spend the rest of her life with Norbert, Gretl did not hesitate. "Despite everything, I immediately answered yes with complete conviction," she recorded. "I expect other people to be more considerate to me than I am to them," she observed the following morning in one of those flashes of self-knowledge that punctuated her diary. If Norbert's dog was so important to him, Gretl would let him have his way, albeit grudgingly. Her sacrifice would be "*very* great," she maintained, "far greater than anyone, especially Norbert, recognized."

Again they made up, though Gretl lacked the words to convey how sorry she was. Norbert and she promised each other to treat their quarrel as a bad dream. He brought her a particularly gorgeous bunch of long-stemmed red roses. That night she reflected at unusual length about the kind of marriage she wanted: "I do not want the type of husband who accedes to all his wife's wishes," she declared, as if such men were easily found in Vienna in 1915. "I need to respect and look up to my husband as I can with Norbert," she continued, prepared to accept his superiority. "I do not want to be a decorative doll," she went on, probably with Ibsen's *A Doll's House* in mind. Her goal—influenced both by her parents' marriage and by contemporary feminism—was equality. Gretl hoped Norbert and she might be "true comrades for life."

Gretl began to think that her engagement might be a mistake when she began arguing with Moriz, which particularly disturbed her because they had always been so close. Because she sensed Moriz's opposition to her engagement was the cause, she asked him what he thought. While Moriz avoided declaring himself against Norbert, he acknowledged that he was not for Norbert either. Economics was the key. Moriz would have preferred Gretl's husband to be able to keep a wife and family. He warned that Norbert would watch his money more than she liked. "Now I am full of doubt and regret," she concluded, "having been so happy until now."

A question of etiquette caused more conflict. When Hermine turned forty-five that June, Norbert sent a four-pound box of chocolates with a card that read, "With all good wishes Architect Norbert Stern." Hermine had no complaints about the chocolates, but she was "enraged," Gretl recorded, not only by the "strange and impersonal" wording of the card but also because it had been written by a shop assistant rather than Norbert himself. When Norbert arrived later in the day, bringing a large bunch of flowers for Gretl as usual, oblivious to the outrage he had provoked, she had the "frightful task" of reprimanding him on behalf of Hermine, who was visiting her parents in Hietzing.

This situation was compounded because Gretl, for the first time, felt that Hermine had "good reasons" to be incensed. Norbert refused to concede he had erred, accusing Hermine and Gretl of being ridiculously sensitive and challenging their conception of good manners. He also questioned Gretl's love for him, which was too much for her. As she later described it, she could not contain herself. "*Ich bin ich*"—"I am I"—she wrote, "and was terribly angry." Although Norbert begged her forgiveness and telephoned Hermine to apologize to her, Gretl identified their exchange as something she would not forget. "The sting remains," she declared. "A hidden wound hurts most of all."

Her parents confronted Gretl a few days later. When Hermine warned Gretl that nothing good would come from her, Gretl was unmoved. "As if I had not long known that!!!" she observed sardonically. The same was true when Hermine exclaimed, "That such a person should marry! When her behavior was so immature!" But then Hermine advanced into new territory by dwelling on her financial sacrifices in letting Gretl buy on credit on her accounts. She stung Gretl for being overweight and having a stupid face. Above all, Moriz spoke as if his agreement to Gretl's marriage had always been reluctant, predicting that he would live to regret having "given in and let her have her way."

5

Hoffmann

Many Viennese families chose to live close to each other at the turn of the century, often occupying apartments in the same building. The Gallias and Hamburgers followed this pattern. When Hermine's brothers Otto and Guido moved to Vienna, they lived in the Schleifmühlgasse. When Moriz and Hermine erected their building in the Wohllebengasse, they expected that as Erni, Gretl, Käthe, and Lene married, each of the children would occupy a floor so the entire family would always be under the one roof. But Mrs. Stern upset this plan because she had similar ambitions for her house in Vienna's Second District, or Leopoldstadt. When she offered Norbert and Gretl the upper floor of her two-story building on the Untere Augartenstrasse, they accepted, though Gretl was yet to see this apartment.

The location was an issue. The Second District was the site of Vienna's seventeenth-century ghetto and, as the city's Jewish population swelled in the late nineteenth century, again became its most Jewish district and a ghetto in the popular imagination. While the families who lived on its main streets, such as the Untere Augartenstrasse, were generally prosperous, most of its residents were poor. In 1880 almost half of the city's Jews lived there. In 1910 more than one-third did. Moriz and Hermine would have been against any of their family living there even before they converted, let alone afterward. They did not want Gretl's new home to be where a high proportion of stores closed for the Sabbath, Yiddish was widely spoken, and many men and women dressed in accordance with Jewish tradition.

The apartment's design created more trouble. Just as when Melanie Gallia married Jakob Langer in 1902 and Guido Hamburger married Nelly Bunzl in 1907, the convention was that wealthy couples occupied architect-designed apartments with custom-made furniture. Moriz and Hermine expected Gretl and Norbert to do the same. Because Hoffmann remained their favorite architect, they probably looked forward to his designing all their children's homes. If the children stayed in the Wohllebengasse, their house could become the site of not just one Hoffmann apartment but an unprecedented quintuple stack.

Norbert's expectations were very different. As an aspiring architect, he wanted to design his own home and, within two days of his engagement, was planning it. Before long, Gretl and he were doing so together, to her delight. "My love for him is beyond words," she wrote after their first design session, when she still had not seen the apartment. "I love my dear one more and more from day to day," Gretl wrote after another session, when she had seen it. They soon had planned three rooms, incorporating furniture owned by Norbert's grandmother to reduce the cost, but Moriz and Hermine were contemptuous. "I am terribly hurt," Gretl wrote in late April. "The parents have absolutely no hope for the apartment."

Ten days later Moriz and Hermine staged a dinner attended by Josef Hoffmann and Gustav Klimt and two of their biggest patrons, the Moravian banker Otto Primavesi and his wife, Eugenia. While the Primavesis employed Franz von Krauss to design their villa in Olmütz, Hoffmann furnished two of its rooms, redesigned the ground floor of their local bank, and designed their country villa in Winkelsdorf. The Primavesis also acquired five paintings by Klimt, including portraits of Eugenia and their daughter Mäda. They invested 100,000 crowns (now about $750,000) in the Wiener Werkstätte when it became a private company and soon replaced Fritz Waerndorfer as its principal underwriters.

The invitation from Moriz and Hermine allowed the Primavesis to see something like what they had in Olmütz—a Krauss building containing Hoffmann rooms hung with Klimt paintings and filled with Wiener Werkstätte objects. Yet for all this similarity, when the Primavesis inspected the apartment in the Wohllebengasse, they identified just one familiar object, a small leather basket with a handle intended for house and pantry keys. Otto had commissioned the first of these baskets from Hoffmann for Eugenia, whose monogram Hoffmann had placed on the handle. Hermine had a later version with no monogram.

Gretl was distracted for much of the evening because Norbert and she had quarreled, but her excitement at the family's guests that night was still manifest when she listed them with an exclamation mark. While Hermine and Moriz had entertained Klimt and Hoffmann before, this dinner was the first attended by Gretl as an adult. The way she described Klimt was revealing. As he did not have a title, Klimt's admirers often gave him one. The Primavesis' daughter Mäda referred to him as "Professor"—a position he aspired to but never secured. Gretl identified him as "Master"—a term of reverence for the greatest artists, writers, and musicians. She had no idea that, after Norbert and she retired, Moriz and Hermine offered Hoffmann a new commission. It was to design six rooms in Norbert and Gretl's apartment—Hoffmann's first commission in the Second District, which implicitly underlined how Gretl was defying the expectations of her class by moving there.

Norbert and Gretl discovered what Moriz and Hermine had initiated when Norbert came to dinner three days later. Many sons-in-law-to-be would have been delighted to receive an apartment by Vienna's most fashionable architect. Norbert took immediate offense because he had different taste, wanted to design the apartment himself, and Hoffmann's commission would come out of Gretl's dowry, which Norbert had been expecting would make up for his own lack of capital. The more Moriz talked, the more upset and quieter Norbert became. "No one leaves us alone even for a second," Gretl lamented, after Norbert finally went home. "It was hideous."

This conflict resumed the following evening when Norbert again came to dinner, causing "disaster" for Norbert and Gretl. The twins also took such pleasure in picking on Norbert after he left that Gretl thought they "would only stop when they had torn him apart." When Gretl started to cry, Moriz turned on her in a way that was utterly out of character, declaring her the most stupid person he had ever met.

The next day was at least as bad. Gretl found it "truly painful" as Norbert "unfortunately" identified a hundred flaws in Hoffmann's work, drawing most likely on Adolf Loos's critique of Hoffmann in "Ornament and Crime," which Loos had delivered most recently in Vienna at the city's Engineers and Architects Association in 1913. In doing so, Norbert not only denigrated the taste of Moriz and Hermine but also implicitly condemned the Gallia apartment in the Wohllebengasse and expressed his abhorrence of the environment in which he had wooed and won Gretl. As Moriz and he engaged in "the bitterest battle of principles for and against Hoffmann," she looked on without saying anything or being asked her opinion.

The next contestation between Moriz and Norbert—their fourth in four days—was "oh so wearisome," Gretl recorded, but it was the last. As they all knew, Norbert could not refuse Moriz's offer. As much as Norbert needed Moriz's help when it came to his military service, he had to accept whatever Moriz would give him as part of Gretl's dowry. After Norbert left, Gretl wrote: "Prof. Hoffmann is to design the apartment. I unfortunately do not know whether I should be happy about this. As far as I am concerned, there is no one better at designing apartments than Hoffmann but Norbert is terribly against him and is very put out because he thinks that Father has no confidence in him as an architect. I hope and believe that Norbert will accept this decision more easily than he expects and that everything will end well."

Mothers-in-law were notorious for their interference in early twentieth-century Vienna. When Gretl became engaged to Norbert, she feared Mrs. Stern would conform to this stereotype. To Gretl's relief, Mrs. Stern confined herself to criticizing Gretl's headwear and trying to improve it. At the start of April, Mrs. Stern took Gretl on a shopping expedition in the city where, despite the international campaign against the slaughter of birds for their plumes, she bought Gretl a small black hat adorned with egret feathers. Such experiences led Gretl to revise her opinion of Mrs. Stern until she was "not at all afraid of her anymore" and "loved her more from day to day." This good fortune was offset by Moriz's determination to govern how Norbert and she lived. "With us," Gretl observed, "Father is the mother-in-law."

What part did Gretl and Norbert play in this commission after Moriz prevailed? When and how did they shape Hoffmann's designs? Gretl's diary suggests they had no say. They neither talked directly to Hoffmann about what they most wanted nor discussed these matters with Moriz so that he might pass on their requirements to Hoffmann. While there is no record of what Moriz and Hoffmann discussed, most likely Moriz simply specified which rooms Hoffmann should design and how much he was prepared to spend, then left everything else to Hoffmann.

Moriz's decision to commission six rooms was remarkable not just because Hoffmann had designed only five in the Wohllebengasse but also because the war had sent the Austrian economy into a severe recession. When Moriz approached him in May 1915, Hoffmann had received no big commissions all year and was to receive only one more. The Wiener Werkstätte was also struggling, prompting Otto Primavesi to become its managing director in the hope of revitalizing it and Moriz to become chairman of its board—a mark of his commitment to the Werkstätte and admiration for Hoffmann, who remained its chief designer.

Norbert could neither forget his defeat nor leave it alone. A week after Moriz prevailed, Norbert told Gretl that Hoffmann was ridiculously expensive. A week later he showed Gretl a range of architectural publications with designs that he admired. By then the apartment was a topic that Gretl feared because she knew it always ended with them arguing. She also accepted Norbert's judgment that she had been spoiled by the lavishness of the family apartment in the Wohllebengasse and wished, like Norbert, that she had not become accustomed to its opulence. Meanwhile, Hoffmann and his staff worked on the commission. Emil Gerzabet, who had supervised the construction of Hoffmann's most spectacular building—the Palais Stoclet for Hoffmann in Brussels—began by visiting the Untere Augartenstrasse so he could draw up a plan of the apartment's rooms. A month later the designs for the apartment were ready. As usual, these renderings were highly finished watercolors showing what each room would look like. While Norbert's name was on the floor plan as if the commission was his, Gerzabet implicitly recognized that it was not when he delivered the watercolors to Gretl.

The rendering of the kitchen was the only one signed by Hoffmann alone, indicating that this watercolor was entirely his work. The other five, typical of Hoffmann in this period, were also signed by one of his staff. While Wilhelm Jonasch was just twenty-three, six years younger than Norbert, he had already achieved a significant reputation as a designer in his own right as well as one of Hoffmann's assistants. Most likely, Hoffmann gave Jonasch broad instructions, then left these watercolors to him. They included many features, such as diamond patterns, stylized rose sprigs, and circular mirrors, that were familiar to Gretl from her parents' apartment. The kitchen was much more austere than any room in the

Wohllebengasse—almost everything in it was white apart from a black-and-white checkerboard floor. The other rooms were much more decorative. The greatest influence on them was folk art. When Gretl first saw the designs, they filled her with "almost unbearable enthusiasm." When she showed them to Norbert later that day, he fell silent, overcome by anger and resentment, then declared he could never be happy in such an apartment. Far from being sympathetic, Gretl saw his response as yet more proof that he was a dunderhead.

The following day, when the Gallias left to spend the summer in Alt Aussee, Norbert was at the station to see Gretl off, bearing flowers and presents as usual, while she was swallowing tears. Before boarding the train, she suggested they try to forget the apartment until he visited Alt Aussee, where they could discuss it in a more relaxed fashion. A week later he was there, staying at the village's one grand hotel while spending most of each day at the Villa Gallia, where he found Gretl in a new outfit that her parents had bought. It was a dirndl, a peasant costume worn by many wealthy Viennese when in the Austrian countryside, which Norbert characteristically disliked.

Their first conversation about the apartment was "peaceful and without ill-feeling!" Gretl recorded with surprise and delight. Their next, on July 8, her nineteenth birthday, was not. While Norbert derided every aspect of Hoffmann's work, Gretl could imagine nothing better. "I love Prof. Hoffmann," she wrote, "and find the drawings especially beautiful." When she refused to accept Norbert's criticisms, he accused her of having no confidence in him and she left the room in tears. Because it was her birthday, everything was magnified for her. When her parents asked why she was so upset, she told them without hesitation. While she knew it would fuel their opposition to Norbert, she did not care because she was beginning to think of breaking their engagement. When the next day was even worse, she thought of nothing else.

"A miracle happened," Gretl started her next entry. "Norbert apologized." She should not have been surprised. Norbert had asked her forgiveness whenever they quarreled. Because Gretl knew how much Norbert wanted to design their apartment and abhorred Hoffmann's work, she particularly appreciated his apology and, for the next two days, it was as if they had never argued. They talked happily, went for walks, and played tennis. As Norbert returned to Vienna by train, he wrote Gretl a letter that she recognized as his most passionate, thanking her for their many beautiful hours in Aussee and suggesting that they should forget the few hours that were not beautiful.

She transcribed her response into her diary in clear recognition of its significance, the first time she had done so. "You should know that I do not forget quickly," she wrote. "That is not my nature. I can forget only with great difficulty if someone has hurt me, especially if it has been someone I have loved with all my heart." She reminded Norbert of the pain he caused her on her birthday. She concluded that they both would have to change and make concessions. If they had another such disagreement, she did not know what would happen.

Norbert would not concede that he had spoiled her birthday. Having hoped to put their argument behind them, he now wondered whether they could. He took her conclusion as a threat that she would break their engagement, and he responded with a list of his aspirations, which began with him looking for good health, a stimulating job, financial prosperity, professional recognition, and freedom from serious worry. It ended with his embracing the language of "comrade," which Gretl also used. "Last but not least," Norbert wrote in English, he wanted a wife who would be his "*very best comrade* for wandering through life." While Gretl thought that they would be equals if they were comrades, Norbert did not. "*You only,*" he declared, "can know whether you have the courage to have confidence in my leadership!"

Gretl fainted after reading this letter. When she replied two days later, she railed: "Your first priorities are *your* health, *your* profession, *your* financial well-being, *your* reputation, and for you to live without worries. You come first, then you again and then nobody and only in the end, in your very last line, after a long pause, comes your wife." While Gretl liked the idea of being Norbert's comrade if it meant they were to be equals, she would not countenance being his inferior. Norbert, she declared, was not the devoted, considerate person she thought she had discovered on their many excursions but an immense egotist who did not love, understand, or know how to appreciate her. "Consider our engagement dissolved!"

Gretl stressed that she reached this conclusion after sleepless nights and reading and rereading his letters. She added—expecting Norbert would presume otherwise—that she had made her decision "free of influence of others and quite alone." She also admitted that she was so despondent that she could hardly recognize herself and, after signing herself "your dear Gretl," addressed herself to Mrs. Stern. "I kiss your mother's hand and am sorry to cause her grief as I love her," she concluded, then mailed this letter by certified post.

She resumed her diary four days later at the request of Moriz, who wanted her to transcribe all her correspondence from Norbert. Most likely, Moriz thought she should make her diary as complete a record as possible of this turning point in her life. He may also have thought she would find the transcription salutary because it would make her dwell on what had happened. In all, she had fifteen letters and cards to copy from the twenty days that Norbert and she had been apart, with three more letters already in the mail, as Norbert typically lost his nerve after challenging Gretl to express confidence in him. He wanted his "sweet, dear, treasure Gretelein" to know that he thought much more about her than she had ever realized, carried her photograph everywhere, and was planning to meet Hoffmann as soon as possible so that their apartment—and marriage—could proceed. "I l. y. s. m!" he exclaimed in abbreviated English. "I love you so much!"

Gretl expected Norbert to respond to her letter breaking their engagement, but the only reply came from her own uncle Adolf, who became involved at the behest of Mrs. Stern, who was close to Adolf's wife, Ida. When Norbert received Gretl's letter, Mrs. Stern rang Ida and met her the following morning, while Norbert consulted Adolf in his chambers. Rather than just talk to Adolf, Norbert brought him Gretl's letter, which Adolf might have recognized was something pivate. Instead, he scrutinized the letter as if it were a legal document and was dumbfounded by it. Adolf could not understand how Gretl could want to end her engagement yet feel lost as a result of doing so. He thought her letter typical of the illogicality of women.

While Norbert wanted to send a telegram to Gretl acknowledging that their engagement was over, Adolf advised him to go to Alt Aussee to talk to her. Norbert responded that he had a higher duty to study telegraphy, which was vital to Austria's war effort and could see him avoid being sent to the front and secure his rapid promotion. Adolf countered by offering to respond to Gretl's letter, which meant he became Norbert's advocate, even though Adolf probably saw himself as giving both Gretl and Norbert one last chance to resolve their differences. Adolf proposed that Ida and he meet Moriz and Gretl that Sunday in Bad Ischl, between Aussee and Vienna. If Gretl still loved Norbert as he still loved her, Norbert was willing to do anything and everything to regain her and achieve happiness with and through her. If Gretl no longer loved Norbert, he would not hold Gretl to her promise. If Norbert did not hear from Gretl within a week, he would accept that their engagement was over.

Adolf wrote all this to Moriz because he had no confidence in nineteen-year-old Gretl. Presumably, Adolf expected that his letter would be read only by Moriz or he would not have been so critical of Gretl. But Moriz immediately showed Gretl the letter, which strengthened her resolve. She was outraged at Adolf's assessment of her. She was incensed that Norbert had persuaded one of her relatives to act for him. "Had Norbert come here for a face-to-face discussion, everything could have been reconciled," she observed improbably. As it was, Gretl not only thought Norbert arrogant, inattentive, insensitive, and moody, she now also despised him. "I am not sorry at all," she wrote, even more convinced that she was right to break her engagement.

The correspondence continued man to man with another letter that Moriz asked Gretl to copy, even though it was as critical of her as of Adolf. In most matters Moriz deferred to Adolf, to whom he owed his opportunities in Vienna. On this occasion, Moriz declared he might have expected Adolf's letter from a twenty-year-old but never from a man of Adolf's experience. Moriz reminded Adolf that he should not have been shocked by the news since Moriz had told him from the outset that he was unhappy with Gretl's choice. Moriz went on to blame himself for his weakness in not opposing Gretl's engagement. He reiterated that Gretl had broken the engagement as a result of seeing for herself how things were.

The result, Moriz maintained, was the best possible. Norbert was so petty, moody, and illogical that he could not imagine anyone being happily married to him, especially someone as impulsive as Gretl. If the repeated arguments between Norbert and Gretl did not demonstrate their incompatibility, Norbert's unsuitability was plain from his failure to find the twenty-four hours to come to Alt Aussee to talk to Gretl. Moriz concluded that the last few days had provided him with more than enough excitement, Gretl was exhausted, and Hermine and he would be spending the weekend in Moravia. In short, Moriz did not want to discuss the matter further.

Adolf was undeterred. Since Moriz would not bring Gretl to Bad Ischl, Adolf and Ida traveled to Alt Aussee for a family conference. Adolf began by analyzing Gretl's letter, which Norbert and he had marked with red pencil, highlighting all the passages they thought unclear and confused. Ida went on to reveal that Mrs. Stern had cried all night and broken into a rash when she heard the news, while Norbert had cried like a child when he met Adolf in his chambers. Adolf explained that while Norbert thought Gretl had been acting strangely for weeks, he still loved her, was desperate to talk to her, and admitted that he had been insufficiently attentive and overly concerned about money. He also feared the gossip they would excite by breaking their engagement.

Gretl was enraged to see how Norbert and Adolf had treated her letter, which she regarded as deeply personal. She was appalled that Adolf and Norbert had not just highlighted her inconsistencies but also defaced the original rather than annotating a copy. She was shocked to learn Adolf had told Norbert many things about her that she thought should never have gone beyond her family. She regretted only the embarrassment she was causing Moriz, Hermine, and Mrs. Stern and would herself suffer from gossip. Yet surely it was better to have discovered Norbert's nature before she married him than to return to her parents' house as a divorcée after two or three years.

Moriz and Hermine helped Gretl to carry out her decision the following day by returning all those gifts of Norbert's that she had with her in Alt Aussee. They included her engagement ring, a pearl ring, two brooches, a pendant and chain, two silver baskets, two enameled boxes, a silk bag, a doll, one Easter rabbit, two wooden boxes, an engraving, a framed photograph, a notebook, a calendar, six books, and the *Song of Hatred Against Italy.* They filled a large box, which Gretl sent to Norbert in Vienna. By then, a small parcel from Norbert was in the mail and arrived in Alt Aussee the following day. It contained his engagement ring and a letter in which he relieved her of her promise, declared that further explanations and recriminations were pointless, wished her good luck with all his heart, and sent his best regards to her dear parents and sisters. "Thus finished my love," Gretl wrote later that day. "God alone knows how much I have loved him and how little responsibility I bear for the outcome. He was not worth it."

Norbert sent Gretl only his ring because that was all he expected her to return. When he received the box from her, he returned everything the Gallias had given the Sterns. He began with an even bigger box that contained a packet of letters, two briefcases, a writing case, three portfolios, two books, a clock, a notebook, a spinning top, a pillow, two pincushions, a pearl handbag, and the six Hoffmann designs for the Untere Augarten-strasse. He followed with another parcel containing a walking stick with a gold top that Moriz and Hermine had given Mrs. Stern. He insured each parcel for 1,000 crowns (now about $8,300), a third of his annual income.

The summer ended with Moriz and Hermine taking Gretl, Käthe, and Lene to Prague, where, despite their conversion to Catholicism, they immediately embarked on Jewish tourism with a Jewish guide. While the American essayist James Huneker thought Prague's Jewish sites were to be visited only "if you should happen to be in the mood antiquarian or ethnographical," they were the Gallias' priority. They visited the Old-New Synagogue, the oldest Jewish building in central Europe. They went to the neighboring Jewish cemetery with its chaos of old headstones, where Gretl was impressed by the grave of the first Jewish *Regierungsrat,* whose title was hereditary, unlike that acquired by Moriz. They inspected the Charles Bridge, where Gretl was struck by the statue of Christ on the Cross, erected by the Prague Jew Elias Backoffen in 1696 as a punishment for allegedly engaging in blasphemy, which symbolically humiliated all Jews because of its acknowledgment in Hebrew of Christ as the Lord.

This visit to Prague changed Gretl's sense of what it had been like to be a European Jew. The cemetery contained Jews who had died as "martyrs to their beliefs," Gretl observed. "There must have been shocking persecutions of Jews in Prague." Yet Gretl continued to display her ignorance of Jewish tradition. When she had first visited her grandparents' grave in the Jewish cemetery in Bisenz with Moriz, they had laid wreaths, in keeping with the Catholic tradition of floral tributes. If Gretl had visited the grave of her uncle Wilhelm in the Jewish section of Vienna's Central Cemetery, she would have known that, like many neighboring Jewish graves, it came with a flower box. She discovered that Jews generally did something different in Prague, prompting her to record, as something new to her, "Jews visiting graves leave pebbles as a form of tribute."

Her exchanges with "Engineer Stern," as she reverted to calling Norbert, continued in Vienna when she sent him another parcel containing the rest of his gifts and he sent her three more filled with the rest of hers. Meanwhile, Moriz and Hermine ensured that Gretl went out more than ever to keep her busy and to show that she was not embarrassed by what had occurred. At her most frenetic she attended six performances in eight nights, including three of Wagner's Ring Cycle. She also reestablished herself within her old circle in Vienna, despite initially expecting difficulties.

"I know the Mandls, Klingers, von Engels, and company will cut me," she wrote of some of the families whose balls she had attended after finishing school. But the only ones to do so were the von Engels, who were related to the Sterns.

Gretl saw Norbert once more by chance in November 1915, when Moriz and Hermine took her to the Vienna Woods. As the Gallias walked through the park at Neuwaldegg, where Mrs. Stern had her villa, they encountered Norbert, who was wearing his new Austrian infantry uniform. While he had snubbed one of Gretl's cousins a few weeks before when they encountered each other in Vienna, Norbert greeted Moriz, Hermine, and Gretl. Their perfunctory exchange gave Gretl even more confidence in her decision. Although it was just four months since they had last seen each other in Alt Aussee, Norbert appeared like a stranger to her. "I had to ask myself how I could have fallen in love with a man like him," she wrote. "He has an angry face and I realize now that people must have talked behind my back about my lack of taste."

It was just one of many entries in which she focused on her good fortune in escaping Norbert and told herself that she was no longer concerned about their breakup. Her marriage, she wrote, would have lasted at most a few years. It could have seen her in the mental asylum, Steinhof, on the edge of the Vienna Woods. Friends and family similarly dwelled on Gretl's prospects by suggesting millionaires she could marry. They emphasized Norbert's idiosyncrasies by telling Gretl how he was the only man not to wear black at her aunt Henny's funeral. Her father, Moriz, declared Gretl very lucky. Her brother, Erni, expressed his delight by getting drunk. The one exception was Käthe, who declared that Gretl shared Norbert's character and temper and, by implication, was just as flawed. While this barb was typical of Käthe, Gretl was still shocked. "I would never have thought," she observed, "my own sister could be so tactless."

6

Death

Austria was in crisis throughout 1918. Just as most of its troops were mal-nourished, so were a majority of its civilians. When the government announced at the start of the year that it was cutting the daily flour ration from seven ounces to five ounces, ten thousand workers at the Daimler armaments plant in the industrial town of Wiener Neustadt downed tools, triggering the one big Austrian working-class revolt of the war. Vienna was brought to a standstill as two hundred thousand workers, including many clerical staff and shop assistants, joined the protest. While Gretl usually ignored political events, she started her diary entry for January 17 with "Strike!"

The food shortages prompted Hermine to acquire one of the first Austrian austerity cookbooks. Published by the magazine *Wiener Mode,* it had a fashionable silk cover embellished with stylized floral sprays, resembling a product of the Wiener Werkstätte, which gave no hint that Austria was at war. Its text dwelled on how to use less flour, rather than how to do without. While emphasizing the need to use more vegetables, it still expected its audience to be eating meat. The pencil markings in this book suggest the family's cook used it regularly.

Most Viennese suffered profoundly as staples such as butter and rice disappeared from legal trade, and ersatz products (such as meat containing pulverized bark of birch trees) proliferated. The city's shops often could not even supply the meager rations of flour, meat, potatoes, jam, and fat to which all Viennese were entitled. While several suburbs experienced food riots, a man who had bought potatoes outside the city was kicked to death by several would-be purchasers enraged at having been turned away empty-handed. Yet as the novelist Thomas Mann observed in Germany, "It was thought an impeccable, respectable thing to break the law, live beyond one's rations, and pay insanely for what had been acquired illicitly." Erni, who took part in spectacular advances, terrible retreats, and protracted trench warfare on the eastern front before Moriz possibly intervened and he was deployed behind the lines training new recruits on account of poor eyesight, was the Gallias' procurer when he was in Vienna. One day he secured fifteen pounds of veal and forty-eight pounds of potatoes, another day 250 eggs.

The silver wedding anniversary of Moriz and Hermine in May 1918 reveals how little the Gallias were affected, at least when it came to major occasions. The celebratory lunch in the Wohllebengasse was five courses, a feast compared to what most Austrians were eating. The entrée was *Einmachsuppe,* a soup based on a roux of fat and flour with a piece of calf's head as its main ingredient. One of Hermine's favorite dishes, it was served with ordinary bread rolls as well as the long salt sticks known as *Salzstangerln.* Duck liver pâté in aspic followed and then roast fillet of beef with rice and bacon salad. The first dessert was *Hindenburgtorte*—one of many manifestations of the cult of the Supreme Commander of the German and Austro-Hungarian armies, Paul von Hindenburg. The second dessert, a compote of pears and peaches, was a creation of Austria's newest enemy, America. Everyone drank champagne.

Just as Moriz and Hermine continued to reserve the best seats at the opera and theater, so they still shopped at the Wiener Werkstätte, which became even more of a family concern when Moriz began chairing its board in 1915. While the Gallias' WW collection had been diverse when they moved into the Wohllebengasse, they came to own objects made of almost every material used by its workshops, including gold, silver, sheet metal, enamel, leather, ceramics, beads, lace, and fabrics. Like the Werkstätte's other main patrons, the Gallias were surrounded by WW objects at home and often wore and carried WW products when they went out. Gretl went to the Werkstätte as often as three times a week. She also received at least one piece of WW every birthday with the occasional gift in between, as she continued to be lavished with presents despite the war. One birthday it was a WW purse and WW book stamp. Another year it was a WW silk box. Yet another it was a small WW bag and travel case.

The work of the Werkstätte in this period was even more decorative and less functional than before. The artist whom the family employed most was Fritzi Löw, whose speciality was eighteenth- and nineteenth-century scenes populated by men in top hats, frock coats, and stockings and women in bonnets carrying parasols. After Löw joined the Werkstätte in 1916, Moriz and Hermine immediately commissioned her to produce a book stamp showing a young woman in a ruff playing a lute, a reference to Gretl's musical interests, which they gave to Gretl on her twentieth birthday. They also bought a set of Löw's watercolors, many of her postcards,

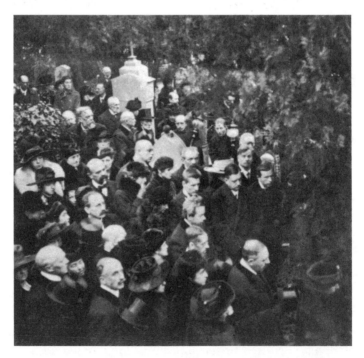

Klimt's funeral at the Hietzing cemetery, February 9, 1918. Moriz is toward the back in the top left, just visible over the shoulder of a bearded man. Emilie Flöge and Josef Hoffmann are at the head of the procession on the lower right.

and a mirrored, glass-topped box that had one of Löw's bonneted young women on its lid.

This attachment to the Werkstätte took many other forms. When the workshop's fashion department began to design costumes for Viennese theaters late in 1915, Moriz, Hermine, and Gretl went to one of the earliest productions at the Residenztheater, where Ida Roland wore WW in the title role of Ibsen's *Hedda Gabler*. When the Werkstätte opened a new outlet in the Palais Esterházy on the Kärntnerstrasse, the family attended concerts it staged in the palace's large empire hall, where it otherwise presented fashion parades.

Käthe's diary confirms that the Werkstätte was the family's favorite place for present buying. When the twins turned nineteen in April 1918, they each received a WW pendant and chain from Hermine's parents, a WW brooch from Gretl, and a WW pearl bag containing an ebony comb from Moriz and Hermine, who also gave Käthe a WW manicure set. When Moriz and Hermine had their silver wedding anniversary that May, the twins commissioned Fritzi Löw to design the book stamp celebrating their parents' marriage, while Hermine's brothers combined together to buy a much grander present—a silver coffee service designed by Hoffmann— which was the Gallias' most significant acquisition of his work since they moved into the Wohllebengasse.

Gustav Klimt, who suffered two strokes at the start of the year, also remained important to them. On January 23, when Klimt's health was still a matter of private interest rather than public discussion, Gretl recorded that Carl Moll's wife, Anna, had told Hermine that Klimt's prospects were bleak. On February 6 Gretl noted that he had died at six that morning. Three days later, Moriz attended Klimt's funeral in the Hietzing cemetery while Hermine stayed in bed with a severe cold. In the one surviving photograph of the cortege, Moriz is the bald, mustachioed man toward the upper left of the procession led in the lower right by Emilie Flöge and Josef Hoffmann.

The only major contemporary publication about Klimt contained fifty spectacular elephant folio collotype prints of his most significant pictures, including the portrait of Hermine and the family's beech forest landscape. While the first edition of *Das Werk von Gustav Klimt* was published by Carl Moll at the Galerie Miethke between 1908 and 1914, a second edition was published in 1918 by Hugo Heller, who succeeded Moll as one of Vienna's great cultural entrepreneurs. This portfolio became

Klimt's last work when its printing, which he supervised, was completed on the day his strokes saw him confined to Vienna's Sanitorium Fürth. Its cheapest edition sold for 500 crowns (now about $290); the most expensive, which came in a boar spear–backed box with silk endpapers and included an original Klimt drawing, cost three times as much. If Klimt had not died, he would have signed the title page and all the plates. As it was, Heller had to make do with a facsimile of Klimt's signature. When Hermine and Moriz celebrated their silver wedding anniversary, she gave him one of the thirty-five copies.

The majority of Klimt's patrons, including Moriz and Hermine, did not buy the work of the next generation of Viennese artists. The first one-man exhibition of Egon Schiele—held by Moll at the Galerie Miethke in 1911, when Schiele was just twenty—attracted almost no purchasers. Schiele's conviction in 1912 for displaying indecent drawings where children could see them fueled his reputation for immorality. But by the end of the war, Schiele's status had changed as his old work found more admirers and his new work became less confrontational. When Schiele compiled a three-page address book in 1918, Moriz was in it. When Schiele organized an exhibition of Austrian art at the Kunsthaus Zürich that May, which the imperial government hoped would bolster its image in neutral Switzerland by countering widespread reports of Austrian barbarism, Moriz lent two paintings.

The Secession's forty-ninth exhibition that March was also organized by Schiele, who again made it Vienna's most exciting contemporary gallery. His poster for the exhibition showed him at the head of a table of artists— in effect, as leader of the Secession—with one chair vacant, symbolizing the death of Klimt. He filled the main room of the exhibition with forty-eight of his own paintings, watercolors, and drawings. The result, Schiele declared triumphantly, was "an unbelievable interest in new art." While critics acclaimed his extraordinary draftsmanship, collectors competed for his work and the public flocked to see it. Gretl went three times.

The Secession's next exhibition, that April, was remarkable for one monumental painting by Albin Egger-Lienz, the greatest Austrian painter of the war. *To the Nameless Ones* was part of a series of battlefield pictures in which Egger-Lienz went from depicting swaggering, individualized, heroic soldiers to crouching, faceless, anonymous figures and then fields of the slain. If not for the war, the Secession would have held special festivities to mark the exhibition, which was its fiftieth. Instead, it simply held a private view one Saturday morning, which Gretl went to with Moriz. Twenty years after he started patronizing the Secession, Moriz was still attending its openings.

If only Moriz had been well. In December 1917, Gretl came home one afternoon to find her fifty-nine-year-old father in bed with a sore throat and "*Schüttelfrost*," or shivers. The following day Moriz was still there and, even though he got up a day later and soon seemed his usual self, he began experiencing renewed shivers and fevers early in the new year. As he continued working regardless, he occasionally went to the Graetzinlicht Gesellschaft, which was trying to make up for the declining market for its gas mantles by selling other gas appliances, including cookers, ovens, and heaters. He usually went to Johann Timmels-Witwe, a producer of liqueurs, spirits, punch, vinegar, and methylated spirits, with two factories but just nineteen employees, which he had bought when he stopped working for Auer von Welsbach. At the start of March Moriz stayed in bed for over a week. By late March Gretl was keeping a daily record of his temperature, which was low almost as often as it was high.

Moriz's doctors were Vienna's best. Friedrich Piniles was a Galician Jew, closely connected with many of the city's cultural elite, who became Vienna's foremost specialist on nerves and glands, resulting in his appointment as a professor at the university. Otto Zuckerkandl, the senior surgeon at Vienna's Jewish hospital, the Rothschild, shared Moriz's artistic taste. While Otto had his smoking room designed by Hoffmann and became a shareholder in the Wiener Werkstätte, his wife, Amalie, was painted by Klimt. When Piniles and Zuckerkandl first examined Moriz together, they thought he was simply suffering from a nervous condition.

They were wrong, but a host of other doctors were no more able to diagnose Moriz's condition than cure it. Moriz occasionally had better days, when he went for short walks in the gardens of the Belvedere across the road from the Wohllebengasse. More often he had worse days, when he could not get up, let alone leave the family apartment. By early April, he was largely confined to his sickbed, from which he tried to control his companies by giving instructions to his senior employees and saw friends such as Maximilian Luzzatto, Carl Moll, and the architect Franz von Krauss. When Hermine and Moriz had their silver wedding anniversary in

May, they restricted their celebratory lunch to their immediate family due to his illness and Moriz went to bed as soon as it was over. By then, Gretl was recording his temperature up to five times a day.

The start of summer saw Moriz and Hermine abandon their usual practice of going to the Villa Gallia with Gretl, Käthe, and Lene. Instead, they went alone to the Kurhaus Semmering, a sanitorium outside Vienna that Franz von Krauss had designed a few years before the Wohllebengasse. This sanitorium was an immense, luxurious establishment, including a music room, reading room, billiard room, and gaming room among its five floors, which promoted itself as a site of winter and summer cures, offering dietary and medicinal treatments under the supervision of three resident doctors. When Moriz and Hermine went there, they hoped the mountain air and sunshine would succeed where Vienna's best doctors had failed, enabling them to spend the rest of the summer at Alt Aussee.

There was no cure. When Moriz arrived at the sanitorium, he was still able to write in a firm, clear hand and oversee Johann Timmels-Witwe by dictating detailed instructions to Hermine for the twenty-three-year-old Erni, who had gotten leave from his regiment in order to run the company. A month later, Moriz did not even want to talk about his investments. As Hermine and he spent day after day on the terrace of the sanitorium, which offered a spectacular alpine view of the Semmering, Moriz lay in his deck chair, his eyes closed even when he was not asleep, wanting only to be left alone. In a letter to their children, Hermine acknowledged that he would never fully recover.

Gretl observed this decline when she made three day-trips from Vienna to the Semmering to see Moriz, to whom she otherwise wrote every day and talked to on the telephone, which still seemed to him a "wonderful discovery." Yet Gretl was dismayed when Moriz returned to the Wohllebengasse in early July to find him so weak, short of breath, and shrunken. Where he had set out by taxi, he came home by ambulance. Soon miserable days were followed by awful nights and times of crisis when Moriz's doctors—two, three, even four at a time and thirteen in all—wondered whether he would survive. It was "*furchbar,*" Gretl wrote, "frightening," especially as his doctors remained unsure what was wrong beyond their discovery of two bacteria, diplococcus and streptococcus.

Wealthy Viennese in a critical condition were beginning to be institutionalized rather than stay home. Gustav Mahler died in 1911 in the Sanitorium Loew, the preferred domain of the well-to-do. Moriz's brother

Wilhelm died there in 1912. Hermine's sister-in-law Henny Hamburger died there a year later. After Moriz's sharp decline in the Kurhaus Semmering, he remained in the Wohllebengasse, where his doctors oscillated between prescribing sedatives and stimulants, sometimes trying morphine, sometimes caffeine. From late July, Moriz often was only semiconscious. On August 12 he went on a lung support system and a day later he lost consciousness. He died on the morning of August 17 with Hermine, Erni, Gretl, Käthe, Lene, and Hermine's brother Otto at his side. The official cause of death was heart failure. He was fifty-nine.

The long-standing Viennese preoccupation with the "*schöne Leich,*" literally the "beautiful corpse" but in fact the "beautiful funeral," shaped how Gretl described what followed. Much as her uncle Otto described his wife Henny as "having died beautifully," so Gretl recorded that, after washing Moriz's body, they dressed him in his best businessman's garb and laid him out "beautiful and smiling!" When his coffin arrived that afternoon, they placed Moriz in it. "He lay there in his black suit so beautifully," Gretl repeated. Then Erni and Otto accompanied his coffin to the Hietzing cemetery together with Adolf and Ida, while Hermine, Gretl, and the twins stayed home. Gretl ended her diary that day by addressing him. "Live well, but not for always!" she wrote, confident they would meet again in another life. *"Aufwiedersehen!"*

The following day and the next, Gretl went to the cemetery and was struck again by how peaceful and relaxed Moriz looked in his coffin, which had glass at one end so his face remained visible. Meanwhile, Hermine bought a triple plot in the cemetery's Catholic section that could accommodate Moriz and her and their four children, if not also their husbands and wives, so the family would be together in death, just as Moriz and she had wanted them in life in the Wohllebengasse. Moriz's funeral was held on August 20. While the "*schöne Leich*" usually involved an elaborate, even pompous funeral, Moriz did not want one. In his will, Moriz asked for his funeral to be simple because "even in life I was no friend of formalities." In a codicil he went further, specifying that his funeral be private and announced only afterward. "It was beautiful and festive," Gretl wrote after it took place as Moriz had instructed. "We all cried for Papa."

The lead obituary in Vienna's *Neue Freie Presse* the following day provided a short account of Moriz's career, devotion to art, and illness. The notices recording his death and funeral and announcing his Requiem Mass were much bigger, filling almost a page and a half of the newspaper, more than anyone else who died that year. The family's notice identified Moriz as a *Regierungsrat* and a great industrialist. The three other notices, taken out by the Hamburger family company, the Graetzinlicht Gesellschaft, and Johann Timmels-Witwe, identified him not only as a director of these companies and the Trient-Malé railway but also as chairman of the Wiener Werkstätte.

Gretl's diaries suggest that the family's formal Catholic observance remained negligible. When she listed a series of family principles, she noted, "One uses Sunday to be rested for the week," rather than for churchgoing. In the first seven months of the year she had attended Mass and taken Communion just once at the Karlskirche, Vienna's finest baroque church, a few blocks from the Wohllebengasse. Moriz's Requiem Mass was celebrated there, too, because it was the family's local church and could hold the vast gathering of Moriz's friends, acquaintances, business associates, and employees. Afterward, a small group of relatives joined Hermine, Erni, Gretl, Käthe, and Lene at the Wohllebengasse for supper.

The following night Hermine called all four children together. They knew that Moriz had taken out insurance policies that entitled each of them to 100,000 crowns. While Gretl's policy had matured in 1916, when she turned twenty, the other policies were due to mature in 1919, when Käthe and Lene turned twenty and Erni, twenty-four. But Erni, Gretl, Käthe, and Lene were unaware that while Moriz had left the bulk of his estate to Hermine, he had given each of them an additional 400,000 crowns. This sum had constituted a fortune when Moriz made this provision in 1912—bringing each of their entitlements to about $4 million in today's money—but by the time Moriz died it had been slashed by inflation, so the children's individual entitlements were the equivalent of about $290,000.

The only other beneficiaries were charities. Moriz's four bequests of 1,000 crowns were token given the size of his estate and the collapse in value of the crown, but these bequests were still revealing: none went to Catholic organizations, while two went to the Jewish communities in Bisenz and Vienna, confirming Moriz's enduring attachment to Jewish institutions. Hermine divided another bequest of 20,000 crowns (or $58,000) among three charities, including the Jewish Institute for the Blind, as Moriz would have wanted.

Hermine returned to the cemetery the day after the funeral, together with all her children and both her parents. The next day they all went again, and then the next. It was too much for Nathan Hamburger, who had never recovered from a series of heart attacks late in 1917, prompting Hermine, Gretl, Käthe, and Lene to visit Nathan at least every second day at his apartment, while he never went to the Wohllebengasse. When Nathan died on August 26, Hermine had lost her husband and father, the children their father and grandfather, within nine days.

Convention dictated that the dead required attendance. As Moriz's grave in Vienna had to be visited and Nathan wanted to be buried in the Jewish cemetery in Freudenthal, which he had established, Hermine divided her family. Erni accompanied Hermine to Freudenthal for Nathan's funeral. Gretl, Käthe, and Lene stayed in Vienna to visit Moriz's grave every day, each of them always carrying a spray of aster, the flower that Austrian Catholics most often used for commemorating the dead. It provided a stark white contrast to their black clothes and veils.

Like other Viennese architects, including Adolf Loos and Franz von Krauss, Josef Hoffmann accommodated his clients not only in life but in death. When Henny Hamburger died in 1913, Hoffmann designed her grave in Vienna's Grinzing Cemetery. When Nathan died in 1918, his grave in Freudenthal was designed by Hoffmann, too. But Hermine, surprisingly, decided against giving Hoffmann another commission for Moriz's grave in Hietzing. Instead, she had a temporary stone erected.

Twenty-two-year-old Gretl was devastated by Moriz's death. She knew her place at home and in society would never be the same. She wondered what would become of her in a household headed by her mother. "It was the worst that could happen to us," she lamented at the end of August. "My only dearest father is dead. I have lost my best friend, my dear father, my greatest advocate, who has always helped and supported me."

Her entry a few days later was most turbulent. She railed that Käthe should have suggested that Gretl was simply playing the part of a grieving daughter. She accused Käthe of projecting her own lack of grief onto her. She recognized that, since Moriz's death, she had become "shockingly bad and vengeful." She concluded, quite bereft, "Father lost, everything lost."

She used the rest of her diary to transcribe her pocket diary from the end of 1917, as she had done with Norbert's letters after she broke their engagement. As Gretl revisited what had occurred, she underlined the critical points in Moriz's illness. She also gave her entries for 1918 a new title, which, even if she was thinking only of the deaths of Moriz and Nathan, had much broader application because of Austria's defeat in the war and the loss of its empire, as well as the deaths of Klimt and Schiele, which ended Vienna's extended period of artistic greatness. She looked on 1918 as "*Das Unglücksjahr,*" "the year of misfortune."

7

Sex

Gretl was unhappy even before Moriz fell ill, acutely envious of her siblings. Erni was generally with his regiment, but when he was in Vienna he spent most of his days at Johann Timmels-Witwe and was out most nights. Käthe and Lene belonged to the first generation of Austrian women to attend university, studying chemistry together, having benefited from the new educational opportunities for girls in Vienna that allowed them to graduate from a gymnasium. Gretl was still waiting to be married, with no prospects and fewer social opportunities than ever because of the war. She was also recording her weight regularly as she exercised with some effect.

Two of her most exciting invitations gave her rare opportunities to mix with Vienna's "first society." One was an afternoon tea at which almost all the women were *"Excellenzen,"* or "your Excellencies," and Gretl thought—she was not sure—that one was even a niece of the emperor. The other invitation was a supper for twenty-eight, where, Gretl recorded with amazement, the lowliest men were *Hofrats,* while all the others were either "vons" or members of the aristocracy, and they paid exceptional attention to her because, apart from Maria Mayen, a star of the Hofburgtheater, she was the only young woman present.

Her one suitor was Fritz Bunzl, a relative of Guido Hamburger's wife Nelly. After one encounter in 1910, Gretl described him as disgusting. When he came to the Wohllebengasse several times after Gretl broke her engagement with Norbert, she thought him much nicer and immediately sensed his interest. "Fritz would like to . . . but he can't or rather does not yet dare," she observed. As he became more forward, she enjoyed flirting with him but thought him too conceited, knew he got on her parents' nerves, and suspected his motives. "I have no intention of getting married for my father's money," she declared.

Her one infatuation was with Carl Lafite, who occupied a succession of prominent musical positions in Vienna, directing the Singakademie, running the Gesellschaft der Musikfreunde, and playing the piano as the accompanist of celebrated singers, but was still forced to bolster his income by taking private pupils and performing at private parties. Gretl met Lafite in 1916 at a dinner held by the parents of her best friend, Lili Pollak, where Lafite accompanied several of the guests while they sang. After Gretl twice seized the opportunity to perform her favorite song, Schumann's "Der Hidalgo," to Lafite's accompaniment, she declared the evening her most enjoyable since the start of the war, as if Norbert had never existed.

Lafite was soon testing her voice and finding it worthy of further exploration. After six sessions, he was sure she should develop it. Before long she had completed her first exercises, then mastered her first song as she immersed herself in music in a way she had not done before. A few months later, he was no longer "Professor Lafite" in her diary but "La." After he came to dinner at the Wohllebengasse, Gretl was full of exclamations, declaring him "charming," "delightful," and "divine." She described herself as intoxicated with him, a sensation she had never recorded while engaged to Norbert. "It was," she wrote, "as if I had drunk too much wine."

So she continued. When Gretl first saw Lafite accompanying the German bass Paul Bender in the Musikverein, she thought Lafite had eyes only for her as he entered the auditorium. "He looked at me so lovingly," she recorded, prompting her to declare this concert the one she had most enjoyed that season. After seeing Lafite accompany Bender again, she cried and cried. After encountering him at another concert, she observed, "If La had not been there, I would have cried with disappointment." After she saw him again at the Pollaks', she declared him "a dear, good, noble human being," just as she had described Norbert when they first met. "God, what an evening!" she exclaimed.

The relationship between an acclaimed musician and his female pupils was the stuff of Hermann Bahr's *Das Konzert,* which Moriz and Hermine saw in 1910. The play starts with the virtuoso pianist, Gustav Heink, about to leave for an illicit weekend with one of his students, arousing near hysteria among his other pupils, who are as riven by envy at her good fortune as they are appalled that she should be starting an affair when not yet married a year. Heink's assumption is that such adulation—and adultery—is his due as a musical celebrity. His pupil imagines he may be the love of her life. His wife begins by tolerating his affair in return for domestic harmony but, by the end of the play, has put an end to it.

Gretl was used to being in raptures over music and musicians. When she first experienced the work of Arnold Schönberg in February 1916, a week before she met Lafite, she was characteristically excited. It was a performance of Schönberg's first major composition, *Verklärte Nacht,* or *Transfigured Night,* from 1899, which initially provoked outrage because of its dissonance but soon appeared conservative when compared to Schönberg's twelve-tone music. Although Schönberg and Klimt are generally seen to have been part of opposing modernist groups in Vienna, exemplified by how Schönberg was championed by Karl Kraus, who derided Klimt, Schönberg's early works have occasionally been likened to Klimt's paintings. After a performance by Vienna's leading string group, the Rosé Quartet, Gretl exclaimed in her diary: "Schönberg is for me the Klimt of music. *Transfigured Night* is for me *The Kiss* by Klimt. Long Live the Rosé Quartet! Long Live Arnold Schönberg!"

Another concert by the Rosé Quartet a week later prompted Gretl to express her emotion before the entire audience in the great hall of the Musikverein. As Gretl described it, she suddenly found herself on stage, holding a red tulip that she happened to have been given earlier that day, and pressed it into the hand of the cellist Friedrich Buxbaum. While embarrassed by her actions, Gretl still thought this experience "too beautiful."

Gretl told herself that her infatuation with Lafite was more of this "*Musikrausch,*" or "musical intoxication." Gretl thought her infatuation was harmless because Lafite was twice her age and recently married to one of Vienna's leading women journalists, Helene Tuschak, who was at the forefront of Austrian feminism. When Gretl encountered Tuschak during the interval at one of Lafite's concerts—the first concert, Gretl recorded delightedly, she had ever attended alone—Tuschak and she talked together amicably. Lafite himself spoke to Gretl at their second dinner at the Pollaks' like a father figure who had no designs on her. "He thinks that one of these days I will make a very good wife," she recorded. "All I have to do is find the right husband."

Yet Gretl was sure that Lafite had eyes only for her, even when Tuschak was with him, and his response when they saw each other at yet another dinner party confirmed his interest. While Tuschak was present for the first part of the evening, she had left before the gathering broke up at three in the morning and Gretl needed to be escorted home. She recorded that when another married man wanted to take her, Lafite was very annoyed, made all sorts of claims, and prevailed, though he did not get to do so alone. Instead, the pair was accompanied by a niece of their hostess, whom twenty-one-year-old Gretl dismissed in a characteristic invocation of English as an "old maid."

Her most exciting evening in 1918 was a dinner held by her aunt Ida and uncle Adolf before Moriz's illness. Gretl wore her red dress. The prime attraction was Flieger Rittmeister Fix, a member of Austria's small air force, which was finding it even harder to replace its men than its machines as it lost all its officers every year. As Gretl described Fix, he was already divorced, a "*Mordsflirt*," or "devil of a flirt," but very nice and entertaining. Although one of her cousins had taken her to the dinner, Fix took her home—unchaperoned—and "courted her very much." She thought the evening "brilliant."

Moriz's sickness constrained her. After he fell ill, Gretl went to just two more concerts, one play, and a performance by one of Europe's leading exponents of modern dance, the Swede Ronny Johansson who, Gretl observed, was not just a "dancing genius" but had "beautiful legs and a wonderful figure," suggesting that, for all Gretl's efforts, she would have liked to be thinner. She also went to one afternoon party, one dance concert, and one private ball before Moriz's decline prevented her from going out.

Otherwise Gretl had private tutoring in English and French and spent part of each day practicing them. She devoted even more time to music, learning the violin and flute early in the year and the guitar later on, while the piano remained her main instrument. Her teacher, Malwine Brée, was best known for her book *Die Grundlage der Methode Leschetizky,* published in English as *The Groundwork of the Leschetizky Method,* which drew on her experience as principal assistant of Theodor Leschetizky, the world's most celebrated piano teacher, whose pupils included Ignacy Paderewski and Artur Schnabel. Until Moriz became seriously ill, Gretl had weekly lessons, practiced at least two hours daily, often played four hands, and occasionally played chamber music.

She also did the occasional piece of work for Moriz as he indulged her long-standing desire to be his secretary. Moriz would usually dictate two or three letters that she would record using the shorthand she had begun learning as a girl and continued to practice. She would then type up these letters. After Moriz was confined to bed, she did more of this work, occasionally taking dictation from him all afternoon, until he was too sick to run his companies.

Housework was almost entirely foreign to Gretl because the family had so many maids. But when the war led many women to leave domestic service for other work, reducing the Gallias' number of servants, Hermine required Gretl to do much more. Gretl usually worked in the family's front rooms, where she polished the floors, cleaned the windows, and treated the carpets with camphor to protect them against insects. She sometimes worked in the kitchen, where she did more cleaning, hung up the meat, and tidied the linen cupboard. She occasionally worked in the family's attic, which housed their laundry, and in the cellar, which was their storeroom. "Twice in cellar," she noted one morning as she began to think of herself unhappily as "very domesticated."

Hermine fueled this unhappiness. Where Gretl felt she deserved praise, Hermine criticized her and, when they quarreled, either yelled or refused to speak to her. The twins added their own barbs by emphasizing their superiority as university students on their way to obtaining doctorates, which meant they were largely exempt from helping around the apartment. Gretl's exasperation was apparent that Easter, which she celebrated by preparing eggs and sweets but without going to church. "I would really like to know why I am alive?!" she exclaimed. "If I at least had a profession, it would be very different. But I am not allowed to work as a stenographer-typist. The family looks on my piano playing as something utterly superfluous. And to help Mama?! That also is not straightforward! Sometimes I wish with all my heart that I had married."

A photograph of Hermine, Gretl, Käthe, and Lene, taken in late 1917 or early 1918, is revealing. Hermine is looking surprisingly similar to her Klimt portrait, with the twins on either side of her, dressed in identical

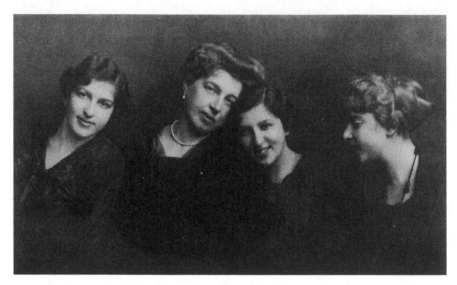

Lene, Hermine, Käthe, and Gretl, late 1917 or early 1918.

clothes with identical hair. Hermine's attachment to them is underlined by how she leans her head on Käthe, who also leans slightly toward her, a small smile of delight on her face, while Lene also leans in to the center, framing her mother and focusing attention on her. All three look at the camera, unlike Gretl, on the far right, whose face is in profile. Gretl's relationship with her mother and sisters is suggested by how marginal she is to the photograph. If she were cropped, we would not miss her.

Gretl's uncle Otto was her closest relative to flout conventional morality. When his wife Henny died in 1913, Otto recorded that only their "faithful maid" Dagmar and Henny's doctor were with him. Before long, Dagmar was not only Otto's housekeeper but also his lover, and by 1915, when Otto was serving as an officer in the Austrian army, she was pregnant. Rather than stay in Vienna, Dagmar returned to her native Denmark to have their baby, Gudrun, and then remained there at Otto's insistence. He did not want his family and friends to know that his housekeeper had borne him a child.

  Gretl's diary suggests that Dagmar's status with Otto's family in this period was more than that of a servant. When Dagmar occasionally visited Vienna while Otto was on leave, they went out together, accompanied sometimes by Otto's son from his first marriage, Robert. Just before Christmas 1917, Otto, Robert, and Dagmar, as Gretl always listed them—not only separating Dagmar from Otto but also putting her last—visited Otto's parents. Early in the New Year, Otto, Robert, and Dagmar came to the Wohllebengasse for dinner. That June, Otto and Dagmar again visited his mother and father before going with Robert to visit the Gallias.

All this occurred while Otto persisted in telling his family nothing of Gudrun. He probably had little opportunity to see her until she was two because of his service in the army. He also saw little or nothing of her after the war, when Dagmar and he went to live in Bruntal, as Freudenthal was renamed after the war when it became part of the new Czechoslovakia. As Otto and Dagmar purported to live in Bruntal as master and servant rather than as man and mistress, they left Gudrun in Denmark with Dagmar's mother until late 1919 or early 1920, when Hermine discovered what had occurred.

Her ideal would have been for Otto to emulate his brother Guido by finding a wife such as Nelly Bunzl, who was Christian, came with a big dowry, and had the social graces and cultural accomplishments of the middle class. After Guido and Nelly started married life in their Hoffmann apartment in Vienna, they moved to Fulnek, in northern Moravia, where Guido grew wheat and raised livestock until the Czech agricultural reforms of the mid-1920s, managed the Hamburgers' powdered-milk factory, and owned a sawmill and crate-making plant. The family's sixteen-room, three-story villa was maintained by a large staff, including a governess and chauffeur. Guido and Nelly mixed with local aristocracy, kept hounds, and went hunting.

The family member's fear of being wed for their wealth is patent in a story recounted by my mother over seventy years later about Hermine's youngest brother, Paul. He was one of many Jewish converts to Christianity in central Europe who thought of himself as marrying down to find a Christian partner. The Gallias and Hamburgers focused instead on the ambitions of his wife, Felizitas, usually known as Fely. "It was said," my mother wrote, that Otto's son from his first marriage, Robert, "courted Fely and possibly had an affair with her but that she, coming from a lower-middle-class family, preferred the wealthier Paul." Fely was "a very pretty, poor girl who wanted a rich husband."

If Otto had not been attached to Dagmar, the solution would have been simple. Like many middle-class men who fathered illegitimate children, he would have sent his mistress away, making some financial contribution to their child's upkeep. But Otto wanted Dagmar with him as a companion and lover while avoiding the shame of marrying his housekeeper. Hermine objected; she believed that Gudrun should be raised by her parents. While dismayed at how the family's reputation would be damaged by one of her brothers' marrying in such circumstances, Hermine demanded that Otto marry Dagmar and, because he was increasingly dependent on Hermine's wealth, Otto complied and brought Gudrun to Bruntal but left behind Dagmar's mother because she would provide even more proof of how badly he had married.

Gretl breached convention much more profoundly than her uncle. As with her engagement to Norbert Stern, she wrote at length about what happened in her diary. Her entries describing how she came to have sex before marriage were her prime reason for instructing Anne to destroy her diaries when she died. These entries were also why Anne kept Gretl's first three diaries and destroyed those that followed. Gretl's affair with Dr. Erich Schiller was the episode in her life that she was most ashamed of. She would have been especially upset that it should be revealed by one of her grandsons, whom she taught to be a "little gentleman."

The only surviving accounts of Gretl's affair were written by Anne, who otherwise knew nothing about Schiller. Her accounts follow the cliché of the experienced man and innocent woman, the predatory male and vulnerable female, of men wanting sex and women obliging them. In an early draft of her story, Anne wrote that Schiller "enticed Gretl to come to his apartment and seduced her." In her final version, Anne elaborated: "Schiller seems to have seduced her while promising to marry her. (It was probably not possible to celebrate an engagement while in mourning, and mourning for a father was worn for a year.) I am guessing that he may have suggested to her that waiting for more than a year was very painful to him. As she loved him, she gave in. After he had achieved his aim—I do not know how long the affair lasted—he declared that she was immoral and that he would have nothing further to do with her. She would, in fact, have made an excellent wife, it was just that she was totally inexperienced and unprepared for life."

The official period for mourning may not have been quite the obstacle that Anne suggested. As Gretl's relationship with Schiller seems to have developed in the first half of 1919, they would only have had to wait until

August before getting engaged and could have married soon thereafter. But Moriz's death almost certainly shaped what occurred by making Gretl even more vulnerable and volatile than usual—especially because of the intensity with which the family went about mourning Moriz. As Gretl recorded, they marked Christmas 1918 by visiting his grave six times in ten days.

Gretl may also not have been as ignorant about sex as Anne implied. In a lecture in 1905, Hermine's friend Elisabeth Luzzatto considered it self-evident that women of the future would fully understand the physiological side of marriage. At a meeting in 1906 chaired by Luzzatto, the speaker declared it much better for children—both girls and boys—to have proper sex education than receive more or less bad instruction on the street, from servants, or through illicit books. When Hermine and Moriz saw Wedekind's *Spring Awakening* in 1908, it was widely understood to be preaching the same message. Far from mothers corrupting their daughters by informing them about conception, they had a responsibility to instruct them.

Yet knowledge of sex was one thing for young women; having it was another. Erni exemplified the enduring double standard for men and women. When he was trying to act as my brother's de facto father after our parents' divorce, Erni drew on his own experiences as a young man in order to introduce Bruce to the ways of the world. He recounted how, as a young officer during World War I, he was often billeted with poor farming or peasant families and almost always had sex with their daughters—a typical instance of middle-class men of this era exploiting lower-class women. For Erni, these successes, as he looked on them with pride, were a normal precursor to married life.

Insofar as Moriz and Hermine knew about Erni's conduct, they do not appear to have minded, considering it acceptable for unmarried men to have a string of affairs. Gretl was in a different position. Had her affair with Schiller become public, her reputation would have been ruined and her prospects of marriage destroyed, regardless of her dowry. As it was, the loss of her virginity was a private disgrace. Anne wrote, "The family had not been able to prevent it and she now had to find a husband in what was regarded as her dilapidated condition." Hermine was scandalized. For all her appetite for representations of the "woman question" at the theater, she was appalled to be confronted by this question in her own household.

8

Marriage

A common image of Jews who converted to Christianity in turn-of-the-century Austria is that they expected not just to change their identity but to do so immediately. One day they would be members of the Israelitische Kultusgemeinde, part of the Jewish community, a widely despised minority; the next they would be Catholics or Protestants, accepted as complete members of the Christian faith, freed from prejudice and discrimination, incorporated into the dominant culture. When this acceptance did not occur, they felt even more rejected and alienated than before they converted. Yet could these men and women have expected their baptisms to achieve so much so fast? For all the outrage that their actions excited among some Jews, the converts' ties to the Jewish community, if not the Jewish religion, ran too deep. The process of exchanging one identity for another was too complex. Anti-Semitism in Austria was too intense. When these men and women converted, their hopes were probably much more modest. They knew their baptisms were simply a first step toward securing a Christian identity.

Their choice of spouse was vital in this process. If they married Christians, as Hermine's three brothers did, it reinforced their new religion. If their partners were *Konfessionslos,* or Jews, it undermined their conver-

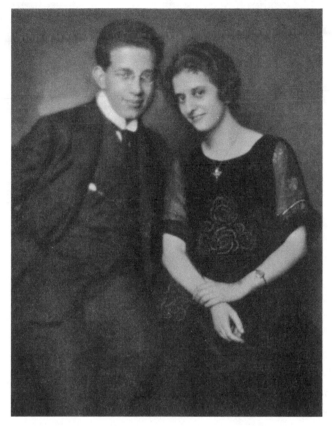

Erni and Mizzi, around the time of their marriage, 1921.

sions. Hermine wanted her children to marry Catholics and give her Catholic grandchildren. But Gretl failed to do so when she finally married in 1921, as did Erni when he married a few months later. Their spouses both came from families who were also part of the great Jewish influx into late nineteenth-century Vienna but, unlike Moriz and Hermine, retained their religion.

When I started this book, I knew that Erni met Marie Jacobi (known as Mizzi) during the summer of 1920 when she was visiting one of the many Jewish families who owned and rented villas in Alt Aussee. I also knew that, like Käthe and Lene, who were the same age, Mizzi was a student at the University of Vienna, although she discontinued her studies when she married Erni, in keeping with convention. She expected that she would never put her degree to use because, as a married woman, she would never enter the workforce. She thought it would embarrass Erni if she were Frau Dr. Gallia when he was Herr Gallia. Yet I knew nothing about the Jacobi household in Vienna and, when I began wondering about it, I thought my questions would all go unanswered. Who could I find sixty-five years later to remember anything about how the family lived in Vienna? On my brother's fiftieth birthday, in 2004, we visited Mizzi's one surviving cousin in Melbourne, Hans Low, who, it turned out, not only had occasionally been to the Jacobis' apartment in Vienna, but his sister Lore had lived with them for a few years in the 1930s and his sister Katia had also visited them. Hans offered to put my questions by e-mail to Lore in Slovakia and Katia in England, then translate their responses.

Only about one in ten of Vienna's 215,000 Jews was strictly observant. The Jacobis were among the majority who were not. They may not even have observed the High Holidays, attending synagogue only for weddings, funerals, and b'nai mitzvah. They did not keep a kosher household. Yet as Hans's sisters remembered it, their household still felt Jewish because Mizzi's mother, Anna, was a typical "Yiddishe Mama" who appeared concerned only for the well-being of her husband and three children. They recalled that Anna had no outside interests, never attending the theater or cinema, coffee shops or bridge parties. Her main conversation was: "Have some more. . . . Can I give you another piece of . . . You must have some. . . . Don't you like my cooking?"

The Jacobis' wealth was Mizzi's great redeeming feature. Mizzi's father was an industrialist who, while not as successful as Moriz, made good in Vienna. Adolf Jacobi's company manufactured corrugated cardboard and cigarette papers. He also owned a vast block of land in the Piaristengasse in the Josefstadt or Eighth District, a wealthy bourgeois area where Jews were almost as rare at the start of the century as in the Fourth District, but gradually became more common. The front of the block was occupied by a modern apartment building where the Jacobis lived on the *Nobelstock*. The other eighteen apartments and the two factories were tenanted. Two factories lay behind.

Paul Herschmann, whom Gretl married, came from a much less prosperous family. They met during Gretl's second ball season, when Paul was doing his compulsory military service after completing a chemistry degree in the German city of Freiburg im Breisgau. "Dr. Horschmann," a misspelling suggesting that Gretl had just been introduced to him, first appears in her diary at a "*thé dansant*" held by another family in December

1913, where he came last in a list of five men whom Gretl danced with and did not feature among those she particularly enjoyed talking to. "Dr. Herschmann," correctly spelled, was at the Wohllebengasse for the Gallias' soiree that Saint Stephen's Day. He was there again for their ball the following January, although, as Käthe later described it, all Paul remembered was "two small pink things running around"—in other words, Lene and Käthe herself, then aged thirteen, both wearing pink because it was Hermine's favorite color. Gretl, occupied with her Officer of Dragoons, was oblivious to Paul.

Gretl and Paul encountered each other again after the war, which he spent in the army. When Gretl went to see Käthe and Lene at the university one day, Paul happened to be there. When they met again at the Chemists' and Technicians' Ball, Paul escorted her home and, after seeing much more of her over the following months, he proposed. Their first extended period together was a trip to Berlin with Adolf and Ida as chaperones. A crisis, reminiscent of those punctuating Gretl's relationship with Norbert Stern, occurred when Gretl received an "indifferent" letter from Paul that left her crying, but this time there was a rapid "correction." Had his father not died in September 1920, they might have married sooner. As it was, they did not wait for the full year of mourning but married after six months in March 1921.

In their own terms, the Herschmanns had made good. Paul's paternal grandmother was a peddler in the Riesengebirge, the mountainous region on the border of Silesia and Bohemia, who had gone from town to town and market to market in order to support her children after her husband died young. Paul's father, Ludwig, came to Vienna, where he ran a bookshop in the Leopoldstadt before establishing a leather business buying and selling hides, a common Jewish occupation. By 1878, the thirty-year-old Ludwig was in a position to marry another Bohemian Jew, Anna Schick. Paul, the fourth of their five sons, was the first Herschmann to go to university. His youngest brother, Otto, followed a few years later.

Yet far from accruing the wealth to buy their own house in Vienna, like the Gallias and Jacobis, the Herschmanns rented their apartment in the Gredlerstrasse, a minor street in the Leopoldstadt where they lived from 1899. The family leather business was also relatively small and, when Paul's father died, he left it to his five sons regardless of whether they worked in the business and at least two did not—Bernhard, who had tertiary syphilis, and Otto, who was still studying chemistry. Once the profits were divided between all five, Paul may have earned no more than Norbert Stern—and he had none of Norbert's prospects of inheriting significant real estate.

Bernhard's illness was an embarrassment to Paul and a cause of fear and loathing among the Gallias. As Bernhard's health deteriorated and he began engaging in inordinate expenditure and arguing violently with his family, the Herschmanns placed him in one of Vienna's leading private clinics. A medical report reveals that he walked abnormally. His speech was impaired. He prayed extravagantly in Hebrew for more decent people of Jewish faith. He damned his doctors, accusing them of betraying him. He thought he could work miracles. He believed that all of Tolstoy's predictions had come true. He had become a sadist. He screamed. He ranted.

Gretl later wrote that she was very much in love with thirty-year-old Paul, who was the right age to be her husband, was handsome, and had the prestige of a doctorate in a culture where titles continued to be taken seriously. Gretl was also keen to marry and have children and probably feared she otherwise would not, as she was twenty-five and growing as stout as her parents. But Paul's antipathy toward Catholicism soon divided them. When he reluctantly attended the Gallias' Christmas celebrations after Gretl and he were engaged, he looked on the family's candlelit tree with a mocking smile, contemptuously lit a cigarette, and was generally scathing. While Gretl was hurt by his response, Hermine never forgave him.

Gretl had reason to be more tolerant of Paul's identity because of her enduring ties to Judaism. Her occasional use of Yiddish in her diaries was a mark of her origins. Another change in religion in the Gallia family was at least as significant. It involved her uncle Adolf, who was one of many Viennese converts to return to Judaism. Yet Gretl displayed clear signs of prejudice. Like Alma Schindler at the turn of the century, she disliked finding herself among too much Jewish company. After an evening at the opera, she observed, "All of Israel was there along with all of Aussee," then added, "One does not exclude the other!" When she went to *Le prophète* by Giacomo Meyerbeer, who was one of the prime targets of Wagner's essay "Judaism in Music," she declared the opera beautiful but still concluded, "I have no time for Jewish music!"

Under the Hapsburgs, a Jew could not marry a Christian without one of them becoming *Konfessionslos,* or embracing the faith of the other. While this law left it to each couple to decide which of them altered their religion, it was intended to encourage Jews to leave the Kultusgemeinde and generally had this result, so intermarriage became one of the prime vehicles for loss of Jewish identity and assimilation. When Austria became a republic following the end of World War I, this law was repealed so couples could retain or change their religion as they chose. While Mizzi was intent on remaining a Jew, she pressed Erni to abandon his Catholicism. His experience of anti-Semitism as a schoolboy at the Theresanium inclined him to do so—prompting him to regard his conversion as futile. But for Erni to leave the Church was still a profound step because it was such a rejection of Hermine's ambitions for him. Between his engagement to Mizzi and their marriage, he became *Konfessionslos.* Meanwhile, Paul and Gretl stayed as they were. He continued to identify as a Jew. She remained a Catholic.

Gretl's past became an issue after they were engaged. When she told Paul that she was not a virgin, he could have refused to marry her, although he was probably not a virgin himself. Alternatively, he could have declared that her affair with Schiller did not matter to him. Instead, he turned it to his financial advantage. Having already agreed on the size of Gretl's dowry, Paul demanded that Gretl and Hermine increase it on the basis that Gretl's loss of her virginity was a liability in the marriage market. Once again the Gallia family conferred. Erni tried to persuade Gretl to reject Paul because his demand suggested he was simply after her money. But Gretl was in love. She also felt guilty about her affair and, having braved the embarrassment of one broken engagement, knew a second would destroy any chance of her marrying. In March 1921, four days before Gretl and Paul married in a civil ceremony, they entered into a prenuptial agreement, a common arrangement when there were great discrepancies in wealth.

The agreement was complicated because the value of the Austrian crown was plummeting due to hyperinflation, which impoverished many members of Austria's middle class. Whereas 16 Austrian crowns bought one American dollar in 1919, it took 177 in 1921. Gretl, who provided most of her own dowry, drawing on her inheritance, contributed assets valued at 1.5 million crowns, which were highly vulnerable because they included bonds and treasury notes paying fixed interest. She also undertook to furnish and equip a bedroom, dining room, living room, and kitchen, including all utensils and linen. Hermine contributed another 1 million crowns in cash.

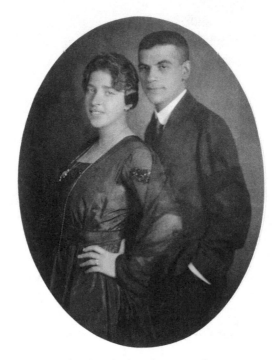

Gretl and Paul when they married, 1921.

Austrian law had long given husbands the power to administer their wives' property unless they entered into a legal agreement to the contrary. When Moriz married Hermine, he became responsible for the management of her dowry. The agreement between Gretl and Paul empowered Paul to do the same, entitling him to invest the 2.5 million crowns contributed by Gretl and Hermine as he thought fit. The agreement also specified that if Paul predeceased Gretl, the entire 2.5 million crowns would revert to her—a provision consistent with Austrian general law, which provided that the property a woman took into a marriage remained hers. If Gretl predeceased Paul without having children, his entitlement depended on the length of their marriage, like a reward for long service. If Gretl died within three years of their wedding, three-quarters of her dowry reverted to her heirs while Paul retained one-quarter. If she died between three and six years, Paul kept half. If she died between six and nine years, Paul got three-quarters. After nine years, Paul would retain it all.

Another provision governed what was to happen if Gretl died after they had children. Had there been trust between them, Gretl would have left Paul the full dowry, expecting him to use whatever he needed from it to care for their children and leave the remainder to them when he died. If she had doubts, she would have required him to preserve the capital while authorizing him to use the income for their children. The agreement provided that he was to get nothing, regardless of how long their marriage lasted. A final clause specified that if they separated, Paul was to vacate their apartment, leaving all the things the agreement identified as hers, and pay maintenance sufficient to sustain Gretl's usual standard of living.

According to my mother, Gretl bought ready-made furniture for her new apartment. After the arguments between Norbert Stern and Moriz over Josef Hoffmann proved so destructive, it is easy to imagine that Gretl did not want to risk repeating this experience. Yet a floor plan of the apartment drawn up by Franz von Krauss, who designed the family building on the Wohllebengasse, suggests that Gretl employed him again to fit out some of the apartment's rooms, while she bought mass-produced furniture for the rest. This question of design matters because the manner in which Viennese couples fitted out their apartments remained one of the prime ways in which they displayed their taste and standing. Architect-designed furniture enhanced the individuality of its owners; mass-produced furniture made them look common. Erni and Mizzi provide the most immediate yardstick. While Hoffmann designed two of their rooms, another two were by Wilhelm Legler, who exhibited with Carl Moll at the Galerie Miethke.

If Gretl employed Krauss, Paul and she started married life much like Erni and Mizzi. Both couples rented apartments in Hietzing, the fashionable outer Viennese suburb where Nathan and Josefine Hamburger had lived. Both couples commissioned architect-designed furniture, displaying an almost complete dearth of independent taste. Both couples employed one servant who did most of their cooking, cleaning, and shopping. Yet Gretl was acutely aware that she would have been living much more grandly had she married Norbert Stern. Rather than containing a salon, dining room, smoking room, and boudoir, the apartment included just a salon and smoking room. Krauss probably fitted out only two or three rooms rather than six, and whatever he designed lacked Hoffmann's cachet.

The greater wealth of Erni and Mizzi fueled Gretl's sense of disadvantage. The key was Erni's position as her father's successor, which saw him briefly replace Moriz on the board of the Wiener Werkstätte and immediately become the manager of the family liqueur company, Johann Timmels-Witwe, and acquire a half share in it. Although Erni displayed little aptitude as a businessman, this company was much bigger than the Herschmann leather business and Erni received half its profits, whereas Paul received just one-fifth of what the leather company earned.

Gretl's sensitivity about her situation and status is revealed by an exchange she had with Otto Hamburger's former housekeeper and new wife, Dagmar, who had just become the mistress of her own house with servants in Bruntal. The inversion of the two women's circumstances—the rise of Dagmar and fall of Gretl—was pivotal. When Dagmar observed, "You are living just like the proletariat," Gretl retaliated with, "You ought to know." Yet Gretl felt profoundly lucky in one respect. While Erni and Mizzi proved unable to have children, Gretl was pregnant within two months of her marriage and, in February 1922, she gave birth to a girl whom Paul and she named after his late mother, Anna.

The diary that Gretl kept about Anna is imbued with a sense of order and progress—of everything happening in the right way at the right time, with both sides of the family engaging with the new baby. Gretl recorded Anna's first sounds, first laugh, and first outing. She recorded Anna's first significant presents from the Gallias and the Herschmanns—a gold heart on a gold chain from Hermine and a bloodred coral necklace from Paul's wealthiest brother, Franz. She recorded Anna's first independent steps at ten months, while they were at a restaurant. She recorded the appearance of Anna's first tooth, a fortnight after her first birthday.

Everything else suggests the marriage of Gretl and Paul turned sour very fast. When she looked back on what occurred, Gretl thought their great mistake was their failure to escape their interfering families when Paul was offered a tutorship in Germany. Instead, they remained in Vienna, where the Herschmanns no more accepted Gretl than the Gallias accepted Paul. Hermine was especially difficult. When Gretl and Erni married, Hermine required them to ring her every day, bring their new spouses to the Wohllebengasse for lunch every second weekend, and spend part of each summer in Alt Aussee. While Mizzi dutifully went to the Villa Gallia every year, Paul never did.

The economy was another source of stress: Austria's defeat in the war saw the Allies strip it of much more territory than its main ally,

Germany—transforming Vienna from the epicenter of a multilingual empire of 55 million people to the capital of a nation-state of just 7 million, with borders more or less determined on linguistic lines. As hyperinflation accelerated and the value of the Austrian currency fell faster than ever, it took 83,000 crowns to buy an American dollar in 1922, compared to 177 a year before, so it became essential to spend what one earned as soon as one received it. Rather than taking a weekly salary from the family leather business, Paul began paying himself daily so Gretl could buy what they needed before prices escalated again. Since she had never managed a household before, Gretl found doing so under pressure particularly challenging.

Their different religions became even more of an issue as anti-Semitism intensified and Paul and Gretl had to decide Anna's religion. Had Paul followed Jewish matrilineal tradition, Gretl's religion would have been determinative. Since she was a Roman Catholic, Anna would have become one, too. But just as Paul insisted that she be named after his mother, so he insisted that Anna be brought up Jewish and Gretl again gave way. For him it was a matter of continuity, an extension of tradition. For her it was a reversion to something her parents had rejected.

Their first Christmas as a family of three exacerbated this conflict when Gretl wanted to celebrate it with a richly decorated tree and presents. Many assimilated Viennese Jews happily did so, just as they celebrated Easter with eggs. Paul maintained the antipathy toward Christian festivities that he had demonstrated before they married. He not only stopped Gretl from displaying any Christian symbols in their apartment but also denied her a candelit tree. All he allowed was one pine branch decorated with hearts, which, as Gretl described it, left her crying, with ten-month-old Anna licking her tears "like a faithful dog." Gretl and Paul probably separated shortly thereafter.

The *Scheidung von Bett und Tisch,* or "separation of bed and table," involving property settlement and alimony but not allowing remarriage, was the closest thing to divorce available to Austrian Catholics such as Gretl. Austria's civil code made it relatively easy to secure when both parties consented. If they had no children and the parties agreed on the terms of their separation, the courts would approve their agreement. If there were children, the courts had to examine the agreement in order to ensure it protected the children's interests. While the prenuptial agreement between Gretl and Paul simplified matters, as it identified Gretl's property and required Paul to pay her "decent maintenance," the courts had to weigh Anna's interests before they agreed to the *Scheidung* of Gretl and Paul in December 1923.

One of Gretl's ways of trying to convince herself she had made the right decision after breaking her engagement with Norbert Stern was her expectation that she would otherwise have been back under her parents' roof within a few years—the usual lot of upper-middle-class women whose marriages did not last. Gretl must have remembered this prognosis as her marriage to Paul ended and there was no question what she would do. Her inheritance and maintenance from Paul were insufficient to allow her to keep the apartment in Hietzing for long. It also ran counter to all social norms for a woman such as her to take a job while she had a small child. Less than three years after her marriage, Gretl was back in the Wohllebengasse with Hermine as well as Käthe and Lene, who had just completed their chemistry degrees after six years at the University of Vienna. To this household of women, Gretl returned with Anna, whom the Gallias promptly renamed Annelore, or Lorle, in a deliberate rejection of the name that Paul had given her.

The Gallia apartment looked much the same as a decade before when it was new. Whereas Adolf Loos did not mind if his clients rearranged his rooms, Hoffmann dictated how his patrons lived and Hermine was one of the most obedient. While she turned the smoking room into her study after Moriz died, Hermine changed nothing else. Although she could have afforded to buy new paintings or furniture, she did not do so. Instead, she maintained her attachment to the art and design of turn-of-the-century Vienna, regularly participating in their commemoration and celebration while ignoring what followed. When she lent her portrait to the Secession in 1918, it was the first time Klimt's work had been shown there since he led his Klimtgruppe out of the society thirteen years before. In 1921, she contributed two paintings to a retrospective of Moll's work held at Vienna's Künstlerhaus to mark his sixtieth birthday. She participated as both a shareholder and a patron when the Wiener Werkstätte reached its twenty-fifth anniversary in 1928, after once again almost going bankrupt, and Hoffmann and Eugenia Primavesi marked the occasion in style over four days, including a characteristically grand feast. She attended the exhibition in 1930 at the Museum für Angewandte Kunst, or Museum of Applied Arts, that marked Hoffmann's sixtieth birthday.

Hermine's fortune was in decline for reasons beyond her control. The introduction of rent control during the war cut her income from the other apartments in the Wohllebengasse. The taxes introduced by Vienna's socialist government required her to pay much more to the city. The triumph of electric lighting slashed the value of her stake in the Graetzinlicht Gesellschaft. The biggest blow was that Austrian war bonds became worthless when the Hapsburgs fell, depriving her of one-eighth of her capital. While Hermine was fortunate that many of Moriz's investments withstood the economic turmoil of the era, she struggled with her new status and responsibilities. One of the family's names for her was Minerl, a diminutive of Hermine. She came to think of herself as "*das arme Minerl,*" a woman who needed help.

Her establishment was still lavish, especially by the standards of the 1920s, when the number of women in domestic service dropped markedly. The most senior was the cook, who had a room to herself on the ground floor and was the one employee to be called Frau rather than by her Christian name, but, as in many wealthy Viennese households, she had access to the pantry only when Hermine unlocked it. Hermine's personal maid was the only servant to live on the first floor, so she could be as close as possible to her mistress. Two junior servants, who shared a bedroom below, cleaned and dusted the apartment and helped with the meals. Although Hermine took pride in how well she accommodated the servants, they worked from before breakfast until after dinner, with just half a day off every second weekend.

Several other women worked regularly for Hermine without living in. A hairdresser came every morning to put waves in her hair before pinning up her long plait. Two other women spent one week in every four doing the washing and ironing. A specialist lace cleaner cared for Hermine's collection, which she began forming when she married in the 1890s and then extended in the early 1900s when Austrian lace excited almost as much international attention as the Wiener Werkstätte. One of Hermine's former servants assisted on special cleaning days, polishing the parquetry floor with a brush strapped to one foot and a cloth under the other.

Frau Dr. Herschmann, as Gretl continued to be known, retaining both Paul's name and title, was a beneficiary of Hermine's wealth when she returned to the Wohllebengasse. Gretl did not have to pay rent and had few other expenses. Almost everything was done for her. Hermine even added to her staff by employing governesses to look after Annelore until she started her primary schooling. Gretl used this freedom to play the piano and take chamber music lessons with an accomplished violinist. She joined one of Vienna's leading choirs, the Singakademie. Like Hermine, she took up bridge, which became fashionable in the 1920s, and played at least once a week. She extended her range of languages by learning Italian and went on holidays by herself to Germany, France, and Italy.

Like other members of the family who benefited from Hermine's money, the privileges enjoyed by Gretl came at a price that Mizzi and Anne, if not Gretl herself, came to think excessively high. For all that Moriz and Hermine shaped the way she would be seen by posterity when they commissioned Klimt to paint her portrait, they could not control the stories told about her by members of the family who felt they suffered from the way she wielded her power.

As Mizzi saw it, Käthe was a victim of Hermine's rule when Lene died in 1926, at age twenty-seven, after another illness that Vienna's best doctors could not diagnose. As Lene's death traumatized Käthe because the twins had been so close—always sharing the same bedroom despite the size of the family apartment and maintaining their identical appearance by wearing the same clothes and cutting their hair in the same style—the last thing that Käthe needed was for her world to be diminished even further. But Hermine feared Lene had been poisoned by chemicals in the Viennese factory where Käthe and she worked following a stint at the family's powdered-milk business in Fulnek. Hermine insisted Käthe leave the factory and work for another family company, the Graetzinlicht Gesellschaft, which had been reduced to an outlet for gas stoves. Instead of pursuing her career as a chemist, Käthe became a shop manager who, at weekly cooking demonstrations, showed customers how to roast and bake.

Mizzi also blamed Hermine for Käthe's failure to marry, even though it was part of a much larger phenomenon: in the 1920s, marriage and children lost some of their traditional importance for members of Vienna's middle class. Women such as Käthe, who completed their university degrees, were particularly unlikely to marry and, if they did, usually married late and often had no children. The dilemmas faced by them even became the stuff of two popular Austrian novels featuring young chemists who decide that they would prefer marriage and a family to their career, though only one fulfills this ambition. Mizzi fixed on how Hermine obstructed Käthe's opportunities, recalling that whenever Käthe attracted a suitor after Lene died, Hermine went to bed, demanded attention, and prevented Käthe from going out so she would always have her favorite surviving daughter under her roof.

Hermine exercised her power over Gretl in other ways, requiring her to run errands in the city and deliver her instructions to the servants. She expected Gretl to be present when she had guests for lunch or afternoon tea and allowed Gretl to have visitors only if she was also present. She controlled Gretl's appearance by insisting she wear her hair long. She forbade Gretl from playing the Steinway grand piano in the salon—restricting her to a modest upright in her bedroom—even though Gretl was by far the most accomplished musician in the family.

Hermine's preference for Käthe and the enduring antagonism between Gretl and Käthe made Gretl's return to the Wohllebengasse even more difficult. Hermine's names for her daughters were indicative. She referred to one by the diminutive Käthelein, the other as plain Gretl. Hermine also reprimanded and criticized Gretl repeatedly and, because Käthe generally sided with Hermine, Gretl usually had no one to defend her. A rare exception, which Gretl treasured, was when Annelore did so as a small girl, inverting the hierarchy of the house. "No one," Annelore admonished Hermine, "speaks like that to my Mutti."

The rooms that Hermine allocated to Gretl and Annelore were even more telling. Since its construction, the apartment's two floors had created a clear divide between the family who lived above and the servants who lived below. Hermine could easily have maintained this divide by giving Erni's and Gretl's old rooms on the first floor to Gretl and Annelore. While Gretl's old room became Annelore's playroom, Hermine made Gretl and Annelore share a bedroom on the ground floor intended for servants. Following Gretl's broken engagement with Norbert Stern, affair with Erich Schiller, and divorce from Paul Herschmann, Hermine considered Gretl a social embarrassment and moral failure deserving of punishment and, even though Annelore was blameless, treated her the same.

Their stigma was acute. Gretl and Annelore were probably the only mother and daughter in Vienna from such a wealthy family who shared a bedroom for so long, let alone one on the servants' floor. The position of their room shaped how they were treated by family, friends, acquaintances, and servants and how they saw themselves. Gretl and Annelore were, of course, superior to the servants, yet they were inferior to Hermine and the twins. For all the privileges that Gretl and Annelore enjoyed within the Wohllebengasse, they were also pariahs.

The stairs provided one of the great metaphors of class relations and social position in the homes of the rich in the early twentieth century. There was not just the language of "upstairs," "downstairs," and "below the stairs." There were also the servants whom the English dubbed "twee-nies," or between-stairs maids, who assisted both the cook and the house-keeper and thus were constantly moving between floors. As Gretl and Annelore were also required to do so, Gretl drew on this metaphor to evoke their place in Good Living Street. According to Gretl, they lived on the stairs.

III

ANNELORE

Memory

Annelore revealed little of herself in the diaries that she kept as a ten- and eleven-year-old. Her opening entry, made in Alt Aussee in August 1932, was typically bland. "Before lunch I went to the swimming school," she wrote. "The weather is beautiful. In the afternoon I went to the Sommersbergersee with Mutti and Käthe." No wonder she opted to rely on her memories when I asked her to write about her life. Yet when she read these diaries carefully after working on her story for a year, they disturbed her more than any other family papers. The difference was that the papers of Moriz, Hermine, Gretl, Käthe, and Lene contained more or less what she expected. Even though many of the incidents they described were new to her, she did not find them surprising. Her diaries were a shock because of the gulf between her entries and her memories—a gulf that made her wonder what she had done and how she had acquired her identity.

As Anne remembered it, her childhood was abnormal in its isolation, which came not just with being an only child and the one Gallia or Herschmann of her generation but also with having almost no friends her own age. As she thought of herself as having "virtually only adult company," she blamed Hermine. She recalled that when she invited one of her classmates to the Wohllebengasse, Hermine was scandalized to discover her friend was illegitimate, stopped Annelore's seeing her again, and began vetting all invitations that Annelore wanted to extend or accept. Just two girls met Hermine's standards.

The diary entries made by Annelore in Vienna were consistent with these memories. She went just twice to visit other girls and had only one girl over to the Wohllebengasse in seven months. Annelore's entries for Alt Aussee could not have been more different. They showed that far from being alone during the summer of 1932, she played with other girls almost every day. She swam in the lake, learned to ride a bicycle, played Ping-Pong and tennis, and cooked with them. They sometimes came to the Villa Gallia; she sometimes went to their houses. While she occasionally described herself as bored, her happiness was usually clear. "I can ride a bike," she recorded one day. "It was fun," she wrote after another.

Many of Anne's other childhood memories related to the grave in the Hietzing cemetery where Moriz and Lene were buried. As Anne remembered it, she had to go to there every Sunday, as well as on religious festivals such as All Souls' Day and All Saints' Day. While she occasionally went with Käthe, she generally accompanied Hermine, who turned these outings into social events with a competitive edge. As they walked around the cemetery so Hermine could meet acquaintances and confirm that the Gallia grave was decorated with the most beautiful flowers, Annelore's boredom and frustration grew. She hated how these visits ruined her Sundays, the one day of the week in Austria when there was no school.

Her diaries tell a different story. They record one visit to the grave of Otto Hamburger's first wife, Henny, in Vienna's Grinzing Cemetery "obeying Grandmother's command"; another to the Gallia grave in Bzenec, as Bisenz had become known following the war; and a third to the Hietzing cemetery on All Saints' Day. That was it. During the seven months that Annelore recorded her daily life in Vienna, she did not go once to the Hietzing cemetery on a Sunday, let alone every week. For the one period when Anne could test her memories against a contemporaneous record, they were wrong.

Anne's solution was to write a chapter about what her diaries revealed, while leaving the rest of her story based on her memories intact. She wrote: "It could be that my memories are wrong but it could also be that the seven months covered by the diary are atypical. Perhaps there was one summer in which I had playmates, but the other summers I had none. Perhaps the compulsory cemetery visits that I remember came later." Otherwise she was unforgiving. If her diaries were typical and her memories were wrong, she had only this explanation: "I was so spoiled that if I did not like anything I exaggerated it and it stuck in my memory in that form." She accepted one of Mizzi's observations about her that characteristically combined affection with criticism. Mizzi always said, Anne wrote, that after her upbringing in the Wohllebengasse, it was a wonder she turned out at all.

Most of her memories were unhappy. They started with Gretl's twenty-ninth birthday in the summer of 1925 when Gretl and she were in Alt Aussee as usual. Annelore, who was already being schooled in etiquette—required not just to say "*Küss die Hand*," or "kiss the hand," but to do so every morning and evening, just as Gretl had done as a girl—went outside to play, climbed a fence, and tore the pink frock that Hermine had just given her. "The outcry at this awful deed was such that it has stayed with me for over sixty years," Anne wrote. "Although I was only three, I was dressed up and expected to behave like a lady."

Hermine controlled her in many ways—prohibiting her from eating bananas because she thought they transmitted polio, requiring her to wear her hair in plaits over her ears throughout junior high school when the fashion was for girls to have their plaits behind their ears, and insisting that she wear pink or red, which made her prefer white and blue. Gretl, full of fears after Annelore nearly died of a blocked intestine as a one-year-old, instructed Annelore to go to the toilet as often as possible at school and insisted that she place a paper cover on the toilet seat to avoid infection. Käthe was more liberal, occasionally buying Annelore a banana in Aussee, although only when Hermine was not there.

Annelore particularly resented her skating outfit because Vienna's largest outdoor rink, the Eislaufverein, was the place where she most wanted to look stylish. She wanted to impress her German teacher, Ilse Hornung, who was one of Europe's leading figure skaters when Austrians took immense pride in their success on the rink. As Annelore developed a crush on Hornung, she wrote repeatedly about her idol's "sweet" clothes, such as very short pants and Yugoslav slippers or tight trousers and a very short sweater that exposed Hornung's midriff. Annelore longed for a new pair of white skates and a new skating dress with a flared skirt that would "fly." Instead, for all of her expensive new outfits, she had to make do with Gretl's brown skates and one of Käthe's velvet dresses.

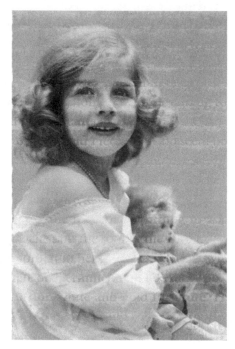

Annelore, aged three, 1925.

As Anne remembered it, the only clothing that she received despite Hermine's disapproval was a pair of tennis shorts that were cut so that they looked like divided skirts. While the American Alice Marble created a sensation when she introduced these shorts to the international tennis scene in 1932, within a year they were nowhere near as controversial. Annelore still wore a knee-length skirt that summer and the next, but got the shorts she wanted in 1935 from Käthe, who exploited the privileges that came with being Hermine's favorite to help make herself Annelore's favorite. Had Gretl wanted to give these shorts to Annelore, Hermine would have stopped her, even though Gretl was Annelore's mother.

This competition between Gretl and Käthe was so much part of Anne's life that she took it for granted when writing her story, neither discussing its oddity nor exploring how it came to be. The answer, most likely, lay not just in Käthe's own failure to have children but in the death of Lene. As Käthe looked for a substitute for her twin, she fixed on Annelore and, whether consciously or not, took every opportunity to supplant Gretl. The theater was a prime example, as Annelore became what

Käthe described as a "*Theaternarr*," or "theater addict." While Gretl took Annelore to her first evening performance not long after she turned ten in 1932, Käthe was soon using Christmas to give Annelore ever more theater outings, until Gretl trumped Käthe in 1936 by promising to take Annelore to the Burgtheater fifteen times, so as to stop Käthe from eclipsing her in Annelore's affection.

The earliest photographs of Annelore suggest a very different childhood. The Viennese studio Jobst, which took two or three portraits of her every year until she was four, created compelling images of her as a radiantly happy girl. A series from 1925 showing the three-year-old Annelore in the pink frock that she was soon to tear is particularly striking. Whereas this dress represented the start of her overly controlled childhood in Anne's memories, Jobst showed her looking self-assured, eager, excited, and full of wonderment at the world.

Two portraits of Annelore from 1931 are much closer to her later image of herself. They both were taken by Vienna's leading celebrity photographer between the wars, Trude Fleischmann. One shows the nine-year-old Annelore almost pouting, not quite sulking, in her first theater dress, a sleeveless satin outfit, and wearing lipstick and a string of pearls. This portrait brings out the wealth and sophistication of Annelore's upbringing, making her look like a starlet. The other, which shows her in a sailor suit and the same string of pearls, makes Annelore appear older than her nine years, even though the sailor suit establishes this portrait as an image of childhood. Sad, serious, and resentful, she stares at the camera, one eyebrow raised, challenging the viewer. Why, she seems to ask, do I have to be here? Why are you making me do this?

Anne recalled nothing about Fleischmann when I asked her. She was photographed far too often for any of her portrait sessions to stick in her memory. But her clothes were another matter because they caused her such resentment and embarrassment as a girl. At the end of her life, she could recall who had given her most of what she wore in her childhood photographs and when she had been forced to wear these outfits and could add color to these sepia and black-and-white prints, recalling that her theater outfit was blue with red flowers and that the sailor suit came with a matching blue cap and a white blouse. She remembered even more about her string of pearls, which exemplified for her how she had been overindulged as a child. She received these pearls one Christmas when she decided that, rather than opening her presents all at once, she would extend her pleasure and excitement by opening one each day. She started on Christmas Eve and finished on the ninth of February. The pearls were in the last parcel. By then, she was bored and there was a new swag of presents, since February 9 was her birthday.

The Christmas was either 1929 or 1930—the first years of the Great Depression. Hermine's finances must have been affected, the turmoil was so great. Yet just as much of the family fortune survived the inflation of the war years and the hyperinflation of the early 1920s, so it survived the crises of the late 1920s and early 1930s. Hermine retained the houses in the Wohllebengasse and Alt Aussee. The family companies—Johann Timmels-Witwe, the Graetzinlicht Gesellschaft, and Hamburger and Co.—continued to operate. So did many other companies in which Hermine had shares. Although Hermine's shareholding in the Wiener Werkstätte became worthless when the Depression forced it to close, its disappearance in 1932 had emotional rather than financial significance for Hermine. While she was one of just three remaining shareholders in the Werkstätte, she owned only 1 percent of it.

Anne was too young to know much of how the adults around her responded to the Depression. She remembered that Erni and Mizzi joined a scheme that saw the well-to-do invite a hungry child for lunch once a week, while Hermine would simply throw a coin to the beggar who sat on their street corner. Just as Gretl had gone through World War I getting ever more presents, so did Annelore during the Depression. Most were new, bought regardless of the economic conditions. But nearly all of the jewelry, including the string of pearls, was old, bought in the early 1900s by Moriz and Hermine for Gretl, Käthe, and Lene.

The transmission of this jewelry from one generation to the next was a goal that Gretl expressed already as a girl, most likely echoing Moriz and Hermine. When she received an exceptionally beautiful bracelet on her eleventh birthday, Gretl wrote that she looked forward to giving it to one of her daughters one day. By the time she became a parent, Gretl had turned this wish into a matter of principle and point of pride. "*Schmuck kauft man nicht, Schmuck hat man*"—"One does not buy jewelry, one has it"—she would say. Its transfer to Annelore demonstrated the Gallias' enduring wealth and capacity to withstand the greatest economic crises. Christmas for Annelore in the Great Depression started forty-seven days of presents that ended with pearls.

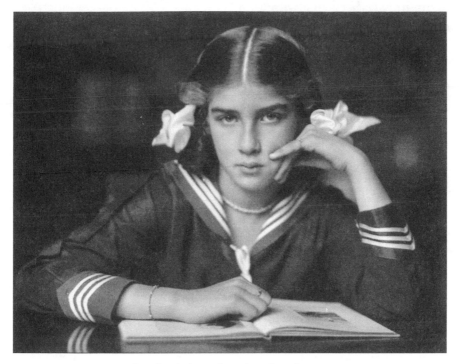

Annelore in her sailor suit and pearls, 1931.

The best opportunity for Gretl and Annelore to leave the Wohllebengasse came when Gretl's aunt Ida died in 1929, almost five years after her husband, Adolf. Because Ida and Adolf had no children of their own, they divided their property among their nephews and nieces. The smallest beneficiaries received one forty-second of the estate, which was a large sum because Adolf and Ida had been so rich. The greatest beneficiary was Gretl, who was bequeathed two twenty-firsts because Ida and she were particularly close. Ida also felt Hermine had mistreated Gretl after Gretl's divorce from Paul, and she wanted to put thirty-five-year-old Gretl in a position where she could rent an apartment of her own. But Frau Herschmann-Gallia, as Gretl increasingly styled herself, lacked the nerve.

Gretl's custody of Annelore immediately became an issue since her separation agreement with Paul gave her Annelore only until she turned seven—a custody arrangement adopted in many countries as the absolute rights of fathers began to be displaced on the basis that mothers were better suited during children's "tender years." Anne thought Paul had no desire to have her living with him. Most men of Paul's generation paid scant attention to small children and had little idea what to do with them. Paul also had no one to look after Annelore while he worked. But when Ida died, Paul thought Gretl's inheritance justified a reconsideration of his maintenance payments and threatened to exercise his right to take Annelore. Rather than call his bluff, Gretl accepted reduced payments.

Paul's visits to the Wohllebengasse to see Annelore were complicated by Hermine, who prohibited him from using the building's main entry, not only to ensure she never encountered Paul again but also to humiliate him. Just as Hermine forced Gretl to occupy a room next to the servants, so she made Paul use the servants' stairs and stay on the ground floor. When Annelore was little, he would see her in the bedroom she shared with Gretl in the Wohllebengasse. Later, he usually took her out. Her diaries reveal that she wrote to Paul twice while she was in Alt Aussee over the summer of 1932, then saw him every week or two after she returned to Vienna but saw much less of him the following year.

What did a forty-year-old divorced father do with his ten-year-old daughter on such outings in the Viennese autumn and winter of 1932 and the early spring of 1933? He took her to four films and always bought her the program, which she stuck into her diary. He took her twice to Gerstner, the old imperial patisserie on the Kärntnerstrasse in Vienna's First District. He took her twice to see other members of his family. He took her twice to the circus, once to a park, and once for a walk. If he took her to his own home in the Gredlerstrasse, she did not record it. If he told her about the death in December 1932 of his brother Bernhard in Vienna's main asylum, Steinhof, where Gretl imagined she might be incarcerated had she married Norbert Stern, Annelore also failed to note it.

Her best memory of Paul involved Goethe's *Faust*, which she first encountered in 1933 when Gretl took her to a bowdlerized production at Salzburg's puppet theater. When eleven-year-old Annelore responded by wanting to read Goethe's text after returning to Vienna, Hermine characteristically tried to exercise control and refused permission. Because of Faust's seduction of the beautiful young Gretchen, which results in her falling pregnant and killing her baby, Hermine ruled that Annelore was too young, only for Paul to read *Faust* with Annelore, leaving out the Gretchen story. He did so as a matter of family tradition. Just as Goethe was one of the favorite authors of Paul's father, so *Faust* was one of Paul's favorite plays. He also enjoyed the opportunity to demonstrate that while

Hermine could make him use the servants' stairs, she could not entirely control him. Annelore was delighted to defy Hermine. Like Paul, she came to know much of *Faust* by heart.

Annelore's diary reveals that she enjoyed some of her outings with Paul. She described her visit with him to see his mother's one surviving sister, Elisabeth Schick, as "very nice," their other family visit as "quite nice." She must have relished their visits to Gerstner as she had great memories of its food, especially its ice creams in the shape of fruits and birds. Yet she also recorded that she was "very pleased" when Paul called to say that he would not be taking her out one public holiday and underlined the "very" for emphasis. She thought one of her afternoons with him was "pfui!"— her most common exclamation of disgust. After he collected her on Christmas Day, she asked him to come upstairs, knowing he would not, and she was right, so they were together only half an hour. "I was delighted," she concluded.

As Anne recalled it almost sixty years later, she wanted Paul out of her life. The catalyst was her decision to learn the cello, inspired by her cousin, Hans Troller, a grandson of Moriz's sister Fanny, who displayed great promise as a musician. After Hans spent part of the summer of 1935 in Alt Aussee, Annelore wrote to Paul asking for his cello, which he had not played since he was a young man. While Paul obliged, he gave it to her exactly how it was after years of neglect, devoid of strings. After she wrote to him expressing her outrage, having never received a present in such a state, he stopped their outings, which, she declared, was what she had been "aiming for in any case."

Annelore's connection with Judaism was always tenuous. Her only Jewish instruction was at school, when she attended the Jewish classes held twice each week. She never practiced Judaism at the Wohllebengasse, where she was surrounded by Christians. She never went to synagogue. While Paul insisted that she stay home from school on most of the Jewish High Holidays, she otherwise ignored them. Her observance of Yom Kippur in 1932 was probably typical. While Orthodox Jews ate much more than usual the day before Yom Kippur, then fasted from before sunset until the first stars appeared the following night, many Liberal Jews treated it like any other day. After Annelore spent the morning at the Wohllebengasse, Paul took her to Gerstner, her favorite café.

She came to regard his identification as a Jew as a form of hypocrisy since he had little or no faith. She lambasted him for failing to introduce her to Judaism in such a way that she was glad to be a Jew. Yet she wanted less Judaism as a girl, not more. Far from appreciating being able to stay at home on the Jewish High Holidays, she resented not being able to attend class with her Christian classmates. She was at least as unhappy about having to attend the Jewish religious instruction classes at school. When her teacher tried to introduce her to Hebrew, she misbehaved. Paul's insistence that she be a Jew was central to her rejection of him.

"Let Mummy tell you how she was Saint Joseph once and an angel another time," Gretl suggested to my brother, Bruce, in the early 1960s, implying that Annelore happily played these roles as a girl. Anne's memories were different. She recalled just one Nativity play staged by her class after she started high school, like Gretl, at the Frauen-Erwerb-Verein. Another Jewish girl was chosen to be Joseph, while Annelore was delighted to be an angel. Gretl supported her participation by giving her one of her best nightdresses as a costume. Then, to Annelore's distress, her religious instruction teacher discovered what was afoot and objected to his pupils celebrating a Christian festival. This "huge row" meant she never took part in such a play again.

Her favorite books included Felix Dahn's *Ein Kampf um Rom,* or *A Fight for Rome,* one of the most influential German novels to contrast Jews and Germans. While the Germans in Dahn's book are beautiful, blond, blue-eyed, virtuous, and courageous, the Jews are generally ugly, untrustworthy, more or less perverted, exploitative, and incapable of spiritual feeling. When Anne reread it in Australia, she was struck by its "very Germanic outlook," characterizing it as "Wagner without music." She also recognized that she had not realized as a girl that it was a political tract designed to mythologize the German race and fuel antipathy toward Jews. "I did not really understand what I was reading," she observed.

Annelore embraced Christian festivals because of the presents she received, the special food she got to eat, and her sense of participation rather than exclusion. One highlight was her *Namenstag,* or feast day in July. Another was Alt Aussee's *Kirtag,* or church day, in September. The most entrancing was Christmas, which started each year for Annelore with one or more visits to the Christkindlmarkt outside Vienna's cathedral, St. Stephen's, where the stalls sold toys, Christmas decorations, and roast chestnuts. Then she would watch as Hermine supervised the installation of a richly decorated tree in the family's apartment, and presents for each member of the family were piled high on separate tables. As Christmas Eve approached, Annelore would wait impatiently for the candles on the tree to be lit because Hermine would then ring a bell, signifying the start of the *Bescherung,* or exchange of presents, allowing Annelore to open her gifts. One year she even had a vision of the Christ child with a Christmas tree in hand running over the roof of the house opposite toward the Wohllebengasse.

Her first visit to a major Catholic site was with Ida, who went on the same religious journey as Adolf so long as they were married, converting from Judaism to Catholicism and then reverting to Judaism, only to re-embrace Catholicism almost immediately after Adolf died. Four years later, when Ida sought the intercession of the Virgin at Austria's most important place of pilgrimage, Mariazell, she was accompanied by Gretl and Annelore, who went to see a mechanical crib made by a local craftsman in the late nineteenth century. This crib, which depicted the life of Christ from the Annunciation to the Ascension through dozens of scenes containing hundreds of figures with moving parts, captured seven-year-old Annelore's imagination. The representation of the Crucifixion was most extraordinary. A red liquid fell from the wounds of Christ and was caught at the base of the cross by a woman with an open book, which she closed once the blood was in it.

While many Jewish children in Vienna had Christian governesses who sometimes took them to Christian events such as the Christkindlmarkt and occasionally even took them to church, Annelore's engagement with Christianity was unusually great, far exceeding her exposure to Judaism. While Paul Herschmann never went to synagogue, Hermine sometimes went to church and had masses said for Moriz and Lene on the anniversaries of their deaths. Annelore's governesses, who were all Catholics, wrote Christian stories and drew Christian pictures for her. In 1931, nine-year-old Annelore herself drew crosses on the cover of her school drawing book, and she filled its pages with even more Christian imagery, including a drawing of two female Christ Childs.

Yet there were profound limits to her Catholic experiences, as illustrated by the confirmation in St. Stephen's Cathedral in 1933 of her cousin Lizzi Hamburger, the only daughter of Hermine's youngest brother, Paul, and his wife, Fely. Annelore attended the celebratory lunch at the Wohllebengasse of calf's head soup, asparagus in breadcrumbs, ragout of sweetbreads and pancreas, bacon, duckling with new potatoes, cream cake, ice cream, sherry, champagne, and coffee. She also joined the entire family when they hired a *Fiaker,* or horse-drawn coach, to go on an outing to Vienna's pleasure park, the Prater. But to her disappointment, she could not attend the ceremony in St. Stephen's because of her Judaism. As she recalled it, she wished she could have been confirmed, too.

Hermine could have comforted Annelore by drawing on her own childhood. Hermine might have explained that when she fell under the influence of the nuns from the Order of German Knights as a girl in Freudenthal, she, too, had been drawn to Catholicism and wanted to participate in the annual Corpus Christi procession, but her parents had stopped her because of their Judaism. Instead Hermine compounded Annelore's sense of exclusion. As they watched the procession that went through Vienna's Fourth District on Corpus Christi Day, Hermine would tell Annelore how wonderful it would be if she were part of it, carrying one of the pillows with a crown on it or holding one of the ribbons attached to these pillows. It was another way Annelore learned she was the wrong religion.

Hermine maintained her guest book until early 1936. She had visitors on New Year's Day and then again on the fifth, seventh, tenth, and fourteenth of January, when seven women joined her for two tables of bridge, accompanied by the usual tea and sandwiches with heated cheese pastries. It was her last bridge party. A week later she was in hospital for a gallbladder operation and, though her doctors initially declared it a success, she died of a blood clot on February 6 at age sixty-five and was buried on February 8, which the Gallias otherwise would have celebrated as Erni's forty-first birthday. A day later Annelore turned fourteen.

Annelore had many memories of these events. She remembered how Hermine left the Wohllebengasse on a stretcher, carried from her bedroom down the hall of the apartment, and how she thought Hermine would never return. She remembered being very frightened when she was taken to the hospital after Hermine died and had to kiss Hermine's hand one last time. She remembered being taken to see Hermine in a coffin with a window at one end so her face remained visible. She remembered that Erni, Gretl, and Käthe led the vast funeral procession at the Hietzing cemetery, she followed with Mizzi, and Hermine's three brothers, Otto, Guido, and Paul, walked behind. Anne remembered that she wore a black hat and a black armband that Gretl bought for her for the funeral. She remembered that she cried bitterly, although she was not really sad. She also remembered that while Hermine usually gave her things she did not like and forced her to use them to her annoyance and embarrassment, that year she had received two embroidered pillowcases bought by Hermine before she fell sick that were exactly what Annelore wanted.

Hermine left Käthe most of her shares and bank deposits and all of her stake in the Graetzinlicht Gesellschaft because she had not received part of a factory like Erni or a dowry like Gretl. Hermine also specified how her silver was to be distributed. She gave the remainder of her estate to Erni, Gretl, and Käthe in equal shares and left it to them to decide what to do with it. They agreed to remain joint owners of the Wohllebengasse and the Villa Gallia while dividing the rest, a process that was sometimes complicated, sometimes simple. One of Hermine's most spectacular pieces of jewelry—a string of huge pearls from the Adriatic—was so long that Gretl, Käthe, and Mizzi could split it in three and each wear one of these thirds.

Hermine addressed how her daughters should live through a provision that was as controlling as it was perceptive. Rather than leave it to Gretl and Käthe to recognize that they got on too badly to continue living together, Hermine stipulated that they live separately, an instruction they obeyed. Their new apartments were both in the Third District, a middle-class area much less prestigious than the Fourth. While Gretl rented a pre-war apartment on the Landstrasser-Hauptstrasse, the Third District's main shopping street, Käthe chose a modernist block almost Stalinist in its severity, overlooking a railway line in the Rechte Bahngasse.

Only the Hoffmann dining room survived more or less intact in the Wohllebengasse. While Erni, Gretl, and Käthe probably removed the marble-topped side table under the window, they left the marble wall fountain and the built-in marble buffet. They also left the massive dining-room table, along with fourteen of its eighteen chairs, as the apartment's new tenants were eager to convert the dining room into a boardroom and wanted the table for their meetings. The other rooms were all dismembered: Erni, Gretl, and Käthe took not only their furniture but, in accordance with contemporary practice, almost everything else including all the Hoffmann chandeliers and most of the Hoffmann wall hangings and wallpapers. While Erni and Mizzi selected just six chairs, a carpet, a chan-

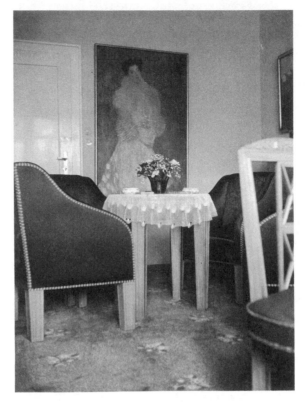

The Klimt portrait of Hermine and some of the
Hoffmann furniture from the salon in Käthe's
apartment in Vienna's Third District, c. 1938.

delier, and some silver when they moved to a new apartment in the Eighth
District, Gretl and Käthe divided the rest because they had no furniture of
their own.

The siblings also divided Hermine's pictures. There were three family
portraits, so Erni, Gretl, and Käthe each took one. Käthe chose the Klimt
since she had been closest to Hermine, Erni exploited his position as the
sole son to take the Andri portrait of Moriz, and Gretl got the painting of
the Gallia children. Otherwise Gretl and Käthe again took more because
Erni and Mizzi had their own collection, though they each received several
pictures. Erni's prime acquisition was Klimt's *Beech Forest*. Gretl and
Käthe divided the pair of portraits by Waldmüller, which remained particularly valuable. Gretl took the Orlik portrait of Mahler because she had
been closest to Theobald Pollak and was the most musical.

Their new apartments were nowhere near as elegant or spacious as the Wohllebengasse. Käthe's bedroom was so full that she could not close the door. Yet when Gretl took the smoking-room furniture, the room she put it into was so large that she could put the five ebonized bookcases along a single wall. She similarly was able to keep almost all the white-and-gold boudoir furniture together in a room that also accommodated the family's Steinway grand piano in a music corner where she hung eight of Carl Moll's woodcuts of Beethoven houses. Käthe kept the salon furniture together in one room with its original carpet, while she put the hall furniture in another, albeit with a chandelier from the salon and the carpet from the dining room.

Gretl was thrilled to be freed from the "*Goldener Käfig,*" or "Golden Cage," as she called the Wohllebengasse, running her own household again fifteen years after she first left. While she thought of her childhood as very happy, Gretl came to look on her time in the Landstrasser-Hauptstrasse with Annelore as the best period of her life. Annelore was delighted to have a bedroom of her own that she could have decorated as she wanted. Yet she preferred Käthe's apartment and went there whenever she could. She felt that she had two homes and two mothers who competed for her love and attention. The guest book kept by Hermine until her death, which Käthe continued in the Rechte Bahngasse, is particularly revealing. Lorle, the family's usual abbreviation of Annelore, was Käthe's most frequent visitor. While she sometimes went with Gretl, she was there by herself once or twice each week. She occasionally came for breakfast, sometimes for lunch, but usually for supper and then stayed the night. Käthe's delight at these occasions is apparent from her most common formulation for them, "Lorle alone."

The sisters' division of Annelore and competition over her was manifest in 1937, a year after Hermine's death. First Gretl took Annelore to Eisenstadt, the capital of the Austrian province of Burgenland, then Käthe took her to Budapest. While Gretl had often taken Annelore on short holidays before, Käthe had never done so and their trip was intended as a trial, designed to determine whether Käthe should take Annelore on even longer holidays. When Käthe and Annelore had a wonderful time eating in restaurants by the Danube, listening to gypsy music, and visiting relatives, Gretl and Käthe divided the summer, making it the first since 1922 when Annelore did not go to Alt Aussee, as well as the first when Gretl and Annelore were apart on Gretl's birthday.

Annelore's holiday to the Austrian and Italian alps was her best ever—especially her week in Hinterbichl, a tiny village at the end of a remote valley in the East Tyrol. Käthe took Annelore there because Hinterbichl was the summer retreat of the Vienna Boys' Choir, which was established in 1924 as the successor to Austria's imperial choir. Within a few years, the Vienna Boys were as famous as their predecessors, acquiring an international reputation that made them a subject of nationalist pride. When Gretl took Annelore to one of the choir's concerts as another Great Depression birthday present, along with her string of pearls, the Vienna Boys became one of her passions. All she wanted was "to see them again and to know more and more about them."

Annelore's religion was her great constraint. The choir was a Catholic institution that sang mass each Sunday in the old imperial chapel, the Burgkapelle. Because she was a Jew, Annelore could not go there. But she saw the choir wherever else she could—in concerts, operas, and films. She was at the choir's jubilee tenth anniversary concert in 1934, at which all of its sixty choristers for once performed together and its founder, Joseph Schnitt, spoke about it. She loved Max Neufeld's film *Singende Jugend,* or *Singing Boys,* which included a host of well-known actors but for Annelore was "a film with the Vienna Boys' Choir." Because it was largely set at the Hotel Wiener Sängerknaben run by the choir in Hinterbichl, it fueled her desire to go there.

Annelore found Hinterbichl all the more enjoyable because of the contrast with her annual holidays in Alt Aussee. Even one summer at the Villa Gallia involved a high degree of repetition and, after fourteen summers, she was bored by it, whereas Hinterbichl was new. Her love of the Alps started when Käthe and she spent a day climbing toward the Grossvenediger, one of Austria's highest peaks, then spent the night in an alpine hut at an altitude of almost ten thousand feet. She was equally excited by her first close contact with the choristers whom she continued to idolize, even though they were all younger than she. She loved their performances, which included Strauss's *The Blue Danube* and *Tales from the Vienna Woods* and the chorus from Wagner's *Rienzi.*

Gretl took Annelore to much more famous places in Italy. After taking the train to Genoa, they went by boat to Pisa, Naples, Pompeii, Palermo, Monreale, Syracuse, Taormina, and Venice. Yet sixty-five years later, the Staglieno Cemetery in Genoa, a site of no particular renown, was all that Anne remembered finding impressive. Her list of disappointments and dislikes was long. She was annoyed to learn that, as a fifteen-year-old girl, she was not allowed to visit the houses in Pompeii containing pornographic frescoes. She was shocked and frightened to find fully clothed skeletons in the catacombs in Palermo. Italy was too hot and smelly, she complained.

The religious component of Annelore's holidays with Gretl was also very different from her holiday with Käthe. While Gretl took Annelore to Christian sites, she also paid more than usual attention to Jewish ones. This Jewish tourism was greatest in Eisenstadt, the site of Austria's oldest continuous Jewish community, where Gretl and Annelore inspected the ghetto, the Jewish cemetery, and the home of a prominent Jewish family. They continued it in the Staglieno Cemetery in Genoa, where Annelore photographed an interior dominated by a menorah, a seven-branched Jewish candelabrum. This tourism suggests that her upbringing by Gretl was not as antithetical to Judaism, or removed from it, as Anne later remembered.

2

Austro-fascism

The first great crisis of the Austrian republic was Bloody Friday on July 15, 1927. The catalyst was the trial of three *Frontkämpfer,* right-wing veterans of the war set on undermining the republic and its democracy, who had killed a socialist in a village in the Burgenland close to the Hungarian border. As with four similar right-wing killings over the previous two years, the *Frontkämpfer* escaped punishment when a jury acquitted them. But this time the city's socialists and communists marched in protest on the Palace of Justice, where the police opened fire, the crowd set the palace alight and stopped fire engines reaching it, and the police retaliated by killing at least eighty-five of the demonstrators and wounding up to one thousand.

Gretl was there by accident, caught up in the conflict and carnage as she happened to be making her way across the city. Her entanglement in Bloody Friday exemplifies how, for all that the Gallias' wealth cocooned them, political events and political violence were inescapable in Austria through the 1920s into the 1930s. The republic was divided. Its national governments were always led by the Christian Socials, once the party of Karl Lueger, which was the biggest right-wing party. The Social Democrats, the dominant party of the left, were not only the country's largest political group but also the strongest socialist party in the world, securing 42 percent of the vote in Austria's general election in 1927.

The Social Democrats' stronghold was Vienna, the home of over one-third of Austria's shrunken population after it lost its empire. "Red Vienna," as it became known, was the international showcase of democratic socialism. It was famous for the municipal government's provision of worker housing, welfare payments, medical services, education, sports facilities, and culture. It was also famous—and in many places notorious—for how the city council funded this program through a system of property and luxury taxes, one of which applied to domestic employees and forced Hermine to reduce her four full-time servants to three.

Mass events were integral to the city's political culture. The first attended by Annelore occurred one May Day, which was an occasion for a celebration of worker power until Engelbert Dollfuss became Austria's chancellor with a majority of one vote in the country's parliament and established a regime often dubbed Austro-fascist, though it was not as extreme as its German and Italian counterparts. When Dollfuss declared presidential rule in 1933, he forcibly prevented parliament from sitting and instituted press censorship. He also banned all mass meetings and demonstrations, including the workers' celebration on May Day.

Dollfuss used these measures to try to control the National Socialists, or Nazis, Austria's dominant far-right party in the early 1930s, which won between 10 and 15 percent of the vote. When the Nazis embarked on a wave of terror to destabilize his regime, Dollfuss closed the Nazis' regional offices, arrested thousands of their members, and banned the party, but with little effect because the Nazis simply went underground. Dollfuss was much more effective when he stopped the Social Democrats' meetings and parades, disrupted and broke strikes organized by their members, censored their main newspaper, and outlawed their armed Schutzbund, a paramilitary organization. When the Social Democrats responded with force in February 1934, the Christian Socials crushed their ill-coordinated uprising in four days, outlawed them, and arrested many of their leaders.

The celebrations attended by Annelore that May Day were initiated by Dollfuss to mark his introduction of a new constitution that put an end to Austrian democracy and attempted to legitimate his rule. If twelve-year-old Annelore's response is any guide, the Gallias sympathized with Dollfuss. After spending the morning along with thousands of other schoolchildren watching a pageant staged by the Christian Socials at the stadium in the Prater, Annelore described the proceedings as "really wonderful." That she spent the afternoon watching and photographing the triumphal procession that went through the city suggests even more interest in it.

Dollfuss's treatment of Jews was one attraction. While anti-Semitism was part of Christian Social ideology, Dollfuss did not persecute Jews, tried to protect them from Nazi attack, and chose not to exploit anti-Semitism for populist ends. This stance was particularly important to the Gallias because they remained unable to escape their Jewish origins, as revealed by a Viennese residency certificate filled out by Gretl. While required to identify herself as born within the Israelitische Kultusgemeinde, she had no opportunity to record her Roman Catholic identity of more than thirty years.

Dollfuss was dead twelve weeks after the May Day celebrations, assassinated by members of Austria's banned Nazi Party as part of an attempted putsch in July 1934. In three days of fighting, there were 269 killings. Over half were on the government side, but the army's loyalty enabled it to suppress the revolt. When Annelore attended the May Day rally staged by the Christian Socials in the Prater a year later, the proceedings were much the same as in 1934, except that they ended with a speech by Austria's new chancellor, Kurt von Schuschnigg, followed by a minute's silence in honor of Dollfuss. As a memento of the occasion, Annelore bought a postcard of the rally in the stadium.

Annelore received a rare lesson in viewing political events critically when the Italian dictator Benito Mussolini, a close ally of Dollfuss's and Schuschnigg's, embarked on his long-planned conquest of Abyssinia in 1935. As the international community toyed with imposing sanctions on Italy, Annelore's geography teacher observed, "There is a war against Abyssinia, and Austria is neutral and friendly to Italy—think what that means." The discussion that followed taught Annelore that "neutral" and "friendly to Italy" were mutually exclusive terms and that what politicians said required analysis.

The Salzburg Festival was more than a cultural event. From 1920, it sought to strengthen, if not create, a distinctive Austrian identity. This political dimension was magnified in 1933, when the festival became the focus of conflict between the new Nazi government in Germany and the Christian Socials. Hitler began when he deprived the festival of much of its audience by imposing a special tax on German visitors to Austria and stopped German artists from performing there. Many Austrians, led by Dollfuss, responded by attending the festival, which became a symbol of Austrian independence. By one account, "those people who wished to help Austria in her fight against National Socialism, and who were perhaps indifferent to the existence of Mozart, flocked to Salzburg." While Gretl was far from indifferent to Mozart, she must have been alive to these politics when she gave Annelore her first and only experience of the festival that year.

The Burgtheater, which remained a state institution in the new republic, also became increasingly political under the Christian Socials. Its most partisan production seen by Annelore was *The Hundred Days,* which the Italian playwright Giovacchino Forzano based on a sketch by Mussolini. While nominally about the hundred days between Napoleon's escape from the island of Elba and his defeat at the Battle of Waterloo, Forzano and Mussolini intended the play as a statement about contemporary politics, supporting authoritarian rule over Italy. When the Burgtheater staged the drama in Vienna, it strengthened the play's attack on parliamentary democracy so that *The Hundred Days* justified the Christian Socials' dictatorship by denigrating constitutional rule as "self-defeating" when it hindered government.

Annelore's first direct experience of Nazi mayhem was at an afternoon performance at the Burgtheater in late 1936 or early 1937. As she recalled it, she was by herself because Gretl was in mourning for Hermine and so could not attend. When a Nazi in the audience threw a stink bomb, fourteen-year-old Annelore had every reason to be fearful. The performance stopped. Members of the audience rushed toward the exits. Far from joining them, Annelore exploited her lack of adult supervision to stay inside and "watched with fascination" as the theater's stagehands raised the curtain and removed the backdrop, giving her "a wonderful view of the stage machinery."

The family's disregard for politics was most apparent when Gretl introduced Annelore to the work of Wagner at the Staatsoper. After *Lohengrin* in 1933, they saw Moriz's favorite, *Die Meistersinger,* in 1934, *Parsifal* in 1935, and *Götterdämmerung, Der Fliegende Holländer,* and a second performance of the *Die Meistersinger* in 1937. While mother and daughter went as a matter of family tradition, these operas had a new function in the 1930s, as the Nazis interpreted Wagner in line with their ideology. "*Wach auf!*" or "Awake!"—the chorale in *Die Meistersinger* sung by Hans Sachs to greet Luther and the Reformation—was one of the Nazis' most resounding calls to arms. *Die Meistersinger* was the work that Hitler had performed on his most important political occasions. In 1937 his minister for propaganda, Joseph Goebbels, credited Wagner with teaching Germans that Jews were "a subhuman race."

The lure of the second *Meistersinger* that Annelore attended was immense because of its guest conductor, Wilhelm Furtwängler, whom the Gallias had seen already in 1922 when he performed in Vienna for just the second time at a concert staged to mark the twenty-fifth anniversary of Brahms's death. Having been "very enthused" by Furtwängler's "splendid" performance, the family bought the first book about him published that year. A decade later, Furtwängler was one of the most famous musicians in the world—eclipsed as a conductor only by Toscanini. As Gretl, Käthe, and Annelore probably knew, Furtwängler had displayed courage in publicly protesting against the Nazis' expulsion of Jewish musicians such as Bruno Walter, prompting Goebbels to respond, "There isn't a single filthy Jew left in Germany that Herr Furtwängler hasn't stood up for." Unlike many German and Austrian cultural figures, Fürtwängler had not joined the Nazi Party, yet he served the Nazis by conducting at many of its most significant occasions, starting with a performance of *Die Meistersinger* as part of the celebrations that marked the inauguration of the Third Reich in 1933.

Furtwängler later maintained that, far from doing the Nazis' bidding, music was his only master. He even cast his interventions to protect Jewish musicians as symbolic of his devotion to high art. Yet Goebbels effectively made this stance an impossibility when he wrote an open letter to Furtwängler declaring that music in Germany was political. Furtwängler must also have realized that whether he criticized the Nazis or conducted at the occasions that mattered most to them, his actions were politically significant because the greatest classical musicians continued to be revered and idolized through the 1930s. Had Furtwängler followed Toscanini's example and refused to conduct in Germany after the Nazis came to power, he would have undermined their legitimacy. By working for the Nazis, he boosted it.

The performance by Furtwängler that Anne remembered was the second of two concerts she attended—the first in 1936, the second in 1937— at which he conducted Beethoven's Ninth Symphony in the Great Hall of the Musikverein. Because of Furtwängler's celebrity, the tickets were unusually expensive. Although Anne generally displayed no interest in her seats in the auditorium, she recalled that she was in the front row, so close to Furtwängler that he sweated onto her program. When *Taking Sides,* the film of Ronald Harwood's play about Furtwängler, was released in 2001, this experience made her want to see it.

Like Gretl, Annelore started her first ball season at age fifteen but, instead of going mainly to private balls, she attended public ones. Gretl had been preparing Annelore for this moment for years, hoping she would enjoy Gretl's own delight on the dance floor. After starting classes when she was five or six years old, Annelore continued in high school when Gretl sent her to the Elmayer, Vienna's most fashionable dancing and deportment school, which segregated its Jewish and non-Jewish clients, placing them in different classes at its premises next to the Spanish Riding School in the First District. By 1937, Annelore could waltz, fox-trot, and tango.

Georg Schidlof, Annelore's main partner during this season, was a Jew from a much poorer family—another mark of the Gallias' failure to live up to Hermine's aspirations. She knew Georg because his mother, Lizzi, had lived in the Wohllebengasse for at least two years as the twins' last governess. When Georg became Annelore's escort, it was because their mothers arranged it, not because of any romance between them. As Gretl looked for a young man to take Annelore, she approached Lizzi because nineteen-year-old Georg was the right age with the right status as an officer cadet in the Austrian army doing his compulsory military service. Just before the season started, Georg's father gave him a gala uniform so he could attend the balls in style.

Annelore's dress was another Christmas present from Käthe, who retained the best eye for what her niece most wanted and also had the means to indulge her. Rather than being pink or red, which Hermine had repeatedly chosen, the gown was white with blue velvet ribbons. It was Annelore's first piece of Viennese high fashion—made by the Berger sisters, Hilde and Fritzi, who also designed textiles and fashion postcards for the Wiener Werkstätte. Käthe, who bought a series of Fritzi's watercolors, took Annelore to the sisters' salon because it was where she bought many of her own best clothes.

Annelore's outfit prompted her fifth photographic session with Jobst. Instead of taking place in the studio, it was in Gretl's apartment in the Landstrasser-Hauptstrasse. In one portrait Annelore sits on a sofa with her dress spread out, her hair up, which was the fashion for girls in senior high school, still wearing the pearls of the Trude Fleischmann photographs, staring sternly at the camera. In another she stands at a window, pulling back the curtain and looks over her shoulder, smiling. In the third she sits in an armchair next to the white-and-gold Hoffmann vitrine, her dress spills over the chair's arms, and she has a rare, dreamy look of contentment. As Anne remembered it more than fifty years later, the last two photographs caught her mood. She loved going out and loved her new dress.

Anne thought these photographs were taken at the end of 1937, before she went to her first ball, when the dress was brand-new. But an album compiled by Gretl in Vienna reveals that these photographs were from March 1938, at the end of the season. The different dates are significant. In December 1937, Austria was still independent, though under intense pressure from Hitler, who declared he could not ignore the fate of Germans outside the Reich. In March 1938, he annexed his birthplace. The photographs of Annelore in her ball dress were the last of her taken before the Anschluss. They appear indicative of the obliviousness of so many Austrians of Jewish descent to what was about to befall them. Here is my mother in the most sumptuous of gowns, a debutante seemingly thinking only of dancing as the Nazis prepared to invade.

One of Anne's own stories reinforces this impression. It was about the annual Scout Ball, the one occasion when Georg and she danced the polonaise that started every ball. Because Georg had been a Scout throughout high school, he was able to arrange for them to be among the opening pairs. The convention was that these couples were all listed in the program but Georg and Annelore were not. Far from wondering why they had been omitted, Annelore was "too carefree and happy" to think about it. She realized only later that Georg and she were excluded because they were Jews, and the Nazis were already so powerful that they controlled who appeared on the program.

Schuschnigg, meanwhile, oscillated between accommodating and rejecting the Nazis' demands. When he saw Hitler at his mountain retreat near Berchtesgaden in Bavaria in mid-February, Schuschnigg agreed to accept the Austrian Nazi leader, Arthur Seyss-Inquart, into his cabinet as minister for the interior. Less than two weeks later, Schuschnigg announced that he was committed to maintaining Austria's independence and would make no further concessions to the Nazis. As he for once proved a passionate, powerful speaker, the crowds on the Ringstrasse

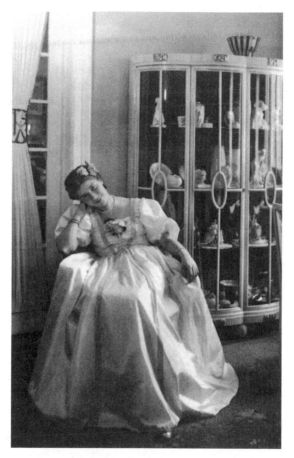

Annelore in her ball dress with the Hoffmann
vitrine behind, in the Landstrasser-Hauptstrasse,
March 1938.

broke into the old imperial anthem in an outpouring of nationalist fervor
and Schuschnigg excited adulation wherever he went.

Annelore was at the opera two days later for a new production of *Dalibor* by the Czech composer Smetana, which was another instance of the
intersection between culture and politics. The conductor was Gretl's
childhood idol, Bruno Walter, whose employment at the Vienna Opera,
after Hitler prevented him from performing in Germany, was immediately interpreted as a symbol of the Christian Socials' acceptance of Jews.
When Schuschnigg entered his box before the start of the second act, he
received a standing ovation from the audience and was lauded again when

he attended a festive, optimistic gathering in the foyer at the end of the performance. While Annelore could not see Schuschnigg from her seat, she was so struck by the audience's response that she recorded it in her concert book.

She remembered being frightened not so much by Hitler but by his young Austrian followers about her own age who belonged to the Hitler Jugend and Bund Deutscher Mädchen. As these young Nazis became increasingly aggressive, some Jewish students in Vienna responded by imitating their distinctive outfits. The writer George Clare, who was in his final year of school in 1938, maintained that, when he donned "white knee-socks, a black raincoat and Tyrolean hat, very much the sort of clothing the Nazis liked to be seen in," he did so as a sign of his readiness to fight. "Looking like a Nazi as much as possible," Clare wrote, "instilled a feeling of toughness in oneself." Annelore did the same for very different reasons. She recalled: "I wanted to look like everyone else, including the Nazis whose dirndl outfits and white socks I liked to copy in the hope of blending in and being inconspicuous."

Annelore, who had persuaded Gretl to let her change schools because the Frauen-Ewerb-Verein had become so anti-Semitic, was among the few Jews in Vienna who recognized that it was time to flee. When the Gallias received an offer to buy their house in the Wohllebengasse at the start of 1938, Annelore pleaded with Gretl to accept it and to emigrate with the proceeds. But the offer was low and, like other Viennese of Jewish origin, Gretl had good reasons to stay. Her attachment to Vienna was intense. All her close family and most of her friends were there. After eighteen months in the Landstrasser-Hauptstrasse free of Hermine and Käthe, she could imagine nothing better than to remain there and dismissed Annelore's fears as those of a "silly child."

Anne was scathing about this response in her story. She maintained that Gretl had spent too long in the Wohllebengasse, "a closed world insulated against the outside" where "everyone was busy following the established routine and did not envisage that things would ever change." But Gretl may not have been quite so blind; that February, she had her passport amended so it became valid for travel to all European countries, as Annelore's passport had been since she obtained it the year before. While Gretl may simply have secured this change as part of planning their next holiday abroad, she may also have been preparing in case they had to emigrate quickly.

According to Anne, Käthe was even more intent on staying in Vienna because she wanted to remain close to Lene, who was buried along with Moriz and Hermine in the family grave in Hietzing. Because the twins had done everything together in life both as children and as adults, Käthe did not want to leave Lene in death. Yet the grave—and Käthe's myriad attachments to Vienna—probably formed only part of Käthe's considerations. Her position as manager of the Graetzinlicht Gesellschaft, which she half owned, was a powerful reason for her to stay.

The opportunity for Gretl, Käthe, and Annelore to leave with relative ease disappeared a few weeks after Annelore's ball season ended, when Schuschnigg called a plebiscite on Austrian independence and Hitler responded by mobilizing the German Eighth Army, which he had stationed close to the Austrian border in order to force Schuschnigg to call off the vote. Once Schuschnigg complied on March 11, Germany demanded his immediate resignation as Austrian chancellor. That evening, like most Austrians, Gretl and Annelore listened to Schuschnigg's farewell speech, broadcast on the radio, in which he announced that he had resigned "because he was determined at all costs not to see German blood spilt." By the end of the night, most of the country was in the hands of Hitler's Austrian followers. At dawn, the German army crossed the frontier to be greeted by tens of thousands of Austrians who showered the German troops with flowers. By midnight, the first German tanks were in Vienna, where they staged an impromptu parade along the Ringstrasse before an ecstatic crowd.

3

Anschluss

"*Stürmisch*" was how Käthe described the ringing of her doorbell. Not just loud but stormy. Insistent. Incessant. At least it was the middle of the afternoon, not the middle of the night. Käthe could have sent her maid, but the intensity of the ringing prompted her to go herself. Keeping the door on its chain, she opened it and found two men, one in civilian clothes, the other in black uniform, who demanded to be let in. Instead, Käthe shut the door and telephoned the police for an officer to come immediately. Then she told the men what she had done and, through the space between the chained door and its frame, watched the man in civilian clothes become increasingly angry.

In the month since the Anschluss, the Nazis had attacked Jews and Jewish converts to Christianity in Vienna in a way that they had not done in Germany. Many had been assaulted and killed. The stores and apartments of others had been invaded and plundered. Hundreds more had been humiliated in front of enthusiastic crowds—forced to spit in each other's faces or made to scrub the streets using water mixed with caustic soda or hydrochloric acid, which burned their fingers. Thousands had been arrested and jailed in police prisons in Vienna or sent to the Nazis' first concentration camp in Dachau outside Munich. Because the Nazis'

Nürnberg Laws identified everyone with three Jewish grandparents as a Jew regardless of whether they or their parents had converted, Erni, Gretl, and Käthe were in immediate danger. While the Nürnberg definition applied in Austria only from May 1938 as a matter of law, in practice it applied from the time of the Anschluss, transforming the Gallias from Austrian citizens into German Jews.

Hundreds of Viennese of Jewish origin responded by immediately escaping Austria while its borders were still open, fleeing by train, car, and even taxi. Thousands of others were soon trying to secure visas so they could leave, often queueing through the night at foreign consulates to increase their chances, only to be attacked as they waited. Käthe had particular grounds to flee because she was among the first targets of the Nazis' *Arisierung,* or Aryanization of businesses owned by men and women of Jewish origin, which resulted in the sale of these businesses at a fraction of their true value. By the end of March 1938, Käthe had been stripped of her job at the Graetzinlicht Gesellschaft. Otherwise she would have been at work, not at home, when the two men rang her doorbell a fortnight later.

Yet men and women of Jewish origin, such as Erni, Gretl, and Käthe, had good reason to hope the first weeks of Nazi rule would prove an aberration; after all, the Nazis had not engaged in such assaults in Germany. When the violence diminished and a semblance of normality returned to Vienna during the first weeks of April, it looked as if those who expected a return to calm might be right. According to Anne, her mother, uncle, and aunt were among those who "thought their pleasant life in Austria would continue." When Käthe found the men at her door, she was preparing to go to the theater.

Käthe's account of what happened that day was one of many forwarded by victims of the Nazis to Vienna's new gauleiter, Josef Bürckel, in the hope that he would remedy the wrongs done to them. Most of these letters were sent directly to Bürckel, which meant that he never read them. Käthe looked to get Bürckel's attention with the help of the Nazi commissar who was Aryanizing the Graetzinlicht Gesellschaft. While most of these men were set on plundering the businesses under their control and humiliating their original owners, some were more decent. Käthe's commissar appears to have been among the latter. In her letter to Bürckel, she maintained that "because it was only a month after the Anschluss when the men came to her door, the black uniform of the SS was still new to me." By implication, she did not realize whom she was keeping waiting when she rang the police. She also explained that she "had read notices published by the Nazis in Viennese newspapers which advised that, as communists masquerading as officers were gaining entry into apartments and stealing their contents, the city's residents should not open their doors to anyone in uniform but ask the police to check the men's credentials." In other words, she was a good citizen complying with official instructions when she telephoned the police.

This naïveté fits Anne's later view of Käthe but is still hard to believe. Could Käthe really have been so ignorant in April 1938 that she did not know what the SS wore, or was she trying to make herself appear as innocent as possible so the Nazis would not conclude that she had deliberately resisted them? And could she really have believed, after five years of Christian Social dictatorship and a month of Nazi terror, that Vienna's communists were still capable of raiding apartments? What did she hope for when she called the police? Did she still trust them, even though many policemen had immediately joined in the Nazis' persecution of Vienna's Jews, or did she ring the police simply because she had no one else to turn to?

According to G. E. R. Gedye, the Viennese correspondent of the London *Daily Telegraph* at the time of the Anschluss, the notices in the newspapers were a sham. In *Fallen Bastions,* the most influential contemporary book about Austria's annexation, Gedye maintained that Jews "naïve enough" to take the notices seriously found that, when they rang the police, "in some cases the exchange refused to answer their telephone call, in others the reply from the police station, when they had explained what was going on, was that all the police were out and that only a caretaker was on the line." The norm most likely was very different because, as was often the case with anti-Semitism, the new regime's persecution of Jews was motivated by economics as well as racism. While no communists were looting Viennese apartments by masquerading as officers, low-level Nazis and street gangs were doing so and the government wanted to stop this freebooting so it could expropriate the property of men and women of Jewish descent for itself. As the government looked to the police to stop "illegal" searches of Jewish apartments, they did exactly as the Nazis' public notices suggested: they answered Käthe's call, advised her that she had followed the right procedure, and reiterated that she should not open the door until an officer arrived. Within a few minutes a policeman was there, checking the men's papers.

The one in black was a member of the SS, as his uniform suggested. The other in civilian clothes was a member of the Gestapo, the Nazi secret police. Because they were whom they claimed, the policeman went from being potential protector to assailants' assistant. He helped the SS and Gestapo search Käthe's apartment, then accompanied them when they took Käthe and her maid to the Hotel Metropol on the Danube Canal, where the Gestapo conducted their interrogations, tortured many of their victims, and held Kurt von Schuschnigg in solitary confinement for eighteen months. After interrogating Käthe about her finances, the three men took her and her maid back to the Rechte Bahngasse, then resumed their search.

An unusual proportion of Käthe's property was in her apartment in keeping with Gallia tradition, which saw Moriz and Hermine keep two strongboxes in the Wohllebengasse rather than rent a safe or deposit box in a bank. After the officers brought Käthe back to the Rechte Bahngasse, she revealed her safe to them, which contained all of her important financial papers and best jewelry. When she attempted to list them from memory a few months later, she recorded that there were sixteen different types of Austrian, Hungarian, Czech, Swiss, and French securities. There were also six accounts in Viennese banks, 2,000 new German reichmarks in cash, and small sums of foreign currency. There were three pearl necklaces and another of diamonds. There was a big diamond brooch in the form of a bow with two pearls hanging from it. There was a pair of long diamond earrings and another of pearls. There were four bracelets and seven rings studded with diamonds, pearls, rubies, and emeralds. There were two diamond pendants, a diamond pin, and a sapphire pin. There was a platinum wristwatch set with small sapphires and diamonds.

She listed much more. Käthe had at least nine gold brooches—some with semiprecious stones, others with Saint Cecilia underneath. She also had a pair of earrings made of artificial pearls with a platinum clasp and small diamonds and another pair made of rose quartz. She had seven more gold bracelets embellished with semiprecious stones. She had two more gold rings—one with small sapphires, the other with small diamonds. She had several gold pendants in the form of miniature books, knives, medallions, and guardian angels. She had a set of shell jewelry consisting of brooches, pendants, armbands, rings, earrings, and necklaces, along with a small pearl pin, a twisted string of pearls, two small pearl armbands, a platinum armband decorated with pearls and small diamonds, several wristwatches made of gold and silver, and an Easter egg case containing a key and heart made of tiny diamonds.

The Nazis had fixed on Käthe as part of targeting the wealthiest members of well-to-do families so they could seize their property and intimidate them and their relatives into abandoning most of their wealth and fleeing. The contents of Käthe's strongbox confirmed she was worth victimizing further. That she had broken no law was irrelevant. The Nazis arrested her under suspicion of intending to transfer her assets out of the country illegally. When her uncle Paul Hamburger happened to arrive at her apartment, they arrested him, too. They also seized Käthe's securities, bankbooks, and cash, which were worth a total of 80,000 reichsmarks, but returned her jewelry to her strongbox while retaining the key. Then they sealed up the flat apart from its back room, which they left open for her maid, and took Käthe to a police prison in the Hahngasse in Vienna's Ninth District. Built to hold common criminals, the Nazis had turned it into a jail for "undesirables"—Jews, communists, socialists, supporters of Schuschnigg, and monarchists who wanted to restore the Hapsburgs.

Käthe's cell was crammed, the only toilet was a bucket, and there was little opportunity to wash. On several occasions she was taken back to the Hotel Metropol for interrogation by the Gestapo, who by now had removed all her jewelry from her apartment while ignoring her paintings, which were nowhere near as valuable. Her questioning, she recorded, took place in room 383. Her interrogator was an officer called Kreipl. Yet she was lucky to be imprisoned in Vienna rather than in the concentration camp at Dachau, where conditions were much worse. She also was fortunate that while the Nazis were trying to force all Jews to leave Austria as soon as possible after stripping them of most of their property, they still displayed an occasional sliver of respect for the law and readiness to negotiate, which meant the Gestapo did not entirely dictate what all its victims had to do. Like members of other wealthy families, Erni and Gretl sought the best legal help, which meant the strongest Nazi connections. They found an experienced defense counsel, Stephan Lehner, who was a party member.

Käthe's willingness to stand up to the Nazis was still remarkable. Far from immediately accepting their terms, she rejected them, though it meant she had to stay in prison longer. The Gestapo began by pressing Käthe to sign an agreement in which she relinquished her shares, bonds, jewelry, and cash and undertook to leave Greater Germany within two days. She refused, most likely on the advice of Stephan Lehner, because she could neither have secured the necessary visas nor organized her affairs so quickly. The Gestapo then offered her a fortnight to leave, which she still refused because she could not have complied. The Gestapo finally gave her three months and suggested that, by petitioning for her jewelry, she might recover it. She agreed and was released after seven weeks.

The Nazis generally denied their prisoners access to family and friends. While Käthe was in the Hahngasse, all the Nazis allowed was for someone to bring her clean clothes and toiletries and collect her laundry once a week. As with almost every other aspect of Jewish life under the Nazis, this weekly process involved queuing, often for extended periods, which made it particularly frightening and dangerous. Anne recalled that she did so for Käthe "because people tended to be nicer to children than to grown-ups." Many Jewish girls and boys as young as twelve performed similar tasks for this reason. Yet Gretl may also have thought that a sixteen-year-old girl on the verge of womanhood would stand a better chance of winning over male officialdom than a stout middle-aged matron like her.

Most accounts of the Anschluss depict the Nazis as all-powerful and their victims as utterly compliant, overlooking how men and women of Jewish origin were quick to defy the new regime, if only in small ways. The bridge-playing, choral-singing Gretl, shop manager Käthe, and schoolgirl Annelore were among them. Just as Käthe discovered that she could smuggle messages out of the prison concealed in her laundry, so Gretl and Annelore found that they could smuggle food into the jail to supplement Käthe's prison diet. They probably began doing so almost immediately to help Käthe celebrate her thirty-ninth birthday in the Hahngasse in late April. Their ruse was to disguise cream as toothpaste in the toiletries that Annelore brought her.

The document securing Käthe's release at the end of May stated that she voluntarily relinquished her property and wanted to leave the new Greater Germany. The first part of this statement was false, the second true. Because of her imprisonment, Käthe was eager to emigrate, as were Gretl and Erni, who was also losing much of his property through Aryanization. Less than seventy years after their uncle Adolf Gallia became their first relative to move to Vienna, drawn by the opportunities it offered and its unprecedented tolerance of Jews, Erni, Gretl, and Käthe knew they had to leave. For all the difficulties of their relationship, Gretl and Käthe decided to flee together so that they could jointly care for Annelore, if not always for each other.

Like all schools in Vienna, Annelore's gymnasium in the Albertgasse closed for several days after the Anschluss. When it reopened, a number of Annelore's teachers were gone, either because they had fled the Nazis or because the Nazis had stripped them of their positions on religious or political grounds. As at other schools, the remaining teachers had sworn an oath of allegience to Hitler. If they had been illegal members of the Nazi Party before the Anschluss, they came to school flaunting their party insignia, perhaps wearing SA or SS uniforms. Annelore was particularly shocked to find that Ilse Hornung, whom she had idolized at the Frauen-Erwerb-Verein, had been a party member when it was illegal.

The Jewish students at the Albertgasse were immediate targets. Annelore was accustomed to sitting at the front of her class with her two best friends, who were both Aryans. After the Anschluss, the class was segregated. While the Aryans occupied the front rows, the Jews, including Annelore, were relegated to the back. If they came too close, the Aryan girls would draw their clothes to their bodies in ostentatious displays of fear of contamination. The two girls who had been Annelore's best friends were at the forefront of this ostracism because they felt obliged to make up for their previous support of Schuschnigg. According to Anne, these girls "did not know her any more."

This exclusion extended to Nazi symbolism and ceremony. The Aryan students at Viennese schools started each day by raising their right arms to "*Heil Hitler.*" The Jewish students were prohibited from doing so. They had to listen while the other pupils learned the Nazi anthem: "When Jewish blood spurts from the knife, then everything will be double fine." They were banned from donning swastikas, which everyone else wore. Anne particularly remembered the response of one of her classmates whose Jewish father was imprisoned by the Nazis while her Aryan mother was not. Anne recalled, with a mixture of envy and contempt, that this girl varied the size of swastika she wore according to the teacher, choosing the biggest for the most fervent Nazis. "It was dreadful," Anne wrote, "to be an outcast and live in this changed atmosphere."

She still thought herself relatively fortunate because many of the Aryan pupils and teachers at the Albertgasse were long-standing Nazis who did not feel obliged to engage in extreme acts of anti-Semitism in order to prove themselves to the new regime. She also could have been excluded altogether from the gymnasium, as a new Nazi law prohibited Jews from going to the schools they had been attending and required them to move to eight new schools restricted to Jews. But as with many of the Nazis' anti-Semitic measures, the enforcement of this law proved uneven. At some schools they evicted Jews as soon as the law came into effect at the end of April. At others they placed Jews in separate classes and required them to use separate entrances and toilets. Some, including the Albertgasse, allowed Jews to stay where they were.

Annelore's great solace was the Staatsoper, which replaced the Burgtheater at the start of 1938 as her favorite place to go. The catalyst was her sixteenth birthday, a month before the Anschluss. Until then, Annelore had always been taken to the theater and opera at night by adults, usually occupying very expensive seats. Her ambition was to attend as many performances as possible regardless of where she sat. When she turned sixteen, Annelore was allowed to go alone and buy tickets to the opera's standing areas, the one democratic feature of this elitist institution. In all there were five hundred standing places against twenty-five hundred seats. Some were at the front of the Gods, the opera's fourth and highest tier. Others were at the sides of the third tier. The best were at the back of the parterre, or ground floor of the theater, offering a perfect view of the stage for a token schilling or two. Annelore first stood for a performance of Mozart's *Don Giovanni* at the end of February 1938. She thought it "outstanding!"

The chaos caused by the Anschluss closed the opera, and when it reopened at the end of March, many people stayed away regardless of their religion. Gitta Sereny, best known for her book on Hitler's architect, Albert Speer, was among them. As Sereny recalled in an autobiographical essay, she and her best friend, both Protestants, both aged fifteen, were forbidden by their parents from walking home at night and, even when they went out in large groups, did not attend any performances. Because Annelore was a Jew, she had even more reason to stay away or seek protection in numbers and Gretl, one of the most anxious of mothers, had particular cause to insist that her only child do so because of Käthe's arrest. Yet Gretl usually gave Annelore what she most desired, and before long Annelore was going more than ever. While Käthe was imprisoned in April and May, Annelore went to fourteen performances and then another nine in June. At her most intense—just before Vienna's operas, theaters, and concert houses closed for the summer—she went out four nights in succession and five nights out of six.

She was free to attend these performances as a matter of law since Nazi legislation prohibiting Jews from attending places of public entertainment only came into force at the end of the year. In practice, the opera was already forbidden to Jews, as the Nazis made plain following the Anschluss when they dismissed eleven "racially unworthy" members of the orchestra and tried to arrest Bruno Walter, only to find that he was performing in Amsterdam. Annelore thought of the opera as *Judenverbot*, a place where Jews were forbidden. Although she went for her own pleasure, these outings were another form of defiance of the Nazis, like the food she illicitly brought Käthe in prison. As much as she was alive to the hazards, she probably was thrilled by them. She wrote in her memoir: "There was one thing I insisted on. Even though Jews were not permitted in the opera or theater, I went there, never mind the risk. It was in that time of my life that I discovered the charm of the standing room. I stood throughout the operas, loved it, and forgot the dismal world outside."

More than seventeen hundred Viennese Jews became Roman Catholics in the first five months after the Anschluss. Annelore was one of them. "It was decided that I should not be Jewish," she recalled. "Many people felt the same and a Franciscan priest conducted a large class of would-be converts." She would have jumped at this opportunity a few years before because of her antipathy toward Judaism and her desire to share the Catholicism of Hermine, Gretl, and Käthe. But by 1938, aged sixteen, Annelore was skeptical about organized religion, whatever its form. Just as the novelist Felix Dahn probably fueled her rejection of Judaism in *A Fight for Rome,* so he expressed if not shaped her view of Christianity when he wrote: "To believe in God is childish. To deny the existence of God is madness. To search for God is the answer." The decision that Annelore should convert was made by Gretl and Käthe.

They knew that under the Nürnberg Laws Annelore would remain a Jew so far as the Nazis were concerned, but Gretl and Käthe still hoped her conversion would help to protect Annelore in Vienna. They thought Catholicism might make her life safer and easier wherever they went as refugees. Her conversion was also a matter of belief for Käthe, though not for Gretl, whose Catholicism had become nominal. Anne wrote that

Käthe was "very pleased that she was about to become a member of the Catholic church." Her conversion was "something Käthe had always wished for."

I asked once about Anne's father, Paul Herschmann. Had he tried to stop her baptism? Anne was not sure whether Paul was in Vienna when she converted or had already fled the Nazis. She reminded me that their confrontation over the cello meant that they no longer had any contact. They had, she recalled, never said good-bye. In fact, Paul not only was still in Vienna but remained in touch with Gretl if not with Annelore. When Annelore submitted a list of her property in July, in accordance with the Nazis' Ordinance for the Registration of Jewish Property, Paul signed her form as her father and legal guardian. Paul may have played the same role when she converted a month later. At any rate, he did not interfere.

Any other summer, Annelore would have persuaded Gretl or Käthe to take her to Hinterbichl, as her passion for the Vienna Boys' Choir remained intense, even though the Nazis had dismissed the choir's director, Rektor Schnitt, because he opposed them. As Anne remembered it, the Anschluss meant that Gretl and Käthe could not take her. In fact, many families of Jewish descent tried to treat the summer of 1938 like any other, either going to their own houses, renting villas for the summer, or staying at hotels or guesthouses. Gretl and Käthe probably did not want to do so in case there was something they could do in Vienna to accelerate their departure. They knew it would be foolish to holiday when they needed to flee. Käthe's lawyer was also trying to recover her jewelry. In the account that she sent Gauleiter Bürckel about what happened when the SS and Gestapo raided her apartment, Käthe stressed that she wanted this jewelry for its sentimental significance as much as its monetary value. She also emphasized that the seizure of this jewelry was unwarranted when her official identity as a Jew was simply a matter of legal definition resulting from the Nürnberg Laws. By implication, Käthe resented being declared a Jew.

Annelore began her formal Christian instruction at the Franciscan church in Vienna's First District by acquiring a copy of the New Testament, a missal containing the masses for all the Sundays and church festivals of the year, and a catechism, which she annotated in several places. One of the questions that prompted a long marginal note was: Why does God let us suffer? Another was: Are all sins equally great? This instruction, Anne recalled, had no effect on her. While she liked her teacher, Father Elzear Wangler, she did not believe anything he taught. Catholicism

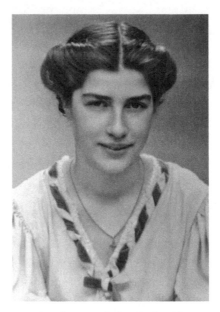

Annelore, newly baptized, with
her crucifix, September 1938.

remained strange, even alien, to her. She still had no faith when Father
Elzear baptized her with Käthe as her godmother and Gretl looking on—
Gretl's first attendance at a service since Hermine's Requiem Mass two
years before. Yet when Annelore took Holy Communion the following
day, she not only believed for reasons she could never explain, but her
faith was so intense that she insisted Gretl and Käthe also become regular
churchgoers.

Gretl was accustomed to having Annelore's portrait taken to com-
memorate significant events in her life, particularly ones involving special
clothes and jewelry. The occasion of Annelore's baptism prompted Gretl
to do so that September, despite the Anschluss. As usual, they went to
Jobst, who photographed Annelore with her hair up in a roll and a thin
chain around her neck, wearing the light purple dress she wore for her
baptism. The most beautiful of Jobst's three photographs shows her in
profile—the simplest classical pose. In another her body is turned more
toward the camera but she looks up and away to the side. The last, which
shows her with rounded shoulders, looking straight at the camera, is the

least attractive but the most telling—revealing that the chain around her neck bears a small gold crucifix.

Before she left Vienna, the newly converted Annelore bought a copy of *Der Ewige Jude,* or *The Eternal Jew,* one of the Nazis' most virulent pieces of anti-Semitism. Its 128 pages, replete with 265 photographs, opened with an account of the origins of the Jewish nose and ended with an attack on Zionism. In between it cast Jews as dishonest, dirty, perverted, treacherous, and murderous. The picture on its cover, which also was featured on banners, posters, and postcards, depicted an "eastern" Jew in a caftan with a whip in one hand, gold coins in the other, and a map bearing the hammer and sickle under his arm, a figure designed to be as threatening because of his Bolshevism as his avarice. The title was in red— its lettering reminiscent of Hebrew script.

The exhibition that formed the basis of this book opened in Munich in November 1937. Over the next twelve weeks, it was seen by five thousand people a day and delighted the Gestapo by heightening anti-Semitism and inciting attacks against Jewish businesses. When it moved to Vienna in August 1938, the crowds were even bigger. Meanwhile, the book became a bestseller. When Annelore bought her copy, one hundred thousand had been sold and another thirty thousand printed. She wanted a copy so she would never be homesick for Austria or grow nostalgic about it—to remind herself that Austria was a country she would be lucky to escape.

4

Visas

Like many children in the 1920s and 1930s, Annelore collected stamps. When I went through what remained of her collection, two envelopes caught my eye because of their sender, John Osborn, an American long resident in the Philippines, to whom Gretl turned for help with visas after Käthe was released from the Hahngasse in 1938. These envelopes suggested that Gretl, who met Osborn in Italy on one of her holidays without Annelore in the early 1930s, remained in regular contact with him, making it plausible for her to ask his help. The stamps and frankings on these envelopes also suggested that Gretl must have told Osborn about Annelore's childhood interest in collecting. While their contents had long been destroyed, the envelopes were part of the chain of connections that gave Gretl, Käthe, and Annelore hope of escape.

The official talk after the Anschluss, as often with refugees, stressed the need for queues and orderly processes, with everyone taking their turn and being judged by the same criteria. Yet there typically was much more disorder than order as refugees used their connections to improve their prospects and governments bent and broke their own rules. As Anne remembered it, Gretl called on three people for help. One was an American woman of German descent who had corresponded with Gretl from the time they became pen pals as girls thirty years before. She responded that Austria's Jews were "getting what they deserved." Another was Osborn, a well-connected government official in Manila, whose initial response was vague, though he soon wrote again to say that he had secured visas for them. The third was Eugénie Luke, the Austrian widow of an English businessman, who had been close to Hermine.

Gretl was eager to draw on this friendship because Mrs. Luke's son, Harry, was even better placed to help them than Osborn. Gretl hoped that Sir Harry Luke, as he became in 1933, would exploit his position as a senior British diplomat to secure British visas for them. But Britain defined itself as "not a country of immigration." Its government was interested only in Jews whom it deemed likely to be an asset to the United Kingdom—a very narrow class. Jews with international reputations as scientists, doctors, researchers, or artists, such as Freud, passed the government's test. So did successful industrialists with businesses that they could transfer to the United Kingdom. Other refugees, including Gretl, Käthe, and Annelore, were ineligible. While some senior British diplomats still tried to secure British visas for Jews who did not satisfy their government's specifications, others such as Sir Harry Luke used their influence to get them visas elsewhere. That Gretl, Käthe, and Annelore should go to Australia, a country of immigration since it became a British penitentiary in 1788, was probably Sir Harry's idea.

Australia was readier to accept European Jews than other former British colonies such as Canada, New Zealand, and South Africa but was far from generous. The national ideal, White Australia, rested on racial homogeneity. The population, by some counts, was 97, if not 98, percent British, and the government wanted it to remain so. While it encouraged British migrants through an assisted passage scheme, non-British migrants with no one in Australia to act as their financial guarantor were eligible for entry only if they arrived with £200 (then $800) and intended to pursue occupations that would not deprive Australians of work. When the Anschluss prompted several hundred Austrian Jews with the necessary "landing money" to apply for Australian visas, the government feared twenty thousand might come within a year and imposed an annual limit of fifty-one hundred. Yet the government continued to maintain that so long as applicants were white, it did not discriminate against any nationality, race, or religion. Just as the government refused to acknowledge that Jews fleeing Hitler were "refugees," so it instructed its officials never to describe its restrictions as a "quota."

By June, Australia had such a backlog of applicants that the government advised the British consul general, who represented Australia's interests in Vienna, to warn all new applicants that they had little chance of success. At the international conference on Jewish refugees held at President Roosevelt's initiative at Evian in France in July, Australia was one of many countries that refused to do more. It insisted that it could not give "undue privileges . . . to one particular class of non-British subjects"—Jews facing persecution—"without injustice to others." It declared that Australia had "no real racial problem" and was "not desirous of importing one." A confidential government paper observed that, while there was "no cause for alarm at the moment" about the number of Jews in Australia, which was one-third of 1 percent of the total population, this number would have to be "watched very carefully."

The Jews competing for visas in mid-1938 included Poles fleeing state persecution as well as Austrians and Germans trying to escape Hitler. Of the five hundred applications the Australian government received each week, it approved one in ten. Gretl, Käthe, and Annelore were fortunate that the government gave preference to Germans and Austrians, both because it considered them in greater need and because it expected them to fit into Australian society more easily than the Poles, whom it regarded as "lesser types." After touring Europe, one senior Australian official compared the Poles to Australian Aborigines, dismissing the Poles as the "poorest specimens outside blackfellows" he had seen.

Australia's criteria for determining whether or not to grant visas fixed on the applicants' age, qualifications, occupation, and capital. Käthe's case was strong as she satisfied the Australian preference for applicants under forty, was a university graduate, and had spent almost ten years managing the Graetzinlicht Gesellschaft. Gretl's case—and hence also that of Annelore as her dependent—was weak because Gretl was forty-two, had no degree, and had never worked. But she had the support of Sir Harry Luke, who was about to become British High Commissioner for the South Seas and governor of Fiji. While the Australian government took four months to decide most applications, the Gallias had their permits "in no time," Anne recalled, after Sir Harry wrote to "his representative in

Australia." By mid-August they knew they would be successful. In early September they had their papers.

Osborn's letter arrived in between. As Anne remembered it, he had secured them visas for the Philippines, which remained an American territory in 1938 but controlled its own immigration policies and was very generous to Jewish refugees. Their passports reveal, however, that the visas were in fact for the United States, where Congress was against measures to help Jewish refugees but President Roosevelt assisted them by combining the annual Austrian quota of less than fifteen hundred, which was manifestly inadequate, with the German quota of almost twenty-six thousand, which was not being filled. In early September, the American consul in Vienna issued Gretl, Käthe, and Annelore visas "good for all United States ports" for twelve months.

Like other refugees who had been in the workforce, Käthe needed more documentation. The first step, as one contemporary account described, was for refugees to go to their old universities and employers "to beg for a copy of a diploma or testimonial and to be called a filthy Jew and left standing, once, twice, three times, before the document—on which was pinned the hope of any future—was finally, with fresh insults, produced." Then they had to seek consular endorsement of these papers, which was hazardous since those waiting in line were sometimes subject to Nazi attack. Because Gretl and Käthe were still not sure which visas they would use, Käthe had her qualifications endorsed by the British and the Americans.

The Nazis required refugees to obtain even more papers before letting them go. Many were financial because the Nazis were intent on ensuring that Jews left with as little money as possible. They had to show that they had paid all government charges, including income, inheritance, building, rental, welfare, and departure taxes, both real and fictitious. The most preposterous document was a statement from Vienna's police president that their departure was voluntary. To begin with, Viennese Jews had to queue to get the necessary forms at ministries, boards, and offices scattered across the city. They had to queue to submit them while Aryans who wanted anything from these offices always took precedence. Because most of these permits were valid for only one month, refugees often found that by the time they had secured what should have been their last approval, the first had expired, so they had to start the process again.

Adolf Eichmann, an officer with the SS, simplified this process in August 1938 by creating a Central Office for Jewish Emigration where members of Vienna's Israelitische Kultusgemeinde could obtain all the necessary permits, all valid for the same period. While Eichmann's use of the Palais Rothschild symbolized how the Nazis were victimizing even Vienna's richest Jews, the office not only enabled the Nazis to secure Jewish property with even greater speed but also allowed Vienna's Jews to escape more easily. Gretl and Käthe did not have this option because of their conversions. Either they could try to secure the documents themselves or become part of Operation Gildemeester, which the Dutch Quaker Frank van Gheel Gildemeester created with the Nazis to expedite the departure of former members of the Kultusgemeinde. This operation, which made Gildemeester a fortune while facilitating the flight of thousands of relatively poor refugees, was funded by property from about a hundred wealthy families whose escapes were also expedited. Because the Nazis imposed strict exchange controls on refugees, Käthe went through Operation Gildemeester to obtain the landing money she needed to gain entry into Australia. She recalled paying an "extravagant sum" to secure this £200.

Switzerland was to blame for a new law that complicated the departure of Gretl and Annelore. When Germany annexed Austria, the only benefit for Austrian Jews was an agreement between Germany and Switzerland that allowed their citizens to travel without obtaining visas. As Austrian Jews became German citizens following the Anschluss, they could enter Switzerland on this basis. When forty-seven reached Basel in one day, Switzerland protested at this "inundation" and renounced the agreement with Germany, only to offer to restrict its visa requirement to German and Austrian Jews so long as their passports made plain that they were Jews. The Nazis duly ordered all Jews to hand in their passports so they could be issued with German passports stamped with a big red *J* on their front pages.

Because Käthe had already obtained a German passport at the start of September in which was affixed her American visa, she simply had to have this passport stamped with a *J* in order to satisfy the new law. Because Gretl and Annelore had obtained their American visas in their Austrian passports, they had to secure new German ones. Then they returned to the American consulate, where, to their relief, they found that the visas they had obtained with Osborn's help were transferable.

In the end, Gretl, Käthe, and Annelore chose Australia because Erni, Mizzi, and Mizzi's sister, Fini, appeared set on going there. As Anne remembered it, Australia's remoteness also attracted them. She thought they were eager to go as far from Hitler as they could, though this aspect of Australia probably began to appeal to them only when World War II started and Hitler's military power appeared almost unlimited. When Käthe and Annelore went to see the Vienna Boys' Choir's founding director, Rektor Schnitt, who was the only person they knew who had been to Australia, he recommended Sydney and wrote them a letter of introduction to its most exclusive Catholic girls' school, run by the Order of the Sacred Heart at Rose Bay.

I can see Annelore dreading the daily insults and indignities at her school in the Albertgasse following the Anschluss. I imagine her wanting to stay away to avoid the harassment and victimization. She would have pressed Gretl to let her sometimes remain home if not take her out of school altogether. When the new school year started that September, there was no choice. Annelore could not return to the Albertgasse because the Nazis' exclusion of children they identified as Jewish had finally taken effect. As a new and devout Catholic, Annelore would have refused to attend the one high school in Vienna that the Nazis created for Jews, even if it had been safe to go there. Like most other children of Jewish origin, Annelore stayed home with what she described as "endless days to fill and nothing to do."

Many other refugees spent their last months in Vienna attending language classes, but Gretl had no need to do so because she had been taught English by a succession of governesses, schoolteachers, and private tutors and was a superb linguist. Käthe's English was also good due to similar instruction. One of her birthday presents in 1908—inscribed by Hermine in English "To my darling twins"—was *A Little Mother*, a 294-page children's story that Hermine clearly anticipated her nine-year-old daughters would have read to them, if not read themselves. Annelore's English was also impressive, as revealed by one of her school exercise books from 1936. She wrote of London's policeman: "The so-called 'Bobby' is everyone's friend. He is very kind, but that does not mean that he can not look sharp after transgressors. Little children and prams or bewildered persons, all are directed by his up-lifted hand."

Many other adults and teenagers looking to flee also attended courses in trades and crafts such as pastry making, pearl stringing, sausage making, typing, and shorthand. The men who attended these classes were typically professionals with qualifications not recognized outside Austria who needed retraining to persuade another country to take them. The women who took these courses needed training since they generally had never worked. The teenagers were often just looking for something to keep them busy as a substitute for going to school. Annelore was among them when she began learning how to clean lace—a specialist occupation for which there was still demand in Vienna but none in Australia.

Her teacher was Anni Wiesbauer, who had worked first for Hermine and then for Gretl and Käthe. While the Nazis allowed the Israelitische Kultusgememeinde in Vienna to organize retraining courses for its members, just as the Quakers did for converts to Christianity, it was very different for an individual such as Anni to do so. By aiding a Jew, as Annelore remained in Nazi terms, Anni could be branded a *Volksfeinde,* or enemy of the people. Anni was particularly vulnerable because her assistant, Reserl, was a Nazi who might have informed on her, yet Anni was happy to help. Her offer to teach Annelore was one of a devoted employee to longstanding employers. It was one of a devout Catholic to a new convert. It was one of a middle-aged woman with no child of her own who had known Annelore all her life. In Annelore's last months in Vienna she saw Anni almost every day.

Both Anni and Annelore looked on this time together with similar intensity. Anni thought of Annelore as a younger sister, a little comrade, a soul mate. Anne described her time with Anni as one of her "great" experiences as a girl and looked on Anni as having "rescued" her. She particularly enjoyed the opportunity to do mundane, practical tasks that had always been the job of the Gallias' servants before the Anschluss and remained so after it because the Nazis initially allowed men and women of Jewish origin such as Gretl to keep their Christian maids. They last saw each other on November 11, the day after Kristallnacht, which was also the day before Annelore left Vienna. Annelore gave Anni a silver basket once owned by Hermine and a bottle of liqueur probably made by Johann Timmels-Witwe. Anni reciprocated with a photograph showing her cleaning lace "in memory of our work together." Annelore also left with a photograph of Anni's maid, Reserl, that she later inscribed "Anni's Reserl, a good Nazi."

Father Elzear gave Annelore more to do as he continued baptizing

Jews at the Franciscan church. Because many of the new converts knew no one willing to be their godparents, Annelore served as the godmother not only of younger girls but also of several adults. Either way, she always filled this role for people she had only just met and did not expect to see again. By the time Annelore left, Elzear was very important to her. The last two photographs that she took in Vienna were of him. He gave her a photograph of himself and a postcard of the Franciscan church that he inscribed "in everlasting memory and forever." Annelore found saying good-bye to him very difficult.

Annelore also occupied herself by playing the cello—the one aspect of her conventional middle-class education to continue through these months. Although Annelore did not show particular ability, Gretl followed family tradition by having her taught by an accomplished cellist, Lucie Weiss, who performed with one of Vienna's best quartets. When the Anschluss resulted in Weiss's being stripped of this position because she was a Jew, she continued to teach Annelore while organizing her own escape to New York.

The start of the new opera season in September saw Annelore going out more than ever, usually alone, though accompanied at least once by Anni Wiesbauer. While she would have worn her new crucifix prominently displayed, these outings were fraught with danger. If identified as a Jew, she would be at risk, whether discovered in the opera or on Vienna's streets. Yet Annelore was eager to make the most of a world that was ending for her. Whether Gretl, Käthe, and she went to Australia or the United States, she did not expect to be back in Europe for years, if ever again. Because she could see no prospect of the Nazi rule of Austria's ending, she could not imagine returning. Besides, she was desperate for distractions and the opera offered an escape. By the end of September, she had been eleven times. In October, she spent another eighteen evenings there, attending performances of Wagner's *Tannhäuser, Lohengrin,* and *Die Meistersinger,* which, she remembered, received thunderous applause.

Annelore also saw more than ever of the Vienna Boys' Choir because her conversion meant that she was finally able to go to the Burgkapelle, the chapel of the old Imperial Palace, where the choir sang each Sunday. As she wrote a few years later, she "learned to love and appreciate High Mass there in preference to any other church." While she thought Rektor Schnitt's replacement "knew nothing about the boys and little about music," she still wanted to see them whenever possible. Their program

that October was wonderful. She heard them perform Mozart's Corona-
tion Mass, Schubert's Mass in F Major, Haydn's Theresa Mass, Mozart's
Sparrow Mass, and Schubert's Mass in G Major, which probably were all
new to her. As a result, the Burgkapelle became her symbol of Vienna as
the "City of Music." She thought there never had been "a more perfect
combination of Art and Religion."

Vienna remained the City of Music for her at the start of November.
She attended the Burgkapelle for Haydn's Holy Mass on All Saints' Day
and Mozart's Requiem on All Souls' Day. That night she saw Strauss's
Salome at the opera. On Friday she saw Mozart's *Don Giovanni.* Two days
later she was at the Burgkapelle for another Sunday mass.

Gretl and Annelore knew that November 9 was Blutzeuge, the most
sacred Nazi public holiday. While festivities during the day in Vienna
commemorated the fifteenth anniversary of Hitler's failed Beer Hall
Putsch, three thousand new members of the SS were to parade from late in
the evening until early the following morning, swearing allegiance to
Hitler at the city's Heldenplatz at midnight. These celebrations gave Gretl
particular reason to keep Annelore home but, with just a few days to go
before they were to leave Vienna, Annelore insisted on one last night at the
opera. For the third time in two months, she went to Mozart's *The Magic
Flute.* When she got home, she recorded the performance in her concert
book as usual. About half an hour later, the Gestapo in Vienna received
the order from Munich to instigate the pogrom that became known as
Kristallnacht.

Anne remembered none of this more than fifty years later—or anything of the next two and a half days in Vienna, when she went across the
city several times. While Anne checked her concert book when she wrote
her story, she was misled by her entry for *The Magic Flute* because the date
could be read as either November 3, when the Vienna Opera did not perform *The Magic Flute,* or November 9, when it did. Anne read this date as
the third, which fit her recollection that Gretl and she left Vienna before
Kristallnacht and that Käthe was still there because she wanted to give her
lawyer more time to retrieve her jewelry from the Gestapo. Anne wrote:
"In the end he succeeded and she left a few days after us, but by that time
the Crystal Night had already taken place and I was extremely worried
whether she would make it."

I discovered Anne was mistaken a few days after she died in 2003,
when I began dipping into her Viennese theater books. The last of these

books included her entry for the performance of *The Magic Flute,* which I immediately read as November 9. When I confirmed this date in the library, I briefly was overcome by frustration at not being able to talk to her about what I had found, that it was too late for me to tell her where she had been on Kristallnacht and see if she could remember anything about it. Then I realized that, for all my curiosity, it was probably better that I had not challenged her in this way when she had been so troubled to discover the unreliability of memory while writing her story. I would simply have fueled her doubts about exactly what she had done as a girl and who she had been.

Subterfuge

The most extensive account of the art looted in Vienna following the Anschluss is by the art historian Sophie Lillie. The 1,439 pages of her book *Was einmal war,* or *What Once Was,* document the 148 biggest collections, identifying their owners, what the Nazis stole, and the roles played by key officials. Lillie also reveals where these collections were located, creating a remarkable map of wealth, directory of theft, and geography of loss. One street, the Rathausstrasse in the First District, was home to four confiscated collections. The Wohllebengasse was home to three. The merchant Fritz Wolff-Knize and his wife, Anna, had one of the great collections of modern art, as well as a spectacular ethnographic room. The property magnates Gottlieb and Mathilde Kraus collected nineteenth-century Austrian art. The artist Wilhelm Krausz combined Old Masters with Louis XIV furniture, baroque crucifixions, Persian carpets, and a bronze Buddha.

The proximity of these collections in 1938 is all the more significant because there are just ten houses on one side of the Wohllebengasse and nine on the other. The prominence of the Wohllebengasse in Lillie's book is testimony to the wealth of its inhabitants, their taste for art, and their Jewish origins. Because the Nazis confiscated all of the Kraus and Krauz collections and the ethnographic collection of the Wolff-Knizes, the Wohllebengasse was one of the prime sites of Nazi plunder. Because the Wolff-Knizes hid their paintings in the Romanian embassy in Vienna and Gretl and Käthe fled with all their pictures and furniture, the Wohllebengasse was also the source of the best collection to escape the Nazis while remaining within Austria and the best private collection to get away.

An array of laws, both old and new, governed what Gretl and Käthe took. One was a cultural protection law, which Austria introduced in 1918 in an attempt to stop the pillaging of its art following World War I and then amended in 1923 so that all objects of historic, artistic, or cultural significance could be preserved in the public interest. Another law introduced in Germany to stem a loss of capital during the Great Depression provided for a departure tax, which the Nazis set at one-quarter of the value of each refugee's property. Yet another law, introduced in Germany as a Depression measure but toughened by the Nazis, stopped refugees from converting their remaining property and money into foreign currency. The Ordinance for the Registration of Jewish Property introduced in 1938, provided the Nazis with information about whom to target, as well as a basis for determining the departure tax that refugees paid when they left.

The most valuable pieces of property that Gretl and Käthe had to leave behind were the houses in the Wohllebengasse and Alt Aussee that they owned jointly with Erni. As part of the family's long-standing involvement in the gas industry, Gretl and Käthe had also made big loans to two gas companies that they could not recover. Although Gretl had significant shares and bonds at the time of the Anschluss, she had to sell them to pay her departure tax. While Käthe's lawyer persuaded the Nazis to treat the shares, bonds, and cash that the Gestapo had taken in April as her payment of the departure tax, this decision was of little consequence since Käthe could not take her other money with her. The same was true of Annelore, who had bonds and debentures in Austria's Postsavings Bank.

The art and furniture owned by Gretl and Käthe were a different matter. The sisters were free to take them so long as they received the permission of the Central Office for Monuments Protection, which administered Austria's cultural protection laws. This office was an inconsequential, ill-funded organization through most of the 1930s, largely ignored by those wishing to take art out of Austria. Following the Anschluss, it rapidly grew in size and significance because refugees had to secure its approval before leaving. Whereas it had been accustomed to one hundred applications a year, in 1938 it received 10,500.

The Gallias' Waldmüllers were most vulnerable—not just because Waldmüller was generally accepted as one of Austria's great artists but because he was among Hitler's favorites, leading him to become the Austrian artist most pillaged by the Nazis. Gretl and Käthe had to decide whether to reveal the existence of their portraits in July 1938, when they submitted inventories in accordance with the Ordinance for the Registration of Jewish Property. While Käthe's list of paintings does not survive, Gretl's list is in Austria's National Archives. Like many other refugees, Gretl did what she could to diminish her valuations. Rather than have her pictures appraised by an expert, she took them to a general valuer. Although her portrait was signed and dated by Waldmüller, Gretl claimed it was a copy of one of his pictures, and the valuer accepted this attribution, significantly reducing her departure tax. While Waldmüller's standard portraits were worth 5,000 reichsmarks, Gretl's painting was valued at 66 marks.

Otto Kallir, the owner of Vienna's leading modern art gallery, was one refugee who manipulated the process again when he required the permission of the Monuments Office. Exploiting his exceptional connections in Vienna's art establishment, Kallir had his collection vetted by Bruno Grimschitz, the deputy director of the Österreichische Galerie, who had just been made a member of the Nazi Party in recognition of his support for it when the party was still illegal. Kallir expected favorable treatment from Grimschitz because of their long association and received it even though Grimschitz was set on securing further advancement under the Nazis. While Grimschitz denied permission for Kallir to take a few Biedermeier pictures—"These we must sacrifice to the Gods," Grimschitz declared—he allowed Kallir to take much more valuable, old works. He also allowed him to take all of his twentieth-century pictures in accordance with the Monuments Office's usual policy that these pictures did not yet form part of Austria's cultural heritage.

Gretl did not enjoy such connections. While Grimschitz was a close friend of her uncle Paul Hamburger before the Anschluss, Gretl felt in no position to exploit this friendship when she sought the Monuments Office's permission in August. She probably also knew that Grimschitz had become an eager agent of the Nazi state, at the forefront of pillaging art from Jewish collections. Instead, her collection was vetted through the ordinary process by the office's second-in-command, Josef Zykan, who identified the painting as a Waldmüller and denied permission for its export.

The only remaining basis on which Gretl might be able to take the painting was by claiming it as a family portrait, which meant it would have depicted a Jew. Such paintings enjoyed a partial exemption from the Monuments Office's controls on the basis that the sitter's Jewishness tainted the art. The only pictures that Ferdinand Bloch-Bauer thought the Nazis might release to him after he fled were four family portraits, including Klimt's two paintings of Adele. The only one that Ferdinand regained was an Oskar Kokoschka painting that the Nazis returned to him in Switzerland in 1944—an extraordinary instance of art restitution in the midst of war.

Just as Gretl sent Annelore to the Hahngasse with cream disguised as toothpaste when Käthe was imprisoned there, so Gretl sent her to the Monuments Office to attempt another subterfuge. As was often the case, when Anne later wrote about what happened, her account was casual, conveying nothing of the risks involved and giving no hint that she might have felt any fear. It was as if when Anne wrote her story, she could not see the magnitude of what she had done or experienced. She simply wrote: "I was told to take the paintings to the office where the clearance could be obtained. I brought them, claiming that they were my relatives."

This claim was risible. While the identities of Waldmüller's sitters were unknown when Hermine and Moriz bought them, the portraits could not be family because there were so few Jews in Vienna when Waldmüller painted the pictures in 1837 and none of them were Gallias or Hamburgers. As a diligent official, Josef Zykan might have been expected to recognize Gretl's subterfuge or at least require her to substantiate it. Instead, the painting became one of fifty cases in which the office overturned its initial refusal of permission. Zykan authorized Gretl to take the portrait on the basis that its subject was "from the family of the owner."

Käthe's application was handled by another of the office's senior staff, Otto Demus, who immigrated to Great Britain the following year for a mix of personal and political reasons. While Demus recorded that Käthe had eleven oil paintings, he did not mention her companion portrait by Waldmüller, suggesting that he did not realize she owned one. As this portrait was unsigned, Demus may not have recognized it was by Waldmüller.

Because he did not inspect Gretl's pictures, he had no reason to expect it was the pair to her signed painting. Yet a letter written by Gretl a few years later indicates that the office initially refused export permission for both portraits. Anne similarly recalled that she regained them both. After she explained that they depicted family, Zykan declared, "The old Jews could go."

Klimt was the other artist collected by Moriz and Hermine whose work was celebrated in Austria after the Anschluss. The first book on Klimt in over twenty years was published in Vienna in 1942. The city's new gauleiter, Baldur von Schirach, initiated the biggest-ever Klimt exhibition, staged at the Secession in 1943. Yet even Klimt's largest pictures did not command the same prices as much smaller works by Waldmüller. Many Nazis also abhorred Klimt because of his modernity and dependence on Jewish patronage. The Secession responded by trying to hide these links—retitling Klimt's first painting of Adele Bloch-Bauer as *A Lady with a Gold Background* and his second portrait of Adele as *Lady Standing*.

This mixed regard for Klimt was patent when refugees wanted to leave with his work. While the Gestapo and the Internal Revenue Office often seized his paintings and drawings, they looked on his work as just another form of property that could be realized to pay the taxes that the Nazis imposed on Jews. The Monuments Office never displayed much interest in Klimt and, even though Austria's cultural heritage protection laws applied to artists who had been dead for twenty years—and Klimt had died in January 1918—the office seems to have ignored his work altogether in 1938, perhaps still viewing him as a contemporary artist outside its domain. In keeping with this approach, Otto Demus allowed Käthe to take the portrait of Hermine. She did not need to make anything of Hermine's Jewish origins or identify the painting as a family portrait. The export of the Klimt was as simple as the wastepaper baskets and doormats that Gretl and Käthe took, too.

The Hoffmann collection was similarly straightforward. The Monuments Office ignored the furniture, treating it as ordinary household goods rather than as works of art. While the office paid more attention to the sisters' silver, it approved its export. Despite the Nazis' admiration for Hoffmann, which led them to appoint him a Special Commissioner for Viennese Arts and Crafts and commission him to remodel Vienna's German embassy into a Haus der Wehrmacht for army officers, the Monuments Office regarded Hoffmann's work as contemporary and hence not within its domain.

The Nazis took a different approach to jewelry, prohibiting refugees from taking their collections with them. While Gretl's collection was nowhere near as spectacular as that owned by Käthe, it was still very valuable. The list of the thirty best pieces that Gretl submitted in accordance with the Ordinance for the Registration of Jewish Property started with a diamond and platinum ring, followed by a gold handbag decorated with three diamonds and four rubies, a long pearl chain, a pair of gold earrings studded with pearls and seven small diamonds, and a gold, diamond, and pearl ring. Despite revealing her ownership of these pieces, Gretl hoped to escape with them. She assumed the Nazis would not miss her jewelry if they could not find it.

First she needed a safe place in Vienna in case the Gestapo raided her apartment. She had to find someone she trusted who was not in jeopardy under the Nürnberg Laws. She had few choices because most of Gretl's Aryan friends abandoned her after the Anschluss. Carl Moll, who became an ardent Nazi, was among them. While Moll has become notorious for pillaging the collection of his stepdaughter, Alma Mahler, after she fled Vienna with her third husband, the Jewish writer Franz Werfel, his treatment of the Gallias was also shocking. Even though Moriz and Hermine had been his biggest patrons and he was the godfather and "Uncle Carl" of Erni, Gretl, and Käthe, Moll severed all contact with the Gallias.

Three sisters—Assanta, Marlene, and Gilda Moll, who were unrelated to Carl—behaved very differently. They had met Gretl at Bad Hall, a spa near Linz, when Gretl took Annelore there in 1925 to recuperate from whooping cough, and continued to see Gretl in Vienna, where they soon became honorary aunts of Annelore. Far from the Anschluss putting an end to this friendship, it brought the Gallias and Molls closer together. When Gretl asked their help, the Molls agreed immediately, but thought it too risky for Gretl to come to their house because their caretaker was a Nazi who might report her visit. Gretl probably thought it would be similarly hazardous for the Molls to visit her apartment. They agreed it was safest to transfer the jewelry in public rather than private. They met on the street.

It was then even more of a challenge for Gretl to get her collection out of the country. One of the best conduits for small items was the diplo-

matic bags of foreign embassies. Just before Sigmund Freud left Austria in
June 1938, one of his great admirers, Maria Bonaparte, the wife of Prince
George of Greece, had Freud's collection of gold coins taken across the
border in the bag of the Greek embassy. Gretl turned to a member of the
Bulgarian embassy, which occupied the ground floor of the Wohllebengasse and so was one of her tenants. When he agreed to take Gretl's collection to the Gallias' most trusted friend in Switzerland, Dr. Emil Widmer,
the risks were high. While Maria Bonaparte could ensure that the Greek
diplomats delivered Freud's gold, Gretl had no power over the Bulgarian
official. If he made off with her collection, she had no redress because she
was acting illegally. Gretl was lucky. Apart from one small diamond flower,
he delivered her entire collection to Dr. Widmer.

The conventional image of the refugee would have Gretl, Käthe, and
Annelore jumping on and off moving trains, sailing in creaky boats, crossing borders at night. Yet there have always been refugees like the writer
Vladimir Nabokov, who departed Soviet Russia in November 1917 wearing spats and a derby, traveled to the Crimea Sea in a first-class sleeping
compartment, then learned to fox-trot while sailing to Marseilles on a
Cunard liner. Until November 1938, many refugees, including Gretl,
Käthe, and Annelore, also fled first class because the Nazis allowed them
to spend as much as they liked on their passage but otherwise stopped
them from taking their money with them.

The standard means of departure was by train. The practice was for
refugees to go to the station alone, since it was too dangerous for family or
friends to accompany them. Erni and Mizzi duly stayed away. Having
already put themselves in jeopardy by safeguarding Gretl's jewelry, the
three Moll sisters did so again by going to Vienna's Westbahnhof to bid
farewell to Gretl and Annelore on November 12. As Anne recalled, she was
heartbroken that Käthe was not with them. Her story implies that Gretl
and she begged Käthe to accompany them but Käthe refused because her
lawyer thought he was on the verge of persuading the Gestapo to return
her jewelry and allow her to take it out of the country.

Gretl was also set on leaving with more of her property, spurred by her
fear of being unable to support Annelore and herself in Australia, having
never worked before. She had a small collection of 100-franc coins from
Monaco—typical pieces of investment gold—that she probably acquired
in return for selling some of her other property as she prepared to flee, just

as Freud acquired his collection. As Gretl explained to me when I was a boy, those were the coins she covered with fabric and sewed onto her traveling coat in place of the original buttons.

The risks again were high. Freud's eldest son, Martin, recalled that before he left Austria in May 1938, he was told that a Jew had been taken from a train and shot because stamps had been found in his pocketbook. Martin duly gave his remaining money to a friend in Vienna rather than attempt to escape with it. Other refugees chose to test the Nazis' controls. Women, who often took charge of packing, were particularly ready to do so. Fanny Kallir, the wife of the art dealer Otto Kallir, was one of them. When the Kallirs fled to Switzerland with their two children in June 1938, Fanny hid a small collection of gold coins in a basket under her daughter's hair ribbons without telling Otto. Although Gretl and Annelore were searched before they crossed the border, the guards failed to notice anything unusual about Gretl's buttons.

Their destination was St. Gallen in Switzerland, because Dr. Widmer lived there. When they arrived on November 13, Uncle Emil, as Annelore called him, was at the station to greet them. That afternoon, Annelore wrote letters thanking the three people who had done the most for her in Vienna—Father Elzear, Anni Wiesbauer, and her cello teacher, Lucie Weiss. She also began a new diary with typical economy, describing her escape in a single two-line sentence. Just as she did not express delight or relief at putting Vienna behind her, she expressed neither excitement nor fear at what was to come.

As Gretl and she had no idea if they would return to Europe, they had every reason to treat their journey as an unintended holiday, an occasion to see more of the world. Gretl had been to Switzerland; Annelore had not. Accustomed to pursuing the best of culture and nature when they traveled, they did so on this trip. They began by inspecting St. Gallen's rococo cathedral and viewing the surrounding countryside of Alpenzell with Dr. Widmer. Then Annelore went by herself to St. Gallen's New Museum before going with Gretl to the railway station to meet Käthe's train. When she failed to alight, Gretl started to panic, only to discover Käthe in the last carriage still organizing her many bags.

The timing of the final negotiations between the Gestapo and Käthe's lawyer, Stephan Lehner, over her jewelry could hardly have been less auspicious. On November 12, when Käthe was still in Vienna, a meeting about the "Jewish question" chaired by Göring in Berlin announced new anti-Semitic measures. The most bizarre cast Jews as responsible for Kristallnacht. It attributed all the Nazis' murder, plunder, and destruction to the killing in Paris of a German diplomat by a Jewish boy whose family was among thousands of Polish-born Jews in Germany whom the Nazis had forced from their homes at gunpoint and tried to deport by train, only for the Polish government to refuse them entry. As part of requiring Jews to atone for Kristallnacht, the new *Judenkontribution* was a fine of 1 billion reichsmarks—the equivalent of $5.3 billion today—to be paid by all Jews in four installments.

Stephan Lehner was one of many lawyers who profited from the Anschluss. He was soon involved in the Aryanization of the property of wealthy Jews, including Gottlieb and Mathilde Kraus, who lived at Wohllebengasse 16. He also began acting for the Gestapo. But he represented Käthe well. Having negotiated her release from the Hahngasse, he was equally successful that November, when he secured permission for her to take her jewelry to Switzerland, so long as she bought it back at an inflated valuation fixed by an assessor employed by the Gestapo. While the nominal cost was high, the price did not matter because of Käthe's attachment to her jewelry and because she could not take her money with her when she left Austria.

The risks taken by Käthe in staying behind were acute. Her last three days in Vienna were at least as frightening as her arrest eight months before. To avoid being seized again, she spent these days hiding in Lehner's car. Because she had no way of contacting Gretl and Annelore in St. Gallen, Lehner probably let them know which train she planned to take. But when Gretl and Annelore went to the station, they still did not know whether Käthe had succeeded in escaping. Annelore's diary contains the one hint of their fears, the only expression of their relief. "*Alles in Ordnung,*" she wrote after being reunited with Käthe. "Everything is all right."

The countries that gave transit visas to refugees fleeing Hitler in 1938 gave them very little time before requiring them to move on. When Käthe reached St. Gallen, the Swiss visas of Gretl and Annelore were good for just five more days. Annelore spent part of the first building on her knowledge of lace in St. Gallen's Industrial Museum. She spent part of the next listening to a radio broadcast of Verdi's *A Masked Ball,* the last opera she heard in Europe. Then Gretl, Käthe, and she went sightseeing for the weekend to Lucerne, Küssnacht, and Zurich. That Sunday Annelore attended mass with Käthe, another mark of how Käthe shared Annelore's new faith more than Gretl. The following Monday they had to leave.

Almost no one flew in 1938. The cost was too high. But many refugees had no choice if they were to get to England because they could not get visas to travel across continental Europe by land. For almost all these refugees, this first experience of small, low-flying aircraft with unpressurized cabins was a cause of excitement and fear. Gretl, Käthe, and Annelore, who flew from Zurich, were among them. In her diary, Annelore made most of the beginning of this flight when the weather was magnificent and they had views of the Alps. Fifty years later, all she remembered was how the weather deteriorated and she became sick and scared, while Gretl feared they would be arrested if they were forced to land because they did not have French visas. When they arrived, the stamps in their passports—"Landed on Condition of Direct Transit through United Kingdom to Australia"—underlined that Britain also did not want them. But its officials were much friendlier than their German and Swiss counterparts. "*Nette Zoll,*" Annelore noted. "Nice customs."

All three of them knew where to go and what to see over the next four days. As part of her school exercise about London in 1936, Annelore had described the view from the top of St. Paul's Cathedral, looking up and down the Thames, across Tower Bridge, and over the Houses of Parliament and Westminster Abbey. Gretl, Käthe, and she went to all these places. They watched the changing of the guard at Buckingham Palace, visited Trafalgar Square, Piccadilly Circus, the Tower of London, the Wallace Collection, and the Tate Gallery. They inspected some of London's famous department stores but bought nothing for the first time in their lives, since they had less money than ever. Then they took the train to Southampton, England's main passenger port. Just before they sailed, Käthe sent a letter to the Moll sisters describing the "beautiful things" they had seen.

When I visited the apartment in Sydney as a boy, several of their suitcases survived, plastered with labels from their travels. Now there is only one, Käthe's hatbox, which carries labels recording stays at the Österreichischer Hof in Salzburg and the Grand Hotel Metropole in Milan, and the voyage of Gretl, Käthe, and Annelore from Southampton. This label reveals they sailed on the *Baloeran,* a Rotterdam Lloyd liner that could carry four hundred passengers. They were in cabin 83 on the first-class deck, a domain of privilege that the second- and third-class passengers could not enter.

They sailed across the Mediterranean, through the Suez Canal, down the Red Sea, and across the Indian Ocean to Ceylon, as Sri Lanka was then known, Singapore, and Java. Their first stop was Lisbon, then Tangiers, where they remained aboard the *Baloeran* because the only way to get ashore was by small boat and the sea was too rough. Similar conditions prevented their landing at Gibraltar, but they were able to land at Marseilles, Port Said, and Colombo. Their destination was Batavia, the capital of the Dutch East Indies, now Jakarta, the capital of Indonesia, which they reached on December 22, four weeks after leaving England.

Along the way, Gretl enjoyed the opportunity to show off the jewelry she had recovered from Dr. Widmer at the elegant shipboard dinners and dances that came with traveling first class. Although Annelore had been cared for by governesses and maids all her life, she was embarrassed that they had their own Indonesian servant who sat cross-legged outside their first-class cabin, waiting for their orders. She was happiest when helping out in the ship's kindergarten, which allowed her to do more of the useful work she had enjoyed so much with Anni Wiesbauer. While Gretl, Käthe, and she had many more opportunities to shop when they reached port, they still bought almost nothing. A piece of batik that Gretl used to cover her desk in Sydney was a rare exception.

As they traveled, mail from the Molls awaited them at almost every port. Gretl, Käthe, and Annelore were also welcomed as they traveled—a common experience of refugees in the immediate aftermath of Kristallnacht, when international outrage at Nazi persecution of Jews reached new heights. Some refugees who traveled to Australia via Canada were billeted by members of the Jewish community of Montreal, fed by other Jews as they crossed the prairies on the Trans-Canada Railway, then taken on an excursion by the Bishop of Honolulu as they sailed across the Pacific to Sydney. Gretl, Käthe, and Annelore were cared for in similar fashion thanks to John Osborn, Gretl's friend in Manila. He arranged for them to be met at several ports by members of the Society of Friends, or Quakers, who were at the forefront of helping refugees from Germany and Austria in keeping with their larger concern for assisting persecuted minorities.

Like many other refugees, the Gallias struggled with this reception. As members of the upper middle class, they thought of themselves as givers of

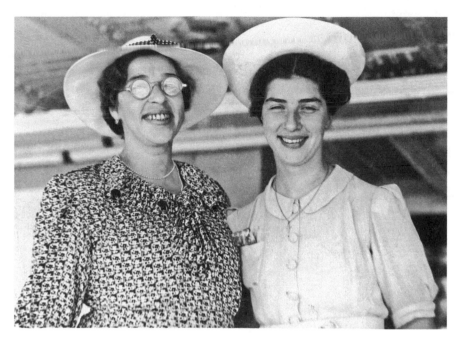

Gretl and Annelore as photographed in Brisbane by the *Telegraph,* January 4, 1939.

charity. They had no experience of receiving it. Their new situation was a cause of embarrassment, even humiliation. Although grateful to be met, they had to learn how to accept help. As Gretl later put it, "The main trouble was that for the first time in our lives we had to accept without being able to give."

The final leg of their journey was on the *Nieuw Zeeland,* one of the "Great White Yachts" of the Royal Packet Navigation Company. Its route took it along the coast of Java to Bali and Makassar and then through the Torres Strait. Its first Australian port was Brisbane, where it stayed just four hours, but the Gallias still made it into the local *Telegraph,* which often published photographs of fashionable women embarking on voyages or returning home. One of these photographs, on January 4, 1939, was "Arriving from Vienna." It showed Gretl and Annelore, both beaming, with Annelore's crucifix prominent. The accompanying text did not explain why they had come. It stated: "Mrs. Margaret Herschmann-Gallia and her daughter Miss Annelore Herschmann-Gallia passed through Brisbane on their way to Sydney this morning." The *Telegraph* revealed more about Käthe, but was still coy, describing her as "a Doctor of Science, who hopes to find scope here for work which was interrupted in Vienna by the German occupation."

The arrival forms, which they filled out in Brisbane, summarized their situation. Gretl and Käthe each had the £200 required of adult non-British migrants, while Annelore had another £100. When they reached Sydney, they expected to stay at the Catholic Women's Association near the center of the city. They knew no one. When asked to provide the names and addresses of two relatives or friends in Australia, the best they could offer was "Sir Harry Luke, Governor of Fiji and Pacific, Suva."

Gretl, Käthe, and Annelore were met in Sydney, where three new organizations were helping refugees. One was the Jewish Welfare Society, founded by Australian Jews of British origin to assist their coreligionists. Another was the Continental Catholic Migrants Welfare Committee, formed by local Catholics. The third was the Germany Emergency Fellowship Committee, which primarily helped Protestant and nondenominational refugees but also assisted Jews and Catholics. While this emergency fellowship committee owed its existence to Quakers, its members also included Protestants eager to help the new arrivals. When the *Nieuw Zeeland* sailed under the Sydney Harbour Bridge on January 6, members of the committee were at Walsh Bay to meet Gretl, Käthe, and Annelore.

Mrs. Nellie Ryan, the wife of a Sydney public servant, with twin daughters a little younger than Annelore, was among this welcoming party. During 1939, she assisted one family of Viennese refugees after another by inviting them to supper, taking them on outings, helping them to find schools for their children, and accompanying them on their first school day. When she heard that Gretl, Käthe, and Annelore were planning to stay at the Catholic Women's Association, she invited them to spend their first Australian weekend in her house on Sydney's inner North Shore, where she had rooms to spare. According to Gretl, Mrs. Ryan saw herself as doing "good in private to three helpless and friendless ladies."

Other refugees helped by Mrs. Ryan found her shockingly English, if only because she was the first British Australian with whom they had significant contact. For Gretl, Käthe, and Annelore, their weekend with the Ryans was not just their first experience of Australian suburbia but also the first time any of them had stayed in a detached single-story house. A letter written a few years later by Gretl records how difficult Käthe, Annelore, and she found it being in a strange land under the roof of strangers. Gretl "nearly died" because the Ryans did not allow smoking in the house as part of their strict Presbyterianism. Yet Gretl also recognized how lucky they were to be cared for by "dear" Mrs. Ryan and her "honorable" family.

Like most refugees who arrived with only their cabin baggage, Gretl, Käthe, and Annelore took a furnished apartment until their containers arrived. While the German Emergency Fellowship Committee had found one for them in Kings Cross close to the city center, it was so filthy and ill-furnished that Gretl and Käthe rejected it. The one they found for themselves in neighboring Darlinghurst was not much better. But they did not have to stay long because their containers were already in Italy, waiting for Gretl and Käthe to authorize their shipment by freighter. Six weeks later, their containers were in Sydney, allowing them to express their gratitude to the Ryans by giving them the largest of their newly arrived silver trays.

Because the £500 that they had brought with them was a quarter of the cost of an ordinary house in Sydney's eastern suburbs, they continued renting. Their problem was that most Sydney apartments were smaller than Gretl's Viennese apartment and they also had Käthe's furniture. While their new apartment in Rose Bay came with a garage, which they used for storage, they could not keep everything. Many other refugees, who arrived at the same time with vast containers but little money, sold their best furniture, creating a brief glut on the local market. Gretl and Käthe could have joined them, but their Hoffmann furniture had not been particularly valuable in Vienna and was worth even less in Sydney, where there was no appreciation of Austrian design. Instead they sold Gretl's Steinway grand piano, which was one of their few possessions to maintain its value across the hemispheres, as well as the hardest to get into their third-floor flat.

They reduced their possessions again when Käthe got a job on the North Shore three years later, prompting them to move to Cremorne, where their new apartment did not have a garage. While wartime austerity meant the market was particularly weak, they sold their Hoffmann desk, two Hoffmann armchairs, and three Hoffmann chandeliers. They also sold their entire set of Flora Danica. Because they still had little money, they did much of the packing and unpacking themselves. Yet they could not do it all because they retained too many things. The extent of what the three of them had succeeded in taking out of Austria was again underlined when they had six haulers work for them one day, three the next, and two more for another two days.

6

Loss

The Australian government did not mind senior British officials such as Sir Harry Luke exerting their influence to get Australian visas for select refugees. That was how the empire worked when Australia was still attached to Britain, though no longer its colony. But the government did not expect "that so many people in Australia would be taking up the cases of the Jews and making representations to the Department." One of these Australians was William O'Sullivan, the owner of a Brisbane company that made cardboard out of recycled materials using the same process as the Jacobis' in Vienna. In September 1938, he secured visas for Erni and Mizzi, who immediately began arranging their departure. They obtained new passports, employed haulers to pack up their apartment so that its contents could be put into containers, and moved to a new, furnished apartment while they made more preparations. But like many couples who fled the Nazis, they did not leave together. When Erni went in January 1939, Mizzi stayed.

The state of their marriage was a factor. Through much of the 1930s, after Erni and Hermine sold Johann Timmels-Witwe, Erni's investment in the Hamburger family business led him to work in Fulnek, where he helped to run the company's vinegar factory. An archetypal playboy, he owned a succession of sports cars, entered rallies, drove recklessly, and had a number of mistresses. The last of them was in Vienna after Erni shifted most of his capital into the Jacobi factories. Anne recalled that when she went skating at the Eislaufverein every Sunday, Erni danced with her until Mrs. Roth arrived. If Erni did not hide his mistress from Annelore, all his family and most of his friends and acquaintances must have known, given that the Eislaufverein was hardly a discreet venue for assignations.

Mizzi's widowed mother was her prime reason for staying. In 1938, Anna Jacobi was sixty-four, an age no country wanted. The dilemma for thousands of Jewish families was acute. They had to choose between remaining together in Austria or having the children leave their parents behind. While Mizzi's younger sister, Fini, left for Australia that November, having secured a place as a guaranteed migrant that required her to work as a governess for a Melbourne dentist, Mizzi and her brother, Fritz, remained in Vienna, and Mizzi decided she would leave only with Anna. When Erni sailed for Australia at the start of 1939—traveling first-class like Gretl, Käthe, and Annelore, and carrying the standard £200 in landing money—Mizzi moved to the Jacobi family home in the Piaristengasse to be with her mother.

Many countries tightened their controls on the admission of Jews following Kristallnacht because they feared a flood of refugees. The Australian government claimed it would take more but in fact reduced the annual number from fifty-one hundred to five thousand. Then the government relaxed its restrictions by creating a new quota of an additional five hundred for men and women over the age of fifty-five who were the parents of refugees already in Australia. This quota gave Anna Jacobi a chance. As soon as Erni reached Melbourne, where Fini Jacobi was already working, he applied for a permit for Mizzi as a guaranteed migrant, then Fini and he applied for permits for Anna and Fritz.

The government was primarily concerned that refugees it accepted did not become burdens on the Australian taxpayer. Erni and Fini had to show that they could support Mizzi, Anna, and Fritz with the test considering capital and income. While Erni was unemployed, he had his £200 of landing money and expected a further £400 "coming in next time." Fini only had £50, which was all she had needed as a refugee with a guarantor, but she was earning £1 15s. a week on top of full board. Between them, it was enough. At the start of June, the government sent Erni three permits.

The hazards of remaining in Vienna were all too clear by then, even to those far away. Annelore's former cello teacher, Lucie Weiss, wrote from New York, "My poor mother remains in Vienna. Otherwise none of my closest family are there. Thank God." Mizzi and Anna put themselves at particular risk by how they managed the family house in the Piaristen gasse. As a Nazi official in the Eighth District reported in March 1939, they helped their fellow Jews by renting the apartments to them, so the building became a Jewish enclave. By June, the Nazis had retaliated by selling the house for a fraction of its value, forcing Mizzi, Anna, and all their tenants to move.

The permits obtained by Erni should have reached Vienna early in July, giving Mizzi, Anna, and Fritz just enough time to escape together before the war started in September. When they did not arrive, Fritz left on a visa from the British government, which responded to Kristallnacht by accepting many more Jewish refugees. But because Anna could not leave, Mizzi stayed, too, and, by the time Erni realized what had gone wrong, the war had started. Their one piece of good fortune was that while the war led the Australian government to stop issuing any new permits to refugees and to revoke many permits it had already granted, the government issued duplicates to Mizzi and Anna.

A host of measures affected Mizzi and Anna while they waited. One required all men and women whom the Nazis identified as Jews to adopt new middle names. While the men became Israel, the women became Sara. This law not only made Jews more identifiable but also cast them as creatures of the Old Testament, whether they were religious or not, and diminished their individuality. Marie Sara Gallia and Anna Sara Jacobi, as Mizzi and Anna became, were barred from public places, prohibited from being out after eight in the evening, and forbidden from listening to the radio. They had to relinquish their furs, woolen clothing, jewelry, and silver apart from their wedding rings, watches, table service for two, and tooth fillings. Like most Jews who remained in Vienna, they were forced to move yet again—a process that generally resulted in several families' being compelled to share the same small apartments. Anna and Mizzi were typical of this community in which the old and the female predominated because they were least able to flee.

Mizzi's worst experience came when the Nazis forced her to sell the Villa Gallia for a fraction of its value early in 1940, and Mizzi had to go to Alt Aussee to hand over the keys to the villa's new owners. Although in constant danger in Vienna, she was entitled to be there. She visited Aussee illegally because it had declared itself *Judenrein,* or cleansed of Jews. Mizzi had never before experienced such fear, but the proceeds of the villa's sale were useful. While a significant portion went to the family's lawyer, Stephan Lehner, the remainder allowed Mizzi to pay the departure tax, which was 25 percent of total assets, and the *Judenkontribution,* which accounted for another 25 percent

By then it was more difficult than ever for Jews to escape. Whereas over 126,000 left Vienna in 1938 and 1939, only 2,000 did so in 1940 and 1941. In April 1940, Mizzi and Anna obtained the papers to leave Vienna and travel through Italy, which had troops fighting in Abyssinia and Spain but otherwise remained neutral. At the start of May, they sailed from Naples on the *Remo,* one of three Lloyd Triestino boats that regularly sailed to Australia. They, too, traveled first-class, though only because they had bought their tickets in 1939, when they had much more money. Their voyage depended on Mussolini. Even before they left Vienna, he was expected to enter the war on the side of Germany. If he did so before the *Remo* reached Australia, its crew would head for the nearest neutral port or scuttle the boat to stop its falling into enemy hands.

Anne's first Australian diaries record her fears. When she heard that Anna and Mizzi were about to leave Vienna, Anne was "trembling" because Italy's forces were massing on the Yugoslav border. When Anna and Mizzi were about to sail, Anne wrote, "We need to pray she arrives safely as the situation in Italy is critical" and duly did all she could by saying the rosary for Mizzi every day. As the *Remo* approached Western Australia four weeks later, her anxiety remained acute. "The ship is still four to five days from Fremantle and one does not know when everything will go wrong with Musso," she wrote. "Everything with Italy is even worse and Aunt Mizzi is still three to four days from Fremantle," was her next entry. "If only Aunt Mizzi had already landed," she continued on June 3.

Mizzi landed in Fremantle two days later. Her arrival form reveals that she came with less than £40—one-fifth of what Erni, Gretl, and Käthe each carried. While some refugees used "Israel" and "Sara" when they landed because these names were on their passports, Mizzi did not. Like many refugees, she probably wondered what to write when asked to give her race. Some, including Gretl, Käthe, Annelore, and Erni, conformed to the White Australia policy by identifying as "white." Others identified in different ways as Jews. One described herself as a "German Jewess," another as "Hebrew (white)." Mizzi wrote "Jude," which the immigration official replaced with "Jew."

The *Remo* was the last boat from Italy to reach Australia before Mussolini declared war on June 10. Because Australian customs officers delayed its departure by requiring it to unload all its cargo, it was still in port on the tenth, enabling the government to seize it as a war prize. While they could have continued with another boat, Mizzi and Anna embarked on a much more remarkable journey across the continent on the Trans-Australian Railway, which included the longest stretch of straight train track in the world, extending 297 miles through the red-soiled, barely populated, almost treeless Nullarbor Plain. When they reached Melbourne, Fini was waiting with Erni, who had just moved to Tasmania. His presence at the station, notwithstanding wartime travel restrictions, was the first sign of his new appreciation of Mizzi. Although far from a model husband in Austria, he was about to become one in Australia.

The most revealing document that Bruce found when Mizzi died was an inventory that she compiled as Erni was preparing to leave Vienna in November 1938. While most of the documents needed by refugees were to satisfy the Nazis' requirements, this "Owner's Declaration in respect of personal or household effects" was required by the Australian government so it could determine the duty the refugees should pay on what they brought with them. Even though Mizzi almost never specified who had designed or made their things, there are few better records of what refugees with money expected to take with them following the Anschluss.

Mizzi's list of 215 household items started with sixteen tables and twenty-four chairs, five bookcases, four cupboards, two sideboards, two commodes, two couches, two beds, a divan, and a bookstand. The tableware included a 277-piece floral dinner service, a 154-piece blue-and-white service, a 150-piece set of silver cutlery, a 110-piece set of glasses, a 100-piece table set of "German silver" (an alloy of nickel, copper, and zinc), and thirty-one pieces of faience pottery. Ernie and Mizzi had almost as much linen—including 264 napkins, 172 kitchen towels, 83 pillowcases, and 42 tablecloths—because Mizzi employed a washerwoman just once a month. They also had thirteen pillowcases, eleven quilt cases, and ten sheets for servants—a mark both of the life they had led and how they hoped it would continue.

The contents of their two display cabinets—"128 fancy goods"—were to come, too. So was everything in their kitchen including two electric coffeemakers (one espresso, one Turkish), a meat-mincing machine, a rotary grater, and a coffee mill. There were also twenty-eight framed paintings—above all, the Klimt *Beech Forest,* which was much more appealing to the Nazis than Klimt's portraits of Jewish sitters, as demonstrated by how the Monuments Office assessed Ferdinand Bloch-Bauer's collection in 1939. While the office expressed no interest in the Klimt portraits owned by Bloch-Bauer, it refused export permission for two of his landscapes, including his *Beech Forest.* But because Erni organized his departure in 1938, when the Monuments Office appears to have ignored all Klimt's work, it gave him permission.

Other items ranged from a wireless and gramophone to opera glasses and binoculars, brooms and brushes, irons and an ironing board, thermometers, bells, and tools. There were five pipes because Erni was a heavy smoker. There was a riding whip that Erni probably inherited from Moriz, who was a keen horseman until he acquired his Gräf & Stift. There were two of Erni's fur coats but just one belonging to Mizzi (who must have decided to retain her other furs because she was staying in Vienna). Their country clothes included a pair of Erni's lederhosen and two of Mizzi's dirndls, which Jews in Salzburg had been prohibited from wearing immediately after the Anschluss. Their one religious object was a menorah belonging to Mizzi—possibly the only Jewish object owned by any of the Gallias at the time of the annexation.

The inventory ended with a list of equipment that Erni bought shortly before he left, just as Käthe bought a laboratory of scientific equipment. They both did so because it was a way of converting money, which they could not take, into possessions that they hoped would transform their lives as refugees. But whereas Käthe wanted to build on her qualifications and experience as a chemist, Erni wanted to abandon manufacturing. He bought everything he needed to establish a photographic studio, including two large-format cameras with tripods and plate holders; a set of silk, muslin, and cloth decoration rags and curtains; and developing tanks, dishes and boxes, and enlargers and draining racks for a darkroom. When asked his expected occupation after arriving in Australia, he answered, "industrial photographer."

The standard *Liftvans,* or containers, used in Germany and Austria were big enough to serve as garages, external bedrooms, or weekend shacks when they reached their destinations. The things taken by Erni and Mizzi filled two of these *Lifts* as well as six crates. When the Nazis allowed Anna Jacobi to leave, her possessions filled two more *Lifts* and two crates, despite Germany then being at war with Australia.

While Gretl, Käthe, and Annelore called for their containers to be shipped as soon as they reached Australia, Erni did not because he was by himself, living in boardinghouses, with no prospects of renting a flat. By the time Mizzi and Anna Jacobi reached Australia in mid-1940, it was too late. Their *Lifts* were in the Italian port of Trieste when Mussolini declared war. They were still in Trieste in 1943 when Mussolini sequestered them as part of his larger expropriation of the property of men and women of Jewish origin. They remained there until 1944, when the Nazis seized them and sent them to Germany to escape the Allied forces that were pressing north through Italy. That was all Erni, Mizzi, and Anna could establish after the war. The paper trail stopped there.

The usual problem of refugees who lose their possessions is that there are no avenues for them to seek redress, no institutions they can sue. But even when they can lodge a claim, the onus of proof generally stymies them because the circumstance of their escape means that they cannot document what they owned, let alone establish its value. Erni, Mizzi, and Anna encountered these problems almost a decade after the disappearance of their consignments when they discovered that they could make claims against the Italian government, which had assumed responsibility for payment of compensation to foreign nationals whose property was lost or damaged in Italy as a result of the war. When Erni approached the Australian government for help late in 1953, it advised him to provide "an inventory of all the items in the lift vans including a description of each item and its value." It also warned that "the Italian authorities require complete evidence of ownership, value and loss and in your own interests, therefore, you should supply the utmost information available to you."

Erni had just one relevant document—the inventory prepared by Mizzi for Australian Customs—and an album of photographs showing their Viennese apartment. In his claim, he had to provide detailed descriptions of objects that he had not seen for fifteen years and estimate their value. When he lodged this claim at the start of 1954, he emphasized that all his figures fell far short of the objects' replacement costs. He also explained how difficult it had been to obtain valuations in Australia

because most of the objects had never been sold there. He offered to provide the photographs to substantiate his claim. The total he sought was
£6,526.

The Italian government began by rejecting his evidence of what had
become of his consignment. Erni had provided typewritten copies of the
documents held by his shipping agents in Trieste; the Italian government
demanded the originals. When Erni asked the agents to forward them,
they refused to do so "in accordance with a ruling of the Association of
Italian Shipping Agents as it would make them liable for any damage
occurred through loss of these documents." When the agents provided
photostatic copies, it was early 1955, prompting Erni to observe: "From the
tone of their letter it would seem that the Italian government does not
encourage Italian firms to be too helpful in these matters."

When Italy finally reached a decision in mid-1955, it ignored all of
Erni's valuations. Instead, the government decided that the "one objective
element" that existed to determine the value of the consignment was its
weight, which was 7,095 kilograms (15,609 pounds). Its next assumption
was that each kilogram was worth 1,000 lire, so the total value of the consignment was 7,095,000 lire or £5,067. It then imposed a discount of one-
third, so Erni and Mizzi were entitled to £3,378 (then about $7,566), just
over half of what Erni had claimed.

Australian officials acknowledged that this process was "somewhat
arbitrary" but advised that it was "difficult to see the grounds on which the
Australian Legation at Rome could ask the Italian Government to recon-
sider the offer" unless Erni could provide new evidence to "substantiate
the quantity and value of the various articles." Erni, of course, could not
do so, as he reiterated at the end of 1955: "It is impossible for me to produce fresh evidence regarding the valuation of my property. This con-
sisted, besides the photographic equipment, of household goods, objets
d'art, etc., bought over a period of nearly two decades. Some were willed
to me by my parents. Whatever bills, etc., I had kept were in the desk
packed in one of the lifts. The pictures, carpets, china, silver, etc., were
bought at art sales and dealers in Austria, as well as England, France, Denmark, Italy, Germany. I doubt these could help me even if I tried. The firm
Wiener Werkstätte which had made some of the silver pieces . . . has gone
out of business."

His anger was palpable a few days later when, having no alternative,
he accepted Italy's offer. "I wish to stress," Erni wrote, that "if the Italian

Government is not prepared to go beyond a certain amount unless the claim is substantiated by invoices, etc., this fact should have been made known. In my case it would have saved me infinite work and trouble in fixing a true and by no means exaggerated valuation on each item." He could not have imagined that it would be over two more years before the Italian government authorized payment or that he would not receive this sum until September 1958, almost five years after he lodged his claim.

7

Capture

The persecution that made Austria's Jews the most unfortunate in the world in 1938 ultimately worked in their favor by spurring the majority to try to leave while there was still time. The assimilation of Austria's Jews also benefited them because it made countries such as Australia more inclined to accept them. As a result, three in four survived the war, almost twice the European average. Yet sixty-five thousand Austrian Jews died, devastating many families. The Herschmanns—the family of Annelore's father, Paul—were among them because they lacked money and connections and their age was against them. Only the youngest Herschmann brother—Otto, who turned forty-four in 1938—succeeded in fleeing Europe for Argentina, where he saw out the war in safety.

The first record of Paul after the Anschluss is from mid-1938, when Jews with property worth over 5,000 reichsmarks had to submit lists of their assets. Paul's list came to 10,000 marks, which was less than one-tenth of what Gretl reported and barely more than Annelore declared. By the end of the year he was below the 5,000-mark threshold as the value of the family leather business plummeted, even though it was yet to be Aryanized. The Gestapo had also seized but then released him. The following April, he obtained a German passport, which shows the forty-

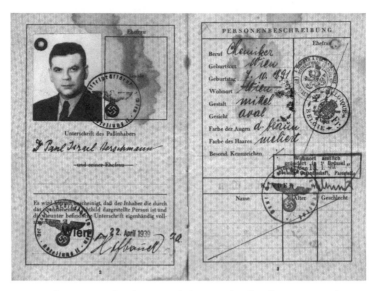

Paul's passport when he escaped the Nazis by illegally entering Belgium without a visa, 1939. The red *J* stamped on the front of the passport has leached through next to his photograph.

seven-year-old Paul looking remarkably young—his face devoid of lines, his hair still dark, though the accompanying description identifies it as mixed with gray. Within a few weeks, he was attempting the only means of escape open to him, set on crossing illegally into Belgium because he could not get a visa. In order to reach Belgium, he had to evade both the German border guards and the Belgian ones, whose numbers had increased markedly when Belgium, like other European countries, began trying to keep out German and Austrian Jews.

The best conditions for attempting the crossing were "*bei Nacht und Nebel*," at night under cover of fog. Most refugees employed what would now be called "people smugglers"—teams of Germans and Belgians looking to make quick money by transporting refugees. Fritz Loewenstein, a Berliner, paid 400 marks or about one-tenth of what Paul owned. In return, a van took Loewenstein into Belgium, where he was met by other guides with another vehicle. As he got out, they were fired at by German guards, despite already being across the border. Then Belgian guards flagged down the car, which evaded them by accelerating through their checkpoint. The crucial distance was nineteen miles beyond the frontier. The thousands of refugees caught within this zone were returned by Bel-

gium to Germany. Those who got farther found Belgium much more generous than most other European countries. While its government sent a
few hundred back, it allowed twenty-four thousand to remain and, from
mid-1939, also supported them.

Paul remained in Brussels for a year. He was there when World War II
started in September 1939 with the German invasion of Poland. He was
there in January 1940, when he had his passport extended for another year
by the German embassy. He was still there that May, when the Germans
put an end to the "phony war" by invading Belgium, the Netherlands, and
Luxembourg, and then France. While tens of thousands of Jews tried to
flee the Germans, Paul was among several thousand more whom the Nazis
expelled from Belgium as part of an ongoing effort to empty their territory
of Jews and foist them onto other countries. The Nazis' new "dumping
ground" was southern France, which the Germans chose not to occupy,
leaving its rule to its French collaborators led by Marshal Pétain.

The Vichy government needed no encouragement to embrace anti-
Semitism. It immediately enacted an array of laws that went beyond those
of German-occupied France, including one authorizing local French officials to arrest "any foreigner of the Jewish race" and put these Jews in special prisons known, as in Germany, as *"camps de concentration."* Paul was
interred in one of these camps but seems to have escaped before security
became too tight. One of his few consolations was that he remained in
regular contact with his favorite brother, Franz, who late in 1937 had
become just the second of the Herschmann brothers to marry. A year later,
Franz was arrested in Vienna on the morning of Kristallnacht, but he was
released after several weeks. When he fled in 1939, it was without his new
wife. By 1941 or 1942, both Paul and he were in Graulhet, a small town in
the Tarn region, about forty miles from Toulouse, which was a major tanning center. Most likely, Paul's long involvement in the leather industry
gave him contacts there—especially among the many French Jewish families involved in tanning.

The "final solution," the Nazis' mass murder of Jews intended to
exterminate them as a race, put Paul and Franz in jeopardy. Instead of
encouraging the departure of Jews from their territory, as they had done in
Austria, or compelling it, as they had in Belgium, the Nazis now set about
their genocide. The SS official in charge of implementing this policy was
Adolf Eichmann, who had established the Central Office for Jewish Emigration in Vienna. In June 1942, he demanded that France hand over Jews

within its borders. While the Vichy government refused to deport all French Jews, it delivered almost all foreign ones, starting with those already in French internment camps, supplemented by many more caught in mass roundups.

The trains carrying these Jews began running with the regularity that the Nazis desired from July, when they left the main Vichy transit camp in the Parisian suburb of Drancy three times weekly, week in, week out. Each convoy carried about one thousand Jews, usually a mix of men, women, and children, in freight cars sealed so they were pitch black. The standard journey lasted five days. Those aboard received neither food nor water. Their destination was southeastern Poland—the concentration camp at Auschwitz-Birkenau, otherwise known as Birkenau or Auschwitz II, where two farmhouses had been turned into gas chambers.

The biggest roundup in the Tarn was on August 26, when the Vichy police caught two hundred German, Austrian, Russian, Polish, Belgian, and Dutch Jews. While Paul escaped, Franz was arrested. Within a day or two he was in Drancy and, on September 9, in a convoy. When he reached Auschwitz-Birkenau on the fourteenth, the waiting SS officials would not have hesitated. While they selected fewer than one in twenty for hard labor and picked out twins so the doctors could experiment on them, they dealt with adults over forty just like they treated babies and children, consigning almost all to the gas chambers. Franz, who was fifty-four, was gassed along with 974 of the other 1,017 members of the convoy.

The Catholic Church was almost totally silent about the Vichy government's treatment of Jews during its first two years in power. However, several clergymen spoke out in the second half of 1942. In a pastoral letter read in most churches in his diocese on August 23, the Archbishop of Toulouse, Jules-Gérard Saliège, reminded his flock: "The Jews are real men and women. They cannot be abused without limit. . . . They are part of the human species. They are our brothers." In another letter read out in every parish in the Tarn following the roundup that caught Franz, Bishop Pierre-Marie Théas declared: "In Paris, Jews by tens of thousands have been treated with the most barbarous savagery. And now in our region we are witnessing a heartbreaking spectacle: families are being dislocated; men and women are being treated like animals and sent toward an unknown destination, with the prospect of the gravest danger. I declare the indignant protest of the Christian conscience." When the Church put these principles into action by giving sanctuary to men and women of

Jewish origin, creating false identities for them, and providing them with food and money, Paul was taken in by a convent in Graulhet. As he later described it, "Life was in constant danger under the Pétain regime but the French were helpful and humane and saved many."

Paul's brother Gustav, who was his partner in the family leather business, had little chance of escaping in 1938 because he was severely injured when knocked down by a motorcycle. He left Vienna in the spring of 1939, but he got only as far as Czechoslovakia, which by then was all Nazi territory, and by 1941 he was back in Vienna. He was there that September, when all Jews over the age of six were compelled to wear yellow Stars of David, which the Nazis forced them to buy. He was there that October, when the Nazis began the mass deportation of Vienna's remaining Jews to the east. He was there in April 1942, when these deportations reduced Vienna's Jewish population to twenty-two thousand, one-tenth of its size before the Anschluss. Then he, too, was deported, on May 6.

This convoy traveled through the former Czechoslovakia and Poland to Maly Trostinec in Belarus, a journey that usually took three days. The train carrying Gustav reached Koydanov, near Maly Trostinec, on the afternoon of May 9. But then it stopped for forty-two hours because May 9 was a Saturday and senior Nazi officials did not want the policemen and SS waiting for the deportees at Maly Trostinec to have to work on weekends. When the train finally arrived at Maly Trostinec on Monday morning, a few of the deportees were selected for farmwork. All the others, including sixty-two-year-old Gustav, were forced to take off their clothes, were stripped of their valuables, and then were shot in front of open trenches.

Many of Anne's other relatives had good reason to wonder at their lot. Guido Hamburger Jr., the older son of Hermine's brother Guido, was particularly lucky—despite having to escape twice, like many men and women of Jewish origin from the Sudetenland. They began, following the Munich Agreement in September 1938, by fleeing to what remained of Czechoslovakia, which should have been easy because they had a right to go there, but in fact was very difficult because the Czech government was loath to take them and the Sudetenland's new Nazi rulers assaulted some, imprisoned others, and seized most of their property. When the Germans occupied the remainder of Czechoslovakia in March 1939, they had to flee again.

Guido Junior found romance in the queue. While he was at the British embassy in Prague one day, the woman in front of him excited his interest. As twenty-nine-year-old Guido and twenty-eight-year-old Anna Schauer waited for visas over the next few months, he took her home to meet his parents, who had also fled to Prague, and she introduced him to hers. Guido and Anna also enjoyed the occasional slice of ordinary summer life in Prague, swimming downstream in the Moldau and then returning upstream by barge. By mid-August they had their permits, enabling them to reach England a fortnight before the war started. They married a few years later.

Guido's younger brother, Friedrich, who remained in Prague, had very different luck. In mid-1942, he and his wife, Helene, and nine-month-old daughter, Jana, were sent to Theresienstadt, a walled fortress town to the northwest of Prague that the Nazis turned into a ghetto. It was in some ways a benign place of incarceration—a "model" settlement under the direction of a Jewish Council of Elders, with lectures, concerts, and schools. Yet food, clothing, blankets, medicines, and heating were as scarce as disease was rife. Overcrowding was also extreme. Home to eight thousand people before the war, Theresienstadt came to hold almost sixty thousand at any one time, even though the Nazis were quick to send many of its inmates to their immediate deaths in extermination camps to the east.

Friedrich, Helene, and Jana were relatively safe for two years as the ghetto's Jewish leaders did all they could to protect adults with young children. Rather than select them for the transports that went east, they kept them in Theresienstadt, where just 80 children under the age of ten died compared to 15,000 men and women over seventy. But when the Nazis sent most of the inmates of Theresienstadt to Auschwitz in 1944, men were often selected without their wives and children, almost all those with tuberculosis were transported, and no one enjoyed special protection. Of the 141,000 inmates of Theresienstadt, only 19,000 survived, including just 150 of 15,000 children. While Friedrich was selected to be transported because he had tuberculosis, a woman without family volunteered to take his place so he could remain with Helene and Jana. When Theresienstadt was liberated in 1945, they all were still alive, a rare nuclear family of concentration-camp survivors.

Hermine's youngest brother, Paul Hamburger, was less vulnerable because his wife, Fely, was Aryan. The Nazis' policy was that if the wives of men of Jewish origin such as Paul stuck with them, and they had children whom they were not raising as Jews, the men would not be sent to concentration camps. But the Nazis put intense pressure on women in this situation to abandon their marriages and, if they did, their former husbands were ripe for deportation. While most of these mixed marriages survived, it was still an act of defiance for women such as Fely to ignore the Nazis' threats and blandishments. Because Fely resisted, she had to move with Paul to a *Judenhaus* in Vienna's Second District, where the Nazis forced almost all men and women of Jewish origin to live. She saw how even Paul's closest friends, such as Carl Moll, severed all contact with him. Still Fely remained true to Paul. Along with their daughter, Lizzi, they were the only family members to live out the war in Vienna. Although the Gallias had denigrated Fely for more than twenty years as a poor girl set on marrying up, Paul owed his survival to her.

Hermine's oldest brother, Otto Hamburger, also benefited from the unintended consequences of his actions more than twenty years before, when his affair with Dagmar led to the birth of Gudrun and Hermine insisted he marry Dagmar to make good his immorality. Because Dagmar was Aryan, Otto was able to stay with her in Bruntal in relative safety after it became part of Germany in 1938. When she died in 1940, the Nazis allowed him to take her remains to Denmark for burial in Copenhagen, though he soon collapsed and, in 1941, died in a mental asylum.

Guido Hamburger Sr. had almost no chance because his wife, Nelly, was another convert from Judaism, and Guido and Nelly were also too old to get visas. They were still in Prague in October 1941, when their granddaughter Jana was born, and Nelly became Jana's godmother. A few days later they were among the first five thousand men, women, and children transported from Prague. Their destination was the Polish city of Lodz, the site of another ghetto established by the Nazis. The conditions in Lodz were far worse than in Theresienstadt, and the new Czech arrivals died particularly quickly. While Nelly survived the winter, she was gassed that spring in Chelmno, the Nazis' first mass extermination camp, where 400,000 Jews were killed in mobile gas vans. There is no record of what happened to Guido.

Age also shaped the fate of Ludwig, or Louis, Gallia, the only son of Moriz's brother Wilhelm, former legal partner of Moriz's brother Adolf and occasional lawyer to the Wiener Werkstätte. When Louis wrote in February 1939 to his favorite niece, Liesl, he was still in Vienna, while thirty-five-year-old Liesl was en route to Melbourne with her forty-two-year-old husband, Erich. Louis, who was sixty-one, stressed that he longed to see Liesl again but did not expect to do so.

Three weeks later, Louis drafted a document that he titled "My Last Will," in which he distributed his remaining property and gave his instructions and apologies to the living. Louis began: "I am to be cremated. No one is to be present at the interment. My ashes are to be taken from the urn and buried in the earth. No stone or other form of memorial is to be erected. No notice of my death is to be published." He continued by addressing his younger sister Friedl, his only surviving sibling, who was sharing his Viennese apartment. "Friedl is to go to England as quickly as possible," he instructed, without explaining how she might get a visa. Louis went on to send his greetings and kisses to all his nephews and nieces. He concluded with a plea to those most important to him. "Friedl and Liesl," he implored, "are not to be angry with me."

Veronal—a product of the German pharmaceutical company Bayer that went on sale in the early 1900s—was the first commercially available barbiturate. While generally taken as a sleeping tablet, it was used as a suicide pill by thousands of German and Austrian Jews, who turned to it out of anxiety and depression and to escape being humiliated, assaulted, and sent to concentration camps. It allowed them to control the occasion of their deaths and die with dignity.

Louis Gallia became one of them after completing his will and going to bed on the night of March 3. By the time he was found the following morning and taken by ambulance to Vienna's Rothschild Hospital, which remained open long after the Nazis closed most other Jewish institutions in the city, its doctors could do nothing for him. When another family member, Arthur Kary, wrote a few hours later to Liesl's brother, Peter Langer, who had already reached Australia, he began: "My news will cause you great sorrow but you must accept it with courage. Your good uncle Olu"—as the family called Louis—"could and would no longer bear this life and is from today no longer."

Many accounts stress how ordinary suicide became in this period. The British journalist G. E. R. Gedye claimed that "Jewish friends spoke to one of their intention to commit suicide, with no more emotion than they had formerly talked of making an hour's journey by train." Yet Louis's family and friends in Vienna were shocked by his death, because he had given no hint of what he was contemplating. He spent his last day work-

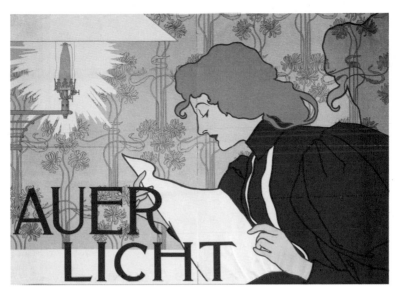

The poster by Heinrich Lefler that Moriz commissioned for Auer von Welsbach's Gas Glowing Light Company.

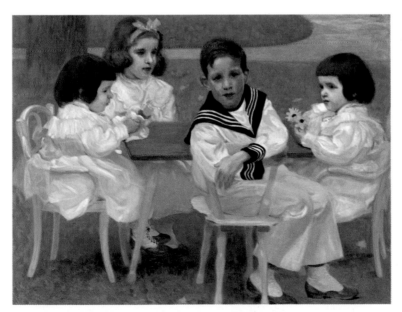

Ferdinand Andri's group portrait of the Gallia children, 1901. Erni, aged six, occupies the dominant position at the front of the picture as the eldest child and only son. Gretl, aged five, is seated behind. The two-year-old twins, with Käthe on the right and Lene on the left, are, typically, almost indistinguishable, wearing identical clothes and jewelry.

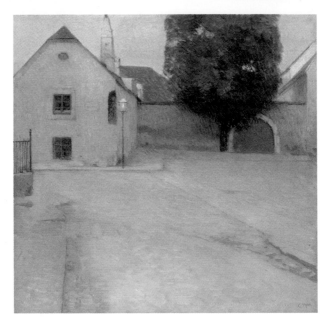

Carl Moll, *Beethoven House, Heiligenstadt*, 1903.

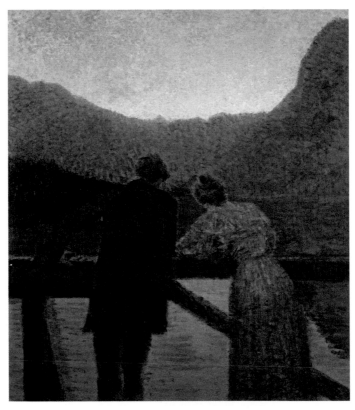

Ernst Stöhr, *Moonlit Landscape*, 1903.

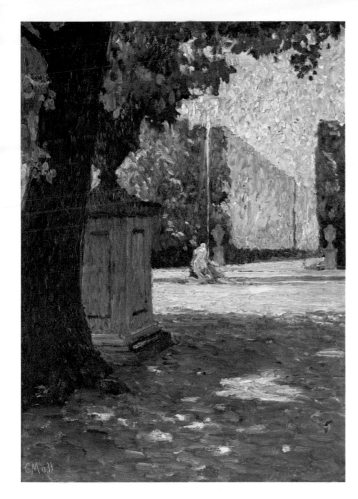

Carl Moll, *In the Gardens of
Schönbrunn*, c. 1910/1911.

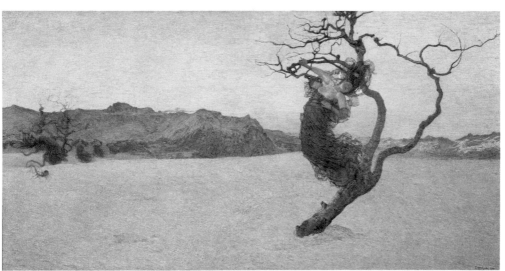

Giovanni Segantini, *The Evil Mothers*, 1894.

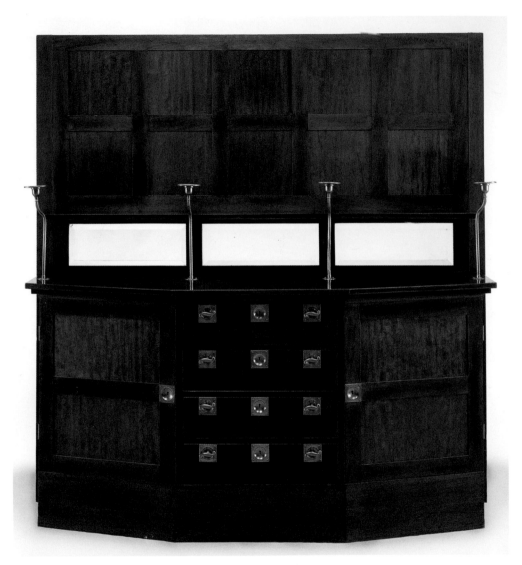

The sideboard designed by Adolf Loos for the Langer apartment, 1902.

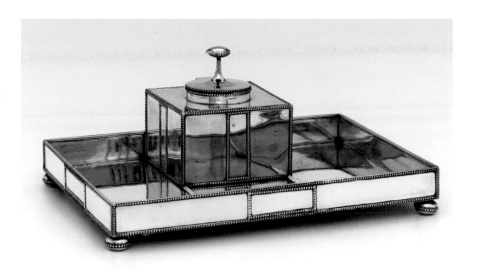

Moriz's inkstand, designed c. 1911 by Josef Hoffmann.

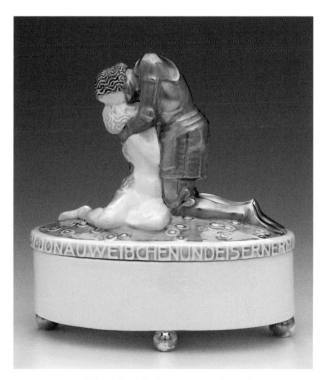

Michael Powolny's ceramic version of
Klimt's *The Kiss*, 1908.

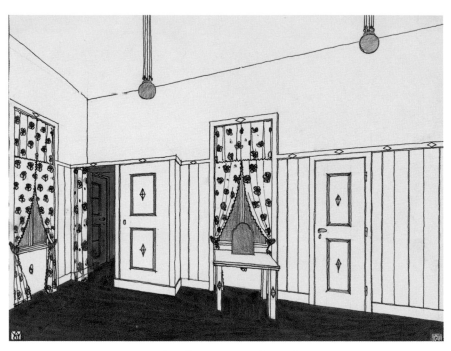

Josef Hoffmann, *Design for Boudoir*,
in the Untere Augartenstrasse, 1915, intended for Gretl
when she was engaged to Norbert Stern.

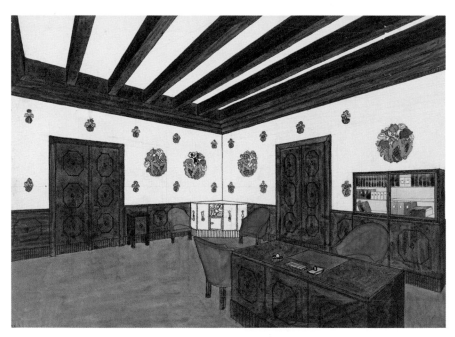

Josef Hoffmann, *Design for Smoking Room*,
in the Untere Augartenstrasse, 1915, intended for Norbert Stern
when he was engaged to Gretl.

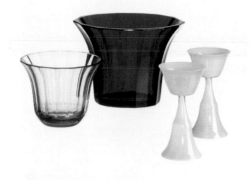

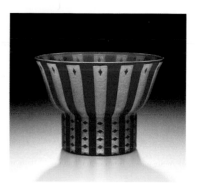

Josef Hoffmann, *Two Vases and a Pair of Goblets*, from about 1915 or 1916 when Hermine was steadily building her collection of Hoffmann glass.

Carl Witzmann, *Bowl*, 1912. One of Hermine's acquisitions as the family apartment in the Wohllebengasse was being built.

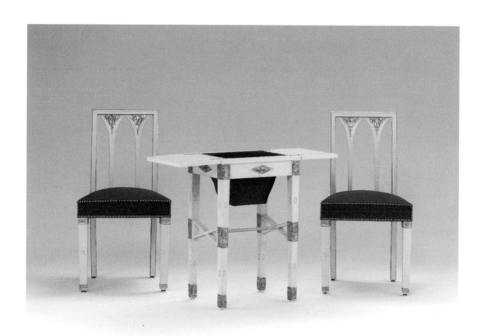

Josef Hoffmann, *Work Table and Two Chairs*, 1913, designed for Hermine's boudoir in the Wohllebengasse.

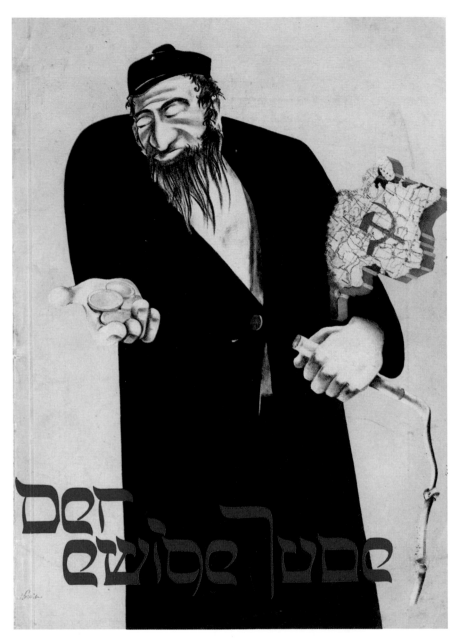

The copy of *Der Ewige Jude*, or *The Eternal Jew*, bought by Annelore before she left Vienna in November 1938 so she would never be homesick for Austria.

ing as usual as a lawyer and went to bed showing no emotion. "No one noticed anything extraordinary," Kary informed Peter Langer. "No one was prepared for it."

The state of his legal practice was a factor. The Nazis began by preventing Jewish lawyers from representing Aryan clients, then barred them from practicing altogether except for one hundred allowed to act as "consultants" to Jews. While Louis was among this relatively fortunate group, he knew this status would not last. Kary observed: "No wonder Olu had had enough. For doctors it is equally horrible; and what about merchants, industrialists . . . it gets more cruel day by day." Louis also knew his prospects were bleak even if he managed to escape. Australia was the one country where he thought he had a chance of continuing to work as a lawyer, little realizing that his qualifications would not be recognized there. Kary wrote: "It is too terrible what we have to endure. It is almost impossible to start a new profession at the age of sixty-one. No one really knows how many people commit suicide. For old people there is hardly a more rational choice."

Carl Moll did the same in very different circumstances. Along with his daughter, Maria, and son-in-law, Richard Eberstaller, he was among the few Austrians to commit suicide when the Soviet army entered Vienna in 1945. By one account, the suicide of Moll and the Eberstallers on the night of April 12 was a consequence of events earlier that day, when the eighty-four-year-old Moll reputedly was wounded by Russian soldiers as he tried to stop them from raping Maria. Yet Moll had written a suicide note on April 10 in which he expressed his belief that he had experienced "all the beautiful things life has to offer" and "would fall asleep without remorse." Richard Eberstaller knew that he had "the worst to expect" because of his work as vice president of the Regional Criminal Court in Vienna. All three saw the fall of the Nazi regime as a catastrophe they did not want to endure.

When my mother wrote her story, she recorded which members of the family were killed by the Nazis but did not explain where, when, or how they died. I wanted to know more. When I read that Gustav and Franz Herschmann "were eventually taken to concentration camps where they died," in what proved to be the final draft of her memoir, I vainly annotated it, "Do you know which?" I began to find out while Googling for material for this book. After discovering Gustav and Franz in lists of unclaimed insurance policies and dormant bank accounts, I came across the Jewish Memorial Center Web site, where I found "Herschmann, Franz, 26.3.88 Vienna—14.9.42 Auschwitz."

It was one of those moments that changed my place in the world. Franz was still the vaguest of men to me. I did not know what he looked like. I knew nothing about his passions, beliefs, tastes, or habits. But in a click I went from feeling barely touched by the Holocaust, because my closest relatives had all survived, to having a direct connection with its most notorious manifestation. That Franz had been one of my great-uncles—the same relation to me as Erni, a key figure in my childhood—brought his death even closer. While I had not been satisfied with my mother's vagueness, I did not expect that to know more could be so shocking.

The material I discovered about Louis Gallia, who at first was just as remote from me, was similarly confronting. His one brief appearance in Anne's story was as the executor of Ida's will. He committed sacrilege in Gretl's eyes when he cleaned out Ida's apartment on the Stubenring and emptied silver frames of their photographs, including a portrait of Moriz. As Anne described it, Gretl "had loved her father and as far as she was concerned his photo was to remain framed. Frames were not just objects for reuse or sale." In characteristic fashion, Gretl never forgave Louis, and Anne inherited her antipathy. In her story, she did not record when or how Louis died.

My connection with Louis began when one of Melanie Gallia's descendants showed me Louis's last letter to his niece Liesl and Arthur Kary's letter describing his death. These letters brought me nearer to Louis than to many other members of the family to whom I was much more closely related. Yet when a Viennese genealogist sent me an e-mail including the wills of Adolf, Ida, and Louis, I started with Adolf and Ida because they remained much more central to this book and I thought Louis's will would be of no interest. When I finally opened it, I was expecting a conventional distribution of property. Instead, I found his suicide note.

IV

ANNE

1939

The refugees who fled to Sydney and Melbourne after Kristallnacht went from one apocalyptic landscape to another, exchanging cities still burning for another fiery environment, because of the effects of a terrible El Niño. A week after Gretl, Kathe, and Annelore landed, the "Black Friday" bush-fires of January 13, 1939 devastated 1.4 million hectares in Victoria, killing seventy-one people. In outback New South Wales the extreme tempera-tures lasted for weeks, resulting in over a hundred deaths from heatstroke. The conditions in Sydney were milder, but it was still over 90 degrees Fahrenheit at ten o'clock at night on Black Friday, while the next day was even worse, as the temperature reached a record 113 degrees.

Many other aspects of Sydney made it a wonderful place to be. Like most refugees, Anne discovered the glory of the city's beaches. After her fears of attack in Vienna, she relished the city's safety, which meant Gretl, Käthe, and she could keep their doors unlocked and walk alone at night without anxiety. Yet even more aspects of Australia were alien to the new arrivals, including the flora and fauna, architecture and urban design, food and clothes. As in most countries to which refugees fled in the late 1930s, the pressure to conform was also intense. The "reffos," as the new arrivals were dubbed when they were not "bloody reffos" or "reffo bastards," immediately learned that they were expected to do "their utmost to acquire a local accent and local mannerisms," become "good Australians," and adopt "the Australian way of life."

Many refugees responded by Anglicizing their names or adopting new ones to mask their origins and to avoid the annoyance of having their names repeatedly misspelled and mispronounced. The Annelore Herschmann-Gallia who appeared in the Brisbane *Telegraph* disappeared almost immediately. Her given name was simple. Just as Käthe became Kathe, so Annelore became Anne. Her change of surname was more unusual because Gretl reverted to Gallia, which was how Gretl thought of herself—though it did nothing to disguise the fact that Anne and she were foreigners in Anglo-Celtic Australia. Gretl's speed was exceptional. While refugees generally took months to alter their surnames, Gretl made this change within a week.

Anne's identity changed again when she resumed her schooling a few weeks later at St. Vincent's College, run by the Sisters of Charity in the inner suburb of Potts Point. While no other member of the family had been so devout since the Gallias and Hamburgers began converting at the start of the century, Anne did not fit in at St. Vincent's because the nuns assumed all their pupils would be born Catholic. When Gretl filled out the school's Register of Admissions, she did not reveal Anne's Jewish origins but gave Anne a complete Catholic identity to satisfy the nuns' expectations and to help Anne escape further prejudice. Gretl recorded that Anne's first Communion was in 1930, when Anne was still a member of Vienna's Israelitische Kultusgemeinde. Gretl gave Anne's confirmation as 1938, when she should have left this column blank.

The prospect of more Viennese culture was immediately before her. The day after Anne landed, the *Sydney Morning Herald* carried a story headed "The Vienna Boys' Choir—Coming Next June." In fact, Sydney was to be visited by the Mozart Boys' Choir, founded in 1936 by Dr. Georg Gruber, a former choirmaster with the Vienna Boys' Choir, after he fell out with Rektor Schnitt. Far from giving the Mozart Boys a new identity, Gruber mimicked the Vienna Boys so he could exploit their reputation when he further emulated them by taking his choir abroad. In 1937, Schnitt accused Gruber of damaging the Vienna Boys' standing, defrauding them, and being a Nazi when the party was illegal. After the Anschluss, Gruber retaliated by ousting Schnitt and briefly imposing himself as the

Vienna Boys' director while maintaining control of the Mozart Boys. When the Mozart Boys' Choir arrived, Anne would have to decide whether to patronize an organization that was the closest copy of her favorite Viennese musical institution, even though it was linked to the Nazi regime.

Tuesday, February 7, 1939, was Anne's first day at St. Vincent's. I imagine her arriving in her first school uniform, ascending the school's marble steps, exploring the grounds, where the most striking feature was a grotto dominated by an oversize statue of Our Lady of Lourdes. I see her entering the school's chapel, where mass was said every morning, going into the class for the first time, knowing no one, and struggling with the cacophany of English. I think of her encountering the one other student who was a refugee from Austria. I know that after being able to put up her hair in Vienna, which she thought of as a mark of maturity, she hated having to cut it above her shoulders or wear it down in plaits, which she considered childlike.

Of course she enrolled in German so that one of her subjects would be simple. But she found it embarrassing that her teacher for most of the year was Gretl, who began working at St. Vincent's at the end of the first term. Anne was shocked to find her English much worse than she expected. She feared she would fail Latin because the other girls had studied it for four years when she had done only one and a half. The schoolwork, the organization of the classes, and even the standard mode of addressing the nuns were very different from what she was used to. She dreaded the Leaving, the public examination at the end of the final Australian year of school, because it was made up entirely of written examinations and she had never taken one.

She continued to use German for all her private purposes but always used English in public and was intent on perfecting it because it was essential in her exams and the key to her assimilation. An anthology of British essays, which was one of her set texts, exemplifies her challenge. Before she could analyze the essays, she had to be able to read them. Her annotations reveal hundreds of words that she could understand only with the aid of a dictionary. But her progress was rapid, as illustrated by an exercise book she started in June 1939. While her teacher returned her first assignments crisscrossed with red marks, by October her work required no corrections. When her school principal wrote Anne a reference, she declared: "Her application to her studies this year has been most remarkable, her victory over new terms and a new language wonderful."

Her expectations of her schoolmates were low after her ostracism at the Albertgasse. She was delighted simply because the other girls did not pick on her. While she made no close friends, she knew that was at least partly because she had vowed not to risk more friendships when her two best Viennese friends abandoned her after the Anschluss. The inclusion in the St. Vincent's magazine of a story by her drawing on her experiences as a refugee is testimony to the school's acceptance of her as well as its eye for novel content. A photograph reveals that Anne was part of the school's chamber music group—showing her with her father's cello. After her final day at St. Vincent's that December, she wrote: "I have experienced much good and beautiful this year."

Her results were a triumph. While she was pleased to have come in third in her class and topped the state in German, her mark in English meant the most to her. When she discovered that she had received an A, she described her result as "unbelievable" and feared for her humility. "I hope," she observed, "I will not be too proud on this ground." Just as Moriz and Hermine had rewarded Gretl with a diamond and pearl pendant when she graduated, so Gretl gave Anne her best watch, made by Patek, one of the most prestigious Swiss watchmakers. That night they had a celebratory supper at Cahill's, a coffee shop in Kings Cross renowned for its caramel ice-cream cake.

Two of Sydney's refugee organizations gave Anne more to do and reduced her isolation. The goal of the Continental Catholic Migrants Welfare Committee was to assist the new arrivals by "receiving, placing in employment and generally attending to the after-care of Catholic refugees." Although the committee's monthly meetings sometimes attracted significant numbers of refugees, it often drew almost none. As Gretl recalled, Anne became "Miss Committee," eager to enliven this small group. When the German Emergency Fellowship Committee, including Mrs. Ryan, organized a harbor cruise for refugees, Anne met Gertrude Angel, who had arrived in Sydney at age fifteen a week after Anne, having also escaped Vienna immediately following Kristallnacht. She became Anne's most enduring friend in Australia.

Anni Wiesbauer, Anne's instructor in lace cleaning, also continued to try to help her from afar. After receiving a letter in which Anne expressed her sense of dislocation in Sydney, Anni responded with passion, stressing that she believed in Anne, recognized her inner worth, and would always care for her—that in a world where Anne had found that almost nothing was safe or reliable, Anni could be trusted. While Anni did not expressly refer to the anti-Semitism that had forced Gretl, Kathe, and Anne to flee, she clearly had it in mind when she wrote that the trials and tribulations experienced by Anne were God's will and would make her a better person.

One of her Viennese schoolmates, Erika Brünn, whom Father Elzear also baptized at the Franciscan church in Vienna, was even more important to Anne. When they began corresponding, Anne was in a far better position than Erika, who had fled without her parents on a *Kindertransport,* the great British humanitarian endeavor initiated by Quakers that rescued thousands of Jewish children from December 1938. But Anne and Erika still had much in common. Just as Anne felt alienated and displaced in Sydney, so did Erika in the English coastal town of Claxton. Much like Anne, Erika found refuge in the Catholic Church when she began working in a hospital run by the Order of the Sacred Heart. They both longed

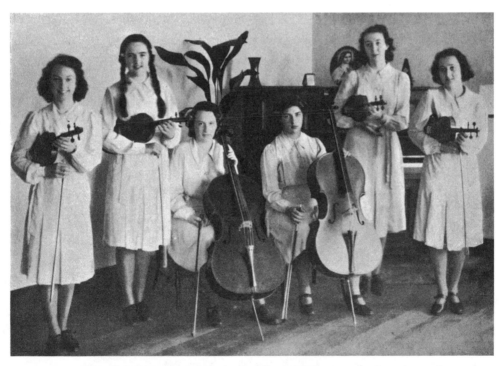

St. Vincent's College, Sydney, run by the Sisters of Charity, 1939. Anne is seated, third from the right, with her cello.

for what Erika continued to describe as "our Vienna" but then would remember why they had fled, as Erika observed after hearing Hitler on the radio. She wrote: "One forgets much, especially when one is out of contact. But now again I have all the horror right before me and it distresses me terribly."

The occasional concert by visiting musicians provided Anne with another link with her past, while also reminding her of what she was missing. The venue was symbolic. While Sydney was a city of almost 1.3 million people in 1939, over half the size of Vienna, it did not have a proper concert hall, let alone an opera house. As a result, most major concerts were staged in its town hall, where the acoustics were adequate but almost everything else was not. Because the hall was almost impossible to heat in winter, most of the audience sat through the performances in hats and gloves. Because the management refused to provide refreshments, many in the audience went to the hotel across the road during intermission. Anne's first concerts there were by musicians whom Gretl had seen as a young woman in Vienna but were new to Anne. The first was the soprano Lotte Lehmann, whose antifascism led her to sever all ties with Germany and Austria following the Anschluss. The second was the piano virtuoso Artur Schnabel, who had taken refuge in the United States.

The arrival of the Mozart Boys' Choir saw Anne put culture before politics, just as she had done before leaving Vienna. For a week, she resumed her old patterns of going out, attending three of the choir's six evening performances and a matinee. Much of the repertoire was familiar, including Mozart's short operetta *Bastien und Bastienne* and Strauss's *The Blue Danube*. A novelty was *Waltzing Matilda*, the choir's one acknowledgment of Australian culture, which they always performed as an encore. That it remained foreign to Anne is suggested by how she listed it once as *Waltzing Mathilda*, once as *Dancing Mathilda*, and once as *Walking Mathilda*.

Anne spent Christmas Eve at home in the apartment in Rose Bay, tidying her room, listening to music on the radio, and reading books in between Sunday mass in the morning and her first midnight mass that evening. She also took the opportunity to reflect on how her life had been transformed over the previous two years. She remembered her last Viennese Christmas in 1937, when her first ball season was about to begin and the Anschluss was yet to happen. She recalled how in 1938, Gretl, Kathe, and she had been sailing toward Australia with no idea what lay before them. Now they were in their own flat decorated with garlands and bells, having eaten good fish, Christmas cake, and gingerbread. They also had even more to look forward to as their "old friend" Mrs. Mabel Ferguson, whom they had met on the *Nieuw Zeeland,* was to visit them on Christmas Day. Anne thanked God for being so good to them.

Kathe, meanwhile, started her new life with high hopes. Because of her training as a chemist and long experience in the workforce, she looked forward to resuming the professional career she had abandoned when Lene died. If she did not establish her own laboratory when her scientific equipment reached Sydney, she would find a job as a chemist. But she soon found that Australian institutions only partially recognized her qualifications, while much of her equipment arrived broken. Her first job, in March 1939, was as a technician in a hospital replacing sick staff for just three weeks. In May she did so again. That was it until the start of the war in September created many vacancies and Kathe found work in a factory that made pencils and carbon paper. While she probably exaggerated when she described herself as an "industrial chemist," she had a full-time, permanent job using some of her scientific knowledge.

Gretl proved more adaptable, like many other women refugees who had never worked before. When required to specify her expected occupation on her arrival form, she wrote, "Unknown as yet." She feared she would be able to get only menial work. But the years of musical training intended to make her a cultured society lady almost immediately created an opportunity. She began teaching German songs at one of Sydney's best music schools, run by the Sisters of Charity on the same site as St. Vincent's, where Anne went to school. While Gretl's position was for only an hour a week, it was skilled work starting just three weeks after she landed.

Her years of language training—again intended to make her a cultured society lady—proved even more useful. By April, she had another part-time position at St. Vincent's as a language mistress teaching German and French, a role for which she had neither experience nor qualifications beyond her command of both languages. In between she took private language pupils and cleaned houses. One of her first employers was a much older Jewish woman who had come to Australia as a refugee a few years before. After Gretl had finished cleaning, they would play four-handed piano together, temporarily transforming Gretl from a servant into an equal.

Australian women's magazines gave Gretl another opportunity. When she discovered they were staging recipe competitions, she tried her luck, despite her limited experience as a cook. The standard format was highly attractive. You did not even have to bake a cake or make a pie. Instead, you simply had to buy a copy of the magazine, fill out the enclosed coupon, submit a recipe, and see if the judges selected it from the thousands of entries. The Viennese recipes entered by Gretl were a small test of Australia's appetite for the new and willingness to embrace the Continental. When one proved successful, Gretl made the most of her surprise. That night, when Käthe and Anne sat down for dinner, they each found one-third of her winnings next to their plates.

The money and public recognition mattered to them. Gretl's part-time teaching position at St. Vincent's paid £2 15s (then $10.15) per week. An orange cream cake, which came in second when Gretl and Kathe entered a competition staged by the *Australian Home Journal,* won £12 10 (then $46.00). The joy of private acceptance was also great. After seven recipes entered by Gretl, Käthe, and Anne in a competition run by *Woman* magazine appeared in its book of *Tested Recipes,* which claimed to represent "the best in culinary art," Gretl received this letter from Mrs. Merle Pateman of Murrumbateman in rural New South Wales: "No doubt you will think that I am presuming in writing to you, but I feel that I must. Some time ago I purchased a copy of *Woman's* cookery book, and on looking through it, I was particularly impressed with your recipes and those also of Dr. Gallia and Miss Gallia, too. I have only been married four months, but the recipes were so simple, yet so delicious, that I was able to follow them easily, without mistake." As a result, Mrs. Merle Pateman wanted more. When she next visited Sydney, she came for dinner.

This unlikely friendship with a newly married country girl was one of many made by Gretl. While most refugees began by moving almost exclusively within refugee circles, Gretl rapidly made friends with Anglo-Australians, including a number of influential figures in the Sydney community. The key was how Gretl, much more than Kathe, satisfied the taste of some Australians for high European culture and their desire for the cosmopolitan. Gretl was the kind of refugee whom correspondents of the *Sydney Morning Herald* had in mind when they emphasized how refugees would enrich Australian society because "cultured people" made the "best immigrants." While Gretl's fluent English was a great asset, her smart clothes and refined manners, her obvious identity as a well-bred woman, gave her cachet.

John Ferguson was a judge of the New South Wales Industrial Court better known as a bibliophile who compiled a seven-volume *Bibliography of Australia*. He was also a relative of the Mrs. Ferguson who had met Gretl, Käthe, and Anne as they sailed to Australia on the *Nieuw Zeeland* at the end of 1938 and then spent much of Christmas Day with them at the end of 1939 in a remarkable display of concern for their well-being. As Mrs. Ferguson looked to do more for Gretl, Käthe, and Anne, she encouraged Justice Ferguson to help them. As part of thanking him "for his kind interest and many a good advice," Gretl later described Ferguson as "the first friend we made in Sydney."

Saul Symonds was a second-generation Australian Jew of mixed British and Russian origin, best known as the president of its Great Synagogue, the foundation chairman of its Jewish Advisory Board, and a member of the executive of its Jewish Welfare Society. When Gretl went to its offices and revealed her Catholicism, as she did not want to receive the society's help under false pretenses, her honesty, along with her impeccable manners and cultural sophistication, impressed Symonds, who introduced her to his family. Their friendship was all the more exceptional because, like similar organizations in the United States, the Jewish Welfare Society was ambivalent about European Jews fleeing the Nazis. As its honorary secretary later acknowledged, the society "wanted to help the refugees but not to mix with them"; its members "would do anything on an official basis but little on a personal basis."

2

Aliens

The war altered the status of Gretl, Kathe, and Anne again. Just five days after it started, the Australian government introduced new security legislation transforming all Germans and Austrians in Australia from foreign nationals enjoying almost the same rights and freedoms as ordinary citizens into "enemy aliens" subject to a welter of restrictions. The government's premise was that some of these Germans and Austrians supported Hitler and hence needed to be subjected to close scrutiny. But while this assumption had substance in relation to those Germans and Austrians who had come to Australia other than as refugees, the categorization of refugees as enemies was bizarre when the circumstances in which they had fled Europe made them staunch antifascists. It also was contrary to Australia's own military interests, as many of the men were eager to fight the Nazis but their classification as enemy aliens prevented them from enlisting.

The Gallias supported Australia's war effort as best they could. They knitted, just as Gretl had during World War I. They gave a pair of Zeiss binoculars to the army as a National Defense Contribution. They became regular donors to the Red Cross Blood Transfusion Service. Meanwhile, they complied with the new law by registering as enemy aliens, carrying their certificates of registration at all times, and reporting to their local police station once a week. Although Anne did not mention these requirements in her diaries, which might suggest they did not affect her, an autobiographical story she wrote a few years later indicates otherwise. She described how "she had to report to the police to obtain a card which told her that she was an alien. Nothing beyond that happened and yet more than anything else this brought home to her the fact that she was a stranger in a strange country."

The Nazis' rapid conquest of the Netherlands, Belgium, and France in mid-1940 fueled fears about refugees. As stories of "fifth columnists" abounded, the new British government of Winston Churchill interned or deported thirty thousand enemy aliens, including many Jews. In Australia, the New South Wales government called on the Commonwealth to intern all enemy aliens because of their involvement in "insidious propaganda" and "the probable existence of plots to neutralize the war effort," and because the continued freedom of refugees engendered a "disturbed state of public mind." Over the next two years a range of groups gathered thousands of signatures on petitions supporting this call, which the Commonwealth ignored while subjecting refugees to ever-tighter controls and greater scrutiny.

The majority of refugees looked back on these events as something to be dismissed with a laugh and treated as trivial. Their sense of good fortune in escaping the Holocaust stopped them from criticizing the country that gave them refuge. But many saw things differently at the time. As one described it in 1940, the war had put an end to their "very kind welcome" because Australians had come to regard them as "enemies" and tried to send them "to concentration camps and imprisonment." Anne's old Viennese dancing partner Georg Schidlof, who escaped to England following the Anschluss, experienced that fate after being sent to Australia for internment. When Georg later explained why he did not contact Anne, he revealed his fear that the Gallias "might not be too pleased to receive a letter from an internee, especially when the anti-alien feeling in Australia was already strong and still growing."

A government report later found that the enforcement of Australia's enemy alien regulations ranged from "unnecessary and overbearing intolerance" to "laxity." As Anne described it in mid-1940, the officers she had to deal with were "especially nice" policemen. When two other officers came to the apartment in Rose Bay to search it and question Gretl, Kathe, and Anne, they stayed for afternoon tea and were again "very nice." But Australia's censors were more concerned when they intercepted a letter to Kathe from one of her Viennese friends who had fled to England. While the text of this letter simply contained news of mutual friends who had also become refugees, the censors reported that "unusual and apparently unnecessary curved strokes occur in many places over various letters," which the censors considered "enough to form some hidden message." The security services immediately ordered Kathe to attend their headquarters in the city, which must have reminded Kathe of her experiences in room 383 of the Hotel Metropol two years before. This time she was allowed to leave, after a short interview with a lieutenant who found her "harmless."

Gretl's security file also grew when, as part of this climate of heightened fear and suspicion, members of the public began informing on refugees. The most notable incident involved a man who rented an apartment in their building in Rose Bay. When Mr. Dunlop found a slip of paper with German writing, he "deduced that it was connected with Mrs. Gallia, and thought it his duty to inform the section." He also reported that the Gallias were using their radio, a key form of communication and entertainment in the era before television, which all enemy aliens had just been prohibited from using without a special license. The lieutenant who dealt with this report found that the sheet of paper revealed that Gretl was trying to get one of her friends out of Austria. He ignored the use of the radio, which Gretl soon made lawful when she became one of the few refugees to succeed in obtaining a license, aided by her invocation of high British authority in the form of the governor of Fiji, Sir Harry Luke.

Kathe's relationship with a teacher at Sydney Technical College was another matter. Anne's diary reveals that while Mr. Rawson occasionally saw Kathe with his wife, he usually saw Kathe alone, sometimes arriving early in the morning and leaving late at night, and visiting up to three times a week. As recalled by Anne, Mr. Rawson continued to see Kathe when his wife thought he had gone to England to work in the Royal Ordnance Factory, but in fact he was still in Sydney. Mrs. Rawson went to the Security Service after Mr. Rawson finally reached England and she discovered that he was in close correspondence with Kathe. Mrs. Rawson warned that Kathe might be using Mr. Rawson "to obtain information which would be of use to the enemy." The security officer was dismissive, concluding: "The matter appears definitely to be one of straightout jeal-ousy, unworthy of any further investigation."

The Security Service responded more seriously in 1943 when one of its own agents reported that Gretl, who had been working as a secretary with the Free French Delegation, had resigned from her job because it was "involved in some dishonest venture." The service began examining all of Gretl's Australian mail, conducted its own investigation, and called Gretl in for questioning. This scrutiny revealed nothing more than Gretl's diffi-culties in adjusting to the role of secretary. Her resignation, the service found, was due to her being "out of place" among her workmates, young girls thirty years her junior, because of her "superior knowledge and cul-ture." Two years later, however, she was still subject to special surveillance.

These controls saw Gretl, Kathe, and Anne live to a certain extent in fear, fueled by uncertainty about what some of the controls involved and whether they could ignore them with impunity. A letter written by Kathe early in 1942, when Anne was on holiday in the country, having secured special permission to go there, provides one example. It reveals that Gretl, Kathe, and Anne began by thinking that they needed permits for their favorite swimming place in Sydney harbor at Nielsen Park and decided sometimes to ignore this requirement, which meant that their swims were clouded by anxiety. Then, to their relief, they discovered that Nielsen Park was within their district so, as Kathe put it, they could "swim without worry."

The Australian government belatedly began relaxing these controls in late 1942, when it decided that enemy aliens needed to report to the police once a month rather than every week and created one large police district stretching fifteen miles from Sydney's general post office, so refugees did not require permits whenever they moved around the city. The next changes came in 1943, when the government reclassified sixty-five hun-dred "enemy aliens," including Gretl, Kathe, and Anne, as "refugee aliens" and then allowed refugees to become naturalized. Gretl, Kathe, and Anne applied as soon as they could and, in March 1944, renounced the German citizenship that had been forced on them by the Anschluss. Because Aus-tralian citizenship still did not exist, they became British subjects.

The war also narrowed Anne's world by putting an end to her correspon-dence with Anni Wiesbauer and leaving Erika Brünn as the only Austrian friend with whom she remained in contact. For all the refugees whom Anne met in Sydney, she regarded them as no substitutes for her "beloved Erika," who shaped her choice of career when Anne decided to become a nurse in the hope that Erika and she might work together in the same hospital after the war. More immediately, the requirement that trainees live at the hospital would allow Anne to leave home, which she was desperate to do, since Gretl and Kathe got on as badly as ever and Anne often fought with at least one of them. While a nurse whom Anne met in Sydney warned her that the work of trainees was mundane and repetitive, Anne still applied.

She soon was struggling. When she sat her first examination in theoretical general nursing, her mark was just 54 percent, which put her second bottom in her class. After all the difficulties of the Leaving, she could not take seriously examination questions such as: "If you were proceeding to make a bed in the ward, how much of the bottom sheet would you turn under the mattress?" But she remained eager to be a nurse—until she began working in the wards. Where she desired challenges and responsibilities, she found herself making beds, changing bandages, emptying bedpans, and washing up. She also had one argument after another with her superiors, especially the deputy matron, who talked repeatedly about "dirty foreigners," Anne's first experience of sustained racism in Australia. For all her good intentions, she worked increasingly poorly by her own account and was dismissed after six months.

Her talents impressed John Ferguson, the judge of the New South Wales Industrial Court who befriended Gretl. When Anne decided that she wanted to go to Sydney University, the fees were an immediate issue. Ferguson offered to pay them. Although Gretl and Kathe did not accept his offer because their combined income had just reached a point where they were able to meet their expenses, Anne always remembered Ferguson's generosity. While otherwise renowned for donating his great book collection to Australia's National Library, Ferguson was celebrated in our household for a very different form of philanthropy.

University was the right place for Anne. She not only worked exceptionally hard, just as when she sat for the Leaving, but also studied with unprecedented pleasure and excitement. As her curiosity, confidence, and ambition grew, she ranged far beyond the subjects she was enrolled in, reading prodigiously and sitting in on lectures in other courses. She also made friends like she had never had before. When one girl wanted to sit next to her in class, another lent her a book, and a third invited her to spend part of the holidays with her family in the country, she was "surprised to be so popular" because she still could not treat friendship as an ordinary experience. In 1943, she observed, "I just love university life."

Her last year, in 1944, was another triumph. Having excelled in history and German during her first three years, she embarked on double honors, which meant she had to write two theses. While she got upper-second-class honors in history, she got first-class honors and a university medal in German, which, her supervisor stressed, owed little to her natural advantage as a native speaker. Her "outstanding achievement," he wrote, was her

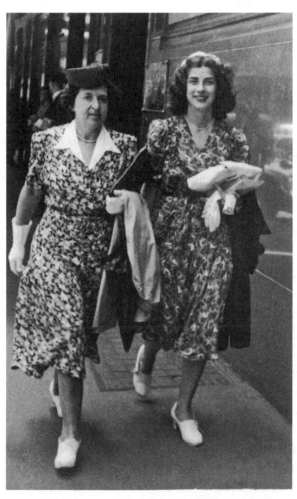

Kathe and Anne, Christmas shopping, Sydney, 1945.

thesis, which exhibited "a grasp of literary method and a power of analysis that were remarkable in an undergraduate." In her diary, an elated Anne saw her result as proof that she was "nearly a true intellectual."

The obvious careers for her in Australia were as a schoolteacher or librarian—the two standard options for young women with arts degrees, regardless of their academic achievements. At the start of 1945, Anne embarked on a Diploma of Education at Sydney Teacher's College, which was a prerequisite to teaching in government schools. But she was soon dreading the prospect of years in the country, which was the lot of many young teachers. She also found the diploma so boring that, just as with nursing, she could not bring herself to concentrate on it. Instead, she wrote letters, read books, and knit in lectures, when she did not skip them altogether, and was not surprised when she failed her exams.

In 1942 Kathe began working as a senior technician in the Medical Research Department of Sydney's Royal North Shore Hospital, prompting Gretl, Anne, and her to move from Rose Bay to the apartment in Cremorne. While Kathe's work at the hospital was a marked improvement on her job in the pencils and carbon paper factory, she was still vastly overqualified for her new position. Whereas she had studied for six years for her degree, the other technicians had obtained certificates after three years of part-time study at technical college. Even the research biochemists typically had only bachelor's degrees after three years' study at Australian universities. While the hospital included Kathe's doctorate when she appeared in lists of its staff, her superiors otherwise ignored it. The result was a profound disjunction between her professional and private identities. At work she was "Miss Gallia." Otherwise, as in Vienna, she remained "Dr. Gallia."

Gretl's position as a part-time language teacher at St. Vincent's led to similar jobs. From 1940, she worked at both Catholic and Anglican schools, transcending a profound religious divide in Australia. But when one of the Anglican schools that employed Gretl closed at the end of 1942, she could find no other teaching positions and so became a secretary. Her first position was with the Free French Delegation, where she looked forward to using her French. The next, where her German was an asset, was through Saul Symonds at the Jewish Welfare Society, underlining her exceptional interdenominational status in Sydney.

Gretl's best job came in 1944, when she secured a job at one of Sydney's most prestigious boys' schools, Shore, which was a male bastion until the war. When several of the school's teachers enlisted, it was forced to recruit three women, including Gretl. Because German was the enemy language, none of the boys wanted to learn it, so she taught only French. For two years, Gretl was intensely happy, making several lifelong friends among her pupils and delighting in the opportunity to teach full time. But when the war ended, Gretl was among many women required to give up their jobs to make way for ex-servicemen, forcing her to seek another post in the country. Just as she felt herself headed for the far end of the earth when she left Vienna in 1938, she felt the same at the start of 1946 when she left for the New England Girls' School, three hundred miles from Sydney by slow train, set amid sheep pasture outside Armidale, population seven thousand.

When she returned to Sydney late in 1948, having found the school as snobbish and mean as she found Armidale lifeless and boring, Gretl knew she would have to work as a secretary. The job she secured was her worst: she found herself in a furniture store working for another refugee set on exploitation. On Christmas Eve he dismissed all his staff to avoid having to pay them for the public holidays and quiet days at the end of December but asked them to resume working for him in the new year. Gretl refused and lost her job.

Many of her evenings and weekends were devoted to a very different venture—a translation of the first part of Wilhelm Hauff's *Märchen,* one of the most famous books of German fairy tales, which had particularly appealed to Gretl as a young woman. While Hauff's tales were the stuff of several English translations, Gretl embarked on an Australian one after her pupils in Sydney and Armidale were entranced by Hauff's stories. The resulting book, published in Sydney in 1949, was a stylish production with color plates and line drawings by one of Australia's most accomplished illustrators, Mahdi McCrae, but it failed to sell.

Gretl finally found satisfying long-term work in the early 1950s as a result of Australia's decision to expand its immigration program to boost its economy and strengthen its defenses. Because the government could not attract as many British migrants as it wanted, it took an unprecedented number from southern Europe. Intent on assimilation, the government funded several forms of English tuition for these men and women,

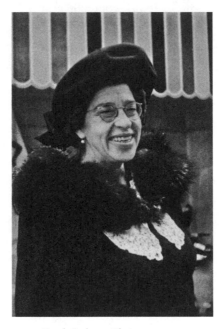

Gretl, Sydney, Christmas 1949.

including correspondence courses for those who could not attend regular classes. For almost twenty years, Gretl was the most popular correspondence teacher in New South Wales.

The sisters' financial situation became easier after they recovered the house in the Wohllebengasse in 1950. They were able to regain it because the Aryanization of the house had resulted in its direct transfer to the Nazi state, and none of the family had consented to its taking in any form or received anything for it. While worth relatively little because Vienna was still a divided city and the Wohllebengasse was in the Russian zone, the house boosted the siblings' capital when they sold it almost immediately. They were unable to regain the Villa Gallia because its Aryanization had resulted in its immediate purchase by a private individual and the new Austrian republic treated this sale as binding despite its being made under duress by Mizzi for a derisory payment. Instead, Gretl, Kathe, and Erni simply received token compensation.

The relationship of Gretl and Kathe was one constant. When the sisters resumed living together in Sydney because their position was so insecure, they agreed on almost nothing. What one embraced, the other almost inevitably scorned. Anyone who became a friend of Gretl's was rejected by Kathe and vice versa. The one exception was Anne, whom they both loved too much, according to Gretl. Far from insisting on the primacy of her relationship with Anne, Gretl repeatedly described Kathe as if they occupied the same position. "Us doting mothers" was one of Gretl's formulations for them. Yet that did not stop Gretl and Kathe from competing for Anne's affections more fiercely than ever.

As relations between Gretl and Anne became increasingly strained, Gretl felt that Anne never adequately reciprocated her intense love and devotion. She was hurt by how, as Anne excelled at university, she followed Kathe in feeling superior to Gretl. In a twenty-first-birthday letter to Anne in 1943, Gretl begged Anne to be patient and love her despite her mistakes and weaknesses. Meanwhile, Kathe's relations with Anne were better, although she, too, was often dissatisfied, rebuking Anne for her lack of kindness. When she wrote a poem for Anne's twentieth birthday, Kathe compared Anne unfavorably to Hermine, expressing her regret that she could discern no trace of Hermine's character in Anne, though she still hoped it might "come with the years passing by."

Anne continued to delight in her new Catholic identity. Her intense devotion saw her go to early morning mass every Sunday, often attend Saturday services, typically record the sermon at length in her diary, and regularly go to confession. But her sense of Christian duty was tested when she received a call from one of her Viennese godchildren whom Father Elzear had baptized at the Franciscan church. As Anne acknowledged in her diary, she had been proud at age sixteen to be godmother to forty-nine-year-old Stella Groak. "It was exactly what I wanted," Anne recognized. In Sydney, Anne wanted to avoid Mrs. Groak because she knew that Anne was another recent convert rather than a born-and-bred Catholic. Their first meeting became even more of a test for Anne when Mrs. Groak asked whether Anne was "completely Catholic," implying that Mrs. Groak was not. After Anne failed to reveal the strength of her faith, she berated herself for not responding: "What should we be? Should we keep changing?"

The dominant Catholic organization for young women in Sydney was the Grail—a lay group founded in the Netherlands in 1929 that described itself as "a pro-God youth movement with the one great object of helping to win the world for Christ." While Anne was attracted to the Grail partly because of the influence of its Dutch founders, which meant that she found it "so European," the Grail also facilitated her assimilation. In a story about her arrival in Sydney, she described how she had dreaded the recurrent question, "And how do you like Australia?" She revealed that she always felt obliged to answer positively, giving no hint of her sense of alienation. This question lost much of its sting once she joined the Grail in 1941 and became one of its most fervent members. She "no longer felt like a stranger in a strange country" because she had "something to work for and dream about and love."

Like many refugees, Anne later wondered how she would have responded to the Anschluss had she met the Nazi definition of "Aryan." Far from considering whether she might have had the courage to oppose Hitler, she assumed she would have accepted the new regime like most Austrians and wondered how enthusiastically she would have embraced it. Would she have joined the Bund Deutscher Mädchen? Might she have persecuted Jews? She could not answer these questions but knew that another part of the Grail's appeal for her was its triumphal, militaristic aspect, its mass displays, marching, banners, and uniforms. She recognized that the Grail allowed her to do what had been impossible for her in Vienna, where she had been "an outcast, not able to wear the swastika like everybody else."

It took a year or more for most young women to be accepted as one of the Grail's lay apostles. Anne was ecstatic when she succeeded in fewer than five months. Little knowing how Gretl had described her own first Communion and confirmation thirty years before, and how patterns of words and responses were transmitted across the generations, Anne declared her initiation the most beautiful day of her life. Before long, her involvement was so great that Gretl feared she was on her way to joining a religious order, which would see Gretl "lose" her only daughter. Having purported to be a complete Catholic since her arrival in Australia, Anne decided that she had to put an end to this deception and, despite Gretl's opposition, she was confirmed in St. Mary's Cathedral. Her closest university friend observed that she had never seen anything like Anne's "complete and unquestioning faith."

It did not last. Her dissatisfaction with the Church was patent in May 1942 when she went to mass on Ascension Thursday and found the priest repeating his sermon from the previous weekend. His exhortation the following Sunday, "We all know that we must love God because we learned it in our catechism," prompted her to exclaim, "Holy Aristotle, what logic." The fourth anniversary of her conversion by Father Elzear in Vienna led her to reflect on how she had become restless in the Church as she continued to seek truth. When she attended the Grail's annual play, which she had appeared in with delight the year before, she dismissed it as "propaganda."

She soon was reading Aldous Huxley's *Brave New World,* which the Church in Australia wanted banned, and Nietzsche on the *Übermensch* and the death of God. She also resumed dancing. As she described it at the time, she had stopped dancing after fleeing Vienna because she "considered it a bit frivolous and too gay but in the end came to the decision that one is young only once and that there is no harm in enjoying oneself." Before long, twenty-year-old Anne was out most Saturday nights, buying new dresses and even going to the Trocadero, a nightclub in the city for Australian and American servicemen featuring a full orchestra.

Sunday, November 8, 1942, was a turning point. While she went to mass as usual with Kathe, she observed that their roles had been reversed so that instead of Anne urging Kathe to accompany her, Kathe had

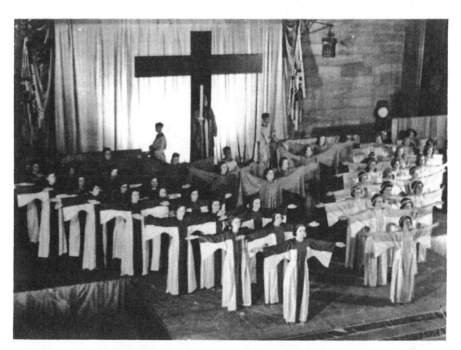

The Grail, including Anne, performing in Sydney in 1941.

pressed Anne to go. A passage in Felix Dahn's *A Fight for Rome,* which so impressed her before her conversion in Vienna, encapsulated what she felt: "To believe in God is childish. To deny the existence of God is madness. To search for God is the answer." After four years of the most intense faith, Anne saw herself as being back where she had started. "I now again finally understand," she observed, "what I already understood as a child."

Sunday, November 15, 1942, was even more momentous. She did not attend mass. Nor did she go again and, while she accompanied Kathe to church on Christmas Day, she did not follow her usual habit of recording the sermon at length. Instead, she transcribed two passages from *This Believing World,* a study of comparative religion by an American former rabbi, Lewis Browne, which she had borrowed from the library. The first passage was, "Theology very frequently is not more than an effort to prolong the life of moribund ideas by interpreting words which no longer mean what they say—and when theology is that it is invariably a confession of secret distrust and skepticism." The second passage started, "Only the great souls, the sages and prophets have ever been able to find salvation in a religion naked of ceremonial adornment. Ordinary men, even today, are incapable of comprehending abstract ideas."

Her distance from Judaism was a constant. If it seems bizarre that at twenty-two I had never heard of a shiksa, the copy of *This Believing World* that Anne bought and reread in 1943 at the age of twenty-one reveals that I was just like her. After four years in Australia, Anne's English was so good that she did not annotate any of the first 250 pages with the meaning of words, in marked contrast to the anthology of British essays she had read for the Leaving. Then, on page 251, she came across this passage: "The Jew clings to his ritual law largely because he senses subconsciously that otherwise he will lose his identity among the non-Jews. In other words, he is god-fearing largely because he is Goy-fearing." Having been formally identified as a Jew for most of her life and gone to Jewish religious instruction classes for ten years, Anne did not know the meaning of the word "Goy." She annotated it "Gentile."

3

Correspondence

The genocide of Europe's Jews is often written about as if those who escaped knew nothing of what was happening during the war. It was not so. Although there was no direct postal service from Nazi-occupied Europe to countries fighting Hitler after mid-1940, there was occasional mail to neutral countries that conveyed some news despite German censorship, and this news eventually reached friends and family elsewhere. The letters that Anne received in Sydney illustrate what was known about the mass murder of Jews, which was widely reported around the world in late 1942, and the fate of individuals. This correspondence also reveals the different ways in which refugees lived with what they knew and what they did not know.

The first of these letters came from Georg Schidlof when he reestablished contact with Anne in 1943, in his new guise as George Turner. While George's sister had escaped to Palestine, his parents had not. One of George's aunts had stayed in touch with them through neutral Sweden until the end of 1940, if not 1941, when they remained in Vienna. While George had since learned that his parents had been "dragged away into Poland," that was it. Despite repeated attempts, George had been unable to make contact with them. He also had been unable to find out exactly where the Nazis had transported them, which was in fact to Riga in the Soviet Union.

George assumed correctly that the Nazis had killed his parents. He wrote: "Of course I know that their fate is the fate of millions but this knowledge does not help." His only solace was that, having been freed from internment in Australia on condition that he enlist—and having opted to join the English rather than the Australian army because he wanted to fight the Germans, not the Japanese—he was "working entirely toward the destruction of Nazism" and would soon be "driving a tank into Austria or Germany." He declared he would "not be satisfied until the people responsible for this mass murder received the proper punishment for their crimes." It was "queer," he concluded, "when I received the news about the fate of my parents I did not feel the sorrow one would expect to feel, but I felt such a hatred, such a desire to kill those inhuman monsters with my own hands."

Another letter came early in 1945, this time from Anne's Czech cousin, Hans Troller, who had inspired her to learn the cello when he had visited Alt Aussee a decade before. Hans wrote that he had left Prague for England in 1939—seen off at the station by his mother under strict orders to keep smiling or at least not to cry as they parted. His grandmother Fanny, the last surviving sister of Anne's grandfather Moriz, had died in 1942. Hans's father, Ernst, had died soon thereafter. He had not heard from his mother since 1944, and not from his two brothers for much longer. Hans observed: "I am afraid that is not cheerful, but I stopped worrying, as with all my worrying I cannot help them under the present circumstances and I really find that the British attitude of 'don't worry' and 'don't show your feelings' is most sensible and makes life a lot easier."

Anne discovered much more once the war in Europe ended in 1945. Before long, Gretl, Kathe, and she were receiving one letter after another about the fate of family and friends. Every time a letter arrived from Europe they wondered what news it would bring. Their excitement at getting mail—so patent in Anne's diaries during the war—became mixed with dread. But particularly when the news was bad, these letters communicated just a sliver of what had occurred, as those who wrote either were in no state to describe in detail what had happened or wanted to spare others from the horror.

Several of these letters came from the Hamburgers. They started miraculously with one from Guido Junior announcing that he had found his brother Friedrich, sister-in-law Helene, and niece Jana all alive. The next was from Gudrun, who reported that her father, Otto, was dead, while her uncle and aunt Guido Senior and Nelly were not to be found. The one after was again from Guido Junior, informing them that Paul and Fely's daughter Lizzi had lived out the war in Vienna only to die of tuberculosis a month after the city fell to the Russians. Before long, I imagine, came another from Fely that Paul, too, had died.

Anne's friend Erika, who married another refugee in England in 1945, evoked what it was like to be searching for family five months after the war in Europe ended without being able to discover their fate. "Otto left his parents, two brothers, and two sisters in Germany and has not been able to find out anything about them so far," she explained to Anne that September. "So, as with him, with thousands of others, hope slowly dies; it is terrible to watch it." A month later Erika reported: "His mother, two brothers, and two sisters are alive and well. His father lost his life in Auschwitz." Her assessment was pragmatic. "As terrible as the point of his father's end is, he is still lucky to know the rest of his family has been saved."

Hans Troller wrote again at the end of 1945, after being reunited with his uncle Norbert, who had been in Theresienstadt with his father, mother, and brothers, and knew more than anyone about their deaths. "I am afraid," Hans wrote, "according to the more detailed information I received from Norbert, there is absolutely no hope at all. I am the only survivor of our family circle. Of about twenty persons of the near family in Czechoslovakia, only three have returned." Hans found it impossible to recount what Norbert had told him: "The stories he told me were absolutely unbelievably horrible and I don't want to think of it if I can help it." He concluded: "Maybe when I am going to meet you one of these days, I will tell you something about the 'Fall of the House of Troller.'" But Anne did not see Hans again before he became one of many refugees to commit suicide.

The end of the war allowed Gretl, Kathe, and Anne to reestablish contact with the few Viennese friends who had remained true to them after the Anschluss. Having heard nothing for five years, they were anxious to discover whether these friends had survived and whether they could do anything for them, as Vienna was a city in chaos, devoid of most services and short of food. The most important for Gretl and Kathe were the Moll sisters, who had hidden Gretl's jewelry, gone to the station to say farewell to Gretl and Anne when they left for Switzerland, and written repeatedly to all three of them as they sailed to Sydney. The most important for Anne was her lace-cleaning teacher, Anni Wiesbauer. When Anne first wrote to her, asking if she needed help, Anni replied that after being caught in fighting on the edge of Vienna for a fortnight as the Russians took the city, she had suffered a nervous breakdown that left her crying for months and unable to work. While she had regained her equilibrium and felt as if she had recovered from a bad dream, she described Vienna as a city where things had never been so difficult—not even at the end of World War I, which Anni had experienced as a girl. She asked Anne to send her tins and tea. While she was five feet seven inches tall, she weighed just 108 pounds.

Anni sometimes wrote over the following year as if she were still no better. She was unable to find peace, doubted whether she would be happy again, could see no ray of light, thought human beings had changed for the worse, doubted the value of life, and imagined it would be beautiful not to wake up in the morning. At other times, she declared that she had found her bearings and was happy—at least, when she worked day and night, and never read a newspaper, so she remained as oblivious as possible to the world around her. Time and again she expressed her shame at asking like a beggar for fat and meat, cocoa and marmalade, despite Anne's obvious delight in being able to reciprocate for what Anni had done for her before the war. In all, Anne sent nineteen fortnightly food parcels that left Anni crying with happiness and gave her renewed hope and confidence.

What of Paul Herschmann? Anne and Gretl must have wondered about him. When Gretl was interviewed by Australia's security services in 1940, she described Paul as "present whereabouts unknown." Once the war ended, Anne and Gretl had the opportunity to search for him through one of the agencies that brought together members of families separated during the war, just as he could have searched for them. Until Anne reread the letters that Paul sent to her after they reestablished contact, she thought he had been the one to seek her out. After rereading these letters, she thought it "most likely" that Gretl, who always retained some attachment to Paul, set out to find him. That it was Anne who did so, as clearly revealed by Paul's letters, made no sense to her when she had always felt she had "a childhood without a father."

Paul's first letter came in January 1948, from the French city of

Toulouse, where he had moved after surviving the war in the convent in Graulhet. He wrote that he had been "completely shaken" on discovering her whereabouts the day before. "Still today," he continued, "I am so overcome by joy that I can hardly grasp it as I had given up hope of hearing news of you." Paul went on to report that his brother Franz had been gassed in Auschwitz, his brother Gustav had been killed in Minsk, his aunt Elizabeth had died in Theresienstadt, his brother Otto was alive in South America, and his own survival was the result of "a remarkable chain of extraordinary circumstances." He asked Anne to give Gretl his warmest greetings, write at length to him soon, and send him a photograph. He concluded, "You are embraced by your father."

Anne responded as if Paul was imposing himself on her. While his letter was not "theatrical," that was how Anne described it in her diary. She still replied immediately, as did Gretl from Armidale. But while Gretl conveyed affection and compassion, so that her letter affected Paul more than any other since the war, he was shocked by Anne's impersonal report, devoid of affection, giving no hint of the relationship of daughter and father. While Paul acknowledged that he was in no position to reprimand Anne because they "had never totally possessed each other," he desperately wanted her to confide in him.

She refused and explained why—accusing him of seeing little of her during her last years in Vienna, and probably much else—which left him struggling to know how to respond. While he declared that he did not want to engage in accusations or defenses, he did. He wrote that he had come to see her often and happily while she was little, even though it sometimes was not easy, but that later he had the feeling that she no longer needed him and he would never force himself on his own dear child. He wanted her to see that they were both very different people. He encouraged her to write again and get to know him because he was part of the puzzle of her life and, if she looked inside herself, would find him.

He could not persuade her and by September was so distraught that he put his grievance to Gretl, prompted by a letter from Anne in which she declared, "I do not have the feeling that I am writing to my father." Paul's hurt was palpable as he asked Gretl, "If that is the case, why did she seek me out?" He concluded, "If I also have made mistakes, I was of the opinion that after such infinite suffering, after the loss of my dearest brother and friend Franz, one must reach out one's hand."

Paul explained in these letters that he had lost an average of six and a

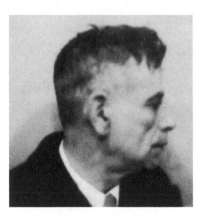

Paul, Toulouse, February 1948.

half pounds a year since leaving Vienna, or fifty-nine pounds in all. He disclosed that in addition to being given injections—the nature of which he did not specify—he had received electric shock treatment. He revealed that he could not stop thinking about the last time he saw Franz and that he dreamed almost every night about Franz's death in Auschwitz. While Paul thought Gretl looked the same as ever when she sent him a photograph of her in Sydney, she must have been shocked when he reciprocated with a photograph of his shrunken, hollow face. When Gretl asked him to write more personally, Paul responded that he had no personal life.

The survival of Paul's youngest brother, Otto, in Argentina did little to alleviate the sense of loss and isolation that came with being the only member of his family left in Europe. When Paul did not hear from Otto for a long time, he could not bring himself to write because he feared another blow of fate. While he was able to forget himself occasionally by attending lectures and operas, this respite was short-lived. Although Paul initially reported that he had many French and Austrian friends, he still described himself as very lonely, and his circle soon shrank when several of his friends moved to Paris. The closest to remain in Toulouse was another Austrian who taught human rights. Paul was surprised when, one evening in 1948, his friend unexpectedly talked about his relationship to God. He killed himself later that night. When Paul tried to deliver the eulogy at his funeral, it proved beyond him.

Paul collapsed on a street in Toulouse in 1950 and was taken to the hospital unconscious. When he recovered sufficiently to write to Gretl a fortnight later, he disclosed that for a long time he had been unable to distinguish fantasy from reality. He also revealed that his doctors attributed his condition to his taking too many tranquilizers and sleeping tablets. At least Paul had company while he was in the hospital. When he wrote another letter to Gretl a few weeks later, he had been visited by a rabbi and a bishop and had enjoyed seeing them both, as his experiences during the war had changed his view of Catholicism. While he did not believe in any God, he was open to both Judaism and Christianity. Anne recorded that Paul had tried to commit suicide but failed.

The awfulness of his situation is patent. Paul was a beaten, broken man—his health ruined, his muscles wasted, incapable of adjusting to new circumstances, afflicted by depression, unable to hold down a job. Just as with Anni Wiesbauer, Anne gave Paul material help. After he wrote that his doctors had advised him to eat more but that he could not get the food he needed because he was unable to buy anything on the black market, Anne joined Gretl in sending food parcels. She even asked for Paul's measurements and knit him a woolen vest. But whereas she conveyed her deep attachment to Anni, she had no love or affection for Paul. Whether fairly or unfairly, she thought he had failed her as a girl and, despite the extremity of his situation, she would not forgive him.

One way in which Paul tried to bridge the gulf between them was by giving her a new sense of family by writing about his parents and grandparents, who had all died before she was born. But while Anne preserved these letters, Paul's family history was of no interest to her. Having always thought of herself as a Gallia in Vienna and finally become one in Sydney, she had no desire to learn about the Herschmanns, let alone identify with them. Paul's other way of trying to find common ground with Anne was by expounding about German literature and theater. By drawing on what he had learned as a young man, he hoped to engage Anne, who had just embarked on a master's degree in German at Sydney University. But she found what he wrote of no interest at best, bizarre at worst, especially Paul's advocacy of Ibsen's *Ghosts,* which she read as a play in which "the heroine . . . had been married to a dreadful man, so much so, that she had her son brought up far from home so that he should have no contact with his father." Anne observed, "Considering that he was so anxious to have contact with me, that was a very odd choice."

Her one expression of interest in Paul came in 1971, when she went to Freiburg im Breisgau, where he had studied chemistry, and sought out his thesis. Otherwise she wanted nothing to do with him. Her last words on

Paul were: "My father died in Toulouse in 1958. After his death I received a letter from a rabbi in Toulouse suggesting that a suitable gravestone should be erected in his memory. But I did not consider this. I never felt that he had been a father to me and in any case the contact I had had with him throughout my life was minimal. I had no idea what his wishes regarding his grave were and my relationship to cemeteries is an ambiguous one. When I was in Toulouse in the early eighties I did not visit any of the cemeteries to find his grave."

4

Eric

The refugees who fled Hitler as children often married other refugees. One American survey suggests that almost half of those who went to the United States did so. In Australia, the number was probably even higher because the society was much less cosmopolitan and much more fearful of the foreign. Anne was eager to do differently but recognized that, because of her origins, there was little chance of a "genuine Australian" wanting to marry her. An incident in 1942 was telling. At a dance one night, she met a young member of the air force who had no idea where she came from because of her success in learning to speak English without an accent. They talked at length and danced together happily. Then she revealed that she was from Vienna and, to her dismay, he lost interest.

My father, Erich, was a refugee from Graz, the capital of the Austrian province of Styria, where his grandfather Salomon and father, Eduard, ran a small leather business. Within days of the Anschluss the Nazis arrested Salomon and placed him in a police prison in Graz where they held him for a fortnight. On the morning of Kristallnacht they arrested Eduard and sent him to the concentration camp at Dachau, where he became prisoner 23,486 on the twelfth of November but was let go that winter, like most of the other men sent to Dachau after Kristallnacht. While the majority were freed at the start of December, the Nazis held those whom they had beaten, such as Eduard, for longer, releasing them only when their injuries had partly healed because the Nazis were still concerned about their image abroad. When Eduard's wife, Edith, finally got word that the Nazis might free her husband, Erich began going to the Graz railway station early every morning so there would be someone to meet Eduard. He went in vain day after day until, one morning, Eduard appeared.

The men whom the Nazis let out of Dachau at the end of 1938 were the last inmates of a concentration camp ever to be released by the Nazis. Just as when they let Käthe out of the police prison in the Hahngasse, a condition was that these men had to leave Greater Germany. Eduard was able to comply because he had applied successfully for Australian visas not long before his arrest. By April 1939, Eduard, Edith, Erich, and his younger brother Friedrich were ready to depart but stayed in Graz long enough to celebrate the start of Passover with Eduard's father and mother, Salomon and Bertha, and brother and sister-in-law, Berthold and Else, who had no means of escaping. Then Eduard, Edith, Erich, and Friedrich set out for Sydney, where they were met by Eduard's sister, Mira, and her husband, Fritz, who had fled while Eduard was in Dachau. Before long, there were no Bonyhadys in Graz, as the Nazis forced Salomon, Bertha, Berthold, and Else to move to Vienna as part of their drive to make Graz *Judenrein*. Seventy-eight-year-old Salomon was dead by the end of the year from natural causes, followed shortly thereafter by seventy-six-year-old Bertha and one of Eduard's brothers, Norbert, whom the Nazis pushed out of a window. By the end of the war, the death toll had grown as the Nazis killed Berthold and Else, Norbert's wife, Alice, and ten-year-old-son, Gerard, and one of Edith's sisters, her husband, and one of their sons.

Had there been no Anschluss, Erich would have stayed at school in Graz until he graduated, then continued on to university and, most likely, embarked on a career as a professional. In Sydney, Eric (as he was renamed) did not even complete the Intermediate examination held at the end of third form, let alone do the Leaving like Anne. Instead, his father put him in school for just six months, then sent him to earn a wage as a process worker on a metal press. Before long, like many other young refugees, he was drawn to communism because it appeared to represent the opposite of fascism. When his family moved from Sydney's eastern suburbs to the city's west, his worldview was transformed by another Austrian refugee, a Social Democrat with a vast library. After attending meet-

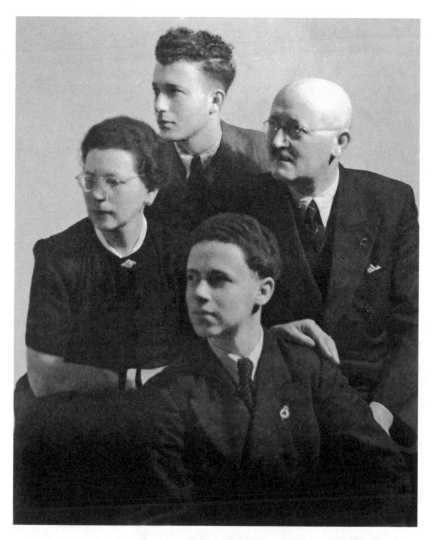

The Bonyhadys—Eric, above; his brother, Fred, below; mother, Edith, and father, Edward—taken in Sydney by Australia's foremost refugee photographer, Margaret Michaelis, 1944.

ings of the Australian Communist Party's Youth League, Eric joined the party itself. En route he lost his belief in Judaism and, though he remained a party member for only a year, his faith did not return. When he met Anne, he was an agnostic but avoided conflict with his father by observing Passover with the family and going to synagogue.

The Bonyhadys' tradition of religious observance was much stronger than that of either the Herschmanns or the Jacobis, the families of Anne's father, Paul, and Erni's wife, Mizzi. The Bonyhadys took pride in being descendants of Meir or Mordechai Tosk, a *dayan,* or religious judge, in Bratislava, whose portrait was displayed in the Bonyhady house. Salomon Bonyhady went to synagogue every morning and occupied ever more significant posts in the Jewish community in Graz until he became president of the *Hevrah Kaddisha,* or Jewish burial society, and a member of the executive of the Israelitische Kultusgemeinde. In Eduard's last three months in Graz following his release from Dachau, he was the Kultusgemeinde's president. In Sydney, Edward, as he became in one more name change, was a member of Sydney's Central Synagogue. Together with Edith, he also joined the local chapter of the Jewish fraternal organization B'nai B'rith and regularly attended its meetings. They kept a kosher household. They always had a mezuzah by their front door, symbolically sanctifying their house as well as announcing their faith.

All this made Eric in many ways similar to Anne as well as very different from her. They both came from Austria. They both were of Jewish origin. The Bonyhadys had not only been engaged in the leather trade like the Herschmanns but had also done business with them. Anne and Eric arrived in Australia within six months of each other. Like Eric, Anne was an agnostic if not atheist. Yet while Anne had acquired intellectual range and ambition at university, Eric's educational aspirations had been stymied. For all the property that Gretl and Kathe lost when they escaped Austria, Eric still thought of them as rich. Whereas Anne knew almost nothing about Judaism, Eric was steeped in it. While she was intent on leaving her Jewish past behind her, Eric remained attached to his.

They met in 1945, when Anne was doing her teacher training and Eric was working as a draftsman, and were soon going out every Saturday night. After he took her to a cabaret at Sydney's Maccabean Hall staged by the Women's International Zionist Organization, Anne recorded how much she liked Eric. After another outing to the ballet, Eric escorted her home to Cremorne for the first time. During another, they encountered

Anne's friend Gerty Angel, who warned Anne that Eric's father was very controlling. Still, when Anne went to meet his family at their house in Bankstown, she was shocked by his father's dominance and mother's subservience. While her friends included several Jews who had retained their faith, Anne was appalled by Edward's religiosity. She described him as a "zealous Jew."

As Anne and Eric continued courting, they still were able to see each other only on weekends because they lived far apart and he was studying at night. While they had wonderful times together, their relationship was usually fraught. When Eric wanted to marry, Anne did not, and vice versa. The same was true when one of them wanted to break up but still wanted the other's agreement. His father was a prime source of tension. Edward Bonyhady loathed Anne, as he despised all converts from Judaism, while Anne loathed Edward's religiosity and his power over Eric, who in turn came to recognize that he let Anne exercise too much power over him. "I gave too much in to you," he wrote in September 1947, "allowed you to take the lead too often!"

They decided to marry that December when Anne was approaching her twenty-sixth birthday and had just begun teaching at the Sacred Heart Convent, while Eric had just turned twenty-four and was still working as a draftsman. Within a week they were looking for a place to live. A week later Eric revealed their plans to Edward and, Anne recorded, the "*Kampf*," or "battle," was on, as Edward demanded that Eric and Anne wait a year while Anne converted to Judaism. When they talked on December 28, she refused to convert but agreed to wait a year, only to fear she had conceded too much. She began a letter to her "dearest Eric" late that night by demanding that he make up his mind at once. He had to choose between his family and her. They needed to marry or part immediately. But by the end of the letter, she was willing to wait so long as Edward fixed the date of their wedding and Eric left home at once.

Eric agreed to marry immediately but did not tell his family. When his aunt Mira pressed Anne to convert, declaring that her marriage to Eric would otherwise be an irredeemable stain on the Bonyhady family's honor, Anne considered Mira a "fanatic." On January 3, 1948, they married at the registry office in the city with just their two witnesses present. As they emerged, a street photographer caught them holding hands, beaming with happiness. They had lunch at the apartment in Cremorne

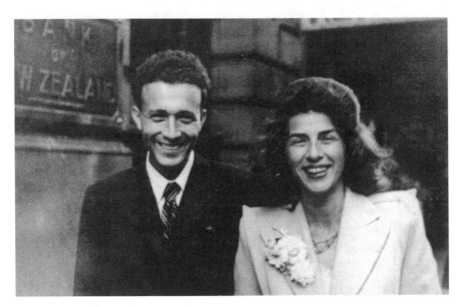

Eric and Anne following their marriage, Sydney, January 1948.

with Kathe and Gretl. They spent the afternoon watching *Black Narcissus,* a new British film, despite Anne having little taste for popular culture. They spent their wedding night in a hotel.

The following day Eric wrote to let Edward and Edith know what Anne and he had done and to try to placate them. "Dear Parents," he began in German, when he usually wrote to them in English. "*Ad meah shanah,*" "For a hundred years," he continued, for once adopting his father's custom of using this Hebrew salutation. "Hopefully you will understand how sorry we are to notify you in writing that we have just married. But if you put yourself in our situation and imagine how much we love each other and that we cannot relinquish our relationship, you will understand that we could not find another way out other than to marry quickly and secretly. This we did on Saturday and look forward to hearing from you when we can personally receive your blessings."

Gretl did her best to ensure that Anne and Eric benefited from what she had learned from her marriage. Because Hermine's criticism of Paul Herschmann had been so destructive, Gretl resolved to side with Eric whenever Anne and he argued. When Gretl received a letter from Anne that April describing her first Passover with the Bonyhadys—almost certainly the first Passover Anne had attended—Gretl was so disturbed that she immediately sent Anne a letter in which she recounted her experience of a similar situation, Paul's obvious contempt for the Gallias' Catholicism when he attended his first Christmas at the Wohllebengasse. Gretl advised Anne that she was incapable of hiding her feelings so, even if Anne said nothing, her response would be clear from her face. She warned that even if Eric said nothing, he would be acutely sensitive to her rejection of Judaism, since he had been raised a Jew. She admonished Anne that "one should never make fun of the religion or beliefs of other human beings."

It was to no avail. Anne was incapable of changing or hiding her animosity toward Edward, just as he could not hide his antipathy toward her. Eric's aunt Mira added to Anne's sense of alienation by persisting in calling her "*Sie*" rather than "*Du*," as if she were still not part of the family. For the next few years, Eric and Anne spent Easter with Gretl and Kathe and Passover with the Bonyhadys. But these occasions were always awkward, if not unpleasant, so after a few years Eric began going to his family's Passover celebrations without Anne. By then it was clear that, for all their similarities, theirs was a mixed marriage.

Their first house created more tensions between them. In keeping with Gallia tradition, they employed an architect, and Anne had a range of furniture designed by a fellow refugee, George Korody, who was at the forefront of modern design in Australia. But when Eric's parents offered to give them a wedding present, and she asked for a bedroom suite from Korody, they went to another refugee, Paul Kafka, whose work was generally much darker and heavier. Just as Norbert Stern was appalled when Moriz insisted that Josef Hoffmann design the apartment in the Untere Augartenstrasse when Norbert and Gretl were engaged, so Anne loathed the furniture that her parents-in-law imposed on her. When Anne and Eric separated, she kept all the Korody furniture apart from the desk used by Eric. He kept the Kafka furniture.

Pregnancy brought out everything that Anne and Eric had not resolved about their religions. While Anne wanted their baby baptized Catholic to mask his Jewish origins and shield him against a recurrence of anti-Semitism, Eric feared his father's reaction. Whereas Paul Herschmann had determined that Anne be a Jew despite Gretl's opposition, Anne insisted that Bruce become Catholic. His baptism, three weeks after he was born in March 1954, may have been the first time that thirty-year-old Eric was in a church. It almost certainly was his first Christian service.

Anne and Eric started the day by going to visit Gretl and Kathe, who celebrated Bruce's baptism by creating a bank account for him into which they deposited £50. Then Anne and Eric went to the Catholic church in Mosman with Kathe, who was to be Bruce's godmother. When the priest insisted on questioning them because he had not seen them before and wanted to confirm their commitment to the Church, they lied. The priest wanted to know where they lived, clearly expecting them to become parishioners, so they gave their address as the flat in Cremorne rather than their own house in Chatswood. He wanted to know where they had been married, and they told him St. Mary's, Sydney's Catholic cathedral, rather than the city's registry office. That afternoon, after returning to Chatswood, they had a terrible argument.

My religious identity was not as much of an issue for Anne. But having had Bruce baptized, she decided I should be, too. Once again Eric had to be involved, he dared not tell his parents, and Kathe was godmother. Once again the priest sensed a lack of conviction, which led him to ask questions. "Who brings this elderly child?" he exclaimed when Anne and Eric took me to the church when I was almost three months old, in December 1957. Kathe made things worse when, feeling the strain of the occasion, she lapsed into German when the priest asked her to recite the Lord's Prayer, prompting him to ask for it in English. Eric—Anne recorded in her diary—was "reluctant and angry."

My Catholicism almost stopped there. Only Gretl built on it when she taught me the Lord's Prayer in German before I even knew it in English. Bruce and I never went to Sunday school or church. For Anne, our baptisms were part of a pragmatic approach to religion that saw us go from being baptized Catholic to having us educated Anglican and then Methodist while she raised us as atheists after Eric and she were divorced. When Bruce found himself being picked on after revealing his Catholic baptism to one of his classmates at the Anglican school we attended in Melbourne in the mid-1960s, Anne instructed him not to talk about his religion. If he was ever asked, she told him, he should say he was Church of England.

5

Return

One of the highlights of the BBC's Christmas Day program for 1954 was a feature on "Good Neighbors," broadcast immediately before the Queen's message to the Commonwealth. As described by the BBC, "Good Neighbors" told the stories of men and women from around the world, some famous, others not, who were "living and working for the sake of others." One was Leonard Cheshire, the most celebrated British bomber pilot of World War II, who became a hero of the peace by establishing the Cheshire Homes for the sick, old, poor, and helpless. Another was the Canadian Marilyn Bell, who had swum "into fame and fortune" by being the first to cross Lake Ontario and then had used her feat to secure donations ensuring the future of a Toronto clinic for crippled children. Nurse Joseph exemplified "the new spirit moving the sons and daughters of India's privileged classes to share the primitive way of life of the villages in which nine-tenths of India's four hundred million people live." Gretl was a "New Australian" helping even newer Australians by teaching them English, repaying "the gift of a new home in a new country by a very practical form of good-neighborliness."

This radio appearance, lasting for one minute and fifty-five seconds—marginally more than the Canadian Marilyn Bell and the Indian Nurse

Joseph—was Gretl's closest brush with fame during her life in Australia. It provided her with an opportunity to represent her new country and to be heard across it. She also reached family and friends who had fled to other parts of the Commonwealth and with whom she had not spoken for at least sixteen years. It was a matter of family pride, as Anne put it, that Gretl was "on the Christmas broadcast with the Queen."

Almost everything Gretl said was an expression of her own situation as someone from a wealthy background who had been forced to adjust to her loss of privilege but was very fortunate to live on Sydney Harbor and had retained her interest in high culture. She declared: "We New Australians have learned a lot here. How to be less fussy. How to keep houses as well as how to live without servants. How to enjoy the sunshine and swimming every weekend. In return we are giving Australia many of our own ideas— ideas about food and furniture and architectural designs. We are keen supporters of music, the theater, the ballet." She also maintained that she had "never regretted that we came here," despite never feeling at home or accepted in Australia. For all her friends in Sydney, Gretl wrote to Anne in 1960, "You know I don't feel comfortable among Australians. I like them as little as they like me."

Wiener Lieder—not so much songs about Vienna but love songs to it—expressed Gretl's homesickness. One of her favorites was "*Meine Mutterl war eine Wienerin,*" or "My Mother Was a Viennese." It describes how a mother takes her small daughter on an excursion to the Vienna Woods, where they look down on the city and the mother has her daughter promise to be true to it. When Gretl played this song in Australia, it brought tears to her eyes. Anne recalled, "It was as if she had been asked to be faithful to Vienna for the rest of her life despite what the city and its people had done to her." Another of Gretl's favorites was "*Wien, du Stadt meiner Träume,*" or "Vienna, City of My Dreams." Vienna remained the city of Gretl's dreams throughout her life in Australia. She called it her "dear, dearest Vienna."

The pictures on Gretl's walls in Sydney may have heightened her nostalgia. The Viennese scenes included the interior of the Peterskirche, the Beethoven house in Heiligenstadt, and a view of the grounds of Schönbrunn Palace. But because these pictures were by Carl Moll, they were also a reminder of how, after being so close to the Gallias for so long, he had rejected Gretl, Käthe, and Annelore following the Anschluss. I wonder whether Gretl was able to separate what these pictures depicted from who had painted them, especially given her strong code of loyalty. What was it like for her to see Vienna every day through Moll's brush?

I wonder, too, what Gretl felt if she heard that when Alma Mahler tried to regain a painting she had owned by Edvard Munch, one of the prime witnesses for the Austrian government was Paul Hamburger's widow, Fely, who drew on her enduring relationship with Moll through the war to argue that, far from stealing this painting, he had acted in good faith. I am even more curious about Gretl's response when Fely married the art historian Bruno Grimschitz who, after being one of the few Austrians subject to de-Nazification—stripped of all his official positions because he was so politically tainted—was reappointed as a professor at the University of Vienna in 1957. What did Gretl make of Fely's first saving Paul Hamburger from the Holocaust, then marrying a rehabilitated Nazi?

Return for Gretl was never a possibility, even as a tourist. Too much of what she missed had been destroyed or dispersed. Austria also was too far away. Yet what she did in life was one thing, in death another. When Gretl decided that she wanted to be buried with Moriz, Hermine, and Lene in the Hietzing cemetery, she arranged for a stonemason to put her name and date on the family gravestone so only her date of death would have to be added. A codicil to her will, written more than twenty-five years after she arrived in Sydney, expressed her alienation from Australia. She declared that if she could not be interred in Vienna as she wished, "I want my ashes to be scattered, but I definitely do *not* want them to be buried in Australia; in death, at least, I do not wish to be a foreigner."

Kathe retained nothing like the same attachment to Austria. For most of her life in Sydney, she looked on Vienna as a place she had left once and for all. After being imprisoned in the Hahngasse following the Anschluss and hiding in her lawyer's car after Kristallnacht, she could not imagine returning. Kathe was also much more interested in Australia. Whereas Gretl traveled only as far as Melbourne, Kathe went by herself to Alice Springs so she could see Australia's Red Center. While Gretl read English novelists such as Somerset Maugham and John Galsworthy, Kathe preferred Australian writers. When Gretl pressed her to be buried in the Hietzing cemetery, too, Kathe agreed because of family, not country.

Kathe's embrace of Australia was most apparent in the early 1960s, when she decided to find a means of expressing her gratitude to Australia for accepting Gretl, Anne, and herself as refugees and being so good to them. While the international revaluation of Klimt's work had only just begun, his work was gaining increasing recognition in the United States, where the Fogg Museum at Harvard, the Museum of Modern Art in New York, and the Carnegie Museum of Art in Pittsburgh had all acquired his canvases. This revaluation meant that the portrait was Kathe's most valuable possession. It also retained emotional significance for Kathe as it kept Hermine in her daily life in the most visible of ways. Kathe offered it to the Art Gallery of New South Wales, Australia's second-oldest art museum, as a gift.

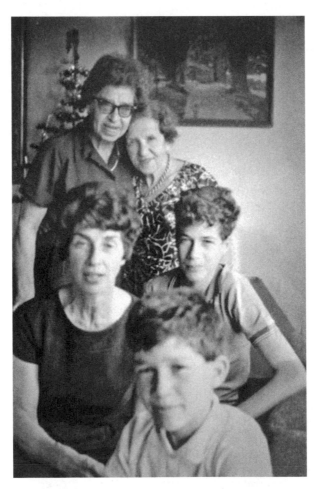

Gretl, Kathe, Anne, Bruce, and Tim in the apartment in Sydney, Christmas 1967. One of Carl Moll's paintings of Hermine's birthplace, Freudenthal, is on the wall behind.

The gallery occupied a spectacular site overlooking Sydney Harbor, but almost everything else about the museum was deficient when Kathe approached it. While it had a director and deputy director, it had neither curators nor a registrar. Behind its neoclassical sandstone facade, embellished in the mid-1870s with the names of the most famous European masters, such as Michelangelo, Rembrandt, Rubens, and Raphael, was a tiny display including none of their works. The gallery's best European pictures were late-nineteenth-century British paintings by Lord Leighton, Sir Lawrence Alma-Tadema, and Ford Madox Brown acquired when the gallery was new. Its strength was its Australian holdings.

They Kill You in the End was how the gallery's director, Hal Missingham, titled his account of his life and times at the gallery. Missingham's twelve chapters addressed the trials, tribulations, and occasional triumphs of his professional life involving the gallery's building, trustees, staff, and exhibitions. The notable omission was acquisitions. A dearth of funds was one reason, but Missingham also failed to make the most of his opportunities to build the collection through philanthropy when he declined Kathe's offer, seemingly rejecting the portrait of Hermine as a work of no value to an Australian collection and of no interest to an Australian audience—one of the greatest blunders of an Australian museum director.

The sharpest record of Anne's views of Austria and Australia is in the letters she wrote to George Turner from 1943. Her first letter revealed her dismay at George's failure to contact her while he was interned in Australia. "I could have wept that I did not know," she wrote. "Not one, not a single one of my old friends is out here, for five years I have not seen anyone at all. And then to hear that an old friend has been so near—and that I did not see him—it just makes me miserable." Still, Anne declared it a "great experience" to hear from George and responded at once at length. Over the next thirty years they corresponded regularly, writing to each other every month for long periods. She typically kept only his first letter, due to her repeated culling of her possessions. He kept all her letters until I came to see him in 2004 while writing this book, and he entrusted them to me after putting them in chronological order and reading them one last time.

Anne's highest praise for Australia was as "a good place to live." She appreciated its material prosperity, abundance of food, and short working week. She delighted in its sunshine, beautiful beaches, and the ease and joy of swimming in a rock pool on the edge of the harbor just a few min-

utes' walk from the apartment in Cremorne. She thought Australia's highest mountain, Kosciuszko, "very beautiful," but emphasized that it was "of
course" nothing like Austria's Alps. Sydney's "low cultural standards" distressed her. "Art treasures may be found only in reproductions," she
lamented after visiting the Art Gallery of New South Wales. "Good concerts, theater, opera, all these things are practically unknown." She did not
expect Sydney to acquire a concert hall because of "local lethargy."

The occasional visit by European musicians did little to alleviate her
sense of deprivation. When an Italian company came to Sydney late in
1948, she seized the opportunity to see professional opera for the first time
since Vienna, attending nine of the fourteen different operas that it performed yet still wanted more, exclaiming, "God knows when there will be
opera again in this country." When the Vienna Boys' Choir toured in
1954, she saw them four times, despite always being tired because Bruce
was only three months old. When the choir returned in 1959, she went
again, taking five-year-old Bruce with her. "This was my first concert
when I was a child and I am taking Bruce," she explained to George,
"though he is still a little young for that."

The Third Man, the film of Graham Greene's screenplay starring
Orson Welles, provided a rare opportunity for her to see what had become
of her old home. "I would love to see some pictures of Vienna," she wrote
when it was released in England in 1949. Yet she knew she would have to
wait because British films took months to reach Australia and, when *The
Third Man* arrived in 1950, she appreciated its award-winning cinematog-
raphy but was disappointed by how little it revealed of the postwar city.
While the most famous sequence of the film, set below ground, lasts only
a few minutes, it had such an impact on her that she wished the film "had
shown more of Vienna than of the sewer."

Her fears and suspicions, as well as her attachment to Gretl and Kathe
and her relationship with Eric, prevented her from returning. Following
George's first visit to Vienna after the war, she asked what had happened
when he encountered men whom he had known who had fought for
Hitler. All she heard made her "very doubtful of the desirability of going
back, even for a short visit," and, when George was there again a decade
later, she thought the same. "Strangely enough I don't feel like going
there," she wrote, when it was not strange at all. "I could not trust the people. I am sure that I would be unhappy if I had to stay there for any length
of time." She otherwise longed to see "all the old places again," the "mag-

nificent culture," "all those beautiful things." "I hope that one day I shall get back if only for a while," she wrote. "I could envy you the chance of going to Vienna," "I sometimes think that I will never be lucky enough to get there."

Erni and Mizzi were the first to return. They began acquiring the means to do so during the war when, having been a business failure in Europe despite his inherited wealth and connections, Erni proved a success as a partner in a Tasmanian liqueur factory that flourished by supplying the American army fighting in the Pacific. When he first visited Sydney in 1944, Anne was amazed to see Erni assume the persona of the rich uncle. While he did not do as well after Mizzi and he moved to Melbourne, Mizzi supplemented their income by taking in lodgers. When he retired at age sixty-five in 1962, they sailed for Europe, where their joy in exploring new ground was intense, their return to familiar places much more complex— especially for Mizzi—whose experience of remaining in Austria so long after the Anschluss haunted her. The one family site that she would not revisit was Alt Aussee—she was too scarred by her experience of going there in 1940 to hand over the keys to the Villa Gallia—so Erni went by himself.

Anne's earliest opportunity to follow with Bruce and me came after she embarked on a new career as an academic in the 1960s, which led to a tenured position in the German Department at the University of New England in Armidale, where Gretl had taught so unhappily twenty years before. By 1970, Anne was bored with language teaching but excited by her development of a course in German culture and history. She was also due for sabbatical leave and feeling "quite adventurous." Although 1971 was Bruce's last year of high school, and many parents would have stayed at home so as not to jeopardize their child's prospects, she decided we would spent eight months in Europe, rightly confident that his results would not suffer.

The strength of the Australian dollar allowed her to make this trip more unusual and ambitious. She decided that, rather than settle in one city, where she could have rented an apartment and Bruce and I could have gone to school, we would travel from town to town, which meant from cheap hotel to cheap hotel. Her goal was not only to discover how German was taught in different universities but also to see as great a variety of theater, opera, and art as possible, while we experienced Europe with her in between studying by correspondence from our hotel rooms.

Far from having a fixed itinerary, she did not know how long we would stay in any one place or where we would go next, as one of her first postcards to a friend in Australia reveals. She gave our address as the flat of Gretl and Kathe in Cremorne with this postscript: "My mother knows where we are."

We flew to Frankfurt in West Germany thirty-two years after she escaped Austria. Our first night at the opera was on January 1, 1971, our third night in Frankfurt. Anne spent the next night, by herself, at the theater. The next night she was there again, not only because it was part of her research for the university but also because her appetite for opera and theater had gone unsated for so long. By the end of January, she had been to twenty-five performances. In February, when her opportunities were diminished by our spending six days in the Bavarian and Austrian countryside, she went to seventeen. In March she attended twenty.

We spent the first month traveling through West Germany, where everything was new for all three of us. Then we crossed into Austria, where Anne found that much of what she thought would feel like old territory seemed new. When she hired a car on our second day in Salzburg, she was not sure where to take it. Her choice was between the professional and the personal—between enhancing her understanding of German history by visiting Berchtesgarten in southern Bavaria, where Hitler had his alpine retreat, or revisiting her childhood by driving through the Salzkammergut to Alt Aussee. She opted for Aussee.

She did not know what to do when we arrived—a common dilemma for returning refugees of her generation. Some sought to regain access to their childhood homes. Others stood outside but could not face confronting the current occupants, however much they wanted to get inside. Almost all found the experience profoundly unsettling. After hesitating over lunch, Anne decided that she wanted to see the Villa Gallia and was not satisfied with looking from the road but walked all around the villa, which proved to be shut for the winter, just as it was when she was a girl. The differences interested her most: "the house made ugly by new windows and a yellow color, the garden changed, tennis court, red currants and gooseberries gone, also the rosebushes near the house and the peonies."

She needed more. Although it was winter, she decided we should walk up the Tressenstein, the smallest of the mountains surrounding Alt Aussee. With snow and ice everywhere, she fell twice but pressed on until we reached a spot with stunning views of the frozen lake and she could see the house where George Turner's family stayed each summer. After we returned to Salzburg, we saw what proved to be our first and only operetta—Strauss's *Wiener Blut,* which she enjoyed despite its "very poor" dancing and "fair" singing, costumes, and lighting. Her summation of the day fell far short of what it must have meant to her. She described it as "silly though most rewarding."

Five days later we were in Vienna, where she was delighted that she could find her way around without a map. She was pleased to discover when she took us skating at the Eislaufverein that she still "could do a few things, though not backward nor the dance step." She found the Burgtheater even better than her memory. She remained so attached to the Vienna Boys' Choir that she bought tickets for us to go to mass in the Burgkapelle every Sunday—Bruce and my first experience of Catholic services since our baptisms. She was disappointed when we celebrated her forty-ninth birthday at the opera for Verdi's *The Force of Destiny* and could get only standing places in the Gods. She was thrilled a week later when, by arriving much earlier, we were able to secure places in the front row of the downstairs standing area for "the most beautiful and richly decorated *Magic Flute* ever."

She could easily have visited the Wohllebengasse but stayed away until we visited Vienna again in July when we found the building locked. Our one visit to the Hietzing cemetery was fraught. While Anne located the family grave as easily as she navigated the streets of the city, she was taken aback to find not just the names of Moriz, Hermine, and Lene, but also those of Gretl and Kathe. Perhaps her mother and aunt had not told her what they had done. More likely she had forgotten. "I suppose I was told this once," she wrote of finding their names, "but the reality of it" gave her a "real shock."

Other parts of the city were full of significance for her. She wrote that the memories came flooding back—the names and identities of many people she had not thought of for years. Almost all were either dead or gone. She found that she had a relative living in Vienna only by looking in the phone book. He was Otto Herschmann, her father's youngest brother, who had returned in 1957 from Argentina and immediately rejoined the Israelitische Kultusgemeinde. Anne's sole contact with Otto had been through lawyers after Paul died intestate in 1958 and Otto unsuccessfully challenged Anne's inheritance of Paul's small estate. When Anne discovered that seventy-seven-year-old Otto was still alive, she did not call him.

The only person whom Anne wanted to see was Anni Wiesbauer, her lace-cleaning teacher, with whom she had not corresponded since the early 1950s. When Anne returned to Vienna and discovered that Anni was still living in the same apartment, she could have sent a letter or telephoned in advance. Instead, typically, she knocked at Anni's door unannounced and was thrilled by their reunion. "Wonderful to know someone like her!" she wrote after seeing seventy-two-year-old Anni. "She was so pleased to see me," she observed after going to see her again without warning. "Had my picture out to show it to a friend," she added, revealing her insecurity and need.

If Anne ever could relax, it was not in Vienna. "I never felt comfortable, let alone at home," she observed in her memoir. Like most refugees who returned, she was suspicious of Austrians old enough to have been part of the Nazi regime. "I looked at people who passed me in the street and were of my own age group," Anne wrote, "and wondered what they had been up to in 1938." When we left for Prague after a stay of almost three weeks, she was happy to go. "Apart from Anni, there is nothing here," she recorded. "I leave it as any other place." Vienna for her was simply a city where she found it "easy to find my way and where I have a real friend."

6

Dispersal

The Klimt revival was gaining momentum as we traveled. Prices for Klimt's drawings, his most commonly available works, had risen from $120 in 1957 to $1,200 in 1964 to $4,000 in 1971. Although Anne, Bruce, and I arrived in England too late to see the *Vienna Secession* exhibition at the Royal Academy at the start of 1971 that identified Klimt as the "star" of the Secession, Anne heard about the excitement that this exhibition generated from Wilhelm Gallia's youngest daughter, Friedl von Hoffmansthal, who was living in London. Anne also went to see the international auction house Christie's, which advised that the portrait of Hermine should fetch between £10,000 (then, $24,200) and £12,000 (then $29,040), a small fortune.

The painting was with Christie's just weeks after we returned. While we had one of the great experiences of our lives, Gretl feared something awful would happen to us all the time we were away. She worried as we flew to Frankfurt. She worried as we traveled around Europe for the next eight months. She worried as we flew back to Sydney in late August. The day we landed, she had a stroke and was hospitalized. As she remained there for weeks, and Kathe's health also deteriorated sharply, Anne looked for ways to pay their medical expenses and fixed on the portrait, which she thought far too valuable to be in an apartment with no security. While Kathe owned the painting, she decided to auction it as the joint property of Gretl.

The portrait was part of a sale of impressionist and modern paintings that included a Picasso from his Blue Period, a Monet of the bridge at Argenteuil, portraits by Degas, Renoir, and Modigliani, and a landscape by Gauguin. These paintings all brought much more than the Klimt, which commentators recognized as "a fine example of his mature style" though "not one of his very greatest works." Yet the Klimt was the work in the auction most discussed and reproduced because it had been identified as lost in the first complete catalog of Klimt's paintings and because very few of his paintings reached the international art market. Christie's estimate after seeing the actual painting was 15,000 to 20,000 guineas, much more than it had advised Anne when she was in England. The London dealers Harry and Wolfgang Fischer bought the portrait for 20,000 guineas, which was then $51,400, a world record for a Klimt.

Anne's horror of almost everything from the Wohllebengasse first appears in a letter in 1948 in which she described the Hoffmann furniture as "all that stuff," "gigantic things very hard to keep clean," that were too big for the apartment in Sydney, making her feel as if she lived "in a furniture store or worse." When she got the opportunity after marrying Eric, Anne sold one of the family's sets of silver cutlery and replaced it with stainless steel because the silver was again "too much work to keep clean." She also sold two of the Hoffmann armchairs and replaced them with much lighter new ones. Because the one surviving Hoffmann table from the salon was too high for these chairs, she got Bruce to cut down the table's legs.

She duly wanted almost everything to go when Gretl had her stroke. Yet how to empty the apartment was far from simple when the furniture excited scant interest in Sydney despite its increasing international value. When a leading local auctioneer inspected the apartment, he advised Anne, "It will cost you a lot to get rid of all this." She looked to Melbourne, where the National Gallery of Victoria was the only Australian museum with a significant European collection. When she approached the gallery early in 1972, she wrote: "My mother and aunt are giving up their flat in Sydney in which they have some furniture designed by Prof. Hoffmann of the Wiener Werkstätte, a lot of Viennese glass and silver, and a number of paintings. They want to sell the contents of their flat.

I am wondering whether the gallery would be interested in inspecting and perhaps purchasing some of these objects."

The gallery fixed on the Wiener Werkstätte collection. After three of its curators visited the apartment, the gallery immediately asked Anne to give it "priority of purchase" because the Hoffmann collection was of "great importance" and the gallery was "the best place in Australia for it." But while Gretl was soon in a nursing home, the sale did not proceed because Kathe remained in the apartment and wanted her possessions around her. Meanwhile, Anne looked for other possible purchasers in Europe where she was surprised by the strength of the Hoffmann market and found the turn-of-the-century section of Vienna's Museum of Applied Arts a revelation. A swatchbook containing examples of Wiener Werkstätte fabrics was, Anne observed, "exactly like" one acquired by Hermine and Moriz—the first time she saw that material in the apartment's cupboards, which she otherwise had considered "useless," was the stuff of a museum display.

The final years of Gretl and Kathe were all the more miserable because they continued to savage each other while needing each other desperately. In a letter to Kathe soon after she moved to the nursing home in Armidale, Gretl observed pointedly, "Nobody contradicts me or makes others believe that I am an idiot!" The pain that they inflicted by maintaining their girlhood practice of deriding each other was even clearer in another letter, in which Gretl promised to stop mocking how Kathe looked and spoke while instructing her, "You will never again be so cruel as to say you will send me to Callan Park," a reference to Sydney's mental asylum. Still, Kathe and she wrote to each other almost daily until Gretl died in 1975.

The responsibility of sorting everything overwhelmed and oppressed Anne when Kathe died in 1976. The first cupboard she opened in the flat was so full that as she pulled open its door, the contents spilled onto the floor, causing her to burst into tears. Many of the other cupboards were no different, as was the safe-deposit box in the city. She kept just a small number of objects particularly important to her, including the gold coins that Gretl had disguised as buttons when they fled Vienna. After almost forty years, Anne had no idea what exactly was inside these buttons and hence had no idea of their value. She implicitly recognized their symbolic significance by leaving them in their original stitching, and so they remained until I finally opened one while working on this book.

As Anne looked to test the market for the collection, she approached the Metropolitan Museum in New York, which suggested the flat contained "enough material for two museum installations" and was keen to secure one. But much as Kathe wanted to give the Klimt to the Art Gallery of New South Wales, Anne wanted "to keep the collection together for the National Gallery of Victoria" so the Hoffmann material would remain in Australia, and she did not mind if she did not secure the best possible price for it. When Wolfgang Fischer of Fischer Fine Art offered £6,000 (or $10,620) just for the furniture in June, and the gallery offered £25,000 (then $30,500) for everything, including the furniture, carpets, silver, ceramics, glass, leatherwork, lace, and jewelry, she accepted.

She also offered to give the gallery the Andri portrait of Erni, Gretl, Kathe, and Lene because she did not want to live with the painting or sell it and thought it should always be with the rest of the collection. While the gallery's curators of paintings refused the portrait, its head of decorative arts, Terry Lane, accepted it, making it the first painting to enter the gallery as a piece of decorative art. Because Lane took the portrait, Anne and he ensured the gallery would be able to break the mold of most museum displays of furniture, which typically are concerned only with materials, design, and workmanship, not who used these objects and how. The portrait allowed the gallery to put faces among the things and to bring the family and furniture together.

Lane was ecstatic after years of being on tenterhooks, uncertain when, if ever, Anne would make up her mind and what she would do. He knew the collection was the greatest acquisition he had made since becoming a curator—perhaps the greatest he would make. His understanding of both the global and local significance of the collection is clear from his acquisition's proposal to the gallery's council. He argued that the gallery needed to acquire the collection in its entirety because of its international importance as part of the "modern movement" and "as a memorial to the contribution of European migrants to the culture of this country."

The remaining pictures from the flat in Cremorne were of no interest to anyone in Australia. If Anne wanted to sell these paintings, it had to be overseas, and, even then, the market for them was not strong. The obvious way to test this market was to auction the paintings in Vienna, but Anne feared that if they failed to reach their reserve, Austria's new cultural protection authority would stop her from taking them out again. Nevertheless, there was competition for the pictures between Wolfgang Fischer and the Viennese opthalmologist Rudolf Leopold, who had amassed the finest private collection of the work of Egon Schiele, leading to Leopold being widely celebrated for his acumen as a collector and, in 2001, having the Austrian government and the National Bank of Austria combine to open a Leopold Museum in Vienna.

Anne was surprised by Leopold's hospitality when she first called him in August 1975, having written to him from Australia after reading a review of his first book about Schiele. In four trips to Vienna, no one new had invited her. Leopold not only suggested she visit him immediately but also spent two hours showing her some of his pictures as well as expressing his interest in those in Sydney. Anne was so moved by this experience that she could think of little else the following day. "I cannot thank you enough for showing me your Schiele collection and so many other beautiful and interesting things," she wrote to Leopold. "It all goes round and round my head," she continued making plain her excitement and awe.

Anne was soon in turmoil as a result of the death of Gretl in Australia while she was in Europe. She also was desperate for company, which Leopold provided by inviting her again to his house and then taking her out for dinner. When she returned to Vienna after a week away, he called her at her hotel. The following night they went out again and, to her obvious delight, "talked very long about art." Two days later, just before she returned to Australia, Leopold expressed particular interest in the Ribarz and Schindler in Cremorne, while denigrating the Viennese art dealers whom Anne had also been to see and emphasizing that everything he collected he kept.

Her return to Australia did nothing to reduce her turmoil because the death of Gretl was rapidly followed by that of Kathe, and then Bruce and I both moved to Canberra, leaving Anne in Armidale by herself. While she believed as a matter of principle that Bruce and I should leave home, in practice she was devastated by our departure. As she became desperate to create a new life for herself, she gave up her university lectureship in Armidale for a job as a schoolteacher in Sydney, where she had not lived for twenty years but still looked forward to finding much more company. She had just arrived in Sydney, late in 1976, when Leopold announced he was coming to Australia to see her pictures.

If only she had been able to read "The Chill of the Hunt," an article about Leopold by the American writer Andrew Decker published in *Art and*

Auction in 1990, which investigated some of Leopold's art dealings from the 1960s and early 1970s. Decker began with Leopold's acquisition of two Schieles from Eduard Wimmer-Wisgrill, a leading member of the Wiener Werkstätte. While Leopold bought these paintings on the basis that he would always keep them, he sold one almost immediately. Decker went on to discuss how Schiele's sister Melanie Schuster, whom Leopold befriended when she was a vulnerable widow, sued him for fraud after Leopold "had her sign a sales contract, which she thought to be an inventory, at 1:30 a.m. when she was exhausted and just wanted him to leave her alone." The result was a settlement in Schuster's favor, although Leopold still got a great deal. It saw him return sixty-eight paintings and drawings and pay Schuster 710,000 schillings (then $30,800), while he kept fifty-one Schiele drawings and Schuster gave him three Schiele paintings.

An article by Judith Dobrzynski in the *New York Times* in 1997, which made looted Holocaust art an issue in the United States, would have disturbed Anne even more. It identified Leopold as someone engaged in "relentless pursuit of his quarry," "who badgered and manipulated owners until they sold him their treasures, often at a very low price." Its focus was two paintings on show at New York's Museum of Modern Art in *Egon Schiele: The Leopold Collection,* which Dobrzynski identified as stolen from their Jewish owners. Her most astonishing revelation involved a portrait by Schiele of his lover Wally Neuzil, which at the time of the Anschluss was part of the private collection of the Viennese art dealer Lea Bondi. Dobrzynski reported that when Leopold began amassing his collection in the 1950s, he had gone to see Bondi in London to ask her help in locating pictures by Schiele. When she in turn asked Leopold to help her recover the portrait of Wally, which the Österreichische Galerie had acquired illegitimately after the war, Leopold not only failed to do so but acquired the portrait for himself in exchange for pictures he owned.

Anne was oblivious to this record in 1976. For her, Leopold's visit was a simple cause of delight, prompting her to invite him to stay, without considering how this would mean they could not negotiate at arm's length over her paintings. But she also telephoned Wolfgang Fischer in London to suggest he make a firm offer for the pictures, since she wanted to have another bidder for them, just as she had for the Hoffmann collection. Four days later, Leopold rang twice more. In early December, he arrived. By Christmas, Anne and he were in court.

$\cdot \quad \cdot \quad \cdot$

According to an affidavit sworn by Leopold, he arrived in Sydney having agreed with Anne that he would pay between 65,500 and 72,500 Swiss francs (then $26,475 and $29,300) for the paintings. The obvious basis on which the actual price would be determined was Leopold's assessment of the pictures when he saw the originals in Sydney. If Leopold is to be believed, Anne and he settled on 67,750 Swiss francs (or $27,385) without his looking properly at the paintings, and it was only after they both signed an agreement for their sale that she allowed him "to look closely at them." If Leopold entered into an agreement on this basis, it must have been because he knew he was getting the pictures so cheaply that it did not matter that he had not inspected them.

The agreement was drawn up by Leopold on December 5, handwritten in German, occupying barely more than half a page. It recorded that Anne was selling ten paintings—the Schindler, the Ribarz, two pictures by Moll, two landscapes by Stöhr, both harbor scenes by Kurzweil, the Andri landscape, and the Russian watercolor by Constantin Somoff, whom Leopold misidentified as "A. Canobz" after misreading Somoff's Cyrillic signature, suggesting that he had no idea what he was acquiring. Leopold was to take these pictures with him to Vienna and, before the end of the month, pay Anne 67,750 Swiss francs. The document concluded: "Their agreement with everything above is attested by their signatures below." After Leopold signed it, Anne followed suit.

Leopold's affidavit suggests Anne was immediately unhappy with the contract, consistent with Bruce's recollection that Leopold badgered Anne into signing it. Because she did not want to let Leopold take the paintings before she received the money, he agreed to let her keep the paintings until she was paid, but then he did not want to proceed on this basis because he did not trust her. Before long, he had found a lawyer and was threatening to institute proceedings to compel Anne to honor the agreement, only for Anne's solicitor to dispute whether it was binding and suggest that Leopold's lawyers consider Australia's foreign exchange regulations, which prohibited dealings in foreign currencies such as Swiss francs without the permission of Australia's Reserve Bank. When Leopold went to court, he did not win, as he maintained in his biography. Instead, he settled, having agreed to pay 25 percent more for the paintings.

The most remarkable aspect of this episode involves a long-distance phone call made by Wolfgang Fischer in London in early December in the hope of persuading Anne to sell the pictures. As Leopold described it in his affidavit, he was alone in Anne's Sydney apartment one evening when the phone rang and he chose to answer it. Leopold recorded: "I spoke to someone I realized was Fischer." As Leopold clearly understood, Fischer wanted to buy the pictures. If Leopold believed that Anne and he had entered into a binding agreement, he could simply have told Fischer that he was too late. He did not. According to Leopold's own affidavit, "I did not identify myself. I think he thought I was a member of the household. He gave me a message to pass on. . . . 'Tell her she should send me a telegram, or better still ring in London and reverse the charges.' " The affidavit contains no apology for this piece of deception. Rather, it makes plain that, while Leopold had always known she was negotiating with other potential buyers, he saw this episode as occasion for interrogating Anne about Fischer. "I said 'Do you have an agreement with him?' This she denied. She said, 'I had only a correspondence with him.' She said she would not telephone him but would write to him and say she would not sell the paintings."

Fischer's version of this story was simpler. Leopold and he had competed "for a collection owned by an Austrian woman who had fled to Australia. One day, I called Australia to ask if my offer was acceptable. I thought I got her son, who said his mother was not available." Fischer did not think further about what had happened until much later when he encountered Leopold, who asked him, "Didn't you ring up the lady?" When Fischer said yes, but that he had spoken only with her son, Leopold responded, "You're wrong. It was me you spoke to." Leopold told this story out of intense competitiveness. He wanted one of his prime rivals to know how he had been outwitted, little realizing that Fischer would get his own back by telling Judith Dobrzynski, who published his account in the *New York Times* as a prime example of how Leopold would go to almost any lengths to enhance his collection.

7

Restitution

The past as much as the present continued to draw Anne to Austria. On her second trip, in 1973, she revisited the house in the Wohllebengasse, which had been bought by a Russian insurance company. She went with trepidation, not because she had any idea that the building's ownership by the "Red Insurance Man" and its use for spying had been investigated by *Time* magazine, but because she was uncertain how she would be received. She could hear her heart beating as she rang the bell, entered, and introduced herself to a secretary who called the company's manager. When he showed her through, she again was interested only in the changes, which ranged from the walling up of the door between the hall and the smoking room to the removal of many Hoffmann door handles and the conversion of her bedroom into a washing-up room.

"Vienna is as wonderful as ever," she exclaimed a year later, only to be "a bit sick of Vienna" within a week. She visited the house in the Landstrasser-Hauptstrasse where she had lived with Gretl. She searched for the building where Kathe had lived in the Rechte Bahngasse but was unsure whether she found the right one. She sought out her favorite teacher, Ilse Hornung, found that she still occupied the same apartment, and rang the downstairs bell. When there was no response, she even went upstairs to confirm no one was there, only to wonder what she was doing. What would she have said had Ilse been at home? Would she have confronted her about being a Nazi?

Anne's worst moment came when Gretl died in 1975, while she was again in Europe. She decided that, rather than return to Australia as soon as possible, she should be at the Hietzing cemetery when Gretl's ashes were interred in the family grave. The only other funeral she had attended there was thirty-nine years before when she was part of Hermine's vast procession. In 1975 Anne was the one mourner. Just as Hermine thought of herself as utterly abandoned or godforsaken when she first went to the theater by herself, so did Anne with infinitely more reason. She, too, described herself as "*mutterseelenallein.*"

Her attitude toward her inheritance remained deeply ambivalent, even as the National Gallery of Victoria prepared to exhibit the Gallia collection. At times she was happy to answer Terry Lane's questions, at other times not. The same was true when it came to lending the few objects that she retained. While she readily organized one of her trips to Vienna so she could bring the apartment to life for Lane, she was clear that she did not want to be associated with the exhibition. As it drew near, she got frightened and withdrew her support, provoking an anxious letter from the gallery's director, Patrick McCaughey. He wrote, as if surprised by Anne's response, that the gallery had always expected "the exhibition would be an occasion of pride for you." More usefully from her point of view, he assured her the gallery would preserve her anonymity.

Mizzi, who had been widowed when Erni died shortly before Gretl and Kathe, felt very differently about her past becoming a public event. She was delighted to invite Lane for afternoon tea so he could ply her with questions. His notes reveal her remarkable recall of fabrics, colors, the use of particular objects and rooms. She also exemplifies the vagaries of memory. When she met Erni in 1920, Hermine was a shareholder in the Wiener Werkstätte, it was less than a year since Erni had been on the Werkstätte's board, and it was less than two years since Moriz had been its chairman. This involvement with the Werkstätte was the kind of information that was vital to Lane, but Mizzi had forgotten it.

The exhibition, in 1984, was the first anywhere to re-create a suite of Hoffmann rooms. While primarily consisting of the gallery's own collection, *Vienna 1913* also included the Klimt from London. As Patrick McCaughey described it, "The exhibition was extraordinary. Terry Lane brought visitors through the front door of the apartment where Madam Gallia, glittering in Klimt's silvery whites, greeted them. The exhibition was set out room by room, interspersed with related Wiener Werkstätte material. . . . It physically re-created the pre–World War I atmosphere of Vienna between secession and modernity, between decadence and innovation . . . it lent credence to the idea that the National Gallery of Victoria was the Metropolitan of Australia, able to collect works that no other museum could touch."

Anne was confounded. While Lane had partly relied on her recollections when he had the furniture restored, she was stunned by its transformation. The silk, wool, and leather coverings of the chairs amazed her after years of so much vinyl. She had no idea that they had ever been—or could again be—so spectacular. While she still wanted to retain her anonymity, she expressed her new attachment to the collection by making the first of what became small annual donations to the gallery. In congratulating Lane, she wrote, "I am sure that the things never looked as good as in your exhibition."

Mizzi was characteristically more effusive. After attending the opening and returning to see the exhibition again, she declared, "It was a memorable impression for me and will remain so for a long time." Uncertain whether or how Anne would respond, Mizzi assumed the role of the family representative. "I want to thank you for the time and trouble you took with the Gallias for the Gallias." She also dwelled on how the re-creation of the Hoffmann rooms transported her across time and space. "I relived the first time I came to the Wohllebengasse more than sixty-three years ago, before I was even engaged." She concluded: "The exhibition means more to me than to anybody else."

One of Mizzi's favorite stories was how, when she was at the exhibition one day looking at Erni in the children's portrait by Andri, a woman about her age of central European origin, almost certainly a refugee, engaged her in conversation. For all the gallery had done to re-create the Wohllebengasse, the woman said these were things one could understand only if one had been to the apartment and known the people. "You are right," Mizzi responded proudly, "I was married to that small boy for over fifty years." Yet despite her sense of proprietorship, Mizzi also felt distanced from the exhibition's contents. She liked to say how strange she found it that, after being required by Hermine to visit the Wohllebengasse, she had to pay to see the apartment in the gallery.

Anne thought she was done with Vienna in 1992. After seven visits in twenty-one years, she declared: "Unless something goes very wrong with the family grave for which I feel responsible, I do not wish to see Vienna again." But because Bruce was living in England, she wanted to see him and, once there, always went to Vienna. As a result, she went more often than ever, returning annually until 1998, even though, with Anni Wiesbauer dead, she had no one to visit. Where the novelist Hugo Bettauer imagined Vienna in 1923 as a city without Jews, and the Nazis tried to make it so, for Anne it became a city without people. While she made a few German friends on her travels who accompanied her to exhibitions, invited her home, and took her on excursions, she never made those connections in Vienna. She spent her days there immersing herself in art, music, and theater, and making her obligatory pilgrimage to the Hietzing cemetery where, even after she discovered that several other refugees had returned to Vienna to be buried, she remained affronted by the decision of Gretl and Kathe to do so when Australia had given them "refuge and kindness."

Other refugees typically returned at most once to their childhood homes. Anne kept visiting the Wohllebengasse. Each time she was delighted to be welcomed by the staff of the Russian insurance company. Each time she focused on the apartment's continuing modifications rather than how it remained fundamentally intact, so it would still have been possible to slot the Hoffmann furniture into the exact spaces Hoffmann created for them. She found that, having revisited the apartment over twenty-five years, it was no longer a place that aroused her memories but one into which she projected them. She still thought it worth recording that it was not where she belonged.

Austria's way of presenting its past continued to occupy her. The Monument Against War and Fascism—the first major Viennese memorial that dealt to some extent with the Holocaust—was one example. Almost everything about this monument was controversial when it was erected in 1988 to mark the fiftieth anniversary of the Anschluss. While political groups on the right regarded its location between the Albertina Museum and the Vienna Opera as too prominent, the left lambasted it for treating fallen Austrian soldiers, civilian casualties of Allied bombings, and Jews as all of a piece. Anne noticed something else. Having always followed the family practice of buying postcards of her travels rather than taking her own photographs, she was struck that there were no postcards of the new monument.

After seeing an exhibition about the Aussee region under the Nazis, she looked forward to the publication of its catalog and ordered it from Australia, only for it to infuriate her. While it listed twenty-nine houses in Alt Aussee and thirty in the immediate vicinity that Jews owned before the Anschluss, the catalog devoted just a page to this community. It did not identify the individuals who profited from the Aryanization of the houses—apart from Goebbels—who was already so infamous that his reputation could not suffer. It said nothing about the fate of the original owners of these houses.

Still, Anne's appreciation of Alt Aussee grew, while most of the Australian landscape became increasingly alien to her. Although she thought that to have gone to Alt Aussee every year as a girl was "a bit much" and she would have preferred its mountains to be higher, she came to see "why one could spend some time" there. She admired the careful management of its forests, which was in contrast to the devastation in Australia, where vast forests of old eucalyptus were being clear-felled for woodchips. She loved how strawberries and blueberries grew wild along Aussee's forest and mountain paths. She thought its meadows and air were wonderful. She described it as "uniquely beautiful."

She first tried to regain access to the villa in 1975, when she knocked at the door without prior warning and asked whether she could look at her childhood home. The man who came to the door refused to let her in. On her next visit, in 1995, she was eager to see the villa but was frustrated that the surrounding trees had grown so high that it was barely visible from the road. Although she walked around the house many times, she did not approach its owners. When she reflected on this visit, her eagerness to see the villa was clear, but so was her uncertainty about whether she would try again. She concluded: "It was an experience. One could repeat it. One does not have to repeat it."

She repeated it two years later much more adroitly. Rather than arriving unannounced and unexpected, she sent a letter in which she introduced herself, enclosed an old photograph of the villa, and offered to tell its occupiers about its history. The reply came by return mail inviting her to afternoon tea. This time the front door opened before she could ring the bell, revealing more of her past than she ever imagined finding. When

Anne entered the main room, sixty years since her last visit in 1937, the table and twelve accompanying chairs, sideboards, grandfather clock, armchairs, rocking chair, paintings, gilt-framed engraving, tapestries, and carved wooden light fitting adorned with four eagles in its salon were all the same. So were the grand piano and a second grandfather clock in the adjoining sitting room. While their owner was different, these parts of the house remained the Villa Gallia in the most material way. When she left that day, Anne wrote in her diary, "Am so happy," "mission accomplished."

What made this experience for Anne was not just the place but the person, Frau Wick, who had acquired the villa with her late husband toward the end of the war. This meant, crucially for Anne, that Frau Wick had not been party to the villa's forced sale by Mizzi in 1940, while it was probably just as important to Frau Wick that Austrian law gave Anne no avenue for regaining the villa and Anne never expressed any claim to it. The more they talked, the more Anne was amazed by how much they had in common. They told each other about their families. They talked about growing old. They discussed the war and contemporary Austrian politics, including the rise of Jörg Haider and his neo-Nazi Austrian Freedom Party. When Anne returned to Australia, they corresponded and sometimes phoned each other. This friendship was the only one that Anne made in her fourteen visits to Austria. While never reconciled with Austria, she could be reconciled with Frau Wick.

I was with Anne when she visited Frau Wick in 1998, on her last trip to Austria—there not only so I, too, could see the villa but also so Anne could show off my son, Nicholas, partner, Claire, and me to Frau Wick. Just before we left, Frau Wick went to a cupboard and took out three coffee cups and two saucers, explaining that they were the last surviving pieces of china that had come with the villa. I was initially nonplussed when Frau Wick gave these remnants to Anne. I knew they would go into Anne's sideboard along with many more impressive objects once owned by Hermine. Then I understood. The cups and saucers were a private, personal piece of reparation, Anne's first experience of genuine restitution from Austria.

A few months later, a parcel arrived in Canberra. Inside was a wax doll that had stood on top of the piano in the villa's salon when Anne was a girl. After returning home, she had asked Frau Wick about this doll. As almost everything else seemed to have survived, Anne wondered what had become of it. Frau Wick's response was to send Anne the doll as a Christmas present, still in its original glass container, though short one arm. When we looked at its base, we discovered it had been given to Moriz as a reward for his investment in war bonds—a manifestation of the patriotism that failed to protect the Gallias in Austria. Unlike the coffee cups, Anne put the doll on show in her display cabinet.

8

Identity

The survivors of the Shoah—whether they became refugees, lived out the war in hiding, or were inmates of concentration camps—almost all reconsidered their identities. Their choices ranged from embracing Judaism more fervently than before to denying their Jewish origins. At one extreme, they could take public pride in their Jewishness, implicitly, if not explicitly, declaring that they would never again submit to anti-Semitism. At the other, they could construct an entirely new identity in the hope of escaping renewed intolerance and persecution—exploiting the opportunities to remake themselves that came with moving to countries where they were unknown, Judaism was much less an issue than in Europe, and Jew spotting was neither an art nor an obsession.

The best-known instance of such invention involved Madeleine Albright, the first woman secretary of state of the United States. Within days of the Senate's confirming her nomination in 1997, the *Washington Post* revealed that two of Albright's grandparents had died in Theresienstadt, while one had died in Auschwitz. According to Albright, who was born a Roman Catholic in Prague in 1937, she had not known. While her parents had told her that they fled Czechoslovakia with her before the war to escape the Nazis, Albright realized that they may have been converts from Judaism only in 1996, when someone sent her a letter about her family's past. Even then she did not suspect how her grandparents had died. She later explained, "If you're eight years old and you are told that your grandparents died, and you think of grandparents as being old people, then you don't question it." She never doubted her parents' account because they "were never mysterious or hesitant about it."

The response in 1997 was widespread incredulity. As described by Albright, "People could not believe that I didn't know my family's past. Instead of being allowed to take in privately the tragic facts I had only recently learned, I was made to feel as if I were a liar and my father, whom I adored, was portrayed as a heartless fraud." Philip Taubman of the *New York Times* wrote a piece that began: "Madeleine Albright must have known." Frank Rich of the *New York Times* suggested Albright was "shading the truth." Yet there was some recognition that Albright's parents were not alone in suppressing their identity. The national director of the Anti-Defamation League, Abraham Foxman, observed, "In Poland, every single day, Jews surface who thought they were Catholics all their lives."

And not just in Poland. Many refugees, who married or remarried after they escaped, told their new families little or nothing about their origins. When one of my colleagues was a boy, his father acknowledged that he was a Jew, but he would not reveal where he came from or what he had experienced. When Hugh asked his father why he was being sent to an Anglican school, his father responded, "Son, religion is never worth dying for." When one of Mizzi's cousins visited Sydney in the 1960s, she went to see another relative who had been married for more than twenty years. When Mizzi's cousin arrived for dinner, her relative whispered as soon as his wife went to the kitchen, "Don't tell her I'm a Jew. I've never told her."

Others did not explain the dead. Much like Madeleine Albright's parents in the United States, Guido Hamburger Jr. and Anna Schauer in England did not tell their children what had happened to Guido Senior and Nelly, or Anna's parents, whom the Nazis also killed. Instead, Guido Junior and Anna led their son and daughter to believe that they had no idea what became of the older Hamburgers and Schauers. Insofar as Guido Junior and Anna talked about them, it was as if all four grandparents had simply disappeared in the chaos of the war. Like Madeleine Albright, the children of Guido Junior and Anna accepted their parents' story for years, though, unlike Albright, they eventually questioned it and discovered how their grandparents died.

Friedrich Hamburger's daughter, Jana, did not even realize where she had been. Because she was only three when Theresienstadt was liberated, Jana grew up with no memories of the camp and her parents never talked about it. Nor did her mother's father, who was another camp survivor. While she had a wooden doll's bed made by her grandfather inscribed "Terezin," the Czech name for Theresienstadt, she did not understand its significance. Her parents raised Jana as a Catholic and never told her that she was of Jewish origin. She found out only when an exhibition of drawings and paintings by the children of Theresienstadt came to Vancouver. As Jana was dating a Jewish boy at the time, she went to the exhibition, began questioning her parents, and discovered their origins.

These stories could come out only because what one generation suppressed, the next generally discovered and was eager to talk about. This generational divide was articulated by the New York writer Kati Marton, who was raised as a Roman Catholic with no awareness of her family's Jewish past, but discovered for herself, at the age of twenty-nine, that her parents were both born Jews and one of her grandparents died in Auschwitz. Soon after the Albright story broke, Marton observed: "As my parents saw it, there were problems enough in being a refugee; why compound them by adding 'Jewish' to the list of things we had to overcome? They had too much history. I did not have enough. They felt that to be American meant not having a past, or at least having the freedom to choose what to remember. I felt the opposite. To me, America means the freedom to unabashedly embrace your heritage, whatever it might be."

Anne did not want to write about her life when I asked her. One of her earliest drafts begins, "Tim has asked me to write my story. I think that it is a rather average tale and that I have no claim to fame. But somehow it interests him and perhaps provides him with a link with the past that he seems to want in quite a different way from me." She also found the writing difficult, since it led her to confront her childhood in a way she had not done before and, while she did not like what she discovered, felt obliged to record it, particularly her sense of her own failings. "I am starting to wonder whether I really want to write this story," she began another draft. "When Tim asked me," she admitted in another, "I didn't know what I was letting myself in for."

Anne persevered because it was something I wanted and because she believed in finishing what she started. She would write, show me drafts, and I would press for more, filling the margins of her drafts with queries and suggestions. When she finally stopped after more than a year, with many of my questions still unanswered, "Anne's Story," as she titled it, ran to over seventy single-spaced typed pages but did not cover a quarter of her life. It concluded in 1939, when she was seventeen, which I thought was because she neither wanted to write about her adult life nor wanted me to read about it. In fact, she wrote more but was unable to give this material the same shape or polish and did not show it to me until just before she died.

Anne would have liked to change almost everything about her childhood. If given a choice of her place of birth, parents, religion, and financial status, she would have kept only her mother. While her attachment to the landscape of her childhood saw her watch *The Sound of Music* whenever it was shown on television and hang one of her own paintings of the Karlskirche in her bedroom, she rejected Vienna as "too conceited" and "too full of lies about its past." Despite writing in Canberra, a national capital one-sixth the size, she embraced the commonplace that Vienna was "too provincial." She went on: "I would have loved a father whom I liked or no father at all. I would certainly never have chosen to be Jewish. It certainly would have been better for me had we been less wealthy and isolated by our wealth."

Anne looked on her childhood in Good Living Street as the worst part of her life—even more traumatic than her experience after the Anschluss under the Nazis. Her account of her first fourteen years until Hermine died is imbued with not just resentment, fear, and anxiety but also a keen sense of the enduringly damaging consequences of how she was raised. Her account of life under the Nazis conveys the shock and horror of suddenly being persecuted and forced to flee. She also acknowledged that her attitude toward other people had been colored by her "Hitler experience." Otherwise, she treated this experience as of no great account both because so many Nazi victims had suffered so much more and because of her good fortune in escaping the wars, genocides, and persecutions that kept recurring. She wrote: "This is a frightening world full of hatred and methods of destruction. I have personally experienced hardly any of this."

Like many other refugees, Anne believed that her forced departure was a godsend. The only good that came from her Jewishness, she wrote, was that it made her go to Australia. For all her attachment to European culture and the European landscape, she was intensely grateful for the chance to start a new life—the opportunity, as she saw it, to be herself. She concluded her story by declaring that she was much happier in Australia than she would ever have been in Austria. Until the government of John Howard began making political capital out of refugees, gaining electoral popularity through its mistreatment of boat people from Afghanistan and Iraq trying to reach Australia from Indonesia, she was proud to be Australian.

This attachment was manifest in 1990 when Austria introduced monthly pensions for surviving refugees who had fled as children as a belated mark of responsibility for what had happened to them. Anne did not apply for years, as she did not want to feel indebted to Austria in any way. Then she decided that this pension provided an opportunity to take from the society that rejected her and give to the one that welcomed her. For the rest of her life, she distributed her pension among Australian charities. She did the same with the small lump-sum payments she received from the National Fund for the Victims of National Socialism created by the Austrian government in 1995.

Anne's decision to redistribute this money was also part of her rejection of her opulent past. As Mizzi once noted, Anne struggled with "the stigma of coming from a rich family" and was intent on living differently, taking conscious delight in how Hermine would have been appalled by much that she did. Even when Anne was in her sixties and seventies, she continued to travel with a rucksack. Until the last years of her life, she stayed in cheap hotels. She avoided good restaurants because she was uncomfortable being waited on. Her last home unit was so modest that, when she died, the government bought it for use as public housing.

One of Anne's enduring ambitions was to be inconspicuous. After working assiduously to get rid of her accent when she arrived in Australia, she was appalled in the last months of her life when taxi drivers began asking where she came from. For more than sixty years she had been indistinguishable in the crowd. Now she was identifiable as a foreigner. She looked on this change as one of the greatest manifestations of her decline caused by a stroke. As much as she was appalled by her diminished, malfunctioning, awkward body, she abhorred her new voice.

Anne was typically reticent about her past when, in 2000, she gave her last public talk at the National Gallery of Australia. When she described how she had come to assist in the preparation of an exhibition of Secessionist art being staged by the gallery, she simply said, "I was allowed to help because of my knowledge of German and because I had some con-

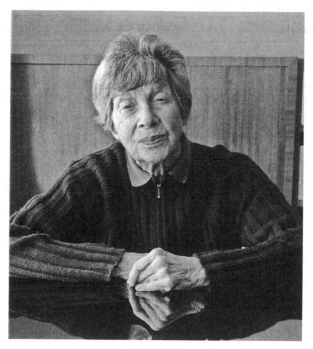

Anne, Canberra, 2002, photographed
by Jon Rhodes.

tacts with the Secession movement before." She did not explain that she
had grown up with a much richer Secessionist collection than the gallery
was exhibiting. Her account of the response of Viennese Jews to the rise of
Hitler was similar. She had her family in mind when she described how
"those who were hated by the National Socialists had no idea what was in
store for them should the Nazis come to power. After all, in their own
eyes, they had done nothing wrong. They were comfortable in Vienna,
and attached to it." She did not reveal that she had been there, let alone
that she had been more perceptive.

Anne was always loath to reveal that she had any Jewish connections
because she feared further persecution. As she thought anti-Semitism
would never go away, she believed Jews should never draw attention to
their identity. If they would not abandon their Judaism, they should suppress it. Anne was delighted that Bruce and I both had children with partners who were not from Jewish backgrounds. She encouraged us to hide
our origins to such an extent that Bruce recalls being fearful when he told

his future wife, Rae. Anne thought it inflammatory for successful Jews to flaunt their wealth and power and was appalled when they acted dishonestly or meanly. It fueled her view that they had not learned from history. She feared they would visit even more anti-Semitism on everyone of Jewish origin.

She could not deny the Gallias' Jewish past because her departure from Vienna in 1938 identified her as a refugee. But she led everyone, including Bruce and me, to believe that since Gretl had converted to Roman Catholicism as a girl, she herself had been born and raised a Catholic. I learned that she had been a Jew until she was sixteen only when I asked her to write about her life. Had she not felt compelled to be as honest as she could in her story, she might not have told me. She never told my father, Eric, her husband for fifteen years, or her oldest friend, Gerty, whom she knew for even longer. Eric and Gerty both found out only after her death when I told them. It was something they never suspected. Anne had been so secretive about her past in her attempt to escape it.

A performance of *Lohengrin* was particularly tempting when I picked up the week's opera and theater program after landing at Vienna airport. While Anne had turned Bruce and me into avid operagoers on our first visit to Europe in 1971, Wagner was the notable exception. Whereas we went to all of Mozart's major operas and most of those by Verdi, the only Wagner that we saw was *Tristan und Isolde* in West Berlin, where Anne found the five-hour performance interminably long, the plot inane, and the singers offensively Aryan. In the thirty-four years since, I had seen none of Wagner's work, which I had come to regard as irredeemably tainted by his anti-Semitism. I knew it would be good for this book if I went.

A day later, I spotted an alternative. While *Lohengrin* was at the opera, the Israelitische Kultusgemeinde was presenting a cantor concert in Vienna's main synagogue to mark the sixtieth anniversary of the Befreiung, or liberation, from the Nazis, in 1945. If I went to this concert, it would be my first experience of Jewish music. It would be the first occasion, other than a sightseeing tour, when I would attend the synagogue where Moriz and Hermine had been married more than 110 years before. It would be an opportunity to join in the commemoration of the destruction and the celebration of the survival of Vienna's Jewish community. I chose the synagogue.

The week went quickly. I saw *The New Austria,* an exhibition at the Belvedere staged to mark the much more popular fiftieth anniversary of the "liberation from the occupiers" in 1955, which saw the United States, the USSR, France, and England leave Austria. I visited the Leopold Museum, where I found that Leopold, characteristically, had retained just half the pictures he bought from Anne—and still wished this half elsewhere because of his manipulation of her and acquisition of Schiele's portrait of Wally when he knew it had been looted. I went to the Wohllebengasse, where I found that Viennese developers, who had acquired the building from the Russian insurance company, had gutted its interiors, destroying most of its Hoffmann features. After making so many visits to Vienna with Anne without talking to anyone Viennese, I met historians, curators, dealers, and journalists.

The cantor concert was on December 8, the Feast of the Immaculate Conception of the Virgin Mary by Saint Anne, a public holiday in Vienna. While that meant that libraries and archives were all closed, I still had too much to do because it was my last day before returning to Australia. For once I gave precedence to present buying. I spent the morning at the Spittelberg market in Vienna's Seventh District and the Christkindl-markt in front of the Rathaus on the Ringstrasse and did well at both. Then I had to decide what to do about visiting the grave.

The Hoffmann grave of Henny Hamburger in Grinzing was gone—removed by the cemetery authorities who took out many old graves to make room for new burials. That still left the shared grave of Moriz, Hermine, Gretl, Kathe, and Lene in Hietzing and those of the Herschmanns, Bonyhadys, and Wilhelm and Eugenia Gallia in the Central Cemetery. When I arrived in Vienna, I expected to go to one cemetery one day and visit the other a day or two later. But I left the cemeteries until last, just as Anne had often done, and then had time only for one. My choice was between Catholics and Jews, between family who were always part of my life and family who I discovered only through this writing.

I knew the Jews particularly needed visiting. When I first went to Vienna to work on this book and told an acquaintance that I would be going to the Central Cemetery, he told me its old Jewish section was very "*romantisch,*" or "romantic," a place of "*wilde Tiere,*" "wild animals." I had no idea what he meant until I went a few days later. When I found an almost abandoned domain—a realm of overgrown, sunken graves, fallen stones, and forgotten paths—it was clear how the area could be considered romantic. Yet I was left wondering about the wild animals until I looked up and for a moment in the distance saw two deer with enormous antlers, completely at home in this wilderness.

The contrast with the adjoining Christian part of the Central Cemetery was a terrible expression of the destruction of the Jewish community, which would otherwise have cared for the graves, a stark indictment of the Austrian government and the City of Vienna for refusing to accept this responsibility when the German government had done so already in the 1950s. Yet the contrast between the Herschmann grave in the Central Cemetery and the Gallia grave in Hietzing also troubled me. While the Herschmann grave had suffered as a result of decades of neglect, the Gallia grave was a model of order as a result of Bruce and my continuing payments that Anne had made for its maintenance. After first visiting the Central Cemetery, my immediate response was that Bruce and I should get the Herschmann grave restored. I wanted to show that at least the occasional person still cared in this landscape of neglect. I felt that we should not be taking care of one side of the family while ignoring the other. But I had not done anything a year later, when I had to decide which graves I would visit. My loyalty to Anne and attachment to Gretl saw me go to Hietzing.

My last visit there had been the previous year, late one November afternoon when the light was beginning to fail. As I made my way into the cemetery, I was pleased, just like Anne in 1971, to find the grave with ease. As I walked toward it, I saw two flickering red lights. Bruce, who was in Vienna at the time, had not only been there earlier in the afternoon but had repaired the two glass candleholders on either side of the gravestone and bought candles for them for the first time in almost seventy years. While I was there alone, the candle was a bond between us, a symbol he had left for Moriz, Hermine, Gretl, Kathe, and Lene that also became one for me. It was wonderfully comforting in the gloaming.

When I returned, I meant to repeat what Bruce had done but struggled by myself, so I decided instead to light candles that night in St. Stephen's Cathedral on my way to the synagogue. Because I was early, I stopped at the Jewish Museum to look at its Mahler exhibition, with the recording of Mahler performing his own piano transcription of the first movement of his Fifth Symphony playing in my ears. I walked to the cathedral, dipped my hand in the holy water as I had learned to do on my first European trip, made the sign of the cross, bought the candles, and sat before them without praying.

I continued to the synagogue, where I was accustomed to finding police at both the bottom and the top of the street to reduce the risk of attack. I expected that, as usual, I would have to show my passport and go through metal detectors to gain access to the building. That night there were more police than ever, in case anyone thought to target the crowd queueing outside on the cobblestoned street. The questioning from the synagogue's security guards was also unusually intense. How had I come to hear about the concert? Whom did I know in Vienna's Jewish community? Why was I there?

I should have struck up a conversation while waiting outside or sitting in the synagogue. I could have explained my connection to the Stadttempel and this celebration. I might have discovered why my neighbors were there. I sat in the synagogue gazing up at its sky-blue dome dotted with golden stars. I found my German stretched by speeches that dwelled on the

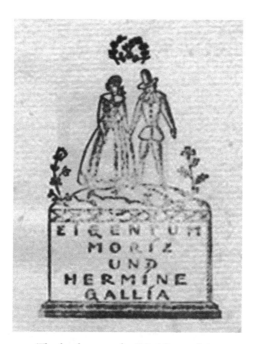

The book stamp by Fritzi Löw of the Wiener Werkstätte showing Hermine and Moriz as a young courting couple.

latest developments in the payment of Holocaust restitution by the Austrian government. I listened to the cantors and wondered whether, as Wagner had argued, there was a distinctively Jewish voice. I felt no sense of community, but was glad that I had chosen the synagogue over the opera.

I found everything transformed at intermission. Instead of the only access being through metal detectors, all the doors on the street were thrown open so members of the crowd could go outside to smoke, just as they would at the opera. While the absence of controls made a mockery of the security before the concert, it was a relief to see the community displaying no fear, acting like any other, enjoying a freedom befitting the sixtieth anniversary of the Befreiung.

I could easily have walked across the city back to my hotel in the Schleifmühlgasse, just a few blocks away from the old gas-glowing light showroom. Instead, I took the tram around the Ring so I could have a different view of the city by night. As the tram took me past the town hall, which had as usual been turned into a giant advent calendar for Christmas, and I alighted at the Opera so I could walk past the Secession to the Schleifmühlgasse, I wondered what Hermine, Gretl, and Anne would have thought of my day. I knew Hermine and Anne would, this once, have agreed. They would have been horrified to see me at the synagogue. I thought Gretl might have been more sympathetic.

Notes

As explained in the Introduction, this book draws heavily on family documents that my brother and I inherited from Anne and Mizzi. The Vienna City Archives holds the wills and probate documents of Moriz, Adolf, and Ida Gallia, Ludwig Herschmann, and Theobald Pollak, along with records relating to the incarceration of Bernard Herschmann, but the will and probate documents for Hermine are, unfortunately, missing. The papers relating to Moriz's designation as a *Regierungsrat* and the military service of Erni are in Austria's National Archives, along with the documents lodged by the family under the Ordinance for the Registration of Jewish Property. The Bundesdenkmalamt holds its approvals for Gretl, Kathe, and Erni to take their collections with them. The Australian National Archives holds documents relating to the family's arrival in Australia, their surveillance during World War II, and Erni's attempt to get compensation from Italy for his *Liftvans,* while the files of the National Gallery of Victoria are a rich source for the Gallia collection. The following notes relate primarily to material I have quoted.

I   HERMINE

1   Klimt
15   Those who attended were primarily women: *Neue Freie Presse,* November 14, 1903, afternoon edition and the cover of *Die Moden-Zeit* for December 15, 1903, reproduced in *Gustav Klimt: Modernism in the Making* (New York: Abrams, 2001), p. 204.
15   "All the tribes of Israel": Alma Mahler-Werfel, *Diaries 1898–1902* (Ithaca, NY: Cornell University Press, 1999), p. 385.
17   "faithful to reality" and "past her prime": Tobias G. Natter and Gerbert Frodl, *Klimt's Women* (Cologne: DuMont, 2001), p. 92.
17–18   "old hag" and "He takes what he can get": Mahler-Werfel, *Diaries,* p. 279.

18   "Just what I'd do": Ibid., p. 235.

19   "an artist who would never be forgotten": Hermann Bahr, *Secession* (Vienna: Wiener Verlag, 1900), pp. 120, 126.

20   While the writer Stefan Zweig recalled: Stefan Zweig, *The World of Yesterday* (London: Cassell, 1953), p. 8.

23   "He paints a woman": Natter and Frodl, *Klimt's Women,* p. 30.

23   The English art historian: Frank Whitford, *Klimt* (London: Thames & Hudson, 1990), p. 140.

24   "sensation": *Neue Freie Presse,* November 14, 1903.

24   It was by Hermann Bahr: Hermann Bahr, *Gegen Klimt* (Vienna: Eisenstein, 1903).

24   "hunt them down": *Die Fackel,* no. 147, November 21, 1903.

25   "as still and discreet": Christoph Grunenberg, "Luxury and Degradation: Staging Klimt," in Tobias G. Natter and Christoph Grunenberg (eds.), *Gustav Klimt: Painting, Design and Modern Life* (London: Tate, 2008), pp. 37, 41.

26   "magical delicacy": Ludwig Hevesi, *Acht Jahre Secession* (Vienna: Konegen, 1906), p. 443.

26   "a product of the most perverted": Tobias G. Natter and Max Hollein (eds.), *The Naked Truth: Klimt, Schiele, Kokoschka and Other Scandals* (Munich: Prestel, 2005), p. 110.

26   "The people rolled about": Alfred Weidinger (ed.), *Gustav Klimt* (Munich: Prestel, 2007), p. 255.

26   "They should be in an exhibition": *Gustav Klimt: Modernism in the Making* (New York: Abrams, 2001), p. 103.

2   God

33   "We in Vienna": Richard S. Geehr, *Karl Lueger: Mayor of Fin de Siècle Vienna* (Detroit: Wayne State University Press, 1990), p. 200.

34   Pollak's religion: Henry-Louis de La Grange, *Gustav Mahler* (Oxford: Oxford University Press, 1995), vol. 2, p. 425, vol. 3, p. 699; *Neue Freie Presse,* March 23, 1912.

34   "The defamatory tactics": Mahler-Werfel, *Diaries,* p. 355.

34   "You Jewish sneak": Ibid., p. 381.

35   "For heaven's sake *don't marry Z*": Ibid., p. 404.

35   "Oh, to bear his child!": Ibid., p. 466.

35   "Evening at Gallias": Alma Mahler-Werfel, *Tagebuch-Suiten* (Frankfurt am Main: Fischer, 2002), p. 641.

36   "the setting of a non-German": Sandra McColl, *Music Criticism in Vienna: Critically Moving Forms* (Oxford: Oxford University Press, 1996), p. 104.

36   "a poem in a foreign language": Stephen McClatchie (ed.), *The Mahler Family Letters* (New York: Oxford University Press, 2006), pp. 5–6.

3 Gaslights

42 He discovered and isolated two of the rare earths: Franz Sedlacek, "Auer von Welsbach," *Blätter für Geschichte der Technik,* vol. 2, 1934; Oliver Sacks, *Uncle Tungsten: Memories of a Chemical Boyhood* (New York: Alfred A. Knopf, 2001), chap. 5.

43 "I soon saw": *The Standard Edition of the Complete Psychological Works of Sigmund Freud* (London: Hogarth, 1953), vol. 5, p. 652.

44 "You all do know this mantle": *Bulletin* (Sydney), April 13, 1905.

45 In the most influential account: Carl Schorske, *Fin-de-Siècle Vienna: Politics and Culture* (New York: Alfred A. Knopf, 1980), pp. xxxvi–xxxvii, 5–6.

45 "Baron Auer von Welsbach and Dr. Gallia": *Die Fackel,* no. 144, October 17, 1903.

47 the German firm Julius Pintsch: John W. White Jr., " 'A Perfect Light Is a Luxury': Pintsch Gas Car Lighting," *Technology and Culture,* vol. 18 (1977), pp. 64–69.

48 Watt, an electric lightbulb manufacturer: Joost Mertens, "The Development of the Dry Battery: Prelude to a Mass Consumption Article (1882–1908)," *Centaurus,* vol. 42 (2000), pp. 109–34.

4 Family

51 "based on mutual respect": Natter and Frodl, *Klimt's Women,* p. 116.

56 The most famous example is Martha Arendt: Elizabeth Young-Bruehl, *Hannah Arendt: For Love of the World* (New Haven, CT: Yale University Press, 1982), pp. 12–15.

59 her most ambitious piece of writing: Elisabeth Luzzatto, *Entwicklung und Wesen des Sozialismus* (Vienna: Brand, 1910).

59 "dedicated her life-work": Richard Luzzatto, *Unknown War in Italy* (London: New Europe Publishing, 1946), n.p.

5 Galas

62 In 1903 Gustav Mahler and Theobald Pollak: Henry-Louis de La Grange and Günther Weiss, *Gustav Mahler: Letters to His Wife* (London: Faber and Faber, 2004), p. 128.

67 Pollak gave Mahler *Die chinesische Flöte:* Richard Specht, "Das Lied von der Erde," *Neue Freie Presse,* December 4, 1914.

67 "the one who persuaded Mahler": Juliane Brand, Christopher Hailey, and Donald Harris (eds.), *The Berg-Schönberg Correspondence: Selected Letters* (London: Macmillan, 1987), p. 46.

68 "intended to ridicule the Jews": Marc A. Weiner, *Richard Wagner and the Anti-Semitic Imagination* (Lincoln: University of Nebraska Press, 1997), p. 143.

69 "greatest musical drama ever composed": Henry Louis de La Grange, *Mahler* (New York: Doubleday, 1973), vol. 1, p. 607.

69 Moriz found the third act *"charming"*: Mahler-Werfel, *Tagebuch-Suiten,* p. 648.

70 "Ah, you should see it at Bayreuth": George Bernard Shaw, "Wagner in Bayreuth," *English Illustrated Magazine,* vol. 7 (1890), p. 49.

71 lauded in Germanic and anti-Semitic terms: Frederic Spotts, *Bayreuth: A History of the Wagner Festival* (New Haven, CT: Yale University Press, 1994), p. 131.

72 Isadora Duncan brought modern dance to Vienna: Frederika Blair, *Isadora: Portrait of the Artist as a Woman* (New York: McGraw-Hill, 1986), p. 52; Hevesi, *Acht Jahre Secession,* pp. 368–70.

74 Tickets for the *"sensationspremiere"*: *Neue Freie Presse,* May 26, 1907.

74 Her first performance in Vienna: Henry-Louis de La Grange, *Gustav Mahler: Triumph and Disillusion (1904–1907)* (Oxford: Oxford University Press, 2000), vol. 3, p. 618.

76 Elise de Vere: Charles Blake Cochran, *The Secrets of a Showman* (London: Heinemann, 1929), p. 100.

76 La Belle Chavita: Jane F. Fulcher, *Debussy and His World* (Princeton, NJ: Princeton University Press, 2001), p. 128.

76 "Because life uses up his strength": David P. Frisby and Mike Featherstone (eds.), *Simmel on Culture—Selected Writings* (London: Sage, 1997), p. 260.

6   Pictures

78 how Viennese couples went about such collecting: Sophie Lillie, "The Golden Age of Klimt: The Artist's Great Patrons: Lederer, Zuckerkandl and Bloch-Bauer," in Renée Price (ed.), *Gustav Klimt: The Ronald S. Lauder and Serge Sabarsky Collections* (Munich: Prestel, 2007), pp. 55–89.

78 A who's who of Viennese art collectors: Theodor von Frimmel, *Lexicon der Wiener Gemälde Sammlungen, Buchstabe A bis L* (Munich: Müller, 1914), vol. 2, p. 9.

78 "the impresario of the Vienna Moderne": Ludwig Hevesi, "Modern Painting in Austria," in Charles Holmes (ed.), *The Art Revival in Austria* (London: Studio, 1906), p. viii; Tobias G. Natter and Gerbert Frodl (eds.), *Carl Moll (1861–1945)* (Vienna: Österreichische Galerie, 1998); Tobias G. Natter, *Die Galerie Miethke: eine Kunsthandlung im Zentrum der Moderne* (Vienna: Jüdisches Museum der Stadt Wien, 2003).

79 "art agent": *Die Fackel,* no. 59 (mid-November 1900), p. 19, quoted in Mahler-Werfel, *Diaries,* p. 348.

79 "nine-tenths of what the world celebrated": Zweig, *World of Yesterday,* pp. 22–23.

83 "proto-Secessionist": Hevesi, *Acht Jahre Secession,* p. 58.

86 "Incredible misery is expressed": Beat Stutzer and Roland Wäspe (eds.), *Giovanni Segantini* (Ostfildern: Hatje Cantz, 1999), p. 53.

86   the first extended psychoanalytical study of an artist: Karl Abraham, *Giovanni Segantini: ein psychoanalytischer Versuch* (Leipzig: Deuticke, 1911).

87   When the Moderne Galerie opened in 1903: *Kunst und Kunsthandwerk Monatsschrift,* 1903, p. 162.

88   "prodigious loss of money on his side": Mahler-Werfel, *Tagebuch-Suiten,* p. 629.

88   "innumerable people immediately began harassing": Ibid.

89   "private means": *Neue Freie Presse,* February 28, 1901; *Ver Sacrum,* February 1904, p. 13.

89   She went to the family's apartment: Mahler-Werfel, *Tagebuch-Suiten,* pp. 641, 647, 648, 728, 732.

7 Rooms

92   one of Vienna's most successful architects, Jakob Gartner: "Villa des Herrn Eduard Hamburger in Olmütz," *Neubauten und Concurrenzen in Österreich und Ungarn,* vol. 2 (1896), p. 55.

92   The Langer family's architect was Adolf Loos: Burkhard Rukschcio and Roland Schachel, *Adolf Loos: Leben und Werk* (Salzburg: Residenz, 1982), pp. 83, 187, 425, 430, 432, 437–38.

93   "an artist with an exuberant imagination": Ronald Franz, "Josef Hoffmann and Adolf Loos: The Ornament Controversy in Vienna," in Peter Noever (ed.), *Josef Hoffmann Designs* (Munich: Prestel, 1992), pp. 11–12.

99   Krauss's most successful designs: A. S. Levitus, "The Architectural and Decorative Work of Franz von Krauss," *Studio,* May 1907, pp. 296–303.

100   The opulence of Hoffmann's work: Terence Lane, *Vienna 1913: Josef Hoffmann's Gallia Apartment* (Melbourne: National Gallery of Victoria, 1984).

106   "why, with moderate foresight on the part of the Dynasty": Henry Wickham Steed, *The Hapsburg Monarchy* (London: Constable, 1914), p. xiii.

106   "new money people": Pieter Noever (ed.), *Yearning for Beauty: The Wiener Werkstätte and the Stoclet House* (Vienna: MAK, 2006), p. 110.

II GRETL

1 Diaries

111   "In a word: a vast amount. Spoilt": Mahler-Werfel, *Diaries,* p. 83.

114   the educational opportunities for girls in Vienna: Marsha L. Rozenblit, *The Jews of Vienna 1867–1914: Assimilation and Identity* (New York: State University of New York Press, 1983), chap. 5.

2 Tango

122   "pornographic spectacle": Marta E. Savigliano, *Tango and the Political Economy of Passion* (Boulder, CO: Westview, 1995), p. 139.

4 War

134 "Only the physically handicapped": Holger H. Herwig, *The First World War: Germany and Austria-Hungary 1914–1918* (New York: Arnold, 1987), p. 129.

136 "went up and got it fixed, of course": Karl Kraus, *The Last Days of Mankind: A Tragedy in Five Acts* (New York: Frederick Ungar, 1974), pp. 29–30.

5 Hoffmann

152 "if you should happen to be in the mood antiquarian": James Huneker, *New Cosmopolis: A Book of Images* (London: Werner Laurie, 1915), pp. 210–11.

6 Death

157 *Das Werk von Gustav Klimt: Neue Freie Presse,* February 10, 1918.

158 When Schiele compiled a three-page address book: Christian M. Nebehay, *Egon Schiele 1890–1918: Leben, Briefe, Gedichte* (Salzburg: Residenz, 1979), p. 493.

7 Sex

167 The relationship between an acclaimed musician and his female pupils: Bruce Thompson, "Ein Furchtbarer Schmarrn? Schnitzler's Reaction to Hermann Bahr's *Das Konzert,*" *Forum for Modern Language Studies,* vol. 31 (1995), pp. 154–64.

III ANNELORE

1 Memory

195 Vienna's leading celebrity photographer between the wars, Trude Fleischmann: *Übersee: Flucht und Emigration Österreichischer Fotografen 1920–1940* (Vienna: Kunsthalle Wien, 1998), pp. 37–39, 106–13.

200 While the Germans in Dahn's book: George Mosse, *Germans and Jews* (New York: Howard Fertig, 1970), chap. 3.

2 Austro-fascism

212 "There isn't a single filthy Jew": Thomas Mann, *Diaries 1918–1939* (New York: Abrams, 1982), pp. 134, 150, 364.

212 Furtwängler later maintained: Sam H. Shirakawa, *The Devil's Music Master: The Controversial Life and Career of Wilhelm Furtwängler* (New York: Oxford University Press, 1992), pp. 145–337.

215 When Schuschnigg entered his box: Bruno Walter, *Theme and Variations: An Autobiography* (London: Hamish Hamilton, 1947), p. 355.

216 "white knee-socks, a black raincoat and Tyrolean hat": George Clare, *Last Waltz in Vienna: The Destruction of a Family 1842–1942* (London: Macmillan, 1981), p. 173.

3   Anschluss

219   Austrian citizens into German Jews: Brian McGuinness and G. H. von Wright (eds.), *Ludwig Wittgenstein: Cambridge Letters* (Oxford: Blackwell, 1995), p. 293.

220   Jews "naïve enough" to take the notices seriously: G. E. R. Gedye, *Fallen Bastions* (London: Gollancz, 1939), p. 304.

225   As Sereny recalled in an autobiographical essay: Gitta Sereny, *The German Trauma: Experiences and Reflections 1938–2000* (London: Allen Lane, 2000), p. 7.

4   Visas

231   "not a country of immigration": A. J. Sherman, *Island Refuge: Britain and Refugees from the Third Reich 1933–1939* (London: Paul Elk, 1973), p. 91.

231   While some senior British diplomats: Louise London, "British Immigration Control Procedures and Jewish Refugees 1933–1939," in Werner E. Mosse (ed.), *Second Chance: Two Centuries of German-Speaking Jews in the United Kingdom* (Tübingen: Mohr, 1991), esp. p. 504.

232   never to describe its restrictions as a "quota": Paul R. Bartrop, *Australia and the Holocaust 1933–1945* (Melbourne: Australian Scholarly Publishing, 1994), p. 86.

232   "undue privileges . . . to one particular class of non-British subjects": Michael Blakeney, *Australia and the Jewish Refugees 1933–1948* (Sydney: Croom Helm, 1985), p. 130.

233   "to beg for a copy of a diploma or testimonial": Yvonne Kapp and Margaret Mynatt, *British Policy and the Refugees 1933–1941* (London: Frank Cass, 1997), p. 15.

234   This operation, which made Gildemeester a fortune: Peter Berger, "The Gildemeester Organisation for Assistance to Emigrants and the Expulsion of Jews from Vienna 1938–1942," in Terry Gourvish (ed.), *Business and Politics in Europe 1900–1970* (Cambridge: Cambridge University Press, 2003), pp. 215–45.

5   Subterfuge

240   The most extensive account of the art looted in Vienna: Sophie Lillie, *Was einmal war: Handbuch der enteigneten Kunstsammlungen Wiens* (Vienna: Czernin, 2003).

240   The merchant Fritz Wolff-Knize and his wife, Anna: Peter A. Knize, "Growing Up with Art: Kokoschka in My Life," in Tobias G. Natter (ed.), *Oskar Kokoschka: Early Portraits from Vienna and Berlin* (New Haven, CT: Yale University Press, 2002), esp. pp. 68–69.

241   This office was an inconsequential, ill-funded organization: Robert Holzbauer, "The Austrian Federal Office for Heritage Protection: Assisting in the Looting during the War, Administering Restitution After the War,"

in Günter Bischof, Anton Pelinka, and Hermann Denz (eds.), *Religion in Austria* (New Brunswick, NJ: Transaction, 2005), pp. 181–88.

242 Otto Kallir, the owner of Vienna's leading modern art gallery: Jane Kallir, *Saved from Europe: Otto Kallir and the History of the Galerie St. Etienne* (New York: Galerie St. Etienne, 1999); Jonathan Petropoloulos, "Bridges from the Reich: The Importance of Émigré Art Dealers as Reflected in the Case Studies of Curt Valentin and Otto Kallir-Nirenstein," working paper, December 1, 2009.

242 Bruno Grimschitz, the deputy director of the Österreichische Galerie: Monika Mayer, "Bruno Grimschitz und die Österreichische Galerie 1938–1945" in Gabriele Anderl and Alexandra Caruso (eds.), *NS-Kunstraub in Österreich und die Folgen* (Innsbruck: Studienverlag, 2005), pp. 59–79. Alexandra Caruso, "Raub in geordneten Verhältnissen," in Anderl and Caruso, *NS-Kunstraub in Österreich und die Folgen,* pp. 90–109.

246 Just before Freud left Austria in June 1938: Janine Burke, *The Gods of Freud* (New York: Alfred A. Knopf, 2006), p. 8.

247 Freud's eldest son, Martin, recalled: Martin Freud, *Glory Reflected: Sigmund Freud, Man and Father* (London: Angus and Robertson, 1957), p. 216.

6 Loss

254 "that so many people in Australia": Bartrop, *Australia and the Holocaust,* p. 83.

7 Capture

264 Fritz Loewenstein, a Berliner: *Fred Lowen: Dunera Boy, Furniture Designer, Artist* (Castlemaine: Prendergarst Publishing, 2001), pp. 14–15.

266 Within a day or two he was in Drancy: Serge Klarsfeld, *Le memorial de la Deportation des juifs de France* (Paris: Klarsfeld, 1978), n.p. (discussion of convoy 30).

266 "The Jews are real men and women": Michael R. Marrus and Robert O. Paxton, *Vichy France and the Jews* (New York: Basic Books, 1981), p. 271.

266 "In Paris, Jews by tens of thousands": Susan Zucotti, *The Holocaust, the French and the Jews* (Lincoln: University of Nebraska Press, 1993), p. 147.

267 This convoy traveled through the former Czechoslovakia: Raul Hilberg, *The Destruction of the European Jews* (New Haven, CT: Yale University Press, 2003), 3rd ed., vol. 2, pp. 485–86.

270 "Jewish friends spoke to one": Gedye, *Fallen Bastions,* p. 305.

IV ANNE

1 1939

276 The prospect of more Viennese culture: *Sydney Morning Herald,* January 7, 1939.

283 "wanted to help the refugees": Suzanne D. Rutland, *Edge of the Diaspora: Two Centuries of Jewish Settlement in Australia* (Sydney: Collins, 1988), p. 187.

2   Aliens

285 "insidious propaganda": Klaus Neumann, *In the Interest of National Security: Civilian Internment in Australia during World War II* (Canberra: National Archives of Australia, 2006), pp. 11–12.

285 "very kind welcome": Lucy Gruder, letter, *Sydney Morning Herald,* June 29, 1940.

285 "unnecessary and overbearing intolerance": Noel W. Lamidey, *Aliens Control in Australia 1939–46* (Sydney: Lamidey, 1974), p. 9.

291 Many of her evenings and weekends were devoted: M. H. Gallia, *Hauff's Tales* (Sydney: William Brooks, 1949).

293 The dominant Catholic organization: Sally Kennedy, *Faith and Feminism: Catholic Women's Struggle for Self-Expression* (Sydney: Studies in the Christian Movement, 1985).

296 "The Jew clings to his ritual law": Lewis Browne, *This Believing World* (New York: Macmillan, 1926), p. 251.

3   Correspondence

299 Norbert, who had been in Theresienstadt: *Terezin 1942–1945: Through the Eyes of Norbert Troller* (New York: Yeshiva University Museum, 1981), and Norbert Troller, *Theresienstadt: Hitler's Gift to the Jews* (Chapel Hill: University of North Carolina Press, 1991).

6   Dispersal

327 If only she had been able to read: Andrew Decker, "The Chill of the Hunt," *Art & Auction,* vol. 12, no. 9 (April 1990), pp. 164–71.

328 "relentless pursuit of his quarry": Judith H. Dobrzynski, "The Zealous Collector: A Singular Passion for Amassing Art, One Way or Another," *New York Times,* December 24, 1997.

329 When Leopold went to court: Diethard Leopold, *Rudolf Leopold— Kunstsammler* (Vienna: Holzhausen, 2003), pp. 141–43.

330 "I spoke to someone I realized was Fischer": *Rudolf Leopold v. Anne Bonyhady,* Supreme Court of New South Wales, Equity Division, 3100/1976.

330 "for a collection owned by an Austrian woman": Dobrzynski, "Zealous Collector."

7   Restitution

331 "Red Insurance Man": *Time,* December 13, 1963.

332 Erni had been on the Werkstätte's board: Noever (ed.), *Yearning for Beauty,* p. 135.

332   The exhibition, in 1984: Terence Lane, *Vienna 1913: Josef Hoffmann's Gallia Apartment* (Melbourne: National Gallery of Victoria, 1984).

332   "The exhibition was extraordinary": Patrick McCaughey, *The Bright Shapes and True Names: A Memoir* (Melbourne: Text, 2003), p. 89.

8   Identity

339   "If you're eight years old": Thomas Blood, *Madam Secretary: A Biography of Madeleine Albright* (New York: St. Martin's Griffin, 1999), p. 272.

339   Philip Taubman of the *New York Times*: Ann Blackman, *Seasons of Her Life: A Biography of Madeleine Korbel Albright* (New York: Scribner, 1998), p. 283.

339   "In Poland, every single day": Madeleine Albright, *Madam Secretary: A Memoir* (New York: Miramax, 2003), p. 240.

340   "As my parents saw it": Kati Marton, "Making Peace with the Past," *Newsweek*, February 17, 1997.

Index

Page numbers in *italics* refer to illustrations.

Abraham, Karl, 86

Abyssinia, 210, 257

Adler, Guido, 69

Albert V, Archduke of Austria, 30

Albright, Madeleine, 338–9

Alpine Triptych (Segantini), 87

Andersen, Hans Christian, 137

Andri, Ferdinand, *18,* 19, 20, 80, 102, *102,* 326, 329, 333

Angel, Gerty, 308–9, 344

Anna Karenina (Tolstoy), 50, 51

"Anne's Story," 340–2

Anschluss, 3, 8–9, 13, 14, 209–29, 230, 234, 236, 241–2, 245, 248, 258, 259, 276–7, 278, 280, 285, 287, 294, 299, 305–6, 314, 328, 334–5, 341

Anti-Defamation League, 339

anti-Semitism, 24, 30–6, 65, 68–9, 79, 132, 174, 178–9, 200, 210, 216, 217, 218–29, 235, 236, 247–8, 263–72, 278, 279, 343–4

Arendt, Hannah, 56

Arendt, Martha, 56

Argentina, 122, 263, 302

Art and Auction, 327–8

Art Gallery of New South Wales, 316–17, 318, 326

Aryanization, 69, 219, 223, 233, 245, 248, 263, 268–9, 292, 294, 335

Ascension Thursday, 138–9, 294–5

As You Like It (Shakespeare), 72

Auer von Welsbach, Carl, 42–9, 76, 87, 88, 159

Auschwitz concentration camp, 266, 268, 272, 299, 301, 338, 340

Australia, 4, 7, 9–10, 110, 216, 230–9, 250–3, 257, 275–81, 284–7, 294, 296, 305, 317–18, 320, 334, 341–2

Australian Communist Party, 306–8

Austria

    aristocracy of, 30, 47, 62, 79, 118, 124, 165

    bourgeoisie in, 19–20, 30, 59, 62, 79, 128, 142–3, 179

    civil service of, 31, 33–4

    constitutional monarchy of, 32, 33

    constitution of, 209

    currency of, 3, 162, 179, 183, 196

    decline of, 104–6, 110

    democracy in, 32, 33, 208, 209, 211

    economy of, 45, 46–7, 95, 106, 132–3, 146, 162, 179, 182–3, 196

    German annexation of, *see* Anschluss

    inflation in, 162, 179, 183, 196

    Jewish population of, 3, 207, 214, 263–72

Austria *(continued)*
  military forces of, 32, 33–4, 86,
    120–1, 122
  Nazi rule in, 3–7, 13, 209–12, 214,
    215, 216–58, 263–72, 322, 332, 342
  postwar period of, 292, 315, 322
  as republic, 32, 33, 179, 208–10, 211,
    217
  workers' strike in (1918), 154
  in World War I, 125, 126, 129, 131–7,
    149, 154, 158–9, 164, 165, 179
  in World War II, 235, 264–5, 284–7
Austrian Freedom Party, 336
Austrian Gas Glowing Light Co.,
    44–9, 77–8, 87, 159, 162, 185
Austrian Women's Suffrage
    Committee, 59
Austro-fascism, 209–10
Austro-Hungarian Empire, 14, 16,
    29–30, 43, 92, 104–6

Backoffen, Elias, 152
Baden, 45, *52*, 92, 127, 128
Bahr, Hermann, 22–3, 24, 72, 167
Baloeran, 249–50
Bayreuth music festival, 69–71, *71*, 98
BBC, 313–14
Beech Forest (Klimt), 26–7, *27*, 80, 100,
    105, 123, 157, 204, 257
Beer Hall Putsch, 238
Beethoven, Ludwig van, 64–5, 80, 84,
    205, 212–13, 314
Befreiung, 344–8
Belgium, 264–5, *264*, 285
Belgrade, 134–5
Bell, Marilyn, 313–14
Berger, Fritzi, 213
Berger, Hilde, 213
Berl, David, 79
Bettauer, Hugo, 334
Biedermeier period, 100, 104, 242
Birkenau concentration camp, 266
Bisenz, 19, 29, 31–2, 33, 37, 44, 162
Bittong, Franz, 68

"Black Friday" brush fires (1939), 275
Bleibtreu, Attilio, 137
Bloch-Bauer, Adele, 22, 51, 78, 81, 84,
    85, ?43, 244
Bloch-Bauer, Ferdinand, 78, 85, 243,
    257
Bloody Friday (1927), 208
Blue Danube, The (Strauss), 206, 280,
    321
Blum (pianist), 119, 122, 123
B'nai B'rith, 308
Bocskai, Stephan, 32
Bonaparte, Maria, 246
Bondi, Lea, 328
Bonnesen, Carl, 104
Bonyhady, Alice, 306
Bonyhady, Anne, *see* Herschmann-
    Gallia, Annelore "Anne"
Bonyhady, Bertha, 306
Bonyhady, Berthold, 306
Bonyhady, Bruce, 7, 8, 11, 200, 258,
    311–12, *316*, 318, 319–20, 321, 323,
    327, 329, 334, 343–4, 346
Bonyhady, Edith, 306, *307*, 308, 310
Bonyhady, Edward, 305, 306, *307*, 309,
    310, 311
Bonyhady, Elsa, 306
Bonyhady, Eric, 305–12, *307*, *310*, 318,
    322, 324, 344
Bonyhady, Fred, 306, *307*
Bonyhady, Gerard, 306
Bonyhady, Mira, 306, 309, 311
Bonyhady, Nicholas, 336
Bonyhady, Norbert, 306
Bonyhady, Salomon, 305, 306, 308,
    309, 310
Bonyhady, Tim, 7, 8, 9, 14, 312, *316*,
    319–20, 321, 323, 327, 336, 340–4
Brahms, Johannes, 212
Brave New World (Huxley), 295
Brée, Malwine, 168–9
Brisbane, 251–2
Brisbane *Telegraph,* 251–2, *251*, 276
Brünn, Erika, 279–80, 287–8, 299

Bruntal, 171, 182, 269
Budapest, 46, 205
Bund Deutscher Madchen, 216, 294
Bunsen, Robert, 42–3
Bunzl, Fritz, 166
Bürckel, Josef, 219, 227
Burckhard, Max, 18, 34–5
Burgkapelle, 237–8, 321
Burgtheater, 195, 211, 225, 321
Buxbaum, Friedrich, 167

cantors, 344, 345, 348
Carl Theater, 72, 75
Catholic Church, 10, 16, 24, 30–41, 73, 132, 266–7, 279, 339, 340, 345, 346
Catholic Women's Association, 252
Central Cemetery, 152, 345–6
Central Office for Jewish Emigration, 234, 265–6
Central Office for Monuments Protection, 241–6, 257
Charles VI, Emperor of Austria, 32
Chelmno concentration camp, 269
Chéret, Jules, 77
"Chill of the Hunt, The" (Decker), 327–8
Chippendale, Thomas, 92
Christian Social Party, 33–4, 45, 208, 215–16, 219
Christie's, 323–4
Christkindlmarkt, 200, 201, 345
Churchill, Winston S., 285
Clare, George, 216
Cody, William F. "Buffalo Bill," 63, 75–6
communism, 220, 306–8
concentration camps, 218–19, 222, 263–72, 299, 301, 305–6, 308, 338, 340
Continental Catholic Migrants Welfare Committee, 252, 278
Crab Apple Tree (Klimt), 26
Czech Crown lands, 29, 32
Czechoslovakia, 171, 267, 299, 338

Dachau concentration camp, 218–19, 222, 305–6, 308
Dahn, Felix, 200, 226, 296
Daimler armaments plant, 154
Dalibor (Smetana), 215–16
Decker, Andrew, 327–8
Demus, Otto, 243–4
Deutsche Kunst und Dekoration, 103
Deutsches Volkstheater, 28, 61, 73–4, 123
Dobrzynski, Judith, 328, 330
Dollfuss, Engelbert, 209–10
Don Giovanni (Mozart), 225, 238
Drancy deportation camp, 266
Duncan, Isadora, 64, 72, 74

Earngey, John, 8
Eberstaller, Richard, 271
Edict of Tolerance (1782), 31
Edison, Thomas, 43–4
Edward VII, King of England, 62
Egger-Lienz, Albin, 158
Egon Schiele: The Leopold Collection exhibition, 328
Eichmann, Adolf, 265–6
Eislaufverein, 193, 321
electric lighting, 42, 43–4, 48, 49, 77, 95, 185
Elisabeth of Austria, Empress, 122
Es war einmal (Zemlinsky), 64
Evil Mothers, The (Segantini), 85–9
Ewige Jude, Der, 229
Exodus (Uris), 10–11

Fackel, Die, 45
Fallen Bastions (Gedye), 220
Familiants Law, 32
Faust (Goethe), 27, 198–9
Ferdinand II, Emperor of Austria, 30
Ferdinand III, Emperor of Austria, 30–1
Ferguson, John, 283, 288
Ferguson, Mabel, 281
Fifth Symphony (Mahler), 65, 346–7

Fischer, Harry, 324

Fischer, Wolfgang, 324, 326–7, 328, 329–30

Fischer Fine Art, 326–7

Fix, Flieger Rittmeister, 168

Fledermaus, Die (Strauss), 75, 113

Fleischmann, Trude, 214

Fliegände Holländer, Der (Wagner), 211

Flöge, Emilie, 17, 20, 25–6, 90, *156*, 157

Flora Danica dinner set, 5, 138, 253

Foxman, Abraham, 339

France, 265–7, 285, 300–3

Franz Ferdinand, Archduke, 95–6, 125, 132, 134

Franz Joseph, Emperor of Austria, 16, 32, 36, 44, 59, 83, 87, 123, 132, 134–5

Frauen-Erwerb-Verein, 113, 114, 200, 216, 224

Frauenstimmrecht, 58–60

Freud, Martin, 247

Freud, Sigmund, 43, 86, 88, 111, 113, 120, 231, 246–7

Freudenthal, 16, 29–30, 32–3, 37, *38*, 47, 75, 82, 84, 95, 138, 163, 171, *316*

Frühlings Erwachen (Wedekind), 73, 173

Fulnek, 47, 171, 186, 254–5

Furtwängler, Wilhelm, 212–13

Gaibl, Alexander, 40

Galerie Miethke, 80, 83, 84, 94, 157, 181

Gallia, Adolf, 5, 38, 44–5, 48–9, 51, 52, 57, 60, 92, 95, 113, 123, 124, 127, 128, 130, 138, 149–51, 161, 168, 178, 197, 201, 223, 269, 272

Gallia, Emmanuel, 29

Gallia, Erni, *39*, 40, 53–4, *54*, *55*, *56*, 57, *57*, 58, 62, 65, 70, 72, 98, 112, 120–1, 125, 126, 133, 142, 153, 155,

160, 161, 162, 165, 173, 175, *175*, 179, 181–2, 187, 202, 203–4, 219, 235, 241, 246, 254–62, 272, 292, 308, 319, 332, 333

Gallia, Fanny, 199, 298

Gallia, Friedl, 124, 128, 270, 323

Gallia, Hermine Hamburger, 3–106

  Alt Aussee villa (Villa Gallia) of, 52–3, 95, 96, *96*, 102, 160, 175, 182, 196, 203, 256–7, 292

  Anne's relationship with, 185–6, 191–2, 193, 194, 196, 198–203, 341

  art collection of, 5–6, 7, 10, 12, 13, 14, 15–28, 58, 77–92, 204, 243, 244, 245, *316*

  assimilation by, 10, 29, 37–41, 90

  Austrian identity of, 14, 16, 83

  author's research on, 12–13, 29–106

  automobiles owned by, 95–6, 98–9, 110–11

  baby book kept by, 54–7

  book stamp for, 157, *347*

  as Catholic, 10, 37–41, 56–7, 80, 161–2, 163, 175, 178, 200–2

  childhood of, 37–41, 202

  correspondence of, 9, 11, 53, 102, 110, 160

  death of, 202–5, 211, 228

  diaries of, 12, 50–7, 63–5, 110

  education of, 37, 202

  family background of, 14, 16, 29–30, 32–3

  funeral of, 202–3, 332

  furniture of, 78, 92–4, 102–3, 122, 130, 184, 203–4

  grave site of, 202, 217, 315, 321, 332, 345, 346

  Gretl's first engagement and, 126, 128–30, 139, 141, 149–52, 153, 173

  Gretl's relationship with, 53–8, 62, 111, 113, 114–18, 126, 128–30, 139, 141, 149–52, 153, 169–70, 173, 182, 185–8, 196, 211

Hoffman as architect and interior designer for, 83, 93–106, 110, 119, 122, 126, 138, 142–8, 152, 159, 184, 203–4, 311, 325

Jewish background of, 10, 15–16, 29–41, 80, 142–3, 175, 244, 348

Kathe's relationship with, 112, 113, 124, 153, 163, 177, 184, 186–7, 293

Klimt landscape owned by (*Beech Forest*), 26–7, *27*, 80, 100, *105*, 123, 157, 204, 257

Klimt's portrait of, 5, 7, 12, 15–28, *21*, *25*, 80, 91, 100–2, *101*, 130, 133, 184, 186, 204, *204*, 244, 316–17, 323–4, 326

Mahler's postcard to, 9, 11, *11*

Mahler's relationship with, 9, 11, 64–8

marriage of, 5–6, 50–60, 155, 157, 158, 159–61, 180, 344

as mother, 53–8, 62, 182, 196

mountaineering expedition of, 52–3

papers of, 11–12, 110, 191

personality of, 50–2, 186–7, 198–9, 293

photographs of, *37*, *39*, *46*, *52*, *54*, *55*, *56*, *57*, *63*, 169–70, *170*

servants of, 53–4, 57, 99, 122, 126, 128–9, 169, 185–8, 198–9, 236

silver sweet bowl of, 90–1, *91*, *101*, 103

silverware of, 90–1, 93, 94, 96, 103, 203, 236

silver wedding anniversary of, 53, 155, 157, 158, 159–60

social life of, 27–8, 35–6, 50–1, 61–76, 82, 90–1, 110, 116–23, 126, 139, 155, 156, 186, 202, 211, 332

theater attended by, 27–8, 50–1, 61–4, 72–3, 82, 155, 156, 332

wealth of, 13–14, 36, 47, 51, 79, 95, 97, 98, 161, 162, 185–6, 196, 203, 342

Wohllebengasse apartment of, 5, *6*, 35, 49, 97–106, *98*, *101*, *102*, *105*, 110, 118, 119–23, 126, 128, 129, 130, 138, 139, 142, 143–5, 146–7, 155–6, 159, 160, 161, 162, 171, 177, 182, 184–8, 196, 198–205, 213, 216, 332–3

World War I and, 133, 154–7

Gallia, Ida, 5, 51, *52*, 92, 95, 113, 118, 123, 124, 125, 126, 127, 128, 130, 138, 149, 150–1, 161, 197, 198, 201, 272

Gallia, Kathe

Anne's relationship with, 191, 192, 193, 194–5, 202, 205–7, 213, 219, 220, 222, 226–7, 228, 293, 295–6, 309–10, 312, 318, 323–4, 325, 331

in Anschluss period, 217, 218–29, 230, 236, 241–2, 287, 299, 314

arrest and imprisonment of, 4, 218–24, 225, 226, 227, 230, 243, 248, 286, 306, 315

art collection of, 4, 5–6, 7, 8, 13, 204, *204*, 241–2, 315–17

as Australian refugee, 110, 231, 232, 234, 250–3, 257, 275, 276, 279, 280–1, 287, 315–16, 334

birth of, 62

book stamp commissioned by, 53

as Catholic, 40, 207, 219, 226–7, 252, 295–6, 312

childhood of, 20, 40, 53, 62, 118, 126, 152, 160, 161, 162, 163

confiscated property of, 218–24, 227, 233–5, 240–8, 260, 292, 308

correspondence of, 219–20, 287, 298–9, 325

death of, 327, 332

departure from Vienna of, 13, 246, 247–8

diary of, 157

education of, 3, 165, 175, 184, 186, 232, 233, 281

"enemy alien" status of, 284–7

Gallia, Kathe *(continued)*
  furniture of, 203–4, *204*, 241–2,
    244–5, 253
  as Graetzinlicht Gesellschaft
    employee, 186, 219, 232
  grave site of, 315, 321, 334, 345, 346
  Gretl's relationship with, 112, 113,
    124, 153, 163, 177, 184, 194–5, 224,
    288, 292–3
  Hermine's relationship with, 112,
    113, 124, 153, 163, 177, 184, 186–7,
    293
  jewelry of, 196, 203, 218–24, 227,
    246, 247–8
  Jewish background of, 216,
    218–24
  name of, 3, 276
  papers of, 110, 191
  personality of, 112, 113, 124, 153, 163,
    177, 184, 194–5, 281
  photographs of, *39, 56,* 169–70, *170,*
    289, 316
  press notices of, 251–2
  Rechte Bahngasse apartment of,
    203, 205, 219–21, 331
  Rose Bay apartment of, 253, 285–6,
    290
  in Switzerland, 247–9, 300
  transoceanic voyage of, 249–50, 281,
    283
  as twin sister, 20, 40, 53, 62, 186–7,
    192–4, 217
  unmarried status of, 142, 186–7
  visa obtained by, 230–9
  wealth of, 203, 218–24, 292
Gallia, Lene, 20, *39,* 40, 53, *56,* 62, 112,
    113, 118, 126, 142, 152, 160, 161,
    162, 165, 169–70, *170,* 175, 184,
    186, 192, 194, 196, 201, 217, 315,
    321, 345, 346
Gallia, Liesl, 269–70, 272
Gallia, Louis (Ludwig), 269–71, 272
Gallia, Marie Jacobi "Mizzi," 175–6,
    175, 179, 181–2, 186–7, 193, 203–4,

    235, 246, 254–60, 292, 308, 319,
    332, 333, 336, 339, 342
Gallia, Melanie, 92–3, 128, 143, 272
Gallia, Moriz
  Andri's portrait of, *18,* 102, 130,
    204
  art collection of, 5–6, 10, 13, 14, 17,
    24, 27–8, 77–92, 102, 130, 159,
    243, 244, 245
  Austrian identity of, 16, 58, 83
  book stamp for, 157, *347*
  as Catholic, 80, 161–2, 163, 175, 201
  conversion of, 38–40, 41
  correspondence of, *81,* 102–3, 110,
    169
  death of, 159–64, 165, 166, 168, 169,
    172, 173
  funeral of, 161–2, 163
  in gaslight industry, 42–9, 77–8, 88,
    95, 104, 159, 162
  grave site of, 192, 217, 315, 321, 345,
    346
  Gretl's engagement and, 129–30,
    139, 140–1, 145–6, 149–52, 153
  Gretl's relationship with, 111–12,
    114–18, 129–30, 139, 140–1, 145–6,
    149–52, 153, 159, 160, 161, 165,
    166, 168, 169, 172, 173, 272, 311
  Herr Regierungsrat title of, 16, 58,
    87–9, 121, 136, 152, 162
  Jewish background of, 29, 38, 80,
    121, 142–3, 162
  marriage of, 5–6, 50–60, 155, 157,
    158, 159–61, 180, 344
  obituaries of, 161–2
  personality of, 51–3
  philanthropy of, 87–9, 106, 162
  photographs of, 19–20, *39, 46, 52,*
    57, 156, 157, 272
  social life of, 27–8, 61–78, 116–23,
    126, 139, 155, *156,* 211
  theater attended by, 27–8, 155, 156
  wealth of, 13–14, 30, 36, 47–9, 87–9,
    95, 97, 98, 102–3, 161, 181–2

as Werkstätte director, 106, 137, 155,
    159, 181–2
will of, 53, 78, 161
World War I and, 126, 133, 154–7
Gallia, Wilhelm, 45, 46, 48, 92, 124,
    152, 160–1, 269, 323, 345
Gasglühlicht ("gas-glowing light"), 43
gaslight, 42–9, 77–8, 185
Gedye, G. E. R., 220, 270
Geisha, The (Jones), 75
Germany, Imperial, 44, 48, 68, 103,
    131, 133, 135, 137, 155, 182–3
Germany, Nazi, 3–7, 13, 209–12, 214,
    215, 216–58, 263–72, 284, 285,
    298, 322, 332, 342
Germany Emergency Fellowship
    Committee, 252, 253, 278
Gesamtkunstwerk, 7, 93, 94, 99–100
Gestapo, 4, 221, 222–3, 227, 229, 238,
    241, 244, 245, 246, 248, 263
Ghosts (Ibsen), 303
Gildemeester, Frank van Gheel, 234
Glück, Gustav, 100
Godowski, Leopold, 51
Goebbels, Joseph, 4, 212, 335
Goethe, Johann Wolfgang von, 27, 111,
    198–9
Goldfish (Klimt), 26
Göring, Hermann, 247–8
Gotterdämmerung (Wagner), 70, 211
Graetzinlicht Gesellschaft, 48, 49, 159,
    186, 196, 203, 217, 219, 232
Gräf & Stift automobiles, 95–6, 99,
    110–11, 125, 259
Grail, 293–6, *295*
Graulhet, 265–7, 301
Graz, 305–6
Great Britain, 136, 231, 232–3, 249,
    256, 268, 279–80, 285, 287
Great Depression, 196, 206, 241
Great Race (1907), 98–9
Greene, Graham, 318
Grimschitz, Bruno, 242–3, 315
Grinzing Cemetery, *66*, 67, 163

Groak, Stella, 293
Gruber, Georg, 276–7
Gustav Mahler (Orlik), 7, 8, *10*, 67,
    204

Hahngasse prison, 222–3, 230, 248,
    306, 315
Hamburger, Anna Schauer, 268, 339
Hamburger, Dagmar, 170–2, 182, 269
Hamburger, Eduard, 38, 92
Hamburger, Felizitas "Fely," 171, 201,
    268–9, 299, 315
Hamburger, Friedrich, 268, 298–9,
    340
Hamburger, Gudrun, 170, 171–2, 269,
    299
Hamburger, Guido, Jr., 267–8, 298–9,
    339
Hamburger, Guido, Sr., *39*, 40, 41, 46,
    95, 100, 112, 142, 143, 166, 171,
    267, 269, 299, 339
Hamburger, Helene, 268, 299
Hamburger, Henny, 67, 128, 153, 161,
    163, 170, 192, 345
Hamburger, Jana, 268, 269, 299, 340
Hamburger, Josefine, 37, *39*, 138, 181
Hamburger, Lizzi, 201–2, 269, 299
Hamburger, Nathan, 29, 32, 37, 38, *39*,
    47, 138, 163, 181
Hamburger, Nelly Bunzl, *39*, 41, 95,
    100, 104, 112, 143, 166, 171, 269,
    299, 339
Hamburger, Otto, 39, *39*, 46, 112, 142,
    144, 161, 170–2, 182, 192, 269, 299
Hamburger, Paul, 40, 171, 201, 222,
    242, 268–9, 299, 315
Hamburger, Robert, *39*, 112, 171
Hamburger & Co., 196
Hamlet (Shakespeare), 111, 136
Hapsburg dynasty, 32, 33, 104–6, 110,
    178–9, 185
Hedda Gabler (Ibsen), 157
Heller, Hugo, 157–8
Henneberg, Marie, 19

Herschmann, Anna Schick, 177
Herschmann, Bernhard, 177, 178, 198
Herschmann, Franz, 182, 265, 266, 271–2, 301, 302
Herschmann, Gustav, 267, 271–2, 301
Herschmann, Ludwig, 177
Herschmann, Otto, 177, 301, 302, 321
Herschmann, Paul, 3, 174–88, *180*, 197–200, 201, 227, 263–7, *264*, 300–4, *302*, 308, 310–11, 321, 341
Herschmann-Gallia, Annelore "Anne," 191–348
  at Albertgasse school, 224–5, 235, 278
  at Alt Alsee villa (Villa Gallia), 191, 192, 193, 198, 199, 205, 206, 298, 319, 320–1, 335–7
  in *Anschluss* period, 209–10, 212–17, 218–29, 230, 234, 287, 294, 299, 314, 319, 341
  art donations and sales by, 323–30, 332–3, 345
  as Australian refugee, 4, 7, 9–10, 110, 216, 231, 232, 234, 250–3, 275–81, 287, 294, 296, 305, 317–18, 320, 334, 341–2
  author's research on, 7, 8, 9, 12–14, 191–5, 238–9, 271–2, 275–7, 340–2
  autobiographical story written by, 285
  baptism of, 228, *228*
  birthday of, 196, 206, 293
  as Catholic, 183, 199, 200–2, 206, 207, 226–9, 235, 236–7, 252, 276, 293–6, 303, 309, 310–12, 321, 344
  cello played by, 199, 237, 247, 256, 278, *279*, 298
  childhood of, 110, 171, 184–8, 191–200, 201, 205–7, 230, 300–4, 341
  confiscated property of, 243, 244, 260, 292, 320–1, 335–7, 342

  conversion of, 226–9, 236–7, 276, 296, 309, 344
  conversions as viewed by, 40–1
  correspondence of, 278–80, 287–8, 293, 297–304, 310–11, 324–5, 336–7
  Cremorne apartment of, 253, 290, 308, 309–10, 317–18, 324–6, 327
  crucifix worn by, *228*, 229, 237, 251
  death of, 12, 344
  diaries of, 13, 191, 192–3, 198, 199, 247, 257, 285, 286, 290, 293, 298, 301, 336
  education of, 193, 199, 200, 216, 224–5, 235, 237, 276, 277–8, 279, 281, 288–90, 293, 303, 308
  "enemy alien" status of, 13, 284–7
  father's relationship with, 197–200, 201, 300–4, 341
  First Communion of, 228, 276, 294
  German spoken and taught by, 277, 289–90, 303, 319, 327, 341
  as godmother, 236–7, 293
  as Grail society member, 293–6, *295*
  Gretl's relationship with, 110, 172, 178, 180–1, 182 191, 193, 194–5, 197–8, 202–3, 205–7, 216, 219, 225, 226, 227, 232, 235, 243, 272, 278, 281, 293, 309–11, 312, 318, 323, 324, 331
  Hermine's relationship with, 185–6, 191–2, 193, 194, 196, 198–203, 341
  jewelry of, 195–6, 203, 214
  Jewish background of, 9–14, 40–1, 183, 199–200, 201, 202, 206, 207, 213, 214, 215, 216–17, 226–9, 235, 276, 294, 296, 303, 308, 309, 310–11, 341, 343–4, 348
  Kathe's relationship with, 191, 192, 193, 194–5, 202, 205–7, 213, 219, 220, 222, 226–7, 228, 293, 295–6, 309–10, 312, 318, 323–4, 325, 331
  lace-cleaning training of, 236, 248, 278, 300, 322

marriage of, 305–12, *310*, 324, 344

memoirs of, 12, 192–3, 200, 226, 271–?, ?85, 340 2

memories of, 191–3, 202–3, 238–9, 321, 334, 335–7, 340–4

music concerts attended by, 212–13, 237–8, 276–7, 280, 318, 321

name of, 7, 184 , 205, 275

operas and operettas attended by, 211–16, 225–6, 237, 238, 248, 318, 320, 344

personality of, 191–6, 278–9, 287–9, 293–7, 303–4

photographs of, *194*, 195, *197*, 213–14, *215*, 228–9, *228*, *251*, 278, *279*, *289*, *295*, 301, 309, *310*, *316*, *343*

press notices of, 251, *251*, 276

relatives lost by, 263–72, 297–9

restitution for, 335–7, 342

Rose Bay apartment of, 253, 285–6, 290

separation and divorce of, 311–12

social life of, 194–5, 211–17, 218, 225–6, 237, 238

teacher training of, 290, 308

theater attended by, 194–5, 211, 225, 320, 321

transoceanic voyage of, 249–50, 281, 283

Vienna revisited by, 318–22, 331–2, 334–7

visa obtained by, 230–9

wealth of, 13–14, 195–6, 203, 204–6, 241, 263, 341, 342

at Wohllebengasse apartment, 184–8, 191–2, 193, 197, 198–202, 321, 324, 331, 334, 341, 345

Herschmann-Gallia, Margarete "Gretl," 109–88

alimony paid to, 183–4, 197–8

at Alt Aussee villa (Villa Gallia), 110, 111, 113, 125, 126, 137, 147–52, 153, 160, 178, 241

Anne's relationship with, 110, 172, 178, 180–1, 182 191, 193, 194–5, 197–8, 202–3, 205–7, 216, 219, 225, 226, 227, 232, 235, 243, 272, 278, 281, 293, 309–11, 312, 318, 323, 324, 331

in Anschluss period, 217, 218–29, 230, 236, 241–2, 245, 287, 299, 314

art collection of, 4, 5–6, 7, 8, 13, 204, 205, 241–4, 314–15

in Australia, 4–8, 232

as Australian refugee, 4–8, 110, 231, 232, 250–3, 257, 275, 276, 279, 280–3, 287, 294, 314–15, 334

author's research on, 7–14, 109–10

baby book for, 54–7

balls attended by, 116–24, *117*, *119*, 129, 176, 177, 213

birthday of, 147–8, 156, 193, 205

birth of, 53

as Catholic, 40, 56–7, 112–13, 116, 127, 136, 138–9, 152, 162, 178–9, 183, 207, 210, 219, 226, 252, 276, 283, 310–11, 312, 344

childhood of, 54, 58, 62, 65–6, 71, 72, 90, 109–15, 205

confiscated property of, 233–5, 240–7, 260, 292, 308

correspondence of, 67, 147–52, 177, 230–1, 244, 282, 287, 298–9, 300, 301, 302–3, 310–11

dancing as pastime of, 116–24, *117*, *119*, 127, 129, 176–7, 213

death of, 327, 332

diaries of, 12, 55, *66*, 109–15, 118, 120–1, 126–7, 134–7, 138, 140, 145–6, 148, 149, 153, 154, 159, 160, 161, 162–4, 170, 172, 178, 182

dowry of, 144, 145, 173, 179–81, 203

education of, 109, 113, 114, 116, 235

"enemy alien" status of, 284–7

English spoken and taught by, 235, 283, 291–2

Herschmann-Gallia, Margarete
"Gretl" *(continued)*
first engagement of (to Norbert
Stern), 125–53, *131*, 163–4, 166,
167, 173, 178, 179, 181, 184, 187,
198, 311
at Free French Delegation, 287
furniture of, 7, 181, 203–4, 205,
241–2, 244–5, 253, 311, 324–5
gold coins hidden by, 246–7, 325
grave site of, 315, 321, 332, 334, 345,
346
health of, 109, 324, 325
Hermine's relationship with, 53–8,
62, 111, 113, 114–18, 126, 128–30,
139, 141, 149–52, 153, 169–70, 173,
182, 185–8, 196, 211
Hietzing apartment of, 181–4
jewelry of, 8, 9, 196, 203, 245,
246–7, 250, 300
Jewish background of, 112–13, 118,
152, 176–7, 207, 210, 216, 217,
219, 283, 348
Kathe's relationship with, 112, 113,
124, 153, 163, 177, 184, 194–5, 224,
288, 292–3
Landstrasser-Hauptstrasse
apartment of, 203, 205, 213–14,
215, 216, 331
love affair of, 172–3, 179, 187
Mahler's symphonies heard by,
65–6, 71
marriage of, 3, 174–84, 185, 300,
310
Moriz's relationship with, 111–12,
114–18, 129–30, 139, 140–1, 145–6,
149–52, 153, 159, 160, 161, 165,
166, 168, 169, 172, 173, 272, 311
as mother, 110, 172, 178, 180–1, 182,
191, 193, 194–5, 197–8, 202–3,
205–7
music as interest of, 65–6, 71, 110,
111, 114, 139, 166–8, 186, 215, 280,
281

name of, 3, 112, 185, 197, 276
passport of, 216, 234
personality of, 109–15, 118, 120–1,
128–9, 139–40, 153, 163–4,
281–3
photographs of, *39, 54, 55, 56, 57,
117, 119, 131*, 169–70, *170, 180, 251,
292, 302, 316*
physical appearance of, 114, 118
prenuptial agreement of, 179–81,
183–4
press notices of, 251, *251*
recipes published by, 282
residency certificate of, 210
Rose Bay apartment of, 253, 285–6,
290
second engagement of (to Paul
Herschmann), 177–81
secretarial work of, 169, 291
separation and divorce of, 181,
183–4, 185, 187, 197–200
siblings of, 112, 113, 114, 118,
165
social life of, 110–30, 139, 157,
165–70, 176–7, 194–5, 213
Sydney arrival of, 252–3
theater attended by, 157, 194–5
translation published by, 291
transoceanic voyage of, 249–50, 281,
283
Untere Augartenstrasse apartment
of, 142–3, 146, 152, 311
in Vienna Woods, 125–7, 128
visa obtained by, 230–39
Wagner operas heard by, 70–2,
71, 98
wealth of, 13–14, 110–15, 128,
129–30, 134, 141, 162, 179–88, 196,
197–8, 203, 208, 263, 292
at Wohllebengasse apartment, 166,
169–70, 171, 177, 181, 184–8, 197,
198–9, 205, 240–1, 311
World War I and, 132, 154–7,
196

Herzl, Theodor, 69
Hevesi, Ludwig, 26, 74, 83
Hietzing cemetery, 138, 141, *156*, 157,
 161–3, 192, 202–3, 217, 315, 321,
 345, 346
Hindenburg, Paul von, 155
Hitler, Adolf, 210–11, 212, 214, 215, 216,
 217, 232, 235, 238, 280, 284, 305,
 318, 320, 341, 342
Hitler Jugend, 216
Hofburgtheater, 27, 50, 61, 62, 73, 99,
 123, 136, 165
Hoffmann, Josef, 5, 10, 12, 24, 34, 65,
 83, 89, 91, 93–106, *102*, 110, 119,
 122, 126, 142–8, 152, *156*, 157, 159,
 163, 181, 184, 203–4, *204*, 214, *215*,
 244–5, 253, 311, 324–6, 331, 332–3,
 345
Hofmannsthal, Friedl Gallia von, 124,
 128, 270, 323
Hofmannsthal, Hugo von, 124, 136
Hofmannsthal, Richard von, 124
Hofoper, 36, 40, 58, 62, 65, 73, 75, 113,
 114, 121, 123
Holocaust, 263–72, 285, 315, 328, 334,
 338–40, 347–8
Hornung, Ilse, 193, 224, 331–2
Hotel Metropol, 221, 222, 286
Hötzendorf, Conrad von, 136
House of Wittgenstein, The (Waugh), 14
Howard, John, 342
Hundred Days, The (Forzano), 211
Huneker, James, 152
Hungarian Gas Glowing Light Co.,
 46, 48
Huxley, Aldous, 295

Ibsen, Henrik, 72–3, 140, 157, 303
Illica, Luigi, 85–6
Internal Revenue Office, 244
International Women's Congress, 59
Interpretation of Dreams, The (Freud),
 43, 120
Israel, 10

Israelitische Kultusgemeinde, 16, 33,
 38–9, 40, 118, 174, 178–9, 210,
 234, 236, 276, 308, 321, 344–8
Itala automobiles, 98–9
Italy, 131, 133, 135–6, 257, 206–7,
 260–2

Jacobi, Adolf, 176
Jacobi, Anna, 176, 254–8
Jacobi, Fini, 235, 255
Jacobi, Fritz, 255
Jewish Institute for the Blind, 162
Jewish Memorial Center, 272
Jewish Museum, 346–7
Jewish Welfare Society, 252, 283, 290
Jews
 assimilation of, 9–11, 29, 30, 36–41,
  90, 178–9, 183, 263
 baptism of, 30, 35, 40, 174, 311–12
 cemeteries of, 32, 38, 152, 207, 345–6
 confiscated property of, 233–5,
  240–53, 257–60, 292, 308, 320–1,
  335–7, 342
 conversions of, 30, 35, 36–41, 58, 69,
  79, 112, 113, 118, 120, 124, 127, 132,
  171, 174, 178–9, 201, 218–19,
  226–9, 236–7, 269, 276, 296,
  309, 311–12, 338–9, 344
 education of, 31, 113, 120
 French, 265–7
 ghettos of, 30–2, 34, 142, 207, 268,
  269
 High Holidays of, 176, 199, 200
 immigration quotas for, 232–3
 Liberal, 199
 marriage of, 30, 32, 174–5
 in middle class, 19–20, 30, 79,
  142–3, 179
 mixed marriages of, 174–5, 178–9,
  268–9, 310–11
 music of, 344, 345, 348
 Nazi persecution of, 3–7, 13,
  209–12, 214, 215, 216–58, 263–72,
  322, 332, 342

Jews *(continued)*
  organizations for, 16, 33, 38–9, 40,
    118, 174, 178–9, 210, 234, 236,
    276, 308, 321, 344–8
  Orthodox, 142–3, 176, 199, 308
  passports of, 234, 263–4, 265
  pogroms and, 4, 13, 30–2, 236,
    238–9, 247–8, 250, 263–72
  property confiscated from, 233–5
  as refugees, 4, 7, 9–10, 216, 250–8,
    275–81, 341–2
  restitution for, 260–2, 335–7, 342,
    347–8
  suicide of, 269–71
  synagogues of, 10, 33, 38, 152, 176,
    199, 201, 308
  taxation of, 3, 31, 32, 233, 241, 244,
    257
  in Vienna, 3–7, 13, 14, 24, 30–9, 65,
    68–9, 72, 79, 97, 113, 132, 142–3,
    162, 174, 178–9, 200, 210, 216,
    217, 218–29, 235, 236, 247–8,
    254–8, 278, 279, 334, 342, 343–8
  visas for, 219, 269, 270
  wealth of, 31–2, 33, 79–80, 343–4
  yellow badges worn by, 30, 31, 267
  see also anti-Semitism
Jobst (photography studio), 195,
  213–14, 228–9
Johann Timmels-Witwe, 159, 160, 162,
  165, 182, 196, 236, 254
Johansson, Ronny, 168
Jonasch, Wilhelm, 146–7
Joseph II, Emperor of Austria, 31
Jubiläumstheater, 69, 99
"Judaism in Music" (Wagner), 68, 178
Judenhaus, 269
Judenkontribution, 248, 257
Jurisprudence (Klimt), 24

Kafka, Paul, 311
Kallir, Fanny, 247
Kallir, Otto, 242, 247
Kallmus, Dora, *82*

Kampf um Rom, Ein (Dahn), 200,
  226, 296
Karlskirche, 162, 342
Karl Stefan, Archduke, 95–6
Karlweis, Oskar, 121–2
Kary, Arthur, 270, 271, 272
Kiss, The (Klimt), 84, 167
Klimt, Georg, 15
Klimt, Gustav, 5, 7, 12, 15–28, *21, 25,*
  27, 51, 58, 79, 80–2, *81, 82,* 83, 84,
  85, 87, 90, 91, 93, 94, 100–2, *101,*
  105, 130, 133, 143, 144, *156,* 157–8,
  159, 164, 167, 184, 186, 204, *204,*
  243, 244, 257, 315–17, 323–4, 326,
  332
Klimtgruppe, 80–2, 84, 184
Klimt Kollektiv, 23–8, *25,* 58, 91, 100
Klinger, Max, 84
Klinkosch, J. C., *102,* 103
Knips, Sonja, 51, 81
Kokoschka, Oskar, 243
konfessionslos ("faithless"), 39, 174–5,
  178–9
Konzert, Das (Bahr), 167
Korody, George, 311
Kraus, Gottlieb, 240–1, 248
Kraus, Karl, 24, 45, 79, 93, 136, 167
Kraus, Mathilde, 240–1, 248
Krauss, Franz von, *98,* 99, 143, 159,
  160, 181
Krausz, Wilhelm, 240–1
Kristallnacht, 4, 13, 236, 238–9, 248,
  250, 255, 256, 265, 278, 305
Künstlerhaus, 5, 86
Kurhaus Semmering, 160, 161
Kursalon, 27, 116
Kurzweil, Max, 19, 84, 329

Lady Standing (Klimt), 244
Lady with a Gold Background, A
  (Klimt), 244
Lafite, Carl, 166–8
Lane, Terry, 326, 332–3
Langer, Jakob, 92–3, 143

Langer, Melanie Gallia, 92–3, 128, 143, 272

Langer, Peter, 270, 271

Last Days of Mankind, The (Kraus), 136

League of Austrian Women's Associations, 58

Lefler, Heinrich, 77

Legler, Wilhelm, 181

Lehár, Franz, 75

Lehmann, Lotte, 280

Lehner, Stephan, 222, 223, 247, 248, 257

Leopold, Rudolf, 326–30, 345

Leopold I, Emperor of Austria, 31

Leopold Museum, 327, 345

Liberal Party, 33, 45

Lied von der Erde, Das (Mahler), 66–8

Lillie, Sophie, 240–1

Lissauer, Ernst, 137

Little Mother, A, 235

Loew, Anton, 25

Loew, Gertrud, 25, 71

Loewenstein, Fritz, 264

Lohengrin (Wagner), 70, 237

Loos, Adolf, 79, 92–4, 144–5, 163, 184

Löw, Fritzi, 156, 157, *347*

Low, Hans, 176

Low, Katia, 176

Low, Lore, 176

Löw-Beer, Marianne, 19

Löwenstein, Arthur, 137, 151

Lueger, Karl, 33–4, 47, 59, 208

Luke, Eugénie, 231, 232–3

Luke, Harry, 231, 252, 254, 286

Luther, Martin, 211–12

Luzzatto, Elisabeth, 58–60, 74, 75, 76, 118, 173

Luzzatto, Maximilian, 58, 60, 74, 75, 76, 118, 159

Luzzatto, Richard, 59

Madama Butterfly (Puccini), 64

Madame d'Ora photography studio, *82*

Magic Flute, The (Mozart), 70, 238–9, 321

Mahler, Alma, *see* Schindler, Alma

Mahler, Gucki, 66

Mahler, Gustav, 7, 8, 9, *10*, 11, *11*, 34, 35, 62, 63, 64–8, *66*, 69, 71, 73, 84, 90, 160, 204, 346–7

Mahler, Justine, 36, 66

Makuzu Kōzan, 104

Mann, Thomas, 155

Mannesmann, Otto, 48

mantles, gas, 43, 48, 77, 159

Marble, Alice, 194

Märchen (Hauff), 291

Maria Theresa (Schöntan), 28, 58

Marishchka, Ernst, 122

Marton, Kati, 340

Masked Ball, A (Verdi), 248

Mata Hari, 64, 74, 76

May Day, 209–10

Mayr, Richard, 114

McCaughey, Patrick, 332–3

Medicine (Klimt), 17, 24

Meine Mutterl war eine Wienerin, 314

Meistersinger von Nürnberg, Die (Wagner), 68, 211–12, 237

Melk monastery, 138–9

Mendelssohn, Felix, 35

menorahs, 207, 259

Merry Widow, The (Lehár), 64

Metropolitan Museum of Art, 325–6, 328

Metropolitan Opera, 65, 73–4

Meyerbeer, Giacomo, 178

Michaelis, Margaret, *307*

Michener, James, 10–11

Missingham, Hal, 317

Moderne Galerie, 86, 87

Moderne Stil, 104

modernism, 59, 92–3, 99, 167

Moll, Anna, 82, 157

Moll, Assanta, 245, 246, 250, 299–300

Moll, Carl, 15, 19, 35–6, 40, 66, 78–82, 83, 84, 85, 86, 89, 91, 94, 157, 159, 181, 184, 205, 245, 269, 271, 314–15, *316*, 329

Moll, Gilda, 245, 246, 250, 299–300

Moll, Maria, 67, 271

Moll, Marlene, 245, 246, 250, 299–300

Monowatts, 48, 77

Monument Against War and Fascism, 334–5

Moravia, 93, 114–15, 133, 171

Moser, Koloman, 5, 24–5, *25*, 34, 89, 90, 91, *91*, 100, *101*, 103

Mozart, Wolfgang Amadeus, 70, 211, 225, 238–9, 280, 321, 344

Mozart Boys' Choir, 276–7, 280

Munch, Edvard, 315

Munich Agreement (1938), 267

Munich Secession, 81

Museum für Angewandte Kunst (Museum of Applied Arts), 2, 184, 325

Museum of Modern Art (MoMA), 316

Musikverein, 51, 64–5, 167–8, 212–13

Mussolini, Benito, 210, 211, 257, 258, 260

Nabokov, Vladimir, 246

Napoleon I, Emperor of France, 211

National Fund for the Victims of National Socialism, 342

National Gallery (London), 12, 23

National Gallery of Australia, 342–3

National Gallery of Victoria, 12, 110, 324–6, 332–3

Nazism, 3–7, 13, 209–12, 214, 215, 216–58, 263–72, 284, 285, 298, 322, 332, 342

Netherlands, 265, 285

Neue Freie Presse, 3, 23, 24, 87, 89, 161–2

Neufeld, Max, 206

Neuwaldegg, 125–6, 153

Neuzil, Wally, 328, 345

New Year's Day, 113, 127–8, 202

New York, N.Y., 44, 65, 73–4

New York Times, 328, 330, 339

Nietzsche, Friedrich, 295

Nieuw Zeeland, 251–2, 281, 283

Ninth Symphony (Beethoven), 64–5, 84, 212–13

"Nirvana of the Lustful Women, The" (Illica), 85–6

Nordpolen, 104, *105*

Nürnberg, 70–1

Nürnberg Laws, 218–19, 226, 227, 245

Olmütz, 38, 92, 143

"On Dreams" (Freud), 43

Operation Gildemeester, 234

Order of German Knights, 37, 202

Ordinance for the Registration of Jewish Property, 241–6

Orlik, Emil, 7, 8, *10*, 67, 204

"Ornament and Crime" (Loos), 93, 144–5

Osborn, John, 230, 233, 234, 250

Österreichische Galerie, 78, 85, 242, 328

O'Sullivan, William, 254

Palais Esterházy, 157

Pallas Athena (Klimt), 26, 27

Parsifal (Wagner), 69–70, *71*, 121, 139, 211

Passover, 306, 310–11

Pateman, Merle, 282

Pétain, Philippe, 265, 267

Peterskirche, 80, 314

Philosophy (Klimt), 17, 24

Piaristengasse, 176, 256

Piniles, Friedrich, 159

Pintsch, Julius, 47–8

Pique Dame (Tchaikovsky), 64

Plain at Auvers, The (van Gogh), 87

Poland, 126, 232, 263, 267, 297, 339

Pollak, Lili, 118, 123, 166, 168

Pollak, Theobald, 9, *11,* 34, 62, 65, 66, 82, 89, 90–1, *91,* 94, *101,* 103, 112–15, 118, 123, 166, 168, 204
Portrait of a Lady (Klimt), 16
Powolny, Michael, 94
Prague, 152, 267–8, 269
Primavesi, Eugenia, 81, 143–4, 184, 345
Primavesi, Mäda, 143, 144
Primavesi, Otto, 146
Primavesi, Robert, 138, 143–4
Prophète, Le (Meyerbeer), 178
Protestantism, 39, 58, 174, 211–12, 253
Przemyśl fortress, 135, 136
Puccini, Giacomo, 64, 113

Quakers, 234, 250, 252, 279

railways, 34, 47–8, 162, 246, 258
Reiffenstein, Bruno, 103, 104
Reinhardt, Heinrich, 75
Reinhardt, Max, 73
Remo, 257, 258
Residenztheater, 157
Rheingold, Das (Wagner), 70
Rhodes, Jon, *343*
Ribarz, Rudolf, 84, 327, 329
Rich, Frank, 339
Richard III (Shakespeare), 72
Rienzi (Wagner), 69, 206
Rigoletto (Verdi), 71
Roland, Ida, 157
Roller, Alfred, 64, 69
Roosevelt, Franklin D., 232
Rosé, Alfred, 66–7
Rosé Quartet, 167–8
Rosthorn-Friedmann, Rose von, 17, 18, 19, 51
Rothschild family, 30, 97, 113, 120
Royal Copenhagen, 5, 104, *105*
Russia, 126, 135
Ryan, Nellie, 252–3, 278

SA, 224
Sabbath, 31, 143

Sachs, Hans, 70–1, 211–12
Sacred Heart Convent, 235, 309
St. Gallen, 247–9
St. Martin's Cathedral, 40
St. Mary's Cathedral, 294, 312
Saint-Saëns, Camille, 40
St. Stephen's Cathedral, 200, 201, 202, 346–7
St. Stephen's Day, 116, 119–20, 127, 128, 177
St. Vincent's College, 276, 277–8, 279, *279,* 281, 290
Saliège, Jules-Gérard, 266
Salome (Strauss), 73–4, 238
Salzburg, 8, 210–11, 320
Salzburg Festival (1933), 210–11
Salzkammergut, 8, 95, 111, 320
Samson et Dalila (Saint-Saëns), 40
Sanatorium Fürth, 158
Sanatorium Loew, 126, 133, 160–1
Schick, Elisabeth, 199
Schidlof, Georg, 213, 214, 285, 297–8, 317, 320–1
Schidlof, Lizzi, 213
Schiele, Egon, 87, 136, 158, 164, 327, 328, 345
Schiller, Erich, 172–3, 179, 187
Schiller, Friedrich, 72, 111
Schindler, Alma, 9, *11,* 15, 17–18, 34–6, 62, 66, 69, 75, 89, 90, 178, 245
Schindler, Anna, 35–6
Schindler, Emil Jakob, 84, 85, 327, 329
Schirach, Baldur von, 244
Schnitt, Joseph, 206, 227, 235, 237, 276–7
Schnitzler, Arthur, 51, 64, 72–3, 75, 79
Schönberg, Arnold, 67, 167
Schöntan, Franz von, 28, 58
Schorske, Carl, 45, 59
Schumann, Robert, 166
Schuschnigg, Kurt von, 210, 214–16, 217, 221, 222, 224
Schuster, Melanie, 328
Scout Ball, 214

Secession, 5, 7, 15–16, 17, 19, 23–7, 25,
  58, 59, 64, 72, 74, 77–82, 83, 84,
  86–7, 88, 89, 91, 93, 94, 158–9,
  184, 243, 323, 342–3, 348
Second Symphony (Mahler), 65, 66
Segantini, Giovanni, 85–9
Serbia, 125, 134–5
Sereny, Gitta, 225
Servaes, Franz, 23, 86
Seurat, Georges, 85
Shakespeare, William, 64, 72, 111,
  136
Shaw, George Bernard, 70, 72–3
Shoah, 338
Siegfried (Wagner), 68
Silesia, 16, 29–30, 32–3, 37–41, 81, 82,
  177
Simmel, George, 76
Simplicissimus, 35
Singakademie, 166, 186
Sisters of Charity, 276, *279,* 281
Sixth Symphony (Mahler), 65
Skywa, Josephine, 138
Smetana, Bedřich, 215–16
Social Democratic Party, 59, 208–10
socialism, 58–60, 185, 208–10
Somoff, Constantin, 83, 329
Song of Hatred Against England
  (Lissauer), 137
Song of Hatred Against Italy
  (Löwenstein and Urbanitzky),
  137, 151
Soulek, Jakob, 102–3
Sound of Music, The, 8–9, 342
Source, The (Michener), 10–11
Soviet Union, 271, 292, 299, 300
Speer, Albert, 225
SS, 4, 219–20, 221, 227, 234, 238,
  265–6
Staatsoper, 211–12
Stadttempel, 344–8
Staglieno Cemetery, 206, 207
Steed, Henry Wickham, 104–6
Steinhof asylum, 198

Stern, Mrs., 125–6, 128, 129, 130, 139,
  140, 142, 145, 148–9, 153, 166, 172
Stern, Norbert, 125–53, *131,* 163–4, 166,
  167, 172 , 173, 178, 179, 181, 184,
  187, 198, 311
Stöhr, Ernst, 80, 329
*Story of the Trapp Family Singers,
  The,* 9
Strauss, Johann, Jr., 27, 75, 113, 206,
  280, 321
Strauss, Richard, 73–4, 238
Sweet Bowl (Moser), 90–1, *91, 101,*
  103
Sweet Girl, The (Reinhardt), 75
Switzerland, 8–9, 86, 131, 158, 234, 243,
  247–9, 300
Sydney Morning Herald, 276, 282–3
Sydney University, 288–90, 303
Symonds, Saul, 283, 290

Taking Sides (Harwood), 213
Tannhäuser (Wagner), 69, 237
Taubman, Philip, 339
Tchaikovsky, Pyotr Ilyich, 64
Théas, Pierre-Marie, 266–7
Theresianum, 120, 179
Theresienstadt, 268, 269, 299, 301,
  338, 340
They Kill You in the End
  (Missingham), 317
Third Man, The, 318
This Believing World (Browne), 296
Times (London), 104–6
Tolstoy, Leo, 50, 51, 178
Toscanini, Arturo, 212
To the Nameless Ones (Egger-Lienz),
  158
Trapp family, 8–9
Tressenstein, 320–1
Trieste, 260, 261
Triple Alliance, 131, 133, 135–6
Tristan und Isolde (Wagner), 69,
  344–5
Troller, Hans, 199, 298, 299

Turner, George, 213, 214, 285, 297–8, 317, 320–1
Tuschak, Helene, 167–8

Universal Exposition (1898), 44
Unser Kind, 54–7
Urbanitzky, Grete von, 137, 151
Uris, Leon, 10–11

Verdi, Giuseppe, 71, 248, 321, 344
Verklärte Nacht (Schönberg), 167
Ver Sacrum, 17, 89
Vichy France, 265–7
Vienna
    anti-Semitism in, 24, 30–6, 65, 68–9, 79, 132, 174, 178–9, 200, 210, 216, 217, 218–29, 235, 236, 247–8, 278, 279, 343–4
    author's visit to, 344–8
    Catholic culture of, 10, 16, 24, 30–4, 73, 132, 345, 346
    cuisine of, 155, 201–2
    as cultural center, 5–6, 10, 13, 27–8, 59–76, 104–6, 244
    Eighth District (Josefstadt) of, 176, 203–4, 256
    First District of, 4, 33, 45, 198, 213, 227, 240
    "first" vs. "second" societies of, 47, 62, 165
    Fourth District of, 5, 43, 81, 97, 176, 202, 203
    gaslight used in, 42–9, 77–8, 185
    ghetto of, 30–2, 34, 142
    government of, 30–1, 33–4, 47, 185
    Jewish population of, 3–7, 13, 14, 24, 30–9, 65, 68–9, 72, 79, 97, 113, 132, 142–3, 162, 174, 178–9, 200, 210, 216, 217, 218–29, 235, 236, 247–8, 254–8, 278, 279, 334, 342, 343–8
    liberation of, 344–8
    Nazi rule in, 230–58
    Ninth District of, 222
    Prater of, 202, 209–10
    Ringstrasse of, 5, 92, 214–15, 217, 345, 348
    Schleifmühlgasse neighborhood of, 35–6, 43, 80, 81–2, 81, 90–2, 94, 96–7, 111, 116–18, 142, 348
    Second District (Leopoldstadt) of, 34, 132, 142–3, 144, 269
    Seventh District of, 345
    Soviet occupation of, 271, 292, 299, 300
    synagogues of, 4, 15, 30, 33, 344–8
    Tenth District of, 58
    Third District of, 95, 203, 204
    Wohllebengasse neighborhood of, 5, 6, 35, 49, 97–106, 98, 101, 102, 105, 110, 118, 119–23, 126, 128, 129, 130, 138, 139, 142, 143–5, 146–7, 155–6, 159, 160, 161, 162, 171, 177, 182, 184–8, 196, 198–205, 213, 216, 332–3
Vienna, University of, 3, 17, 24, 175, 184
Vienna Boys' Choir, 206, 227, 235, 237–8, 276–7, 318, 321
Vienna 1913 exhibition, 332–3
Vienna Opera, 13, 64, 215, 334
Vienna Philharmonic, 64–5
Vienna Secession exhibition (1971), 323
Vienna Woods, 125–7, 153
Villa Gallia, 52–3, 95, 96, 96, 102, 110, 111, 113, 125, 126, 137, 147–52, 153, 160, 175, 178, 182, 191, 192, 193, 196, 198, 199, 203, 205, 206, 241, 256–7, 292, 298, 319, 320–1, 335–7

Wagner, Richard, 14, 68–72, 71, 121, 139, 152, 178, 200, 206, 211–12, 237, 344–5, 348
Wagner, Siegfried, 70, 71
Wahnfried, 70–1
Waldmüller, Ferdinand Georg, 83–4, 85, 204, 242–4

Walküre, Die (Wagner), 69

Walter, Bruno, 65, 66, 111, 114, 215, 226

Wangler, Elzear, 227–8, 236–7, 247, 279, 293, 295

Wärndorfer, Fritz, 24, 26, 27, 34, 91, 106, 143

Was einmal war (Lillie), 240

Waterloo, Battle of, 211

Watt, 48, 77, 95

Waugh, Alexander, 14

Wedekind, Franz, 73, 173

Weiss, Lucie, 237, 247, 256

Welles, Orson, 318

Welsbach Light Co., 44, 45

Welsbach mantle, 43

Werfel, Franz, 245

Werk von Gustav Klimt, Das (Moll), 157–8

"What is German?" (Wagner), 68

Whistler, James McNeill, 20

Whitford, Frank, 23

Widmer, Emil, 246, 247, 250

Wiener Werkstätte, 5, 12, 24, 26, 34, 53, 59, 79, 91, *91*, 94, 97, 103, 106, 118, 119, 122, 133, *134*, 137, 143, 146, 154, 155–7, 159, 162, 181–2, 184, 185, 196, 213, 261, 269, 324–5, 328, 332–3, *347*

Wiesbauer, Anni, 236, 237, 247, 250, 278–9, 287, 300, 303, 322, 334

Wilde Oscar, 63, 72–3, 82

Wimmer-Wisgrill, Eduard, 328

Wittgenstein, Karl, 87, 88, 97

Wittgenstein, Margarete, 51

Witzmann, Carl, 102, 103

Wolff-Knize, Anna, 240

Wolff-Knize, Fritz, 240

Woman, 282

Women's Discussion Club, 58, 59

Women's International Zionist Organization, 308

World War I, 106, 125, 126, 129, 131–7, 149, 154–9, 164, 165, 179, 196, 241, 300

World War II, 12, 235, 264–5, 284–7

Young, Claire, 10, 336

Youth League, 306–8

Zemlinsky, Alexander, 34–5, 62, 64

Zionism, 69, 229

Zuckerkandl, Amalie, 159

Zuckerkandl, Berta, 24–5, 26

Zuckerkandl, Otto, 159

Zweig, Stefan, 20, 79

Zykan, Josef, 243, 244

A NOTE ABOUT THE TYPE

This book was set in Adobe Garamond. Designed for the Adobe Corporation by Robert Slimbach, the fonts are based on types first cut by Claude Garamond (c. 1480–1561). Garamond was a pupil of Geoffroy Tory and is believed to have followed the Venetian models, although he introduced a number of important differences, and it is to him that we owe the letter we now know as "old style." He gave to his letters a certain elegance and feeling of movement that won their creator an immediate reputation and the patronage of Francis I of France.

Composed by North Market Street Graphics
Lancaster, Pennsylvania

Printed and bound by Berryville Graphics
Berryville, Virginia

Designed by Soonyoung Kwon